FOREWORD TO THE FIRST EDITION

This booklet is intended for farmers, advisers, students and everyone else who, frequently or infrequently, find themselves hunting for data relating to farm management - whether it is for blunt pencil calculations on the back of an envelope or for feeding into a computer. The material contained is based upon the sort of information which the author finds himself frequently having to look up in his twin roles as adviser and teacher in farm management. There are several excellent handbooks already in existence, but this pocketbook endeavours to cover a wider field and thus to be substantially more comprehensive. It is intended that most of the data herein contained will have a national application, although there is inevitably some bias towards conditions in the south-eastern half of the country.

The development of farm planning techniques in recent years has outstripped the quality and quantity of data available. It is hoped that this booklet will go a little further in supplying the type of information required. It cannot, however, claim to be the ultimate in this respect. For example, there are many variations in labour requirements according to farm conditions and sizes and types of machine used and there are many more variations in sheep and beef systems than are dealt with here. More detailed data on these lines are gradually becoming available from various sources. It is hoped further to refine the material in this booklet and to keep it up to date in subsequent editions, as the information becomes available. As a help towards this end, any comments or criticisms will be gratefully received.

The author wishes to thank his many friends and colleagues who have given him so much time and help in compiling this information.

John Nix
October, 1966

First published October 1966

Forty-fifth Edition   September 2014

FOREWORD TO THE FORTY FIFTH EDITION

Every year there are considerable changes in agriculture, bringing both challenges and opportunities. The implementation of the Basic Payment Scheme across the EU in 2015 will present further adjustments for farmers and the wider industry. The lower direct payment for most recipients, the added bureaucratic requirements and 'Greening', of course, will all contribute to encouraging the farm business manager to reconsider his resources and opportunities.

Most UK farmers are likely to be receiving almost 25 per cent less direct subsidy by 2019 than in 2014, in real terms. The market and income from diversification will thus become increasingly important to each business. Consequently, a clear and full explanation of the latest CAP reform, with its implications for farmers, is included in this year's Pocketbook.

Certain environmental challenges facing the industry have merited inclusion in this edition of the Pocketbook. The rise in persistent grass weeds in arable rotations is causing major problems to those growing cereals and therefore agronomy is discussed in considerably more detail. Technological advance in precision farming is reflected in a new section.

Economics too are ever changing. Wheat, while generally considered the highest gross margin combinable crop, was eclipsed by oilseed rape only three years ago. This year, the pulse market has found new legs and peas are predicted to show the highest 'broad-acre' combinable crop gross margin, with beans not so far behind.

Figures in this book are estimated for 2015. Thus the crops data relate to the 2015 harvest. The livestock data relate either to the 2015 calendar year (e.g. for milk production) or to 2015/16 (e.g. for winter-finished beef). The yields and prices assume a 'normal' or average season, based on trends. Looking 6-18 months ahead to 2015/16, no one can know what the actual average yield and price for that particular year will be. *The figures should be adjusted as appropriate according to circumstances and price and cost differences.* Assumptions are set out to enable this to be done.

As always, I would like to thank all those who have contributed to the revision of this edition.

John Nix
August 2014

iv

Moreton Morrell Site

£24.61
658.
04
NIX
(D23)

John Nix
Farm Management
Pocketbook

2015 EDITION
Published September 2014

Copies of this book may be obtained from:
The Pocketbook, 2 Nottingham Street,
Melton Mowbray, Leicestershire LE13 1NW.
(Tel: 01664 564 508 Fax: 01664 503 201)
www.thepocketbook.co.uk

PRICE £24.00 + £2.50 p&p
5 to 19 copies: £23.00
20 to 100 copies: £21.00
Over 100 copies: *p.o.a*
*Postage & Packaging free for 5 or more copies
in single deliveries*

ISBN 978-0-9576939-1-3

*We take all reasonable steps to ensure that the information in the Pocketbook is correct.
However, we do not guarantee the correctness or completeness of material within it. We
shall not be liable or responsible for any kind of loss or damage that may result to you or a
third party as a result of your or their use of this book.*

CONTENTS

I.   GENERAL

1.   THE USE OF GROSS MARGINS

DEFINITION

The data on the crop and livestock enterprises in the Pocketbook are based on gross margins. The gross margin of an enterprise is its output less its variable costs. Enterprise output includes the market value of production retained on the farm. The variable costs must (a) be specific to the enterprise and (b) vary in proportion to the size of the enterprise, i.e. number of hectares or head of stock. The main items of variable costs are: Crops: fertiliser, seed, sprays, casual labour and contract work specific to the crop. Non-Grazing Livestock: concentrate feed, vet. and med., marketing expenses. Grazing Livestock is as for non-grazing livestock, plus forage crop variable costs.

POINTS TO NOTE

1. The gross margin is not a profit figure. The 'fixed costs' (rent, labour, machinery, general overheads) have to be covered by the total farm gross margin before arriving at a profit.

2. The gross margin of an enterprise will differ from season to season, partly because of yield and price differences affecting output and partly because variable costs will vary, e.g. the number and type of sprays required. Different soils and other natural factors, as well as level of management, will also cause differences between farms.

3. Items of variable cost may vary from farm to farm, e.g. some farmers have greater weed control costs than others; some farmers employ a contractor to combine their cereals (a variable cost), others employ their own equipment (a fixed cost); some employ a contractor to deliver their sugar beet to the factory (a variable cost), others have their own lorry (a fixed cost). These differences must be borne in mind in making inter-farm comparisons.

4. Provided points 2 and 3 are borne in mind, comparison of gross margins (particularly averages over several seasons) with standards can be a useful check on technical performance.

5. The other main usefulness of gross margins lies in farm planning. This is not simply a matter of substituting high gross margin enterprises in place of low gross margin enterprises. The gross margin is only one feature of an enterprise, albeit an important one. It says nothing about the call the enterprise makes on the basic farm resources - labour at different times of the year, machinery, buildings, working capital requirements, etc. All these factors and more have to be taken into account in the planning process.

6. This is not to argue that these other costs should be allocated. Complete allocation of many farm expenses is only possible on an arbitrary basis, since they are shared by two or more, possibly all farm enterprises. Allocation can therefore be completely misleading when making planning decisions. The same is true even when regular labour and machinery are employed specifically on certain enterprises, if such costs are calculated on a per-hectare or per head basis. This is because when enterprises are substituted, expanded, contracted or deleted, the variable costs for each enterprise will vary roughly in proportion to the size of that enterprise, but other costs will not, except possibly for fuel and some repair costs. Most 'fixed' costs may stay the same, others will change - but not smoothly in small amounts at a time. Either the same regular labour force will cope with a revised plan or a smaller or larger number of men will be needed. The same is true of tractors, other machines and buildings. Such cost changes

must of course be taken into account, but allocating these costs on a per-hectare or per head basis will not aid, and may positively confuse, planning decisions. The only point of making such calculations is for efficiency comparisons, e.g. labour costs per cow.

7. Allocating fixed costs at a flat rate (e.g. per hectare) for all enterprises, deducting this from the gross margin and hence calculating a 'net profit' from each enterprise can also be misleading. It ignores the whole problem of enterprise inter-relationships, differences between enterprises in total and seasonal requirements for labour, machinery and capital, and other factors such as different quality land on the same farm.

8. Changes in the scale of an enterprise may well affect its gross margin per unit, e.g. increasing the area of winter wheat from 30% to 55% on a farm will mean more second and third crop wheats being grown and a smaller proportion of the crop being drilled under the best conditions; hence yields may fall. Even if yields remain the same, variable costs (e.g. fertiliser) may be higher.

9. Gross margins used for planning future changes should also take account of possible changes in price, and the effect of changes in production techniques.

LOW, AVERAGE AND HIGH LEVELS

The levels of production given for most crop and livestock enterprises are meant to indicate differences in managerial skill or natural factors, soil productivity, etc., given the level of variable costs. They refer, to an average for each level over several years taking trends into account. Higher variable costs do not necessarily mean greater output, but depends on other factors too such as timing of applications.

The book is written with the progressive and business orientated farm manager in mind, those wanting to improve their businesses both technically and commercially. It therefore presupposes that the performance of the average Pocketbook user will exceed that of the national average farm performance, albeit only slightly. We therefore don't simply take Defra's average yields but, in most cases, a slightly higher yield. These figures are still thoroughly achievable in most farm businesses. The 'high' yields and performances are set out for those pushing the barriers of production slightly harder.

2.   COMPLETE ENTERPRISE COSTINGS

Gross margins are extremely useful for measuring the output and total costs that are directly attributable to that particular enterprise. This means costs that increase for every additional hectare or head of the enterprise maintained. They are also useful for comparing enterprises that fit into a similar farm system to help identify the most appropriate farm rotation. For example combinable crop rotations are comparable whereas a cereal and a root crop, less so because the farm's overhead requirements will vary with each crop. Each comparison requires interpretation. Gross margins are also useful for each farm to examine their own performance. Comparing gross margins between fields for example or from year to year gives useful feedback on financial and physical delivery.

Much meaningless and arbitrary allocation of 'joint costs' is required to attempt fully costed net margins, and the results are often of limited use in making farm decisions. Another problem in 'complete enterprise costing' is where to stop. For example should interest on capital be included, whether borrowed or not? Further problems of asset valuation and allocation are involved if so. Variations between farms in their financial situations are considerable as, ranging from the farmer who owns all his land without any mortgage and has no other borrowings to the one with both a rent to pay for all his land and heavy borrowings in addition.

The above problems arise when 'costs per tonne' or 'costs per litre' are calculated. Wheat can be calculated to cost anything between £100 and £165 a tonne according to just what costs are included, how they are allocated and their yield.

It is natural to want to know 'unit costs' to compare, for example, with prices received. Sometimes these calculations clarify particular costs and therefore efficiency gains that could be made. For these reasons costs per litre of milk are included, although the calculation of some of the 'fixed cost' items is difficult. If a farm has only one enterprise such calculations on that farm are obviously straightforward. However, even on solely dairy farms followers are usually reared or forage grown, which are separate enterprises to milk production.

If required, a cost per tonne of combinable crops can be calculated by adding the fixed costs per hectare of mainly cereals farms (according to size range, given on page 218) to the variable costs per hectare given in the enterprise gross margin data and dividing by the selected yield. Such calculations need to be interpreted with caution because the allocation of fixed costs per hectare is inevitably crude.

The allocation of specific labour (e.g. a full-time cowman), machinery (e.g. a potato harvester) and buildings (e.g. a grain store) is relatively simple and can provide useful information both for purposes of efficiency comparisons and partial budgeting. For some enterprises on many mixed farms, there are few such specific items and the question of the other so-called fixed cost items remains if a full costing is attempted.

A modern method of calculating total costs of production is to allocate machinery and labour according to fuel use. This is not a perfect science but attributes the various costs more accurately than per hectare or per unit of yield.

3. HISTORIC DATA

It has never been the intention of The Pocketbook to include 'historical data', except for some of the material in the Agristats section. Hence total farm survey results, which are inevitably a year or two old by the time they are published, are not included, although some are used in some sections with interpretation for the forthcoming year. However the Pocketbook is gradually publishing spreadsheet tools with charted historical data on its website in the subscriber's section. This is not exhaustive and is anticipated to gradually increase. Let us know if there is a particular series that is not on the website.

4. FARM BUSINESS SURVEY DATA

ENGLAND

The Farm Business Survey (FBS) is a key source of farm business data in England. It is carried out on behalf of DEFRA by a consortium of Universities. Its site; www.farmbusinesssurvey.co.uk holds a number of sets of FBS data and publications on specialist enterprises.

WALES

The Farm Business Survey in Wales is undertaken on behalf of the Welsh Assembly Government by the University of Aberystwyth. The results are published at - www.aber.ac.uk/en/ibers/enterprise-kt/fbs/

SCOTLAND

In Scotland the data for the Farm Accounts Survey is collected by the Scottish Rural College. It is available in the publication 'Farm Incomes in Scotland'. See www.scotland.gov.uk/Topics/Statistics/15631/8884

NORTHERN IRELAND

The Department of Agriculture and Rural Development for Northern Ireland undertakes the Farm Business Survey in the province. Results can be found at http://www.dardni.gov.uk/index/statistics/statistical-reports/statistics-farm-incomes-in-ni.htm

5.   MAIN ASSUMPTIONS

Budgeting future prices, by necessity requires making several assumptions about how they are likely to move in the future from current levels (August 2014). This Edition of the Pocketbook uses the following key assumptions for 2015:

- The pound: euro exchange rate throughout the book is £1 = €1.25, equivalent to €1 = 80p.

- Fertiliser prices for nitrogen (N), phosphate (P) and potash (K) are the same throughout. A full schedule of fertiliser valuations can be found on page 268. For calculating the gross margins, the following are used:

    o   N: 76.8 p/kg   (£265/t 34.5% N)   (UK Ammonium Nitrate)

    o P_2O_5:   60 p/kg   (£275/t 46% P_2O_5) (Triple Super Phosphate)

    o K_2O: 45.8 p/kg   (£275/t 60% K_2O)   (Muriate of Potash)

- Farm machinery fuel price (red diesel) is taken to be 62ppl.

- Feed wheat price (from which many other commodity prices are benchmarked), is £135/tonne. This is an ex-farm price for November 2015 delivery.

II.   ENTERPRISE DATA

1.   CROPS

WINTER WHEAT

Feed Wheat

Production level	Low	Average	High
Yield: tonnes per ha (tons per acre)	6.75 (2.7)	8.40 (3.4)	9.75 (3.9)
	£	£	£
Output	911 (369)	1,134 (459)	1,316 (533)
Variable Costs:			
Seed...		58 (23)	
Fertiliser...		207 (84)	
Sprays...		233 (94)	
Total Variable Costs		498 (202)	
Gross Margin per ha (acre)	**413** (167)	**636** (258)	**818.3** (331)

Milling Wheat

Production level	Low	Average	High
Yield: tonnes per ha (tons per acre)	6.15 (2.5)	7.75 (3.1)	9.00 (3.6)
	£	£	£
Output	935 (379)	1,178 (477)	1,368 (554)
Variable Costs:			
Seed...		63 (26)	
Fertiliser...		248 (100)	
Sprays...		241 (98)	
Total Variable Costs		552 (224)	
Gross Margin per ha (acre)	**383** (155)	**626** (254)	**816** (330)

1. Prices. The average feed wheat price for the 2015 harvest crop (i.e. 2015/16 marketing year) is £135 per tonne.

    The average milling price is £152/tonne. This is based on a 'full specification' premium of £30 over feed wheat, a 'biscuit' grade milling specification of £15 and a 25% failure rate of achieving the specification. The average premium achieved varies widely according to quality and season: see note 3. Full specification is defined as NABIM Group 1 wheat with a minimum Hagberg of 250, 13% Protein and a bushel weight of at least 76Kg/hl.

2. *Yields.* The average yield is for all winter wheat, i.e. all varieties and 1st and subsequent wheats. See over for more on First and Second Wheats. The overall yield used for feed and milling wheats combined calculates as 8.27t/ha.

3. *Milling v. Feed.* The yield of bread and biscuit wheat (generically known as milling) averages about 8% below that of feed wheat. Slightly higher seed, fertiliser and spray costs are normal for milling wheats. The price premium varies each season according to quality and scarcity. Also, not all deliveries achieve full specification. Grade 2 varieties normally achieve a premium of a few pounds a tonne (£15 used here) but their yields are higher than Grade 1 varieties. Full specification bread-making premium averaged £25.17/tonne from 2008 to 2014 with a range of £6.50 to £66.00 per tonne. The 2013/2014 bread-wheat premium averaged £26/tonne. NABIM wheat group 1

varieties account for about 14% of wheat area (2014), comparable with Group 2 and Group 3 areas. The proportion of Group 4 wheats has been rising steadily to about 59% in 2014.

4. *First v. Second (Feed) Wheat*. The effect of different types and lengths of rotational breaks on subsequent wheat yields varies given the differences between seasons (weather), soils, varieties etc. The table below assumes a yield reduction of 10% for second wheats compared with first and higher input costs as shown (the later the sowing date the less the yield gap tends to be). Only average and high levels are shown. Third wheats could yield 10% below second wheats; variable costs are likely to be similar. Heavy, well-structured, well-drained clay soils are best suited to second wheats.

Comparison between First and Second Feed Wheat Crops

Production level	Average		High	
Year (after break)	First	Second	First	Second
Yield: tonnes per ha (tons/acre)	8.82 (3.6)	7.9 (3.2)	10.238 (4.1)	9.2 (3.7)
	£	£	£	£
Output	1,191 (482)	1,067 (432)	1,382 (560)	1,242 (503)
Variable Costs:				
Seed..............................	52 (21)	75 (30)	52 (21)	75 (30)
Fertiliser..........................	206 (83)	219 (89)	206 (83)	219 (89)
Sprays.............................	230 (93)	248 (100)	230 (93)	248 (100)
Variable Costs	488 (198)	542 (220)	488.33 (198)	542 (220)
Gross Margin per ha (acre)	703 (285)	525 (212)	894 (362)	700 (284)

5. *Straw* is costed as incorporated. Average yield and price is approx. 3·5 tonnes per hectare at £60/tonne (£5 more in small bales); variable costs (string) approx. £3.25 per tonne. Unbaled straw (sold for baling): anything from no value to £170/ha (£70/acre), national average around £37/ha (£14/acre).

6. *Seed*. Rates vary according to soil, season, variety, drilling date etc. Seed: £375 and £385 used for feed and milling respectively (C2) with a single purpose dressing; 175kg/ha in good conditions; Farm-saved included at 36% (feed) 25% (milling) as according to pesticide survey 2010. Includes grain value, cleaning, dressing, testing and BSPB levy (refer to p 274).

7. *Fertiliser* costs are based on P and K replacement cost for an average yield crop, with straw incorporated. RB209 suggests Phosphate and Potash is replaced at 7.8kg/t and 5.6kg/t of grain weight harvested respectively (65 and 47kg/ha respectively in this gross margin). Nitrogen is 190kg/ha for feed wheat and 250kg/ha for milling.

8. *Sprays*. Refer to Agrochemical Rates on page 274

9. This schedule does not account for severe grass weed infestations such as Black Grass or Sterile Brome. The costs associated with managing such problems can amount to up to £150/hectare of additional agrichemical costs. Yield losses increase as infestation rises:

Yield losses from Black Grass Infestations

Grass plants/m^2	Yield loss t/Ha	% yield loss
8-12	0.2-0.4	2-5%
12-25	0.4-0.8	5-15%
100	1-2	15-25%
>300	+3	37%

References:

Roebuck, J.F. (1987). B.C.P.C. and

Blair A, Cussans J, Lutman P (1999).

SPRING WHEAT

Production level	Low	Average	High
Yield: tonnes per ha (tons per acre)	4.75 (1.9)	5.75 (2.3)	6.75 (2.7)
	£	£	£
Output	717 (290)	868 (352)	1,019 (413)
Variable Costs:			
Seed....................................		76 (31)	
Fertiliser................................		157 (64)	
Sprays.................................		138 (56)	
Total Variable Costs		371 (150)	
Gross Margin per ha (acre)	**346** (140)	**497** (201)	**648** (263)

1. *Price*: In general, see Winter Wheat (previous pages). A far higher proportion of spring wheat is sold for milling compared with winter wheat. Here we assume 90% making the average price £151/tonne for 2015 harvest.

2. *Straw:* See Winter Wheat but yields are considerably lower.

3. *Seed:* £400/tonne at 200kg/ha used. Home saved included at 15% including grain value, cleaning, dressing, testing and BSPB levy (refer to p 274).

4. *Fertiliser:* 150kg/ha N used, and P and K replacing off-take at 45kg/ha and 32kg/ha respectively.

5. *Sprays.* Refer to Agrochemical Rates on page 274

Normally, only about 1% of the UK wheat area is spring sown although survey data is unavailable. It is popular after root crops. The percentage is naturally higher after a particularly wet autumn so 2013 had a very high area. The percentage is even lower in Scotland (1% or less) than in England or Wales. The area has risen in recent years by about 7,000 hectares because of new very hard 'Red Wheat' varieties grown to contract.

RED WHEAT

Production level	Low	Average	High
Yield: tonnes per ha (tons per acre)	4.00 (1.6)	5.00 (2.0)	6.00 (2.4)
	£	£	£
Output	840 (340)	1,050 (425)	1,260 (510)
Variable Costs:			
Seed....................................		90 (36)	
Fertiliser................................		185 (75)	
Sprays.................................		206 (83)	
Total Variable Costs		481 (195)	
Gross Margin per ha (acre)	**359** (145)	**569** (230)	**779** (315)

Red Wheat is a relatively new spring crop to the UK. It is a hard, high protein crop. It is used widely in bread-making, with imports of about 850,000 tonnes per year. It is solely grown on contract, and currently priced against the St Laurence (Canada) *fob* (free on board) price. Here it is £210/tonne

Inputs: Seed used here at £575/t at 155kg/ha, Fertiliser at 155:65:60 N:P:K accordingly and for sprays, see page 274.

WINTER BARLEY

Feed Barley

Production level	Low	Average	High
Yield: tonnes per ha (tons per acre)	5.5 (2.2)	6.9 (2.8)	7.9 (3.2)
	£	£	£
Output	688 (279)	863 (350)	988 (400)
Variable Costs:			
Seed..		60 (24)	
Fertiliser....................................		158 (64)	
Sprays.......................................		178 (72)	
Total Variable Costs		396 (160)	
Gross Margin per ha (acre)	**292** (118)	**467** (189)	**592** (240)

Malting Barley

Production level	Low	Average	High
Yield: tonnes per ha (tons per acre)	5.0 (2.0)	6.0 (2.4)	6.9 (2.8)
	£	£	£
Output	710 (288)	852 (345)	980 (397)
Variable Costs:			
Seed..		62 (25)	
Fertiliser....................................		120 (49)	
Sprays.......................................		178 (72)	
Total Variable Costs		360 (146)	
Gross Margin per ha (acre)	**350** (142)	**492** (199)	**620** (251)

1. *Prices.* The feed barley price for 2015 harvest (i.e. 2015/16 marketing year) is taken to be £125/tonne, a £10.00 discount to feed wheat (the average over 5 and 20 years is about 7 per cent). The winter malting price (£142.00/tonne) assumes an average premium over feed of £17/tonne. This accounts for some that don't meet malting standards. For the best malting barleys the premium in the past has been £25 and in some years higher.

2. *Straw* is costed as being incorporated. Average yield is approx. 2·75 tonnes per hectare, value £65 per tonne baled ex-field, higher in the West, (£10 more in small bales); variable cost (string) approximately £3.25 per tonne. Prices rise in years of forage shortage.

3. *Seed.* Winter barley seed averages £375 for feed and £385 for malting at 175kg/ha. Seed includes 25% farm-saved including grain, dressing, testing and BSPB levy (see p 274).

4. Fertiliser costs are based on N at 160kg/ha for feed, 100kg/ha for malting crops. P and K replacement cost, with straw incorporated making 53:38kg/ha for feed and 45:32kg/ha for malting crops.

5. *Sprays.* Refer to Agrochemical Rates on page 274

SPRING (MALTING) BARLEY

Production level	Low	Average	High
Yield: tonnes per ha (tons per acre)	4.6 (1.9)	5.45 (2.2)	6.3 (2.6)
	£	£	£
Output	699.2 (283)	828 (336)	958 (388)
Variable Costs:			
Seed...		63 (26)	
Fertiliser....................................		101 (41)	
Sprays.......................................		138 (56)	
Total Variable Costs		302 (122)	
Gross Margin per ha (acre)	**397** (161)	**526** (213)	**656** (266)

1. *Prices.* Virtually all spring barley grown is malting varieties, grown for a premium. Spring malting premiums usually exceed those for winter varieties. Here the premium over feed barley is £27/tonne. Again, this allows for failed samples making £152.00/t.

2. *Seed.* Spring barley seed used is £400/tonne at a seed rate of 175Kg/ha. 35% is home saved (refer to p 274).

3. *Fertiliser* costs are based on N at 80kg/ha. P and K replacement cost, with straw incorporated making 43:31kg (P:K) per hectare.

4. *Sprays.* Refer to Agrochemical Rates on page 274

OATS

Winter Oats

Production level	Low	Average	High
Yield: tonnes per ha (tons per acre)	5.3 (2.1)	6.3 (2.6)	7.7 (3.1)
	£	£	£
Output	656 (266)	788 (319)	956 (387)
Variable Costs:			
Seed...............................		59 (24)	
Fertiliser............................		114 (46)	
Sprays............................		125 (51)	
Total Variable Costs		298 (121)	
Gross Margin per ha (acre)	**358** (145)	**490** (198)	**658** (266)

Spring Oats

Production level	Low	Average	High
Yield: tonnes per ha (tons per acre)	4.5 (1.8)	5.5 (2.2)	6.5 (2.6)
	£	£	£
Output Feed	563 (228)	688 (278)	813 (329)
Variable Costs:			
Seed...............................		65 (26)	
Fertiliser............................		94 (38)	
Sprays............................		87 (35)	
Total Variable Costs		246 (100)	
Gross Margin per ha (acre)	**317** (128)	**442** (179)	**567** (230)

1. Price used is £125/tonne for the 2015 harvest crop, i.e. the 2015/16 movement year for milling oats. Milling specification requires a minimum bushel weight of 50Kg/Hl. Conservation grade milling oats may obtain a premium of £10-20/tonne.

2. Seed: priced here at £400/tonne and £425/tonne, at 175kg/ha and 185kg/ha for winter and spring crops respectively, both with 40% home saved (refer to p 274).

3. *Fertiliser;* winter costs are based on N at 90kg/ha winter and 70kg/ha spring. P and K replacement cost, with straw incorporated making 50:36kg/ha for winter and 43:31kg/ha for spring.

4. *Sprays.* Refer to Agrochemical Rates on page 274

5. Straw is not included above. Average yield is 3.5 tonnes per hectare; value £65 per tonne according to region and season; variable costs (string) £3.25 per tonne.

6. For Naked Oats refer to page 21

7. The high majority of GB oats are winter crops; the proportion increases from north to south although spring oats has been rising in popularity in recent years; (85% winter in England/Wales but less in Scotland).

OILSEED RAPE

Winter Rape

Production level	Low	Average	High
Yield: tonnes per ha (tons per acre)	2.40 (1.0)	3.40 (1.4)	4.40 (1.8)
	£	£	£
Output	636 (258)	901 (365)	1,166 (472)
Variable Costs:			
Seed..		51 (21)	
Fertiliser...................................		192 (78)	
Sprays.......................................		196 (79)	
Total Variable Costs		439 (178)	
Gross Margin per ha (acre)	**197** (80)	**462** (187)	**727** (294)

Spring Rape

Production level	Low	Average	High
Yield: tonnes per ha (tons per acre)	1.5 (0.6)	2.00 (0.8)	2.75 (1.1)
	£	£	£
Output	398 (161)	530 (215)	729 (295)
Variable Costs:			
Seed..		49 (20)	
Fertiliser...................................		88 (36)	
Sprays.......................................		156 (63)	
Total Variable Costs		293 (119)	
Gross Margin per ha (acre)	**105** (43)	**237** (96)	**436** (177)

1. *Prices.* The price assumed for the 2015 crop is £265/tonne, including oil bonuses at 42% oil content, (£255 before).

2. *Varieties.* Inputs are lower with spring-sown crops, pigeons are less trouble and the late summer/autumn workload is eased. Spring yields average only 60% of those of winter rape; hence normally less than 5% of the total oilseed rape crop is spring-sown. The proportion of the total area sown with hybrid winter rape is about a third.

3. *Seed;* Winter price is 30% conventional merchant's seed (£40/ha), 40% hybrid (£70/ha) and 30% home saved conventional (refer to p 274 For Home Saving costs).

4. *Fertiliser* costs are based on N at 190kg/ha for winter, 80kg/ha for spring. P and K replacement cost, with straw incorporated making 45:35kg/ha for winter and 28:22kg/ha for spring crops.

5. *Sprays.* Refer to Agrochemical Rates on page 274

LINSEED

Spring Linseed

Production level	Low	Average	High
Yield: tonnes per ha (tons per acre)	1.25 (0.5)	1.75 (0.7)	2.75 (1.1)
	£	£	£
Output	358 (145)	501 (203)	787 (319)
Variable Costs:			
Seed..		80 (32)	
Fertiliser..................................		85 (34)	
Sprays......................................		64 (26)	
Total Variable Costs		229 (93)	
Gross Margin per ha (acre)	**129** (52)	**272** (110)	**558** (226)

Winter Linseed

Production level	Low	Average	High
Yield: tonnes per ha (tons per acre)	1.50 (0.6)	2.30 (0.9)	3.00 (1.2)
	£	£	£
Output	429 (174)	658 (266)	858 (347)
Variable Costs:			
Seed..		95 (38)	
Fertiliser..................................		139 (56)	
Sprays......................................		77 (31)	
Total Variable Costs		311 (126)	
Gross Margin per ha (acre)	**118** (48)	**347** (140)	**547** (222)

1. The price for the 2015 crop is £286/tonne (OSR price plus 10%). Contract prices are normally tied to a standard 38% oil and 9% moisture. Some specialist contracts for specific varieties such as Yellow Linseed can be worth more.

2. Most linseed is spring-sown, drilling mid-March to mid-April, no more than 1 year in 5. Too much nitrogen (over 130 kg/ha) can cause lodging, delayed maturity and excessive weed growth and hence difficult harvesting, poor quality and lower yields; it should be applied early. Harvesting: spring normally end Aug-early Sept. Moisture content most likely 12-16%: must be dried to 9% for storage.

3. Inputs: seed, 50kg/ha (sold in hectare bags) minimal home saved, Fertiliser N/P/K of spring 80/25/19 and winter 90:75:50.

Winter Linseed area has plateaued at about 6,500ha grown in the UK because of easier establishment and earlier harvest (late July). Yield is affected by frost heave, disease and thrips (thunder-bugs), most varieties susceptible to lodging; pigeons can be troublesome. Early sowing (early to mid-September) is best.

FIELD PEAS

Blue Peas

Production level	Low	Average	High
Yield: tonnes per ha (tons per acre)	3.0 (1.2)	3.75 (1.5)	5.0 (2.0)
	£	£	£
Output	780 (316)	975 (395)	1,300 (527)
Variable Costs:			
Seed..		99 (40)	
Fertiliser......................................		38 (15)	
Sprays...		124 (50)	
Total Variable Costs		261 (106)	
Gross Margin per ha (acre)	**519** (210)	**714** (289)	**1,039** (421)

Marrowfats

Production level	Low	Average	High
Yield: tonnes per ha (tons per acre)	2.7 (1.1)	3.40 (1.4)	4.5 (1.8)
	£	£	£
Output	891 (361)	1,122 (454)	1,485 (601)
Variable Costs:			
Seed..		191 (77)	
Fertiliser......................................		34 (14)	
Sprays...		178 (72)	
Total Variable Costs		403 (163)	
Gross Margin per ha (acre)	**488** (198)	**719** (291)	**1,082** (438)

1. *Price.* All peas are now grown for a premium market. Only a small proportion (10-20%) are compounded as second grade peas or go for pet food. The high premium for food consumption justifies pea cleaning to remove discoloured and damaged peas. Feed value is therefore not relevant as a base price but a discount. The overall price for Blue peas is £260/tonne, taking account of human consumption premiums (£275/tonne) and a 20% failure rate with feed price of £205. Most peas (70% in 2015) are Blues, used for micronizing and exports.

   Marrowfats can achieve even higher prices. They are not priced with a premium over wheat, as the markets bear no relationship. They are used for canning, packets and export trade. They are almost entirely grown on a contract thus production is restricted by demand. They command a higher price than blues but yield about 10% less. The average price in this gross margin is £330/tonne being £345/tonne for 90% £205 for the 10% that only achieves feed specification.

2. *Seed:* Blues, £550/tonne planted at 200kg/ha, Marrowfats £675/tonne at 300kg/ha. Home Saved rate of 30% for blues and 30% for Marrowfats (refer to p 274).

3. *Fertiliser:* based on 9kg phosphate and 10kg potash per tonne of pea harvested per hectare. No nitrogen is applied making 0:34:38kg/ha Blues and 0:30:34 Marrowfats.

4. *Sprays.* Refer to Agrochemical Rates on page 274

FIELD BEANS

Winter Beans

Production level	Low	Average	High
Yield: tonnes per ha (tons per acre)	3.0 (1.2)	4.0 (1.6)	5.0 (2.0)
	£	£	£
Output	660 (267)	880 (356)	1,100 (446)
Variable Costs:			
Seed...................................		80 (32)	
Fertiliser.............................		40 (16)	
Sprays.................................		111 (45)	
Total Variable Costs		231 (94)	
Gross Margin per ha (acre)	**429** (174)	**649** (263)	**869** (352)

Spring Beans

Production level	Low	Average	High
Yield: tonnes per ha (tons per acre)	2.8 (1.1)	3.7 (1.5)	4.6 (1.9)
	£	£	£
Output	644 (261)	851 (345)	1,058 (428)
Variable Costs:			
Seed...................................		87 (35)	
Fertiliser.............................		37 (15)	
Sprays.................................		109 (44)	
Total Variable Costs		233 (94)	
Gross Margin per ha (acre)	**411** (166)	**618** (250)	**825** (334)

Winter Bean Notes

1. *Price.* The 2015 harvest price for winter feed beans is budgeted at £220 per tonne. This is based on a Human consumption price of £230/tonne achieved by 70% and feed specification for the rest at £205/tonne.

2. *Seed:* 185-220 kg per hectare (200kg used here) at £485/tonne. About 60% is farm-saved as in this gross margin (refer to p 274).

3. *Fertiliser:* 9kg phosphate and 10kg potash/t bean harvested/ha. No nitrogen is applied making 0:36:40kg/ha.

4. *Sprays.* Refer to Agrochemical Rates on page 274

Spring Bean Notes

5. *Price.* Spring beans are all grown for the human consumption market. It is only the poor quality beans (predominantly Bruchid beetle damaged) that are rejected and redirected to feed compounders. Damaged samples can be cleaned if the premium justifies it. A large proportion of the crop is exported (to North Africa). Average spring bean price is budgeted here at £230/tonne comprising 60% at £265/tonne and the rest at £205/tonne.

6. *Seed:* 185-220 kg per hectare (200kg/ha here) at £485/tonne. About 50% is farm-saved. Sprays: as for winter beans.

8. *Fertiliser:* 9kg phosphate and 10kg potash/t bean harvested/ha. No nitrogen is applied making 0:33:37kg/ha.

9. *Winter versus Spring Beans.* The key determinant between which to crop is soil type. Winter beans are more suited to heavy soils and springs on lighter land. As the schedules illustrate, there is little real difference between the gross margins. Spring crops are retained in many rotations to help manage grass weed problems.

Peas or Beans?

For the last decade the area of peas was about 20% of the UK combinable pulse area having fallen from 50% in 1997. High quality and good yields can return high gross margins and offer wider benefits to the farming system although they can be difficult to grow and the unpredictability of pulses had put several growers off in previous years.

LUPINS

The following table refers to spring sown *white lupins*. Differences in yield and price for yellow and blue lupins are given in the accompanying notes:

Production level	Low	Average	High
Yield: tonnes per ha (tons per acre)	2.25 (0.9)	3.00 (1.2)	3.75 (1.5)
	£	£	£
Output	484 (196)	645 (261)	806 (327)
Variable Costs:			
Seed		130 (52)	
Fertiliser....................................		61 (25)	
Sprays		85 (34)	
Total Variable Costs	276 (112)	276 (112)	276 (112)
Gross Margin per ha (acre)	**208** (84)	**369** (149)	**530** (215)

The price used here is £215 per tonne. Few lupins are traded on the open market, but the value tends to be slightly higher than the feed bean price.

A leguminous crop traditionally associated with light land. Their protein content is about 40 to 50% higher than peas and beans, making lupins a good substitute for soya bean meal in livestock feed compounds. They are a non-GM source of high quality digestible protein. The crop can be cut whole for silage, crimped or milled and fed directly to stock or the grain traded as a cash crop.

The area grown in the UK has stabilised in the last few years at around 4,000 hectares (*10,000 acres*). Varieties are virtually all now spring lupins. Around 75% of the total area is likely to be whole-cropped. Determinate varieties (single stem, uniform ripening) can be harvested easily; non-determinate varieties (with multiple heads at various stages of ripening) are more difficult.

Lupins can be grown on all but the heaviest land but are not tolerant of alkaline soils. They need a good cereal seedbed and pre-emergence weed control. Sowing is from mid-March to early April and harvest from mid-August onwards (and can be late September). If the crop is for silage, sowing can be as late as mid-May using an appropriate variety. No nitrogen fertiliser is necessary although 15-25kg per ha is often used to accelerate early stage growth. Replacement P and K at 30-50kg per ha is assumed. There are no serious crop pests. Anthracnose is a potentially serious threat but plant health measures have so far kept it under control. Other diseases are not a problem. Determinant varieties do not generally need pre-harvest desiccants if weed-free, non-determinant ones do.

Appropriate species and variety choice is important depending on area of the country, soil pH, intended end use and growth habit required. There are three distinct species of spring lupins; white (lupinus albus), blue (lupinus angustifolus) and yellow (lupinus luteus). All are suitable for grain or livestock feed. White lupins have higher protein and potentially greater yield than blue lupins but require a longer growing season. Yellow lupins fall between blue and white on both counts.

About two-thirds of the national lupin area is white, 15-20% blue and the remainder yellow. In the South-East and East Anglia 90%+ of lupins are white. In the North of England and Scotland blue and yellow varieties are more common due to their shorter growing season.

Lupin characteristics

	White *Lupinus Albus*	Yellow *Lupinus Luteus*	Blue *Lupinus Angustifolius*
Flower Colour	white or blue	yellow	white or blue
Growth habit	semi-determinate	semi-determinate	fully or semi-determinate
pH tolerance	5 to 7.6	4.6 to 6.8	5 to 6.8
Protein	36-40%	38-42%	31-35%
Oil content	10%	5%	6%
Main use	Combining in Southern England on acidic land. Forage in all areas	Mainly used for forage in the North.	Combining in the North (determinate) Forage in the very North (semi-determinate)
Yield	3.0-3.5 t/ha	2.5-3.0 t/ha	3.0-3.5 t/ha

Acknowledgement: Thanks to - Soya UK, Tel: 02380 696922.

HERBAGE SEEDS

	Italian Ryegrass		Early Perennial Ryegrass	
	Average	High	Average	High
	£	£	£	£
Yield (tonnes per ha)	1.3	1.7	1.20	1.50
Price per 50 kg (£)	55		60	
Output	1,430	1,870	1,440	1,800
Variable Costs:				
Seed	115		105	
Fertiliser	243		243	
Sprays	115		120	
Cleaning / Certification	221	281	206	251
Total Variable Costs	694	754	674	719
Gross Margin per ha	**736**	**1,116**	**766**	**1,081**
Gross Margin per acre	298	452	310	437

	Intermediate Perennial Ryegrass		Late Perennial Ryegrass	
	Average	High	Average	High
	£	£	£	£
Yield (tonnes per ha)	1.2	1.5	1.00	1.50
Price per 50 kg (£)	65		70	
Output	1,560	1,950	1,400	2,100
Variable Costs:				
Seed	100		100	
Fertiliser	243		243	
Sprays	125		125	
Cleaning / Certification	206	251	176	251
Total Variable Costs	674	719	644	719
Gross Margin per ha	**886**	**1231**	**756**	**1381**
Gross Margin per acre	359	498	306	559

	Hybrid Ryegrass		Kent Wild White Clover & Kent Indig. Peren. R'grass	
	Average	High	Average	High
	£	£	£	£
Yield (tonnes per ha)	1.3	1.6	0.09 (Clover)	0.11 (C)
			0.6 (R'grass)	0.8 (R)
Price per 50 kg (£)	55		350 (C)	65 (R)
Output	1375	1,705	1,410	1,810
Variable Costs:				
Seed	105		70	
Fertiliser	231		97	
Sprays	125		115	
Cleaning / Certification	214	259	143	179
Total Variable Costs	674	719	425	461
Gross Margin per ha	**701**	**986**	**985**	**1,349**
Gross Margin per acre	284	399	399	546

1. The following were the number of hectares entered for certified seed production for the main grasses and clovers in the UK for the 2013 harvest;

Italian / Westerwold Ryegrass	147	Cocksfoot	89
Early Perennial Ryegrass............	66	Timothy..................................	0
Inter. Perennial Ryegrass............	1,881	Red Fescue	179
Late Perennial Ryegrass	2,549	White Clover	128
Amenity Perennial Ryegrass.......	388	Red Clover..............................	184
Hybrid Ryegrass	699	Common Vetch.......................	86

The ryegrasses total 5,730 ha (*14,160 acres*).

All herbage seeds total 6,396 ha (*15,800 acres*).

2. The *yields* shown are averages for cleaned certified seed. The crop is risky, i.e. yields are highly variable, depending especially on the weather at, and precise timeliness of, harvesting. However, the use of growth regulators and stripper headers has reduced the risk. A considerable amount of skill is necessary to average the 'high' levels over a number of years. Most grasses give their highest yield in their first harvest year, assuming good establishment. Yields can be increased by up to 30% with a combination of higher Nitrogen applications along with a growth regulator (e.g. Moddus). The cost of the growth regulator is likely to add £15 per ha (*£6 per acre*) to the chemical figure in the margins above, with a similar cost increase for the extra Nitrogen.

3. Prices in the table are estimated prices for certified seed for the 2015 year. Current markets for grass seed are well-supplied after good recent harvests. The figures relate to Diploid varieties. Very little *early* Diploid is now grown. Tetraploid prices are £5-£10 per 50kg lower, but yields should be higher (intermediate and late varieties achieving 1,300-2,200kg per ha). High sugar varieties should command a premium of £10-£15 over the values seen in the tables. Amenity ryegrasses and fescues also command a premium for high quality sports use, and some yield nearly as much as agricultural varieties.

4. No allowance has been made above for by-products. Some crops produce 4 to 5 tonnes of threshed hay, which is, however, of low feeding value. This could be worth £300 or more per hectare. Some grasses, especially spring-sown ryegrass, also provide substantial quantities of autumn and winter grazing. Clovers can be either grazed or cut for hay or silage and do not have to be 'shut up' until mid or late May, or, in some cases and seasons, even early June. More grazing (until end of May) and better quality threshed hay is provided with a combination of ryegrass and white clover than with the specialist herbage seed grasses.

5. The seed rate is 10kg per ha for autumn sown Italian ryegrass. Diploid varieties sown at 8-9kgs per ha and tetraploid 10-12kgs. Spring planting seed rates will be lower. If the seed crop is to be undersown, specialist growers often reduce the seed rate for the cover crop by up to half and restrict nitrogen dressing: the cereal yield may thus be reduced by up to 0.6 tonnes per ha. If this is not done the grass seed yield is usually lower in the first year compared with direct drilling, except for ryegrass.

6. Chemical costs will vary depending on the prevalence of grass weeds. Autumn sown crops will have higher costs than spring sown ones, although yields for autumn crops should be higher in the first year. The margin assumes an autumn-sown crop.

7. Labour: see page 172.

Acknowledgement: Thanks to - British Seed Houses, Tel: 01522 868 714; Herbage Seed Services, Tel: 01962 774 432; NIAB, Tel: 01223 342 238.

RYE

Production level	Low	Average	High
Yield: tonnes per ha (tons per acre)	4.90 (2.0)	6.20 (2.5)	7.50 (3.0)
	£	£	£
Output	711 (288)	899 (364)	1,088 (440)
Variable Costs:			
Seed		95 (39)	
Fertiliser................................		159 (64)	
Sprays		105 (43)	
Total Variable Costs	359 (145)	359 (145)	359 (145)
Gross Margin per ha (acre)	**352** (143)	**540** (219)	**729** (295)

1. The price assumed is £145 per tonne for 2015 harvest. This is based on a £10 per tonne premium over the prevailing feed wheat price at the point of movement, based on Oct-Dec delivery. The price assumes the milling specification is achieved. Deductions are made for low quality, and if it is feed grade, price then falls between feed wheat and feed barley. Only a very small percentage of the crop is grown for the free market.

Largely grown on light, low fertility, sandy or stony soils, not suited to other cereals. Yields would clearly be higher on better soils, but then rye has difficulty in competing with wheat and barley; it could never do so on good wheat land. The average yield in the UK in the five years 2009 to 2013 was around 5.8 tonnes per ha.

The area grown in the UK has ranged between 6,000-7,000 ha for several years. Rye crisp-bread is the major outlet. It is also milled into flour, used in mixed-grain bread and muesli. About two-thirds of UK requirements are imported, mainly from Canada (which produces the highest quality), Denmark, Germany and Spain. Demand for UK-grown rye has been falling in recent years, owing to increased competition in the crisp-bread market.

Rye, which is autumn-sown, is drought tolerant and very hardy, can withstand low temperatures and starts growing early in the spring. It has all-round resistance to wheat and barley diseases, e.g. eyespot, and suffers less from take-all than wheat – hence it is a possible replacement for third or fourth wheat. Its vigour keeps weeds down. Its herbicide, fungicide and fertiliser requirements are lower than for other cereals, except for growth regulators. Rye is harvested earlier than winter wheat (useful for following with oilseed rape).

Drawbacks: it sprouts in a wet harvest: must therefore harvest early, at relatively high moisture content. It grows very tall and lodges easily: hence high levels of nitrogen are not possible; but growth regulators help. Its heavy straw crop means very slow combining (takes about twice as long per hectare as wheat and barley), and difficult straw incorporation. New hybrid varieties, with shorter, stiffer straw, are being developed; these would improve the comparative profitability of rye on better soils.

Drilling: 2nd and 3rd weeks September. Harvesting: by mid-August at relatively high moisture content, then dry to 14-15% (no drying costs included in margin).

TRITICALE

Production level	**Low**	**Average**	**High**
Yield: tonnes per ha (tons per acre)	4.00 (1.6)	5.00 (2.0)	7.20 (2.9)
	£	**£**	**£**
Output	520 (211)	650 (263)	936 (379)
Variable Costs:			
Seed		54 (22)	
Fertiliser..................................		153 (62)	
Sprays		70 (28)	
Total Variable Costs	276 (112)	276 (112)	276 (112)
Gross Margin per ha (acre)	**244** (99)	**374** (151)	**660** (267)

A 'man-made' cross between rye and hard wheat. It combines the hardiness of rye and the marketability of feed wheat. It is used in livestock feed, particularly pig and poultry rations, having high levels of lysine. However it is not widely used by feed compounders. The area grown in the UK has risen over recent years to around 15,000ha. A large proportion of this rise is likely to be in the newer spring varieties (see below).

The price is usually £4 or £6 per tonne below the price for feed wheat, but this tends to vary from season to season; £130 per tonne is assumed above for the 2015 harvest crop.

The average yield in the UK in the five years 2009 to 2013 was just below 4.0 tonnes/ha. But in the five years 1996-2000 the average had been over 5.90 tonnes per ha – showing that the potential of the crop is not always fully realised. The low yields are a result of it mainly being grown on light land, especially thin, drought-prone, poorish, marginal cereal-growing soils. In these circumstances, it can frequently out-yield wheat or barley, especially the former, and it has lower input requirements. Its yields tend to be more consistent on such soil than those of barley. Triticale tends to do well compared with second and subsequent wheats owing to its resistance to drought and fungal diseases. It is also less prone to damage than other cereals where rabbit grazing is a problem.

Lower levels of fungicide are needed because of its good disease resistance, except for ergot, but including take-all (making it a possible replacement for a third or fourth wheat, as indicated above). It is a tall crop, which helps to suppress weeds, but it is susceptible to lodging; growth regulators are beneficial. New semi-dwarf varieties are being developed, to overcome straw strength weakness and susceptibility to rust infections.

The crop is best drilled early (September) on very light, drought-prone soils; otherwise October is satisfactory. Harvesting is at approximately the same time as wheat. There is more straw, which slows combining, and incorporation is difficult; this is less of a problem on poor soils as there is less straw.

Spring Triticale

New spring varieties of this crop have been introduced in the last few years. These have been taken up strongly in livestock areas – the north and west of England, as well as western Scotland, Wales and N. Ireland. Being a spring crop means that winter water logging is not an issue, and it can be grown on a wider range of soils. In total over 5,000 ha of spring triticale may well now be grown in the UK: either on its own or often as part of a mixture.

It has lower yields than winter triticale if it is harvested for grain in the conventional way. However, most is whole-cropped to produce an 'arable forage'. Often it is grown in a mixture with a proteins crop – peas or lupins for example. Inputs for spring triticale will be lower than those for winter varieties.

NAKED OATS

Production level	Low	Average	High
Yield: tonnes per ha (tons per acre)	4.50 (1.8)	5.50 (2.2)	6.50 (2.6)
	£	£	£
Output	824 (334)	1,007 (408)	1,190 (482)
Variable Costs:			
Seed		60 (24)	
Fertiliser....................................		126 (51)	
Sprays		100 (41)	
Total Variable Costs	286 (116)	286 (116)	286 (116)
Gross Margin per ha (acre)	**538** (218)	**721** (292)	**904** (366)

Naked oats have a higher protein, energy and oil content than 'traditional' oats, but the fibre content is lower – as the husk is removed during harvesting. Contracts require a maximum moisture content of 14%, which is also recommended for long-term storage.

The area being grown continues to increase steadily. Naked oats now account for in excess of 10% of the traded tonnage of UK oats (i.e. excluding those grown for on-farm use). The traditional markets such as racehorse feed, dog food, and bird feed markets are all increasing. Over recent years the human consumption market has developed so that at least half the crop is now sold for health foods, fancy breads and breakfast cereals. In future, a further growth area is likely to be from demand for inclusion of the crop in monogastric animal feeds. The poultry industry in particular is looking into setting up supply chains.

The 2015 harvest crop price assumed is £183 per tonne, based on contracts offering premiums 35% above the average feed wheat price. The premium can be reduced according to husk content.

In a normal cropping year, over 90% of the crop is winter sown, although the proportion of spring cropping rises after a wet autumn. The margin above assumes winter cropping. NIAB survey results have suggested that yields average 20%-25% less than conventional oats. New spring varieties have become available that offer yields much closer to winter crops. The actual difference in yield will depend on the particular season, but are likely to be in the range 15%-20%.

The agronomy of naked oats is similar to that of husked oat varieties. Variable inputs are lower than for wheat or barley. Traditionally, high nitrogen use has not been possible due to the risk of lodging, however, new semi-dwarf varieties with stiff straw have been introduced. As well as increasing the scope for higher fertiliser applications, this means the crop is also suited to more fertile soils, and growth regulators may be avoided. Oats provide a break in the take-all cycle.

Harvest is early (coming just after winter barley). New varieties are less susceptible to shedding than in the past, however care needs to be taken with both the timing of harvest, and the set-up of the combine, to ensure a clean, saleable, sample.

Naked Barley

Naked barley, suitable for roasting, flaking or milling as pearl barley, is now rarely heard of. It is grown like normal barley, but yields are reckoned to be some 15% lower. It could be either autumn or spring sown.

BORAGE

Production level	Low	Average	High
Yield: tonnes per ha (tons per acre)	0.10 (0.0)	0.40 (0.2)	0.70 (0.3)
	£	£	£
Output	330 (134)	1,320 (535)	2,310 (936)
Variable Costs:			
Seed		153 (62)	
Fertiliser.................................…...		98 (40)	
Sprays ....…...		40 (16)	
Total Variable Costs	291 (118)	291 (118)	291 (118)
Gross Margin per ha (acre)	**39** (16)	**1,029** (417)	**2,019** (818)

Borage is indigenous to Britain (or at least here since Roman times); it has both grown in the wild, and been cultivated for centuries. It is produced principally for use as a dietary supplement, but it may also be used in cosmetics and pharmaceuticals. The oil has a high gamma linolenic acid (GLA) content.

It was first grown as a field crop in the UK in the early 1980's. The last few years have usually seen around 5,000 hectares (*12,500 acres*) planted per year. However, due to a world-wide surplus of GLA, few, if any, contracts were offered in the years 2009 to 2011. The area has recovered since, partly due to the high quality of the UK crop compared to other sources. The usual area should be contracted for 2015.

The harvest crop price assumed is £3,300 per tonne. This is slightly lower than the past two seasons due to currency movements. As the market tends to be volatile, it is essential for a grower to have a buy-back contract with a reputable company. The crop should not be grown speculatively.

The crop is spring sown (March-April) into a good seedbed. Its aggressive growth gives good weed control with a high plant density. There are no significant pests and diseases, except for powdery mildew. Low rainfall areas are preferred owing to harvesting difficulties in wet conditions. It is combined in late July/early August, after swathing and drying, which takes a minimum of two weeks. The costs of swathing is not included in the margin above. Harvesting can be difficult and seed shedding at maturity is a problem. Seed should be promptly dried to 10% for safe storage. Cleaning may be necessary.

Borage should only be considered by those prepared to invest sufficient time in the crop's husbandry, harvest and storage. Borage is a low yield / high risk crop – yields are from virtually nothing to 0.75 tonnes per ha (*6cwt per acre*); average 0.4 (3.2).

Acknowledgement: Thanks to – Frontier, Tel: 01522 556600; Fairking, Tel: 01206 212330; Premium Crops, Tel: 023 9263 2883.

MINORITY CROPS

Camelina Sativa

Camelina, Gold of Pleasure, or False Flax is a fast growing spring (or occasionally winter) sown crop. It is easily grown and harvested and is drought tolerant. The oil contains a range of essential fatty acids. It can be used as a food supplement or in industry as a drying oil. There is currently no commercial scale production in the UK that the authors are aware of. It is thought that current domestic usage requirements could support around 1,000 ha of the crop in the UK. Yields are in the 1.0-2.5 tonne per ha range. Price is uncertain due to the absence of a domestic market but an indicative price is likely to be around £250-£300 per tonne.

Crambe - Abyssinian Mustard

Crambe is an industrial oilseed that contains high levels of erucic acid. Converted into erucamide it is used as a slip agent in plastics and is a constituent of heat sensitive dyes. The area of crambe in the UK had grown to around 5,000 ha in the early 2000's.. However, the major promoter/buyer of the crop went into receivership and little or none is being currently grown commercially.

Crambe is a cruciferous spring crop managed in a similar way to spring oilseed rape. It has a short growing season, requiring only 100-120 days to reach maturity after emergence. As with oilseed rape, timely harvesting is important. Crambe can be combined direct, desiccated and combined or swathed. The crop should be stored and marketed at a moisture content of 9% or less. Yields are in the 2.5 tonne per ha range. Contract prices offered in the past were £180 per tonne. Growing costs are likely to be around £300 per tonne.

Durum Wheat

As well as pasta, durum is used to produce ethnic foods, semolina, biscuits, etc. Domestic demand is relatively small; UK consumption per head is approx. 4% that of Italy and 10% that of France.

The crop started to be grown in England in the late 1970s and reached a high-point of 11,000 ha (*27,000 acres*) in 1984. The area has fluctuated since then, but had declined to well below 1,000 hectares (*2,500 acres*). At present there are no contracts being offered to produce durum in the UK. In the past, an ex-farm premium for 'Grade A' durum of £50 per tonne over feed wheat was offered.

On average the crop should yield 75%-80% of conventional feed wheat in the same situation. As with milling wheat, there is a risk of rejection if contaminated with excess foreign seeds, especially self-set cereals from previous crop; thus safer as a first cereal crop. A poor price is obtained if quality is too poor for pasta and thus has to go for feed.

Durum Wheat Gross Margin Schedule

Yield 6.2t/ha (2.5t/acre), Price £185/t ex-farm	£/ha	(£/ac)
Output	1,147	(465)
Variable Costs:		
Seed	95	(38)
Fertiliser	176	(71)
Sprays	145	(59)
Total Variable Costs	350	(142)
Gross Margin per ha (acre)	**797**	(323)

The crop is likely to be grown only in the driest parts of the east/south east, where it can best compete with second and third wheats. It may be either autumn or spring sown; around two-thirds is currently autumn sown and this is assumed in the table above. The crop is very sensitive to stress and frost-kill in severe winters; the spring-sown crop is more reliable, and cheaper to grow, but the yield is usually 15-20% lower. Spring crops also allow more opportunities for black grass control. The crop has a higher disease resistance than other wheats, except for eyespot and ergot.

Harvesting is a critical operation; it needs to be done as soon as the crop reaches 20% moisture content, or at most 18%: it is very prone to sprouting and the quality for semolina is reduced if harvest is delayed. Durum must be dried (slowly) to 15%. It is easier and quicker to dry than normal wheat. The straw is of poorer quality and lesser quantity than conventional wheat straw and is therefore rarely baled.

Echium

Echium is a relatively new commercial plant to the UK. It has been cultivated on contract for less than a decade. It is a member of the Boraginacea family and is rich in stearidonic acid, which is used in cosmetic creams to reduce skin wrinkling and the effects of sunburn.

In past years there has been around 1,000 ha or so grown in the UK. A global glut of the active ingredient led to no contracts being offered in the years 2009 to 2014. It is believed that few if any contracts will be offered for 2015 as there is currently little to no demand for Echium oil as it is uncompetitive against marine oil alternatives. It is essential for a grower to have a buy-back contract with a reputable company, and the crop should not be grown speculatively. In the past prices have collapsed to almost nothing due to over-supply in the market.

The crop can be grown as far north as Yorkshire. It has a husbandry programme similar to that of borage but does not shed its seed as readily as borage. The seed is relatively small in size. Echium is suitable for light to medium land whereas borage performs better on a wider range of soil types.

The crop is sown in April and should come to harvest in July/August. There appear to be no significant pests of the crop. Harvesting is carried out with the use of a swather. Yields are approximately 250kg per ha (100kg per acre). Contract prices have been around £3,500 per tonne of clean seed.

Evening Primrose

This crop is an important source of gamma linolenic acid (GLA), but it is no longer grown in the UK and very little is cultivated elsewhere in Western Europe – it has been largely superseded by borage, which is easier to grow. The crop is still widely grown in China where the climate is more suitable, and labour costs are lower. Previous editions have given details of the crop and possible gross margin data.

Flax (cut flax for industrial fibre)

Flax was re-introduced into the UK during the 1990s, not as the traditional, pulled, long fibre variety used for linen textiles but as a cut, combinable crop producing shorter fibres for industrial uses – 'short-fibre flax'. As a natural, biodegradable fibre and a renewable resource it was promoted as a 'green' alternative to synthetic fibres and plastics. New markets were developed and several processing plants set up – the area of flax expanded to 20,200 ha in 1996. Following low prices and reform of the subsidy regime, the area fell to less than 2,000 ha by 2003, and the one remaining processing facility in Wales was closed. Little, if any, is currently grown.

The agronomy of flax is similar to that of linseed but it is harvested earlier. It is spring sown, suitable for most soil types although lighter soil is preferred. It is a low input crop but weed control is essential. It grows best in areas of high rainfall such as Wales and the South-west. There are several harvesting options (described in earlier editions). Currently the preferred option is desiccation followed by combining. The straw is left to rett in the field and then baled. Retting takes 10-21 days, depending on weather conditions. The price paid for straw will reflect quality. The fibre content of a reasonable crop is 20-30%.

Hemp

The traditional use for hemp was in canvas and rope manufacture. New uses have developed over recent years in building materials and producing internal car panels for the automotive industry. The core or pith of the plant is used for horse or poultry bedding.

The area grown had be stable at around 1,000 ha have been in recent years. However, the UK's sole commercial processor of the crop went into administration in autumn 2013. With no buyer for the company, it seems that the processing factory will cease operation, and no contracts will be available in the UK for the foreseeable future.

Hemp is drilled in late April/May and the fibre crop grows 3 to 3.5m (10-12 feet) tall. Hemp Technology suggests a minimum area of 10 ha. A well-grown crop should have no weed or pest problems. The crop is mowed in mid to late August, and then baled when it is dry, bleached, and partially retted after 2-3 weeks. Average yields should be around 7.5 tonne per ha (*3.0t per acre*), with target yields at 9.5 tonnes per ha (*3.8t per acre*). The margin below assumes that the grower will undertake the cutting and baling operations. If contractors are used then the variable costs will obviously be higher. The crop must be stored under cover.

The margin below is based on the past contract price of £160 per tonne delivered. Transport costs need to be taken into consideration. A figure of £15 per tonne is used in the table below.

Hemp Gross Margin Schedule

Yield 7.5t/ha (3.0t/acre), Price £160/t delivered	£/ha	(£/ac)
Output	1,200	(486)
Variable Costs:		
Seed	135	(55)
Fertiliser	175	(71)
Sprays	20	(8)
Haulage to factory (£15/tonne)	113	(46)
Total Variable Costs	443	(179)
Gross Margin per ha (acre).................................	**757**	(307)

Dual Hemp

Hemp may also be grown as a dual-purpose crop. In recent years, up to 10-15% of the national hemp crop was of this type. The crop is left to mature longer, and then the top can be combined for the seed before the straw is mown and retted. A yield of 1.0-1.2 tonne per ha (*0.4-0.5t per ac*) of seed is possible. The seed was worth around £500 per tonne. However, the yield of straw is lower at 5-6 tonnes per ha (*2.0-2.4t per ac*), with the price being the same as 'conventional' hemp. The seed is cold-pressed to produce high-value cooking oil, and is also used for bird feed, fishing bait and in nutritional supplements and cosmetics. Agronomy and costs are likely to be similar to a fibre crop. Because of the time needed to let the seed heads mature, an earlier-maturing variety is used. The later harvest also means that this crop is more suitable for early land in the East and South.

Grain Maize

Maize is one of the major global grains – with world output being higher than that for wheat. However, the climate of the UK has made it difficult to ripen the crop and most maize is grown for forage rather than grain. A combination of earlier varieties, the development of machinery that copes with wet conditions, and even possibly the effects of warmer summers has improved the prospects of this crop.

There is market potential, as well over a million tonnes of grain maize are imported annually. It is used in animal rations, human foods, and in industrial processes. Marketing the UK crop is a problem at present as consignments are generally not big enough to interest the major buyers. The animal feed market is the likeliest outlet for domestic production - a specialised or local market can be developed, for example feed for pigeons or corn-fed chickens. The basis of pricing in the margin is a £15-£25 per tonne premium over feed wheat. This assumes sale into a 'niche' premium market.

There is no fundamental difference between forage and grain maize – the same varieties are simply left in the field for 3-6 weeks longer to let the cobs mature. It is difficult to know how much of the total UK maize area is taken for grain but it could be around 3,000 ha. The crop can be grown south of a line from Bristol to East Anglia, excluding the far south-west. Fields should be below 500ft in elevation and south-facing. To maximise heat units, the crop should be drilled as soon as soil temperatures are above 8°c – usually late April/May. Harvest by conventional combine with an adapted header in October/November. In UK conditions grain maize seldom drops below 30% moisture. The crop needs to be dried to 15% for storage which can be expensive and time-consuming. On good land the crop can yield 8-10 tonnes per ha but the average is not likely to be so high.

Grain Maize Gross Margin Schedule

	£/ha	(£/ac)
Yield 7.5t/ha (3.0t/acre), Price £155/t ex-farm		
Output	1,163	(471)
Variable Costs:		
Seed	155	(63)
Fertiliser	111	(45)
Sprays	70	(28)
Total Variable Costs	336	(136)
Gross Margin per ha (acre)..................................	**827**	(335)
But note high drying costs:		
£15-25/t on-farm; £20-30/t off-farm	113-225	(46-91)

The majority of grain maize is currently stored as a crimped product. This sees the crop cut at 30-35% moisture from mid-October to early November with the 'wet' grain being processed, and an additive added (usually an organic acid). The overall cost of crimping and preservative is around £12-£15 per tonne. The grain is clamped or put into large bales or bags. It provides a very digestible dairy feed of high nutrition content. Yields can be 11-13 tonnes per ha and it sells for £180-£220 per tonne ex-farm.

Acknowledgement: Thanks to - Maize Growers Association, Tel: 01363 775040.

Millet

Millet describes a range of small-seeded grain plants covering a number of different species. The most commonly grown type in the UK is proso (also called white or common) millet. Millet has been cultivated since prehistoric times. It is a major food source in arid and semi-arid parts of the world; predominantly India, China, and parts of Africa. The crop has been grown in the UK for game cover for many years, but it has recently been commercialised to supply grain to the bird seed market.

Millet Gross Margin Schedule

	£/ha	(£/ac)
Yield 3.0t/ha (1.2t/acre), Price £235/t ex-farm		
Output	705	(286)
Variable Costs:		
Seed	100	(41)
Fertiliser	110	(45)
Sprays	60	(24)
Total Variable Costs	270	(109)
Gross Margin per ha (acre)...............................	**435**	(176)

The UK currently imports approximately 25,000 tonnes of millet for bird and pet feed each year. Domestic plantings in 2013 were in the region of 1,000 ha. There is the potential to raise this to around 5,000 ha. Full import substitution is unlikely to be possible as UK seed cannot match the quality of the best imported millet.

The crop can be grown on a range of soil types, but as it is drought tolerant, it is often planted on lighter land. It does not grow well in heavy or very chalky soils. The crop requires warm temperatures to ripen and is therefore best suited to the South of England.

The crop is late drilled, usually in May once the soil has warmed up sufficiently. It can be planted as late as June. It requires a fine seedbed. The crop grows to about a metre high and is ready to harvest after 4½ months in mid to late September. The crop is usually desiccated before harvesting with a conventional combine harvester.

Yields are in the range 2.5-4.0 tonnes per ha. The contract price for 2015 is not known at the time of writing. However, contract values have historically been around £100 per tonne above the feed wheat price and a price of £235 per tonne is assumed.

Acknowledgement: Thanks to - Premium Crops, Tel: 02392 632 883. Soya UK, Tel: 02380 696922.

Navy Beans

Navy beans are the basis for the familiar canned 'baked beans'. Over 100,000t of these are consumed annually in the UK – with the vast majority of these being imported from North America. A few years ago there was some interest in the crop, as varieties adapted to the soil types and climate of the UK were introduced. However, disappointing prices, variable yields, and the lack of area aid discouraged growers. It seems unlikely that the economics will encourage a resurgence of production in the foreseeable future.

The crop requires good fertile land and some care in growing. Sowing is in mid-May when there is no further frost risk. Harvesting is late August/early September. The target yield is 3.0 tonnes per ha but the average is likely to be substantially less. When budgeting, an average of around 2.0 tonnes per ha (*0.8t per acre*) could be assumed. There is very little market information available on price, but it is likely to be in the region of £250-£300 per tonne. Variable costs are likely to be in the range £300-£350 per ha.

Poppies

Commercial growing of poppies in the UK began in the early 2000's. The poppy heads are processed to produce morphine for pharmaceutical purposes. The seeds are sold into the culinary market. A bit less than 3,000 ha of the crop are currently grown – all on contract to the sole UK processor.

The crop needs free-draining alkaline soils; it is planted in the second half of March, and is harvested in early to mid-August. The processor undertakes the harvesting operation with a specialised machine. Seed is included as part of the contract, as is agronomy advice (the processor specifies the pesticides to be used). The grower needs to be able to offer on-floor drying facilities.

The contract for the 2015 harvest has not yet been finalised. In previous years a basic fee of £200 per ha was paid by the processor, which was then topped-up by a bonus based on the yield of the alkaloid from the crop.

Poppy Gross Margin Schedule

	£/ha	(£/ac)
Fixed Area Payment	200	(81)
Alkaloid Bonus Payment	980	(397)
Output	1,180	(478)
Variable Costs:		
Seed	0	(0)
Fertiliser	169	(69)
Sprays	170	(69)
Total Variable Costs	339	(137)
Gross Margin per ha (acre).................................	**841**	(340)

Acknowledgement: Thanks to – Macfarlan Smith, Tel: 01225 793 679.

Soya Beans

Soya is a sub-tropical crop in origin, grown mainly in North and South America, but also to a small extent in southern Europe. The UK imports three quarters of a million tonnes each year as beans and almost a further 2 million tonnes as meal, all for animal feed, so there would appear to be a ready market for the home grown product.

Various attempts have been made to commercialise the crop in the UK. In the late 1990's new varieties were introduced and by the early 2000's the area expanded to 1,700 ha. But after several difficult years the planted area declined. In recent years, less than 100 ha were being grown. However, the plant breeding process has continued and further varietal improvements yield and earliness have been made. Importantly, the soya price has been at high levels, making the economics more attractive. An expansion in area has been seen in the last couple of years, although the amount grown in the UK is still likely to be well below 500 ha. A shift to spring cropping may see the planted area rise once again in 2015.

Soya Bean Gross Margin Schedule

Yield 2.5t/ha (1.0t/acre), Price £400/t ex-farm	£/ha	(£/ac)
Output	1,000	(405)
Variable Costs:		
Seed	145	(59)
Fertiliser	56	(23)
Sprays	75	(30)
Total Variable Costs	276	(112)
Gross Margin per ha (acre).................................	**724**	(293)

The crop is sown in late April or early May, depending on soil temperature, into a fine moist seedbed. The crop has a requirement for high temperatures and cumulative day-degrees of heat (similar to maize). This effectively restricts the crop to the southern half of England. The crop is combine harvested in September, usually after desiccation. The crop should be cleaned and dried to 14% moisture and 2% admixture.

As a legume, soya is a good alternative break crop, largely fixing its own nitrogen. Maintenance P and K is required plus 10-20kg of N to get the crop started. Spray costs also tend to be low.

Target yield is 3.0 tonnes per ha but the average is likely to be less; an average of 2.5 tonnes per ha (*1.0t per acre*) can be assumed. The price is largely determined by the price of imported crop. The UK crop is GM free, for which a premium is paid. A further premium may be paid for Identity Preserved UK crop which goes into human consumption or for organically grown soya. For 2015 harvest the price is estimated to be £400 per tonne.

Sunflower

The UK imports the equivalent of 400,000 tonnes of sunflower seed each year, mainly as sunflower oil. None is commercially crushed in the UK. There has been continued interest in sunflower, but late harvests and low yields have restricted the development of the crop. It is unclear how much of the crop is currently been commercially grown in the UK, but it is likely to be less than 500 ha. This would produce some 1,000 tonnes of seed. Almost all UK production goes into pet-food or bird seed. Producers should satisfy themselves of the end-market before planting the crop. The birdseed market takes 20,000 tonnes of sunflower seed annually, so there is scope for import substitution. Some attempts have been made to cold-press sunflowers to produce a UK-sunflower oil, but this market is still restricted to local and small-scale production.

Extra-early maturing semi-dwarf hybrid varieties are the most suitable to conditions in the UK. The crop needs a relatively mild climate and is best grown south-east of a line from the Wash to east Dorset. Sowing is from April to early May when the soil temperature is 7-8°C. Although sunflower will grow on a broad range of soil types its capacity to do well in dry and sandy soils and areas of low rainfall is a recommendation. Pre-emergence weed control may be necessary; at the right plant density weeds should not subsequently be a problem. As it is a broad row crop, chemical or mechanical weed control is possible. Sclerotina and botrytis, in a wet season, may affect the crop; on areas of less than 6 ha bird damage can be serious. Sunflower has a low nitrogen requirement.

Harvesting is from mid-September by combine harvester. Yields of up to 2.5 tonnes per ha with oil content of 44% are possible. The crop is dried to 8-9% for safe storage, which can be expensive. The price is usually based on a premium over the price of oilseed rape (around £50 per tonne), but other pricing mechanisms may be used in specialist markets. Growing costs will be in the region of £300-£375 per ha.

Others

Other crops that have been in the news in recent years as possible new crops for the future (or present crops capable of substantial development) include the following: chickpeas and lentils, ahiflower, fenugreek, meadowfoam, cuphea, peppermint, quinoa, buckwheat, honesty and herbs for their essential oils. At present there are no reliable data for these crops on average yield expectations and little on prices or variable costs, when grown on a commercial scale in this country. A number of them are either for the health food market or are sources of oil for industry as replacements for whale oil and light mineral oil. Research continues on many of them. More details may be available from the contact listed below;

Contact: National Non-Food Crops Centre (NNFCC): www.nnfcc.co.uk

VINING PEAS

Production level	Low	Average	High
Yield: tonnes per ha (tons per acre)	3.20 (1.3)	4.30 (1.7)	5.18 (2.1)
	£	£	£
Output	1,024 (415)	1,376 (557)	1,656 (671)
Variable Costs:			
Seed..		220 (89)	
Fertiliser...................................		81 (33)	
Sprays......................................		124 (50)	
Total Variable Costs		425 (172)	
Gross Margin per ha (acre)	**599** (243)	**951** (385)	**1,231** (499)

1. The table above relates to vining peas grown on contract where harvesting (approx. £78/tonne) and haulage (approx. £30/tonne) are paid for separately; the average price in this situation ranges from £250 to £370/tonne depending primarily on quality. The average yield is taken as 4.5 tonnes/ha; the national average (fresh weight) for the last five years has ranged between 3.6 and 5.1 although growers are paid on frozen weight. Top quality ('150 minute') peas have to be grown within 40 miles of the factory. More distant 'long haul' peas will be in the lower price range. A pea viner costs in the region of £400,000.

    The average yield of petit pois is lower but the price averages 12 to 15% more.

2. *Fertiliser*. Many growers use no fertiliser; but RB209 suggests P&K. Here P_2O_5:K_2O = 85:65kg/ha respectively.

3. *Sprays*. Both herbicide and aphicide are commonly used with fungicides being used dependant on seasonal requirements.

5. *Total Area:* Around 32,000 ha are grown in the UK annually with a view to vining a 152,000-tonne crop.

MAINCROP POTATOES

Production level	Low	Average	High
Yield: tonnes per ha (tons per acre)	37.0 (15)	45.0 (18.2)	53.0 (21.5)
	£	£	£
Output	4,551 (1843)	5,535 (2242)	6,519 (2640)
Variable Costs:			
Seed..		787 (319)	
Fertiliser.....................................		374 (151)	
Sprays...		703 (285)	
Casual lab. (harvest & grading)............	722 (292)	878 (355)	1034 (419)
Sundries (levy, sacks, etc.)..............	377 (153)	459 (186)	541 (219)
Total Variable Costs	2,963 (1200)	3,201 (1296)	3,438 (1393)
Gross Margin per ha (acre)	**1,588** (643)	**2,334** (945)	**3,081** (1248)

1. *Prices*. The price assumed above is £130 per tonne for ware and £30 for stock feed (assumed to be 7½ per cent), which is £123 per tonne for the whole crop. The actual price in any one season depends largely on the national crop size but also international trade. Variations according to quality and market (as well as season) are considerable. The average GB price for wares between 2003 and 2014 was £138/tonne.

2. *Physical Inputs*. Seed: 60% planted with certified seed: 2.8 tonnes per hectare at £300 per tonne (the price varies widely from season to season); 40% with once-grown seed: 2.6 tonnes per hectare at £240 per tonne. Sprays: herbicide, blight control, and haulm destruction. *Sprays*. Refer to Agrochemical Rates on page 274, but include Nematode (PCN) spray, which accounts for about 60% of potato land. This accounts for £420/ha

3. *Casual Labour*. The figure in the table above is for assistance during (machine) harvesting and for grading/riddling (approx. £19.50/tonne); it is assumed that most of the labour for the latter is supplied by casuals.

4. *Contract* mechanical harvesting: £600-620/hectare (excl. pickers, carting, etc.), £1,000/hectare incl. carting. Other contract work see page 195.

5. *British Potato Council (AHDB) levy*: £42.62/ha (£17.25/acre) for growers to April 2015; exempt from levy if less than 3ha grown. 2015 rates as yet unpublished.

6. *Potato Land Rentals* range depending on the year, location, soil and water availability, ranging from over £650/ha (£260/acre) to as much as £1,200/ha (£500/acre). Potato rents are the product of potato profitability and also cereals as they are the alternative. In addition late harvested potatoes depress yield of following crop. As a result some have tried to increase potato rents on back of increased cereal prices.

7. *Sacks*. Approx. £8.40 per tonne, plus the cost of wire ties or stitching.

8. *Specialised Equipment Prices*: see page 189.

9. *Potato Store Costs*: see page 226.

10. *Labour:* see p. 172.

EARLY POTATOES

Production level	Low	Average	High
Yield: tonnes per ha (tons per acre)	18.0 (7)	23.0 (9.3)	28.0 (11.3)
	£	£	£
Output	3,600 (1458)	4,600 (1863)	5,600 (2268)
Variable Costs:			
Seed...		850 (344)	
Fertiliser......................................		264 (107)	
Sprays..		377 (153)	
Casual labour................................	334 (135)	388 (157)	442 (179)
Sundries (levy, sacks, etc.)...............	230 (93)	293 (119)	357 (145)
Total Variable Costs	2,055 (832)	2,173 (880)	2,290 (928)
Gross Margin per ha (acre)	**1,545** (626)	**2,427** (983)	**3,310** (1340)

1. *Prices and Yields.* The price assumed above is an average of £200 per tonne for a 23 tonne/ha yield. However, yields increase and prices fall as the season progresses. Thus both depend on the date of lifting, e.g. late May to early June, 7 to 12t/ha; July, 20 to 30 t/ha. Prices in late May to mid-June can be up to three times those in July; the very earliest crops (early May) can even fetch more than £1,000 per tonne, but the price could be down to £500 by mid-May and to £250 or even £200 by early June. Thus the average output of £5,290 given above could be obtained from 10 tonnes at £529 per tonne, 15 at £353, 20 at £265 or 30 at £176.

2. *Casual labour for planting*: £145 per hectare, plus help with harvesting/grading (£11.40/tonne). *Sprays.* Refer to Agrochemical Rates on page 274

3. *British Potato Council (AHDB) levy*: £42.62/ha (£17.25/acre) for growers to April 2015; exempt from levy if less than 3ha grown. 2015 rates as yet unpublished.

4. *Labour:* see p. 172.

   The percentages of the total potato area in Great Britain planted in early, second early and main crop, respectively are approximately 5, 31 and 63 in England, 20, 52 and 28 in Wales, 3, 38 and 59 in Scotland and 5, 33 and 62 of the total GB potato area.

SUGAR BEET

Production level	Low	Average	High
Yield: tonnes per ha (tons per acre)*	59.5 (24)	70.0 (28.4)	80.5 (32.6)
	£	£	£
Output	1,756 (711)	2,065 (836)	2,375 (962)
Variable Costs:			
Seed..		190 (77)	
Fertiliser...................................		221 (90)	
Sprays......................................		230 (93)	
Contract Harvest........................		245 (99)	
Transport (Contract)...................	321 (130)	378 (153)	435 (176)
Total Variable Costs	1,207 (489)	1,264 (512)	1,321 (535)
Gross Margin per ha (acre)	**548** (222)	**801** (325)	**1,054** (427)

* *'Adjusted tonnes' at standard 16% sugar content*

1. Note, these figures are for the 2015/16 harvest crop, meaning cultivation in 2015, delivery in 2015/16.

2. *Prices.* The 'all-in' delivered price is falling in 2015/16 to £29.51 per adjusted tonne. This is based on 90% sold 'in contract' 5% industrial contract entitlement (ICE) and 5% non-contract. The 'in-contract' and ICE beet price is forecast at 24.00 plus average transport of £6.00 and £5.50 per tonne and late delivery allowances of 40p/tonne. Non-contract beet price is projected at £12.50/tonne with a £4.50 transport allowance.

   Late delivery bonus. 26 December - 7 January: 0.8% of price; thereafter, the rate rises by 0.3% per day and at 0.4% per day from 1 March onwards.

   An Inter-Professional Agreement between the NFU and British Sugar has historically been the process for negotiating the sugarbeet price. This is currently in place for future years but is not mandatory from this year. The global sugar price has fallen sharply and there is ample sugar in Europe and the UK with export restrictions, hence the expected fall in prices.

3. *Sprays.* Refer to Agrochemical Rates on page 274

4. *Contract.* Excludes carting or £296 per hectare including carting.

5. *Transport.* Contract haulage charges vary according to distance to factory. The figure assumed above is £5.40 per (unadjusted) tonne of unwashed beet including loading and cleaning (dirt and top tare assumed at 14% in total).

TOP FRUIT

The figures indicate a range within which the performance of most (established) orchards falls. The gross margin is calculated as lower yields less lower costs/higher yields less higher costs. In practice yields are not necessarily so directly linked to costs.

	Dessert Apples		Culinary Apples		Pears	
	Low	High	Low	High	Low	High
Yield: tonnes/ha	15	55	25	50	15	30
Price (£/tonne)	525	895	265	525	475	685
	£		£		£	
Output	7,875	49,225	6,625	26,250	7,125	20,550
Variable Costs*						
Orchard Depreciation	300	2,000	167	1,250	133	325
Fertilisers/Sprays	890	1,485	690	1,285	690	1,135
Crop Sundries	160	635	210	530	160	425
Harvesting	948	3,476	1,300	2,600	948	1,896
Grading/Packing	2,020	7,405	3,365	6,730	2,020	4,040
Packaging	780	8,583	780	3,641	624	3,745
Transport	946	5,201	788	3,678	709	2,207
Commission/Levies	710	4,430	600	2,360	640	1,850
Variable Costs*	6,754	33,215	7,900	22,074	5,925	15,623
Gross Margin	1,121	16,010	-1,275	4,176	1,200	4,927

* Excludes Storage

1. *Price:* Average of all grades. Price is not only influenced by grade-out, but also by variety, customer and pack format (which in turn may affect packing, packaging costs).

2. *Orchard Depreciation:* Establishment costs written off over lifetime of orchard. Establishment includes trees and stakes and, in newer plantings, support structures and irrigation. Total establishment costs of £6,200 - £31,000 per hectare at planting densities of 750 – 4,000 trees per hectare.

3. *Orchard Duration:* Traditional dessert apples around 20 years, with culinary and pears frequently 30 years plus. More recently planted denser apple and pear systems likely to be nearer 15 years, with full cropping reached in years 3-5 (6-9 for traditional systems). Figures above include an allowance for 5% immature trees.

4. *Crop Sundries:* Including tree ties, stake replacement, tree replacement, bee hire, picking hods, bin depreciation etc.

5. *Harvesting:* Based on £63.20 per tonne average (to include supervision, Employer's NI & holiday allowance) for dessert apples and pears and £52.00 per tonne for culinary. In practice can vary significantly with variety, yield, fruit size and quality, etc.

6. *Grading and Packing:* Based on £134.60 per tonne. Can vary considerably, particularly with crop quality.

7. *Packaging:* Typical average of between £55 and £160 per tonne, although may be higher with specialist formats (e.g. overwrapped packs). Considerable variations arise from both crop quality (i.e. grade-out), customer and pack format.

8. *Transport:* Includes allowance for farm to packer, as well as delivery to final customer.

9. *Commission/Levies:* Including both marketer's and retailer's commission, as well as levies (e.g. English Apples and Pears, AHDB). A total figure of 9% has been used, although it should be emphasised that charges can vary considerably. N.B. This category **does not** include levy payments under the Producer Organisation regime.

SOFT FRUIT

The figures – for both soil-grown and a tabletop substrate crop - indicate a range within which the performance of many, but not all crops is likely to fall. The gross margins are lower yields less lower costs/higher yields less higher costs. In practice, yields are not necessarily linked to costs.

	Strawberries Raised Bed June bearers (Soil)		Strawberries Ever bearers (Substrate-Tabletop)		Raspberries (Soil)	
	Low	High	Low	High	Low	High
Yield: tonnes/ha	18.0	23.0	28.0	44.0	8.0	15.0
Price (£/tonne)	2,525	3,375	2,525	3,375	5,265	7,105
	£		£		£	
Output	45,450	77,625	70,700	148,500	42,120	106,575
Variable Costs						
Plants/Planting/Substrate/Wirework	3,010	3,855	11,615	19,005	1,480	1,795
Structures (average annual cost)	5,280	8,445	7,390	10,555	5,280	8,445
Fertilisers/Sprays/Predators	1,140	1,900	1,710	2,850	855	1,330
Fieldwork	1,875	4,160	3,120	8,325	3,120	5,200
Harvesting	14,410	18,845	16,260	25,550	15,520	29,100
Grading/Packing	4,680	5,980	7,280	11,440	3,745	7,020
Packaging	6,550	8,370	10,190	16,015	5,825	10,920
Transport	3,220	4,115	5,010	7,875	1,865	3,495
Commission	4,090	6,990	6,360	13,370	3,790	9,590
Variable Costs	44,255	62,660	68,935	114,985	41,480	76,895
Gross Margin	1,195	14,965	1,765	33,515	640	29,680

1. *Strawberries – June bearers:* Plants – assumes 35,000 per hectare with 60-day cropping in year 1 followed by 2 further years in main season production. Plants/planting/sterilisation written off over crop life of 3 years. Bed making not included as a variable cost.

   Structures – annual cost of poly-tunnels including both metalwork (w/o 10 years) and plastic (w/o 3 years). Costs also included for erection, dismantling and venting.

   Fieldwork – weeding, runner removal, leaf thinning etc.

   Harvesting- including supervision, Employer's NI & holiday allowance.

   Grading/Packing at £260/t. Packaging at £364/t, Transport at £179/t.

   Commission/Levies: Including both marketeer's and retailer's commission, as well as levies (e.g. AHDB). A total figure of 9% has been used, although it should be emphasised that charges can vary considerably. N.B. This category does not include levy payments under the Producer Organisation regime.

2. *Strawberries – Tabletop Ever bearers:* Plants – assumes 40,000 per hectare. Plants/planting written off over crop life of one year. Cost of substrate bags w/o 3 years.

Structures – poly-tunnel cost as for June-bearers, together with annual cost of tabletop system (estimated as £20,000 w/o 10 years, although tabletop system costs can vary considerably)

Fieldwork – weeding, runner removal, leaf thinning and tucking, truss support etc.

Harvesting- including supervision, Employer's NI & holiday allowance.

Grading, Packing / Packaging / Transport / Commission - as for June bearers.

3. *Raspberries:* Plants – 8000/ha at 42p per plant. Planting at 12p per plant.

- Structures – as for strawberries.
- Wirework – to include material and labour.
- Plants/planting/wirework written off over crop life of, say 5 years (crop life typically 4 to 7 years).
- Harvesting (including supervision, employer's NI & holiday allowance) – at £1940 per tonne (£1.94 per kilo).
- Grading/Packing – at £468 per tonne (47 pence per kilo).
- Packaging – at £728 per tonne (73 pence per kilo).
- Transport – at £233 per tonne (23 pence per kilo).
- *Commission/Levies:* Including both marketeer's and retailer's commission, as well as levies (e.g. AHDB). A total figure of 9% has been used, although it should be emphasised that charges can vary considerably. N.B. This category does not include levy payments under the Producer Organisation regime.

Blackcurrants

Although a soft fruit, this crop is much more of a field crop grown on arable farms with machine harvesting. The majority of the UK blackcurrant crop is grown for processing into cordial drink. Typical output is 6-7 tonnes/ha sold at £600-£700 per tonne = £3,600-£5,000/ha, with annual variable costs of say £1,430/ha (principally share of crop establishment, fertilisers and sprays) leaving a gross margin of £2,200-£3,500/ha. Establishment costs approximately £7,000/ha for bushes with full production in year 2 followed by up to 10 years cropping.

Acknowledgement (Top & Soft Fruit): Thanks to - Andersons Midlands

FIELD-SCALE VEGETABLES

In order to grow field vegetable crops commercially, certain resources are necessary, the key being good quality land. The overhead structure of the farm is somewhat different to that of combinable crops as is crop marketing. These are more like products than commodities so a market is necessary in advance of cultivation. In some cases major costs such as harvesting, packing and marketing expenses are borne by the produce company taking the crop, although the pricing structure of the product will reflect this.

Per Hectare (acre)	Dry Bulb Onions		Cauliflower		Calabrese	
Yield: tonnes/ha (tons/acre)	41	(16.6)				
Net Price (£/tonne)	140					
	£		£		£	
Output	5,740	(2,325)	4,445	(1,800)	3,765	(1,525)
Variable Costs:						
Seed	753	(305)	972	(394)	840	(340)
Fertiliser	359	(145)	465	(188)	417	(169)
Sprays	629	(255)	213	(86)	247	(100)
Casual Labour			1493	(605)	1493	(605)
Packaging/consumables			266	(108)	266	
Total Variable Costs	1,741	(705)	3,409	(1,381)	3,263	(1,322)
Gross Margin	3,999	(1,620)	1,036	(420)	502	(203)

The unit sale of cauliflower and calabrese can differ according to retailer supplier arrangement. For example some might be sold on a pence per head basis, pounds per tray, or pound per tonne and therefore a general output calculation has been provided. Sizes of heads and percentages harvested vary enormously and therefore yield so an average yield and price calculation is also ambiguous.

Dependant on the system, field scale vegetables have a high working capital requirement relative to other cropping alternatives, and bear considerable risk (both yield of saleable product and price vary enormously according to production and also demand factors). It is therefore necessary to carefully research the potential end market in terms of its expectations and cost structure.

Cauliflower and Calabrese give an example of brassica production. The majority of fresh produce crops such as carrots, parsnips, leeks, lettuce, rhubarb, and brassicas are now grown by a few highly specialised growers with in-house marketing departments. These growers supply the multiple retailers with high volumes and work to exacting specifications. The other key market for fresh produce is the local market, usually on a smaller scale and often tied into a local food chain such as a farm shop.

HOPS

Output Data

Hops are sold to contracts and on the open market, the latter varying greatly in price. They are sold per kilogram or in 50kg lots, (historically known as Zentners). The national area of hops has recently dropped below 1,000 hectares, most of which is in Hereford and Worcestershire. Recent average national yields have been at the low end of this gross margin, but top producers can achieve more.

This gross margin spreads the establishment costs over 11 years and wirework structure over 40. There is no harvest in year 1 but substantial investment.

Hop Gross Margin Schedule

Production level	Low	Average	High
Yield: Kg per ha (Kg/Acre)	1350 (546.8)	1500 (607.5)	1600 (648.0)
	£	£	£
Output	8,640 (3499)	9,600 (3888)	10,240
Variable Costs:			
Establishment		1020 (413)	
Growing Costs		1600 (648)	
Harvesting		3200 (1,296)	
Total Variable Costs		5820 (2,357)	
Gross Margin per ha (acre)	**2,820** (1,142)	**3,780** (1,531)	**4,420** (1,790)
Overheads		2,875 (1,164)	
Return	**-55** -(22)	**905** (367)	**1,545** (626)

Establishment Costs

	£/ha		£/ha
Ground Preparation	250	Ties & Strings	300
Plants	2,400	Fert/Spray	250
Wirework Structure	6,875	Labour	300
Planting	500	Sundries	300
Total	**11,175**	**Cost per Year**	**1,020**

Growing Costs; Fertiliser & sprays £1,100, crop sundries £200, labour £1,100/hectare

Harvesting: labour £1,400, drying fuel £650 per hectare

Overheads: general labour £500, power and Machinery £1,800 inc. harvesting machinery, admin & property costs £575 (rent not included). Costs per hectare

A new hop garden (erecting the poles, wiring and planting) could cost in the order of £25,000 per hectare (£8,500 per acre), which would be expected to last 40 years. About 4,000 plants per hectare (60p each) are planted in a new hop garden, which would be expected to last 10-12 years.

Acknowledgement: Thanks to – Ali Capper, British Hops Association alicapper@mac.com

VINEYARDS

The total planted area under vines in England and Wales in 2013 was 1,884 hectares with 1,571 in production. Plantings have increased from a low point of 773 ha in 2003. This data is collected by the Wine Standards Branch (WSB) of the Food Standards Agency which is under a statutory authority to maintain a Vineyard Register. The 2013 area showed a considerable jump (446 ha) over the 2012 figures, reflecting the efforts of the WSB to update the register. Plantings in 2014 were high and industry estimates put the total planted area, as of June 2014, at least 1,950 hectares. There are 448 registered vineyards of 0.10 hectare or more as at August 2013, plus several smaller ones run as a hobby and not selling wine. The average size of vineyards in the UK is 4.2 ha. However, there are several vineyards of over 100 hectares and the 50 largest vineyards account for around 75% of total production. There is no EU restriction on planting vines in the UK, and in 2008 it was confirmed that there will not be one in the future, whatever level production reaches. Changes to the vine variety legislation also meant that, from August 2009, almost any variety may be legally planted in the UK.

2013 was a good year for UK vineyards, a welcome relief after the very low yields of 2012 and a total of 4.45 million 75 cl bottles of wine, both still and sparkling were produced. The five-year average yield is 1,978 litres per hectare which is low as there are many young vineyards and under-performing and poorly managed vineyards included in the figures. Yields in well-run, favourably sited vineyards would be several times these levels. Most UK wines used to be white, but the proportion of red (and mainly) rosé has risen to around 25% of the total. Industry estimates suggest 60% of the total amount produced is made into sparkling wine. Since the very warm year of 2003, plantings of Champagne varieties (Chardonnay, Pinot Noir and Meunier) have increased significantly, and the majority of plantings in the last decade have been for the production of sparkling wine. Chardonnay and Pinot Noir are now the most widely planted varieties (about 425 ha each) and these, together with Meunier (100 ha), account for around 50% of the total vine area. Bacchus, the most widely planted still wine variety, is becoming recognised as one from which excellent top-quality wines can be made, and is expanding, accounting in 2013 for almost 9% of the UK vineyard area.

The amount of UK sparkling wine available for sale is still smaller than the amount being produced. This is because bottle-fermented sparkling wines take 2 to 5 years to mature and many new vineyards are still building up stocks or only just releasing their first vintages. Still wines come to market faster than sparkling wines – wine for sale ought to be available within 4 years of planting – whereas sparkling wine producers typically have 3-4 years' worth of stock to store (and more importantly, finance) before they can start selling wines. Although UK-grown wines only account for around 0.3% of the UK wine market, sales through the off-trade i.e. supermarkets and wine merchants and the on-trade i.e. hotels, restaurants and pubs, can be slow. Many producers find that at least initially, before they have built up a reputation for the quality of their wines, selling from the 'farm-gate' is their best route to market and helps introduce the public to their wines. However, over the last twenty years, the reputation of UK-grown sparkling wines has considerably improved and with the rising availability of these wines, more and more outlets, both on-trade and off-trade, are now willing to stock them. All wines sold in the UK bear the same level of VAT and duty irrespective of their origin, although the duty on sparkling wines is higher than for still wines.

The overall UK market for sparkling wines is around 100 million bottles a year, of which around two-thirds is Cava, Prosecco, Asti Spumante and other less expensive wines. Champagne (for which the UK is the biggest export market) accounts for about 35m bottles and it is into this sector of the sparkling wine market that UK producers need to sell their wines if their enterprises are to be profitable. Although the amount of sparkling wine available for sale today is small, given the amount of land in the UK already planted with Champagne varieties, this will rise from today's 1.7 million bottles to around 4 million by

2018 and 6 million by 2020. Most of the major producers think increased supply will result in more wine-buyers being exposed to the wines, resulting in increased sales rather than reduced prices. Some of the larger producers have also started exporting their wines and this may be a route to additional sales.

A Quality Wine Scheme for England and Wales was introduced in 1991 and a Regional Wine Scheme in 1997, but in 2010 these were replaced with a new system of wine classification based upon the terms Protected Designation of Origin (PDO) and Protected Geographical Indication (PGI). PDO wines are broadly the same as Quality Wines and PGI wines the same as Regional wines. All PDO and PGI wines have to go through a testing and tasting procedure before they can use the relevant names. There are also 'Varietal Wines' which have to be 'certified' and can then can be labelled with the name of the grape variety and vintage, but not vineyard name. Wines outside of these three categories are known as 'UK Wines' and may not bear vintage or variety names, although they can state their origin. There is also a PDO for sparkling wines made from certain vine varieties which allows the term 'English Quality Sparkling Wine' to be used. The UK Vineyards Association (UKVA) has a marketing arm, English Wine Producers to promote all English wines and organise tastings and events.

The quality of wine depends on the site and, in a cool climate like the UK's, considered 'marginal' by many non-UK growers, the best sites are to be found on south-facing, well-drained and sheltered land, less than 100 metres above sea level. In the UK, these are to be found in the southern half of England or Wales. Yield is a mott subject in viticulture. Low to very low yields in many vineyards, contribute positively to wine quality, but do not help the viability of the business. Most of the longest-established and most successful UK vineyards sell a good proportion of their wine direct to the consumer and often have tea-rooms, restaurants and even small hotels as part of the enterprise. They also make money from guided tours, weddings, parties and corporate entertaining. Therefore any suitable site for vines should be selected with these activities in mind.

High quality vineyard management and marketing ability is essential for a successful enterprise. There is no minimum area for profitable production and a small vineyard selling wine at the farm gate and locally may be just as profitable as a larger one selling wine (at a considerable discount) through wholesalers and retailers. Quite a few vineyards grow grapes under contract for other wineries who wish to spread the source of their grapes for both financial and diversity of supply reasons. The price for grapes has been held up by the moderate size of the 2011 harvest and the very small harvest in 2012. Whilst this buoyancy in grape prices has partly been off-set by the higher than normal 2013 harvest, as new vineyards – planted by both established growers and new entrants – come into production, prices may soften.

Most UK vineyards are now planted with a row width of between 1.75 m and 2.25 m, an intervine distance of between 1.0 m and 1.4 m and use the Double Guyot cane-pruned system. Around 4,000 vines/ha gives the best quality and chances of an economic yield in the UK's condition. Cane-pruned vines, with good establishment, should be partially cropping at the end of their third summer and fully cropping at the end of their fourth summer in the ground, although much will depend on how they establish.

Investment capital (including planting materials and labour for establishment but not the land) of £21,000 to £30,000/ha is typical for the vineyard. A tractor, mower, sprayer etc. would cost at least £40,000-£50,000. There are currently 131 wineries in the UK (August 2014) many of them are small and housed in modest buildings.

Depending on the quality of the site, the vine varieties being grown and the style of wine being produced, a well-sited, well-managed vineyard should yield on average at least 7.5 tonnes/ha (*3 tonnes/acre*) of grapes, with higher average yields possible. For still wine production, around 950 x 75cl bottles will be produced from 1 tonne of grapes. For sparkling wine production will be between 675 and 800 bottles per tonne, depending on quality, with some additional juice/wine available which will not be suitable for sparkling wine, but might be acceptable for blending into still wine, depending on the vintage.

The costs below refer to a commercial enterprise on a suitable site with a broad variety range. Establishment costs could be more if the site has to be drained and provided with windbreaks and rabbit and deer fencing. Annual growing costs can also be significantly greater, depending on planting density, variety, yield and management

	Double Guyot	
	per ha	per acre
Number of Vines . . . . 3,000 - 5,000		(1,210 - 2,020)
	£ per ha	£ per acre
Establishment Costs:	over two years	
Materials	14,700	5,950
Labour	12,500	5,059
Total Establishment Costs	**27,200**	**11,009**
Subsequent Annual Costs:		
Materials	1,500	607
Labour (growing)	6,100	2,469
Harvesting*	1,600	648
Total Variable Costs	**9,200**	**3,723**

* *Harvesting costs are very yield dependent. Growers without wineries will also have transport costs.*

Prices: Grape prices will vary according to the variety and the vintage and whether growers are under contract or not. Prices range from £1,500 to £2,500 per tonne delivered to a winery, with still varieties being less valuable and good Pinot Noir or Chardonnay for sparkling wine at the higher end.

A retail price for still wine of at least £9.40 per bottle is necessary to cover outgoings, before capital or any profit. Minimum prices for sparkling wine would have to take account of higher costs of production, higher excise duty and costs of finance and storage for 2-5 years of production.

Retail price of £9.40 less 20% VAT and £2.05 ① duty = £5.78 ②

Less winery costs (materials and labour) £4.50 per bottle③ = £1.28

At 7.50 tonnes per ha and 950 bottles per tonne = £9,120/ha (£3,691/acre).

① Sparkling wine of 8.5% and up to 15% or more has a duty rate of £2.63 per 75cl bottle; still wines of the same alcoholic strength, £2.05 per 75cl bottle

② If wines are sold via a wholesaler and/or retailer, gross profit margin of at least 10% (wholesaler) and 30% (retailer) on duty-paid prices must be allowed for.

③ Having still wine made under contract costs at least £4.50 a bottle. Sparkling wine will be at least £6 per bottle, plus storage costs.

Acknowledgements: Thanks to:

Stephen Skelton MW, Viticultural Consultant, 1B Lettice Street, London, SW6 4EH. Tel: 07768 583 700 www.englishwine.com

United Kingdom Vineyards Association, Mr Robert Cowley, UKVA, PO Box 284, Cirencester, GL7 9EZ. Tel: 01285 238941 www.ukva.org.uk

2.   GRAZING LIVESTOCK

DAIRY COWS

General Notes:

The notes below are intended to act as an introduction to the dairy section, detailing some of the general points that are pertinent to completing costings for dairy enterprises. A number of gross margins are then presented with more specific detail given relating to each type of dairy production system.

1. *Yield per cow:* Increases in this are usually (though not necessarily) associated with more intensive farming operations. Intensification focuses on higher gross margins per hectare, although more intensive systems will incur higher overhead costs (specifically machinery and labour requirements). Higher milk yields require improved cow genetics (usually Friesian / Holstein's) and increases in concentrate feeding (kg/litre), as well as other inputs.

2. *Yield*: The yield is annual herd production divided by the average number of cows and calved heifers in the herd. The average yield given for each type of production system is an estimated national figure for sizeable herds of black and white cows in 2015.

3. *Milk Price:* the average milk price for 2015 is 30.5p per litre for black and white cows' milk. The prices used for each gross margin are an average for the 2015 calendar year, after deducting transport costs. It incorporates adjustments for milk composition and seasonality assuming an average-size herd. Payments are lower in the spring but constituents higher, making prices per litre similar for each system.

    Smaller herds achieve a lower price due to smaller volume bonuses / larger transport charges and *vice versa*. The average price received by individual producers depends on seasonality of production and compositional quality.

    Seasonality Price Adjustments: These are diverse between the various dairy companies. An increasing number of companies no longer operate 'conventional' seasonal adjustments but instead have payment systems that encourage a level monthly production, with a range of deductions and bonuses related to the individual producer's spring and autumn deliveries. The average adjustments for a selection of companies operating conventional adjustments are as follows in 2015/16 in pence per litre:

April	May	June	July	Aug	Sept	Oct	Nov	Dec	Jan– Mar
–2.5	–3.5	–2.5	0	+1.5	+2	+2	+1.5	+0.5	0.0

Some companies also offer a premium for a level delivery option if supplies in a calendar month are within 10% of an agreed daily volume. Spring calving herds will produce more milk in the spring and summer, therefore receiving a lower price on average, whereas autumn calving herds will receive a higher average price as a result of producing more milk in the autumn and winter.

Compositional Quality Payments: How milk prices are derived now depends largely upon the buyer and its end market. For example, cheese-makers will often derive the majority of the milk price from payments per % of butterfat and protein; whereas a liquid processor may pay largely on a set base price per litre with small adjustments for butterfat and protein in addition. As a result, constituent values vary widely between buyers. A *standard litre* is typically 4·10% butterfat and 3·40% protein.

Within Breed Quality Variation: For Holstein Friesians without going to extremes, the range can easily be: 3.5% to 4.1% butterfat and 3.1% to 3.4% protein. The difference in value between these two levels combined can be up to 3.5p per litre depending on milk contract. This is being achieved by both breeding and feeding for milk quality to meet varying contractual requirements.

Proportional Split of Dairy Breeds and milk Compositions:

	Cows %	Butterfat %	Protein %
Holstein Friesian	96	4.01	3·22
Jersey	1·3	5·4	3·9
Guernsey	1·0	4·7	3·6
Ayrshire	1·4	4·1	3·3
Dairy Shorthorn	0·3	3·9	3·3
All Breeds		4.08	3·25

Data from Dairy Co.

Hygiene Price Adjustments: These vary widely between the different dairy companies. A typical 2015/16 example is as follows:

A. *Bactoscan (bacteria measure)*

Bactoscan Reading	Price Adjustment (ppl)
0- 50,000	+0.5
51-100,000	-0.50
101-200,000	– 2.00
Over 200,000*	– 6.00

*1st month, -10p subsequent months.

B. *Somatic Cell Count (Mastitis)*

Count	Price Adjustment (ppl)
0-250,000	+ 1.00
251-325,000	-1.00
326-400,000	– 4.00
Over 400,000	– 15.00

Several milk buyers have no bonus for top hygiene bands; they expect suppliers to deliver top quality milk in order to receive the standard litre price.

C. *Antibiotics.* Milk in a consignment that fails an antibiotics test is usually worth 1p/litre.

4. *Concentrate Price:* An average of £235/t has been used for dairy concentrate. Blends and straights are typically cheaper than compounds. Spring calving herds tend to have lower protein concentrate as fresh grass has more protein than preserved feeds; conversely, autumn calvers receive higher protein concentrate. An average of £230/t has been used for spring calving herds and £240/t for autumn calving herds.

5. *AI / Bull Costs:* AI is assumed in the gross margins with no bull. However bull depreciation would be approximately £140 a year (£1,600 purchase price less £900 cull value, 5-year herd life); tight calving pattern: average 40 cows per bull; 10 to 15 tonnes silage per year, 0·15 tonnes concentrates a year. Very high yielding herds may use more expensive (dairy) bulls above £2,500 purchase price. Most herds now use AI but rely on bulls as sweeper bulls.

Spring Calving Friesians (per cow per year)

	Average	High
Yield Per Cow (litres)	*5,250*	*6,000*
Milk Output @ 30.5 ppl	1,601	1,830
Calf Value	147	147
Cull Value	96	96
Less, Replacement Cost @ 20% per year	-300	-300
Total Output	**1,545**	**1,773**
Variable Costs		
Concentrate Costs £230/t @ 0.8/cow and 1.02t/cow	184	235
Purchased Bulk Feed	0	0
Vet & Med	53	54
Bedding	43	44
AI	32	33
Recording, Parlour Consumables, Sundries	65	65
Total Variable Costs	377	431
Gross Margin per cow Before Forage Costs	**1,168**	**1,343**
Forage per cow @ 2.4 Cows Per Forage Hectare	114	114
Gross Margin per Cow After Forage Costs	**1,054**	**1,229**
Gross Margin Per Forage Hectare	2,530	2,950
Margin of Milk Over Concentrates	1,417	1,595
Sensitivity Analysis per cow		
Concentrate Price +/- £10/tonne	+- 8.0	+- 10.2
Concentrate Price +/- £20/tonne	+- 16.0	+- 20.4
Milk Price +/- 0.25 ppl	+- 13.1	+- 15.0
Milk Price +/- 0.50 ppl	+- 26.3	+- 30.0

Spring calving herds (80% or more calvings between February and May) typically have a much lower annual average yield than other systems due to a smaller, hardier cow type. As a result, replacement rates will be lower than other production systems. Spring calving herds will normally produce high milk constituents and aim to sell on a cheese/manufacturing based contract to maximise their price, despite the reductions incurred through seasonality. These systems often have low overhead costs (labour, buildings and machinery) and are often focused on milk from grass. Lower costs reflect the lower milk price received.

See notes on page 46.

Autumn Calving Friesian/Holsteins (per cow per year)

	Average	High
Yield Per Cow (litres)	*7,000*	*8,500*
Milk Output @ 30.5 ppl	2,135	2,593
Calf Value	147	147
Cull Value	110	110
Less, Replacement Cost @ 23% per year	-345	-345
Total Output	**2,048**	**2,505**
Variable Costs		
Concentrate Costs £240/t @ 1.68/cow and 2.635t/cow	403	632
Purchased Bulk Feed	43	43
Vet & Med	63	64
Bedding	58	58
AI	37	38
Recording, Parlour Consumables, Sundries	65	65
Total Variable Costs	**669**	**900**
Gross Margin per cow Before Forage Costs	**1,379**	**1,605**
Forage Costs @ 2.2 Cows Per Forage Hectare	127	127
Gross Margin per Cow After Forage Costs	**1,252**	**1,478**
Gross Margin Per Forage Hectare	2,754	3,251
Margin of Milk Over Concentrates	1,732	1,960
Sensitivity Analysis per cow		
Concentrate Price +/- £10/tonne	+- 16.8	+- 26.3
Concentrate Price +/- £20/tonne	+- 33.6	+- 52.7
Milk Price +/- 0.25 ppl	+- 17.5	+- 21.3
Milk Price +/- 0.50 ppl	+- 35.0	+- 42.5

Autumn calving herds (80% or more calvings between August and November) tend to have much higher overhead costs than spring calving herds, mainly associated with winter housing and feeding – buildings, greater silage requirements, slurry and muck handling, plus labour. Autumn calving herds will benefit from a marginally greater milk price than spring or all-year-round calving herds because of seasonality, and will typically (but not always) sell milk to a liquid buyer. The decision between being a spring or autumn calving producer will depend largely upon specific circumstances, such as building facilities available, the ability of the farm to grow forage (wet or dry land) and the nearby milk buyers' requirements.

See notes on page 46.

All-Year-Round Calving Friesian/Holsteins (per cow per year)

	Average	High
Yield Per Cow (litres)	*8,000*	*9,500*
Milk Output @ 30.5 ppl	2,440	2,898
Calf Value	131	131
Cull Value	120	134
Less, Replacement Cost @ 25% & 28% per year	-400	-448
Total Output	**2,291**	**2,714**
Variable Costs		
Concentrate Costs £235/t @ 2.56/cow and 3.61t/cow	602	848
Purchased Bulk Feed	41	42
Vet & Med	73	76
Bedding	60	60
AI	40	42
Recording, Parlour Consumables, Sundries	75	75
Total Variable Costs	891	1,143
Gross Margin per cow Before Forage Costs	**1,400**	**1,571**
Forage Costs @ 2.2 Cows Per Forage Hectare	130	130
Gross Margin per Cow After Forage Costs	**1,270**	**1,441**
Gross Margin Per Forage Hectare	2,794	3,170
Margin of Milk Over Concentrates	1,838	2,049
Sensitivity Analysis per cow		
Concentrate Price +/- £10/tonne	+- 25.6	+- 36.1
Concentrate Price +/- £20/tonne	+- 51.2	+- 72.2
Milk Price +/- 0.25 ppl	+- 20.0	+- 23.8
Milk Price +/- 0.50 ppl	+- 40.0	+- 47.5

All-year-round calving herds have higher costs of production than seasonal producers and so will aim to sell their milk on a liquid premium based (supermarket supply) contract. However, these contracts are limited. Both vet and med and A.I. costs tend to increase with higher milk yield due to greater pressure on the cow and poorer fertility. As a result, herd replacement rates are also considerably higher.

Gross Margin Notes:

1. *Value of Calves:* Average annual value per cow at 10-20 days old, allowing for 5% mortality and an average calving index of 385 days. Average value assumed for spring and autumn calving herds is comprised equally as follows per year

2. :

		Spring & Autumn	AYR
Dairy bull calf	(dairy x dairy)	£ 75	*55*
Dairy heifer calf	(dairy x dairy)	£155	145
Cross bred bull	(beef x dairy)	£240	*215*
Cross bred heifer	(beef x dairy)	£185	*165*
5% mortality, 385 day calving interval			
Average		**£147**	**£131**

* Calves for all-year-round calving herds with higher milk yields normally have less beef genetics meaning dairy bull calves and beef cross animals are less valuable.

3. *Replacement Costs:* The table below demonstrates herd replacement costs.

	Spring	Autumn	AYR	
Yield per cow	*5,250*	*7,000*	*8,000*	*9,500*
Value of new heifers (a)	1,500	1,500	1,600	1,600
Replacement Rate (b)	20%	23%	25%	28%
Herd Depreciation (a x b =c)	**300**	**345**	**400**	**448**
Cull Cow Value (d)	500	500	500	500
Casualty Rate (e)	4%	4%	4%	4%
Annual Cull Value (b x d x e = f)	**96**	**110**	**120**	**134**
Calf Values (g)	**147**	**147**	**131**	**131**
Net Replacement Cost (c-f-g)	**57**	**87**	**149**	**183**

Herd depreciation is the annual cost of replacing the herd i.e. the cost of a down-calving heifer divided by its life expectancy in years (or multiplied by the annual replacement rate). When the value of cull cows and calves are added (both adjusted for casualty and mortality allowance), the net replacement cost can be derived.

4. *Concentrate Costs:*

	Spring		Autumn		AYR	
Yield per cow	*5,250*	*6,000*	*7,000*	*8,500*	*8,000*	*9,500*
Tonnes / Cow	0.80	1.02	1.68	2.64	2.56	3.61
Kg feed / Litre	0.15	0.17	0.24	0.31	0.32	0.38
Concentrate Cost (ppl)	3.50	3.91	5.76	7.44	7.52	8.93
Conc. cost p/marginal L		6.75		15.28		16.45

This table gives the costs of concentrate feed per litre of milk and crucially, the costs of concentrate feed per litre of *additional* milk. In other words, the cost of the extra feed required to move from the first yield to the second yield bracket in each category. The yield difference in the spring and autumn groups is small, but the yield rise for all-year-round (AYR) herds is considerable, the cost of the last litre (to 9,500 in this instance) is always dearest.

5. *Feeding:* Typically, specialist spring calving herds use 0.09 kg per litre / 850 kg per cow per year less concentrates than autumn calving herds. The table below is an example of annual concentrate use for an all-year-round calving herd.

Typical Monthly Variation in Concentrate Feeding (kg per litre, 8,000 litre herd)

Winter		Summer	
October	0.30	April	0.23
November	0.32	May	0.14
December	0.33	June	0.14
January	0.33	July	0.20
February	0.32	August	0.24
March	0.28	September	0.27
Average winter: 0.31		Average summer: 0.21	
Weighted average whole year: 0.26kg/l			

The distribution on farm varies according to factors such as seasonality of calving, milk yield, summer grazing productivity, the quantity and quality of winter forages and bulk feeds, as well as turnout and housing dates. The March figure in particular will be affected by type of soil and seasonal rainfall.

Yield with no concentrates and good quality silage can be 4,000 litres for spring calvers.

6. *Margin over Concentrates (MOC) and Concentrates per litre:* It is important to highlight in the above gross margins the differences between the margin (of milk value) over concentrates per cow; the same large variation can occur with widely differing combinations of milk yield and quantity of concentrates fed.

In the following table, for each production system, figures are given for *(a) margin of milk value over concentrates* per cow (£) and (b) *concentrates per litre* (kg).

Margin Over Concentrates (MOC) and Concentrates per Litre (C/L)

Milking System	Spring Calving		Autumn Calving		All-Year-Round Calving			
Milk Yield (litres)	5,250		7,000		8,000		9,500	
	MOC	C/L	MOC	C/L	MOC	C/L	MOC	C/L
Concentrates per cow	£	kg	£	kg	£	kg	£	kg
0.65 tonne (£150)	1451	0.12	-	-	-	-	-	-
0.75 tonne (£173)	1428	0.14	-	-	-	-	-	-
0.90 tonne (£207)	1394	0.17	-	-	-	-	-	-
1.05 tonne (£242)	1359	0.20	1,893	0.15	-	-	-	-
1.60 tonne (£384)	-	-	1,751	0.23	-	-	-	-
1.75 tonne (£420)	-	-	1,715	0.25	-	-	-	-
1.90 tonne (£456)	-	-	1,679	0.27	1,984	0.24	-	-
2.10 tonne (£494)	-	-	-	-	1,946	0.26	-	-
2.25 tonne (£529)	-	-	-	-	1,911	0.28	-	-
2.40 tonne (£564)	-	-	-	-	1,876	0.30	2334	0.25
2.85 tonne (£670)	-	-	-	-	-	-	2228	0.30
3.00 tonne (£705)	-	-	-	-	-	-	2193	0.32
3.15 tonne (£740)	-	-	-	-	-	-	2158	0.33

7. *Stocking Rate and Forage Costs:* The stocking rates given assume that nearly all requirements of forage/bulk foods – both winter and summer – are obtained from the forage area, i.e. little is bought in. The stocking rates of 2.2 cows per forage hectare (autumn and AYR calving) and 2.4 cows per forage hectare (for spring calving herds) assume good grassland management. Greater stocking rates are achievable, particularly in the West of the UK where natural conditions favour forage production. On average about 55 per cent of the forage area (or production) is grazed and 45 per cent conserved for an all-year-round calving herd. Spring calving herds rely much less on conserved forage. Some high yielding herds are housed all-year-round.

The forage costs are taken from the *Forage Variable Costs* on page 85 as follows:

	Intensive Grass	Maize	Intensive Grass	Maize	Intensive Grass	Maize
			£/Ha		£/cow	
£ Cost /Ha	272	336				
Spring calving	100%	0%	272	0	114	0
Autumn calving	89%	11%	243	37	110	17
All year round calving	78%	22%	213	74	97	34

An increase in stocking density can be obtained not only by intensifying grassland production, but also by buying in bulk fodder (assuming the same level of concentrate feeding in both cases). Theoretically, a zero-grazed farm buying in forage needs no land. In this situation, the gross margin per hectare would be extreme (and meaningless), although the cost of hauling in forage (low dry matter) would be high.

Overheads such as labour and buildings depreciation are likely to increase per hectare and fall per cow as stocking density rises. Management challenges occur with higher stocking rates such as poaching which can be alleviated with good cow tracks. Cross Compliance and Nitrate Vulnerable Zone regulations must still be adhered to.

7. *Quota.* The milk quota policy ends on 31 March 2015 (see chapter III Section 1 for details). The regime is irrelevant in the UK as we have been behind quota for 10 years and quota has minimal value.

8. *Labour*: see page 184.

9. *Building Costs*: see page 226.

Costs of Milk Production Summary (Pence per Litre)

Production type	Spring Calving	Autumn Calving	AYR Calving
Litres per cow	*5,250*	*7,000*	*8,000*
		Pence Per Litre	
Concentrates	3.50	5.76	7.52
Forage and Bought Bulk Feed	2.16	2.43	2.14
Other Variable Costs	3.68	3.19	3.10
Total Variable Costs	**9.34**	**11.37**	**12.76**
Labour: Paid	1.95	2.20	2.24
: Un-paid (farmer)	3.22	2.42	2.12
Power and Machinery*	6.35	5.86	6.09
General Overheads	1.37	1.17	1.22
Rent/Rental Equivalent & Finance	4.22	3.16	2.77
Total Fixed Costs	**17.11**	**14.81**	**14.44**
Less, Net Replacement Cost	1.08	1.24	1.87
Total Costs of Production	**27.53**	**27.43**	**29.06**
Milk Price	30.50	30.50	30.50
Net Profit	**2.97**	**3.07**	**1.44**

* inc electricity & Parlour repairs

1. The *Variable Costs* per litre are derived from the data (and therefore the assumptions made) under average performance in the dairy gross margin tables for each system.

2. The *Fixed Costs* assume average financial performance. The average fixed costs are taken from the medium-sized 'mainly dairying' farm data in the Fixed Costs Section on page 216. Within each system, there will be a marked difference between the costs achieved by the top 10% and the bottom 10% of producers. The difference is simply due to improved management ability. *Labour* includes the farmer and any unpaid family labour. However, there is no management charge included. *Power and machinery* cover all machinery and equipment costs, including the use of farm vehicles, etc. *General overheads* similarly relate to the whole farm, including electricity and property repairs. *Rent/Rental Equivalent and Finance* assumes a modest rental charge on all land plus interest charges on a modest amount of working capital. No long-term debt is included.

3. *Net Profit* reflects the profit from dairying alone. It does not include any other income that the farm will also receive, such as the Basic Payment or income from environmental schemes.

4. All-year-round calving herds will have the highest overheads in absolute terms. However, well-managed high yielding herds can compete with block calving systems due to higher output. Block calving herds will have lower overheads due to lean times of the year i.e. periods when all cows are dry, and the economies of scale of managing animals in batches. Spring calving herds will have the lowest overheads due to a shorter housing period, less demand for winter forage and lower muck handling costs. Rental costs, in pence per litre terms, will be higher though due to the fixed land charge and lower output (litres) per unit area of land.

Channel Island Breeds (per cow per year)

Performance level (yield)	S. Calving	A. Calving	AYR Average	AYR High
Milk Yield per Cow (litres) (1)	*4,150*	*5,000*	*5,550*	*6,250*
	£	£	£	£
Milk Value per Cow (2)	1,473	1,775	1,970	2,219
Calf Value	100	100	100	100
Cull Value	48	55	60	60
Less, Replacement Cost	-250	-288	-313	-313
Total Output	**1,371**	**1,643**	**1,818**	**2,066**
Variable Costs				
Concentrate Costs	216	350	429	588
Purchased Bulk Feed	35	35	35	35
Vet & Med	31	35	39	43
Bedding	36	41	41	41
AI	29	31	31	33
Recording, Parlour Consumables, Sundries	55	55	55	55
Total Variable Costs	**402**	**547**	**630**	**795**
Gross Margin Before Forage Costs	**969**	**1,096**	**1,188**	**1,271**
Forage Costs @ 2.5 Cows Per Forage Ha	109	109	144	144
Gross Margin After Forage Costs	**860**	**987**	**1,044**	**1,127**
Gross Margin Per Forage Hectare	2,151	2,467	2,610	2,818
Margin of Milk Over Concentrates	1,257	1,425	1,542	1,631

1. *Yield.* Average of Jerseys and Guernseys. See Note 1 and 2 for Holstein Friesians (page 42). Guernsey yield averages slightly higher than Jerseys and Jerseys achieve a higher butterfat and protein (see page 43).

2. *Milk Price.* This is 35.3p per litre for spring calvers, 36.3p per litre for autumn calvers and 36.2p per litre for all year round herds (average of Jerseys and Guernseys for a level profile), with adjustments made for spring and autumn production profiles. This is based upon a channel island milk contract, for which a premium is usually paid.

3. *Concentrate Costs.* The average price taken (for 2015) is £245 per tonne (for all-year-round calving herds), £240 per tonne average for spring calving herds and £250 per tonne for autumn calving herds.

Amounts:	*Milk Group*	*Spring*	*Autumn*	*AYR ave.*	*AYR High*
	kg/litre	0.217	0.280	0.315	0.384
	tonnes/cow	0.90	1.40	1.75	2.40
	pence / litre (ppl)	5.20	7.00	7.73	9.41
	pence/ marginal litre*		13.0		20.4

* This is the additional cost of feed between yield groups, and the cost of the additional feed divided by the additional litres of production.

4. *Net Annual Replacement Cost*: Calculated as follows (replacement rates vary by system, 20% for spring, 23% for autumn, 25% for higher yielding all-year-round calving herds):

	£ per cow in herd
Cost of replacements: 25% of herd per year @ £1,200	288
Less Value of culls: 25% of herd per year @ £270	
(allowing for casualties)*	65
Herd Depreciation	223
Annual Value of Calves**	90
Net Annual Replacement Cost	**143**

*Cull cow prices for Guernseys are about £40 higher than for Jerseys.

** Allowing for calving index of 385 days and calf mortality; mixture of pure bred calves and beef crosses. Guernsey calves, especially crosses, fetch more than Jersey calves, averaging perhaps £10 more per head and substantially more for some Guernsey beef crosses.

5. *Forage Costs and Stocking Rate.* See, in general, Note 6 for Holstein Friesians (page 48). A small amount of purchased bulk fodder is assumed at £35/cow (purchased forage) for the higher yielding herds based upon the average stocking rate of 2.5 cows per forage hectare. (See forage section for details of improved temporary grass used here).

At the average stocking rate given above for combined Channel Island breeds (2.5 cows per forage hectare) the average figure for Jerseys would be approximately 2.60 and that for Guernseys 2.40 cows per forage hectare.

DAIRY FOLLOWERS

(per Heifer reared)

Performance Level	Low	Average	High
	£	£	£
Value of heifer (allowing for culls) (1)	1350	1350	1350
Less Value of calf (2)	163	163	163
Output	1187	1187	1187
Variable Costs:			
Concentrate Costs (3)	288	262	236
Miscellaneous Variable Costs (4)	149	135	122
Total Variable Costs			
(excluding Forage)	436	397	357
Gross Margin per Heifer, before			
deducting Forage Variable Costs	751	790	830
Forage Variable Costs (5)	173	132	105
Gross Margin per Heifer	578	659	725
Forage Hectares (Acres) per Heifer			
reared (6)	0.95 (2.3)	0.73 (1.8)	0.58 (1.4)
Gross Margin per Forage Hectare (7)	608	908	1262
Gross Margin per Forage Acre	246	368	511

B. Channel Island Breeds

Performance Level	Low	Average	High
	£	£	£
Value of heifer (allowing for culls) (1)	1125	1125	1125
Less Value of calf (2)	95	95	95
Output	1031	1031	1031
Variable Costs:			
Concentrate Costs (3)	245	223	200
Miscellaneous Variable Costs (4)	134	122	109
Total Variable Costs			
(excluding Forage)	378	344	310
Gross Margin per Heifer, before			
deducting Forage Variable Costs	652	686	721
Forage Variable Costs (5)	156	119	94
Gross Margin per Heifer	496	568	627
Forage Hectares (Acres) per Heifer			
reared (6)	0.68 (1.7)	0.58 (1.4)	0.50 (1.2)
Gross Margin per Forage Hectare (7)	736	987	1253
Gross Margin per Forage Acre	298	400	508

N.B. on average Channel Island heifers calve about three months younger than Holstein Friesian Heifers

1. *Heifer values* are based on the purchase price of down-calving heifers with an allowance for culls and barren animals. Most heifers are home-reared. If heifers are reared for sale, the price of whole batches is likely to be lower than the values given in the tables, by 10 or 15 per cent. On the other hand the purchaser will often take the batch a few months before the average expected calving date, thus reducing the costs incurred by the rearer.

2. *Calf Value;* is based on the cost of a heifer dairy calf, increased to account for mortality of 5%.

3. *Lower levels of concentrate* costs are the combined result of more economical feeding and a lower average calving age. (Other things being equal, including the overall level of management, a lower calving age requires higher levels of feeding.) Average (Holstein Friesians) = £76 to 3 months (see Calf Rearing on page 55) plus 290 kg calf concentrates @ £260/tonne and 500 kg @ £220/tonne = £262 per calf.

4. *Miscellaneous* variable costs include bedding (£47): straw requirements average approx. 0.7 tonnes per heifer reared, but are variable, depending on time of year and age when calved, as well as system of housing and extent of out-wintering. Vet. and med. approximately £46 per heifer reared, and other sundry items £42.

5. *A "replacement unit"* (i.e. calf + yearling + heifer) equals about 1·25 livestock units with an average calving age of 2 years 4 months. The three stocking rates used above are equivalent to approximately 0.75, 0·6 and 0·5 forage hectares (1.85, 1.48, 1.24 acres) respectively per Holstein Friesian cow (Livestock Unit).

6. *Forage variable costs.* Grass for both grazing and conservation, at £284/ha, assuming all home produced. This is the variable costs for 3-5 year leys in the forage section on page 85, thus assuming that less productive grassland is used to rear dairy heifers with the best pasture being retained for the dairy cows.

7. *Higher gross margin figures* can be achieved by intensive grazing methods, particularly if combined with alternative winter feeding systems, such as out-wintering on forage crops such as Fodder Beet or Kale.

8. *Contract Rearing*: see page 70.

9. *Labour*: see page 184.

SELF-CONTAINED DAIRY HERD: COWS AND FOLLOWERS

At average annual replacement rates (25 per cent of the milking herd), nearly one-third of a replacement unit is required for each cow in the herd, i.e. roughly one calf, yearling and heifer for every three cows (including calved heifers), allowing for mortality and culling. At average stocking rates for both, this means more than 1 hectare devoted to followers for every 3 hectares for cows. Since surplus youngstock are often reared and frequently the stocking rate is less intensive the ratio often exceeds this in practice. 1:3 is about the minimum where all replacement heifers are reared, unless their winter feeding is based largely on straw and purchased supplements, or unless there is a combination of long average herd life and early calving, i.e. all at 2 years old.

The table below shows the combined gross margin per forage hectare (acre) for the whole herd (i.e., Cows and Followers Combined) for four different farming systems assuming the same stocking rate for the dairy cows and three levels of performance, including different stocking rates, for the followers. This assumes a 3:1 land use ratio (dairy cow area: followers area) and relates to the dairying systems (gross margins) shown earlier in this section. It is important to note, however, that these are only a guide as the figures (ratio of land areas assumed) do not take account of the different herd replacement rates for each dairying system. In practise, it is likely that the amount of land required for the followers for a block spring calving herd would be much less than that for a high yielding all-year-round calving herd; this is due to the fact that typically a high yielding herd would have a higher herd replacement rate and as such require more heifers and therefore land on which to rear them.

Gross Margin per Forage Hectare for Cows and Followers Combined

			G.M per Forage Hectare (acre) Dairy Cows			
			Autumn	Spring	AYR Ave.	AYR High
			£	£	£	£
G.M. per			2754 (1115)	2530 (1025)	2794 (1131)	3170 (1284)
Forage	Low	608 (246)	2217 (898)	2050 (830)	2247 (910)	2530 (1025)
Hectare	Ave.	908 (368)	2292 (928)	2125 (860)	2322 (941)	2605 (1055)
(acre)						
Followers	High	1262 (511)	2381 (964)	2213 (896)	2411 (976)	2693 (1091)

As an example, the above table indicates that at the average level of performance and stocking rate for an all-year-round 8,000 litre dairy herd (AYR Average) and followers, the whole dairy gross margin per hectare (acre) figure is £2,322 (941) compared with £2,794 (1,131) for the dairy cows alone, a reduction of 17%.

BEEF

There are numerous different systems for producing beef in the UK which are heavily influenced by factors such as feed and forage, breeds, housing, sale weights, market outlets, labour availability and enterprise scale. By virtue, the financial performance of beef enterprises are infinitely variable, more so than any other sector of UK agriculture. The enterprise gross margins shown on the following pages represent some of the most common types of beef systems with output prices and costs based on 2015 budgets.

Calves

The values in the table below are for 2015 and relate to dairy bulls or beef cross calves of average quality, less than three weeks old. These values have been used in the budgets for the following beef systems. There is significant regional and seasonal variation in calf prices.

Calf values of various beef cattle

	Bulls	Heifers
Holstein Friesians	55	-
Hereford Cross	180	160
HF/Continental Cross	240	200

Calf Rearing
Early Weaning - Bucket Rearing (per calf)

	3 months	6 months
	£	£
Value of Calf	380	490
Less Calf Purchase (1)	229	229
Output	**151**	**261**
Variable Costs:		
Milk Substitute (2)...	34	34
Concentrates (2)...	34	100
Hay (3)...	4	18
Vet & Med	16	18
Bedding	7	12
Miscellaneous (Ear Tags etc).........................	3	6
Total Variable Costs	**98**	**188**
Gross Margin per Calf Reared	**53**	**73**

1. *Calf Purchase*: Assumes equal number of male and female calves (Holstein Friesian/Continental beef cross, 1-2 weeks old). £229 average price including 4% mortality assumed, mainly in first 3 weeks.

2. *Milk substitute*: 20 kg @ £1,800/tonne = £36.00. Calf concentrates: to 3 months, 140 kg @ £245/tonne = £34.00; to 6 months, additional 270kg @ £245/tonne = £100. Calves fed on machine or lib milk systems will use more milk powder.

3. *Hay*: 50kg to 3 months, 230kg to 6 months (£61/tonne) See page 87.

4. *Weights*: at start = 45 to 50 kg; at 3 months = 115 kg; at 6 months = 245kg. Contract rearing charge (both 0 to 3 months and 0 to 6 months): £14 per week. Direct labour cost: approximately £28 per head to 3 months, £42 per head to 6 months.

5. *Labour requirements* (all beef systems): see page 184.

Suckler Cows

Single Suckling (per Cow): Lowland (1)

System	Spring Calving		Autumn Calving	
Performance Level (2)	Average	High	Average	High
	£	£	£	£
Value of Calf Sold (3)	503	587	667	732
Calf Sales / Valuation per Cow (3)	458	546	607	680
Less Cow and Bull Depreciation				
Calf Purchases (4)	171	171	194	194
Output	**286**	**375**	**413**	**486**
Variable Costs:				
Concentrate Costs (Cow and Calf)	43	36	74	67
Vet & Med	27	27	29	29
Bedding (5)	42	42	48	48
Miscellaneous	19	20	22	23
Total Variable Costs (excl. forage)	**131**	**125**	**173**	**167**
Gross Margin per Cow, before				
deducting Forage Variable Costs	155	250	240	319
Forage Variable Costs (6)	117	96	128	105
Purchased Bulk Feeds	12	10	20	16
Gross Margin per Cow	**26**	**144**	**92**	**198**
Cows per Hectare	1.80	2.20	1.65	2.00
Forage Hectares (Acres) per Cow	0.56	0.45	0.61	0.50
	(1.37)	*(1.12)*	*(1.50)*	*(1.24)*
Gross Margin per Forage Hectare (Acre)	**47**	**316**	**151**	**395**
	(19)	*(128)*	*(61)*	*(160)*

1. *System*: Relates to performance per cycle, i.e. for the production period. Assumed 390 days average calving interval.

2. *Performance level:* relates to variations in both outputs and inputs.

3.

Calving Period	Spring Calving		Autumn Calving	
Performance Level	Average	High	Average	High
Calf Sale Weights (kg)	280	309	371	385
Sale Age (Days)	250	240	365	340
Sale Prices (£/kg)	£1.80	1.90	£1.80	1.90
Calves reared per 100 cows mated	91	93	91	93

4. *Assumptions.* Herd life: spring calving, 8 years; autumn calving, 7 years. Purchase price £1,700, average cull value £500. Calves purchased: average per 100 cows mated: spring calving 3, autumn calving 4; at £220. Bull: purchase price £4,200, cull value £500; (one bull per 35 cows on average; 5-year herd life). Dairy cross beef cows have better fertility performance than continental pure bred cows, but lower cull sale prices.

5. *Straw*: where yarded in winter, straw requirements average 0.7 tonnes per cow for spring calvers and 0.8 tonnes for autumn calvers.

6. *The Forage Area* includes grazing and conserved grass (silage and hay). Higher stocking rates imply better use of grassland or can be achieved by buying in more winter fodder, or feeding more arable by-products, including straw. Purchased bulk fodder and/or straw balancer concentrates will reduce gross margin per cow but increase gross margin per hectare. Forage cost from *Long Term Ley* in *Forage* at £211/ha on page 85.

7. *Headage Payment*: A payment is made in Scotland on three-quarter breed beef calves from Suckler Cows. The previous Beef Payment Scheme paid a basic fee of approximately £50 per head (with the first 10 calves expected to be around three times the basic rate payment). A headage payment will be available for Scottish beef producers under the reformed Common Agricultural Policy from 2015.

8. In lowland conditions rearing two or more calves per cow is an option, but needs substantially greater labour input. Output is raised by fostering a second purchased calf onto a cow soon after calving, with little impact on costs of keeping the cow. The cow breed needs to be of a quiet temperament and have enough milk to rear two calves.

Single Suckling (per Cow): Upland / Hill

System	*Spring Calving*		*Autumn Calving*	
Performance Level	Average	High	Average	High
	£	£	£	£
Value of Calf (2)	491	532	654	703
Calf Sales / Valuation per Cow (3)	441	489	589	647
Less Cow and Bull Depreciation and				
Calf Purchases (4)	183	183	207	207
Output	**258**	**306**	**382**	**440**
Variable Costs:				
Concentrate Costs (Cow and Calf)	46	39	76	69
Vet & Med	27	27	29	29
Bedding (5)	45	45	51	51
Miscellaneous	19	20	22	23
Total Variable Costs (excl. forage)	**137**	**131**	**178**	**172**
Gross Margin per Cow, before				
deducting Forage Variable Costs	121	175	204	268
Forage Variable Costs (6)	96	81	122	102
Purchased Bulk Feeds	14	12	22	18
Gross Margin per Cow	**11**	**83**	**59**	**148**
Cows per Hectare	1.60	1.90	1.25	1.50
Forage Hectares (Acres) per Cow	0.63	0.53	0.80	0.67
	(1.54)	*(1.30)*	*(1.98)*	*(1.65)*
Gross Margin per Forage Hectare (Acre)	**18**	**157**	**74**	**222**
	(7)	*(63)*	*(30)*	*(90)*

1. *System*: Relates to performance per cycle, i.e. for the production period. Assumed 390 days average calving interval.

2. *Performance level:* relates to variations in both outputs and inputs.

3.

Calving Period	Spring Calving		Autumn Calving	
Performance Level	Average	High	Average	High
Calf Sale Weights (kg)	273	280	364	370
Sale Age (Days)	250	240	365	330
Sale Prices (£/kg)	£1.80	1.90	£1.80	1.90
Calves reared per 100 cows mated	90	92	90	92

4. *Assumptions.* Herd life: spring calving, 8 years; autumn calving, 7 years. Purchase price £1,700, average cull value £500. Calves purchased: average per 100 cows mated: spring calving 3, autumn calving 4; at £220. Bull: purchase price £4,200, cull value £490; (one bull per 35 cows on average; 4-year herd life). Dairy cross beef cows have better fertility performance than continental pure bred cows, but lower cull sale prices.

5. *Straw*: where yarded in winter, straw requirements average 0.75 tonnes per cow for spring calvers and 0.85 tonnes for autumn calvers.

6. *The Forage Area* includes grazing and conserved grass (silage and hay). Higher stocking rates imply better use of grassland or higher can be achieved by buying more winter bulk fodder, or by winter feeding more arable by-products, including straw. Purchased bulk fodder and/or straw balancer concentrates will reduce gross margin per cow but increase gross margin per hectare. Forage cost from *Improved Permanent Pasture* in *Forage* page at £153/ha on page 85.

7. Headage Payment: A payment is made in Scotland on three-quarter breed beef calves from suckler cows. The previous Beef Payment Scheme paid a basic fee of approximately £50 per head (with the first 10 calves expected to be around three times the basic rate payment). A headage payment will be available for Scottish beef producers under the reformed Common Agricultural Policy from 2015.

Store Cattle

Maintenance / Keeping of Young Dairy Store Cattle (per head) (1)

	Summer Keeping	Winter Keeping
	£	£
Store Sales (2)	683	677
Less Purchased Store (incl. mortality) (3)	424	424
Output	**258**	**252**
Variable Costs:		
Concentrates	5	70 (4)
Vet & Med	9	11
Bedding	0	48
Miscellaneous	14	18
Total Variable Costs (excluding Forage)	**28**	**147**
Gross Margin per Head, before		
deducting Forage Variable Costs	231	105
Forage Variable Costs (5)	37	15
Gross Margin per Head	**194**	**90**
Animals per Hectare	5.75	
Forage Hectares (Acres) per Head	0.17 *(0.43)*	
Gross Margin per Forage Hectare (Acre)	**1,115** *(451)*	

1. *System*: Buying dairy cross steers and heifers at 6 months old for keeping / rearing. Animals spend 6 months in system before sale / transfer to a finishing enterprise.

2. *Sales*: at 402kg summer, 398kg winter (liveweight), both at £1.70/kg.

3. *Purchases*: Both systems 245kg purchase weight @ £1.75, plus 1% mortality.

4. *Concentrates*: Winter 270kg concentrates @ £260 per tonne.

5. *Forage Costs*: Based on '*Long Term Ley*' in forage section (page 85) at £211/ha. Winter Keep: 2.9 tonnes per head grass silage consumption. Only silage variable costs are considered and therefore overhead costs of silage production need to be considered. Similarly, bought in silage will increase the forage costs over those shown.

Finishing Cattle

Finishing of Dairy Bred Store Cattle **(per head) (1)**

	Summer Finishing	Winter Finishing
	£	£
Finished Sales (2)	1,105	1,117
Less Purchased Store (incl. mortality) (3)	683	690
Output	**422**	**428**
Variable Costs:		
Concentrates	74	181 (4)
Vet & Med	11	19
Bedding	0	42
Miscellaneous	35	42
Total Variable Costs (excluding Forage)	**120**	**284**
Gross Margin per Head, before		
deducting Forage Variable Costs	302	144
Forage Variable Costs	70	19 (5)
Gross Margin per Head	**232**	**125**
Animals per Hectare	3.00	
Forage Hectares (Acres) per Head	0.33 *(0.82)*	
Gross Margin per Forage Hectare (Acre)	**695** *(281)*	

1. *System*: Finishing of dairy bred store cattle (as shown in previous margin – *summer finishing cattle will have been winter stores and vice versa*). Purchased / transferred in at 12 months old and finished over 7 months (210 days for summer finishing, 220 days winter finishing). Summer finishing takes place entirely out at pasture whilst winter finishing is a housed system for the production period.

2. *Sales*: Finished sale liveweights of 598kg for summer finishing and 604kg for winter finishing. Sale price £1.85/kg in both systems.

3. *Purchases*: Purchase / transfer-in weight of 398kg and 402kg for summer and winter finishing respectively. Cost in both cases £1.70/kg plus 1% mortality allowance.

4. *Concentrates:* 660kg concentrate @ £235 per tonne.

5. *Forage Costs*: Based on '*Long Term Ley*' in forage section (page 85) at £211/ha. Winter Finishing: 3.7 tonnes per head grass silage consumption. Only silage variable costs are considered and therefore overhead costs of silage production need to be considered. Similarly, bought in silage will increase the forage costs.

Finishing of Suckler Bred Store Cattle (**per head**) **(1)**

	Summer Finishing		Winter Finishing
	£		£
Finished Sales (2)	1,202		1,082
Less Purchased Store (incl. mortality)	550		706
Output	**652**		**377**
Variable Costs:			
Concentrates (3)	85		148
Vet & Med	12		20
Bedding	0		48
Miscellaneous	45		50
Total Variable Costs (excluding Forage)	**142**		**266**
Gross Margin per Head, before			
deducting Forage Variable Costs	510		111
Forage Variable Costs (4)	83		17
Gross Margin per Head	**427**		**93**
Animals per Hectare	3.20		
Forage Hectares (Acres) per Head	0.31	*(0.77)*	
Gross Margin per Forage Hectare (Acre)	**1,368**	*(553)*	

1. *System*: Beef suckler progeny purchased / transferred in at 8 months old for summer finishing and 12 months old for winter finishing (*summer finishing cattle will be from spring calving suckler cows, with winter finishers from autumn calving suckler cows*). Summer finishers = 300 days in system, winter finishers = 180 days in system.

2. *Sales*: Summer finishing 639kg liveweight, winter finishing 576kg liveweight. Sale price of £1.88/kg in both systems.

3. *Concentrates*: Summer finishers consuming 360kg, winter finishers 630kg. Concentrate price of £235 per tonne.

4. *Forage Costs*: Based on '*Long Term Ley*' in forage section (page 85) at £211/ha. Winter Finishing: 3.4 tonnes per head. Only silage variable costs are considered and therefore overhead costs of silage production need to be considered (inc. contracting). Similarly, bought in silage will increase the forage costs over those shown.

Maize & Grass Silage Beef Finishing (per Head Produced)

System (1)	Dairy X Progeny		Suckler Progeny	
Performance Level	Average	High	Average	High
	£	£	£	£
Finished Sales (2)	1,196	1,284	1,214	1,348
Less Purchased Store (incl. mortality) (3)	424	424	498	551
Output	**772**	**860**	**715**	**797**
Variable Costs:				
Concentrates (4)	154	146	100	93
Misc Variable Costs (5)	111	108	127	124
Total Variable Costs (excl. Forage)	**266**	**254**	**228**	**217**
Gross Margin per Head, before				
deducting Forage Variable Costs	506	606	488	580
Forage Cost (6)	81	73	75	68
Gross Margin per Head	**425**	**533**	**412**	**512**

1. *System*: An intensive finishing system utilising a housed forage-based system of grass silage and maize silage with heavy finished weights. Dairy cross progeny bought or transferred in at 6 months and suckler progeny at 8 months. Dairy-cross finishing period of 365 days and suckler progeny at 305 days. The gross margins are higher than in other finishing enterprises but overhead costs (fixed costs) will also be high in comparison.

2. *Sales*: Dairy cross = average 647kg liveweight @ £1.85/kg, high 683kg liveweight @ £1.88/kg. Suckler progeny = average 646kg liveweight @ £1.88/kg, high 706kg liveweight @ £1.91/kg.

3. *Mortality*: 1% mortality assumed.

4. *Concentrates*: Dairy cross = average 657kg, high 621kg, suckler progeny = average 427kg, high 397kg. Concentrates @ £235 per tonne.

5. Miscellaneous *Variable Costs*: assumed to be proportionally higher than the store and suckler finishing enterprises shown previously. Assumed 8% premium for average performance and 5% for high performance.

6. *Forage Costs*: Based on silage intakes of; Dairy cross = average 1.90 tonnes maize and 1.85 tonnes grass silage, high 1.71 tonnes maize, 1.70 tonnes grass silage. Suckler progeny = average 1.80 tonnes maize and 1.70 tonnes grass silage, high 1.62 tonnes maize, 1.50 tonnes grass silage. The silage costs relate to the total operational cost of growing and harvesting the forage, but not the costs incurred in preparing/mixing rations as shown in page 85.

Cereal Bull Beef (per Head)

System (1)	*Continental Cross Holstein/Friesian Bulls*		*Holstein Friesian Bulls*	
Performance Level	Average	High	Average	High
	£	£	£	£
Finished Sales (2)	901	955	817	896
Less Calf Purchase (3)	245	244	56	56
Output	**656**	**711**	**761**	**840**
Variable Costs:				
Concentrates (4)	442	428	442	428
Other Feed	22	20	22	20
Vet & Med	20	18	20	18
Bedding	54	54	54	54
Miscellaneous	48	48	48	48
Total Variable Costs	**586**	**568**	**586**	**568**
Gross Margin per Head	**71**	**143**	**175**	**272**

1. A traditional cereal based system for finishing cattle. Animals are housed throughout the production period and fed on a barley concentrate and straw based ration. Production period typically from 2 weeks to 14 months old. This system is highly exposed to swings in cereal commodity prices. Margins are very sensitive to calf price and feed price movements. A £10 per tonne feed price movement equates to a margin change of £22 per head.

2. *Sales:* Cont. cross bulls = average 530kg, high 555kg; Dairy bulls, average 475kg, high 515kg. Prices: Cont. cross bulls, average £1.70/kg liveweight, high £1.72/kg liveweight; Dairy bulls, average £1.72/kg, high £1.74/kg. All year round production is assumed. Average slaughter age is 15 months, with killing out percentages ranging from 54% to 59%, with the better conformation continental cross bulls achieving higher percentages.

3. *Purchases:* £255 for continental cross male calves at 3 weeks of age including mortality; £73 for dairy bulls including mortality. Mortality, average 2%, high 1.5%.

4. *Concentrates:* £116 calf rearing (to 12 weeks: see page 55) + finishing ration. Finishing ration: 17 parts barley @ £120 per tonne, 3 parts concentrate supplement @ £235 per tonne; plus £17 per tonne milling and mixing cost. Total, £154 per tonne.

    Barley ration quantity; average 2,225kg, high 2,140kg (excluding calf feed to 12 weeks – see page 55).

Veal

Veal consumption is very low in the UK - only a small fraction of the per capita consumption of France for example. Continental demand is mainly for white veal, produced in individual veal crates, a system that is illegal in the UK. There is no live calf export activity from the UK to the continent for veal production owing to animal welfare concerns and the risk of spreading Bovine Tb.

There is some activity in UK 'welfare friendly' domestic veal production where calves are kept in groups in straw yards producing heavier calves with 'pink' meat known as 'Rose Veal'. This is a premium product and is considerably more expensive to produce than imported 'white veal'.

SHEEP

Spring Lambing Flocks

Lowland Spring Lambing per Ewe (selling lambs off grass)

Performance Level	Low	Average	High
Lambs Reared per Ewe put to Ram (1)	1.27	1.55	1.72
Finished Lamb Liveweight (kg)		41.0	
Finished Lamb Liveweight Price (£/kg)		1.68	
Store Lamb Price (£/head)		52.0	
Average Price per Lamb (£) (2)	62.8	66.3	69.8
Sales:	£	£	£
Lamb sales..	80	103	120
Wool (3)..	2.6	2.6	2.6
Cull Ewes and Rams (4).................	10.2	10.2	10.2
Sub Total	92.4	115.5	132.8
Less Ewe and Ram Replacements (4)	34.8	34.8	34.8
Output per Ewe	**57.7**	**80.7**	**98.0**
Variable Costs:			
Concentrates (5)	20.6	15.3	13.7
Vet and Med (6).............................	9.9	10.4	12.5
Miscellaneous (7)...........................	13.7	13.7	13.7
Total Variable Costs (excluding Forage)	**44.23**	**39.4**	**39.96**
Gross Margin per Ewe, before deducting Forage Variable Costs	**13.4**	**41.3**	**58.1**
Forage Variable Costs (inc bought-in Forage and Keep) (8)	20.4	15.3	13.9
Gross Margin per Ewe	**-7.0**	**26.0**	**44.2**
Stocking Rate (Ewes with Lambs per forage Hectare (acre))	7.5 (3.0)	10 (4.0)	11 (4.5)
Gross Margin per Forage Hectare	-52	260	486
Gross Margin per Forage Acre	-21	105	197

1. *Rearing Performance Data:*

	Low	Average	High
Ewes in Lamb	90%	93%	95%
Lambing Percentage	160%	185%	201%
Lambs born per 100 ewes	144	172	191
Young Lamb Deaths	8%	6%	6%
Older Lamb Deaths	4%	4%	4%
Total Lamb Losses	12%	10%	10%
Lambs sold per 100 ewes put to ram	127	155	172

These performance figures are assumed for flocks of mature ewes, i.e. shearlings and older. Where ewe lambs or mainly shearlings are included in flock performance adjustment needs to be made. The breed will have a large effect on performance data.

2. *Lamb Prices.* Prices for lambs sold for slaughter are based on the forecast for the 2015 season and assumes a continuation of the robust EU export market without restrictions.

An average market price of £1.68/kg live-weight (equivalent to £3.65/kg deadweight) has been used giving £68.88 per finished lamb at an average live-weight of 41kg.

The average budgeted price in the table above allows for 15% sold as stores. Store price is assumed at £52 per head, making an overall lamb price of £66.30. Low and high performance variation is +/- £3.50 a lamb for variations caused by differences in weights, time of marketing and proportion sold finished or retained as stores.

3. *Wool*: In recent years the wool price has improved. Reasonable, clean wool yields give a small margin over the cost of shearing. Budgeted price assumed for lowland flocks is £2.60 per ewe, based on a price of £1.30/kg at 2kg/ewe. Variations between flocks will occur due to ewe breed affecting wool quality and ewe size affecting weight of wool produced.

4. *Flock Depreciation:* (i.e. Market price of replacements less value of culls). It is assumed that 19% of the ewe flock is culled each year @ £52 each and that, allowing for 4% mortality, 23% are purchased or home-reared at £138 each. Rams: 1 per 45 ewes, 3.5 year life, purchased @ £480, sold @ £50. The net cost (flock depreciation) is £25 per ewe per year. *Cull ewe prices vary considerably depending on the weight and 'fleshiness' of the ewes. Cull values tend to be highly variable but remain robust, partly at least through a strong, consistent demand from the UK ethnic sector. No other changes in flock valuation are assumed.*

5. *Concentrate Feeding*: Concentrate finishing of late season lambs has been common, but there has been a swing to sell as stores (for finishing on winter forage crops) rather than finish on high cost concentrates. Late season grass availability influences the store trade.

6. *Veterinary and Medicine:* includes allowance for wormer (ewes and lambs), vaccines, fly strike chemicals and foot treatments.

7. *Miscellaneous Costs:* include contract shearing @ £1.35/ewe, scanning £0.80/ewe and ewe and lamb tags £1.40/ewe (assuming slaughter batch tags are used), carcase disposal £0.64/ewe, straw £1.45/ewe, minerals and licks etc. £2.00/ewe, marketing, levy and transport £6.10/ewe.

8. *Forage Costs*: Based on *Improved Permanent Pasture (£153/ha)* refer to *forage section, page 85*. Only variable costs are included and therefore overhead costs of forage production need to be considered. Similarly, bought in grass keep and forage may increase the forage costs over those shown.

9. *Other Costs:*

    a. *Prices of Specialised Equipment*

Troughs (2.75 m)	£30 to £42
Racks (2 to 3 m)......................	£210 to £230
Foot Baths (3 m)	£100 to £160
Shearing Machines..................	£460 to £975
Lamb Creep Feeders	£360 to £775
Weigh Crate............................	£490 to £775
Mobile Handling System	£2,550 to £8,600

    b. *Fencing:* Approximately £6.30 per metre *for posts, sheep netting, 2 strands of barbed wired and labour inclusive. Refer to page 265.*

    c. *Labour*: see page 172.

Upland Spring Lambing per Ewe **(selling lambs off grass)**

Performance Level	Low	Average	High
Lambs Reared per Ewe put to Ram (1)	1.22	1.41	1.59
Finished Lamb Liveweight (kg)		39.0	
Finished Lamb Liveweight Price (£/kg)		1.66	
Store Lamb Price (£/head)		48.0	
Average Price per Lamb (£) (2)	58.2	61.7	65.2
Sales:	£	£	£
Lamb sales.......................................	71.2	86.9	103.6
Wool (3)...	2.0	2.0	2.0
Cull Ewes and Rams (4).................	8.3	8.3	8.3
Sub Total	81.5	97.2	113.9
Less Ewe and Ram Replacements (4)	33.4	33.4	33.4
Output per Ewe	**48.1**	**63.8**	**80.5**
Variable Costs:			
Concentrates (60kg ewes, 10kg lambs) (5)	23.29	17.3	13.80
Vet and Med (6)..............................	9.22	9.7	11.64
Miscellaneous (7)..........................	12.32	12.3	12.32
Total Variable Costs (excluding Forage)	**44.82**	**39.3**	**37.76**
Gross Margin per Ewe, before			
deducting Forage Variable Costs	**3.3**	**24.5**	**42.8**
Forage Variable Costs (inc bought-in			
Forage and Keep) (8)	22.8	10.0	8.5
Gross Margin per Ewe	**-19.5**	**14.5**	**34.2**
Stocking Rate (Ewes with Lambs per forage			
Hectare (acre))	4 (1.5)	9 (3.4)	10 (4.0)
Gross Margin per Forage Hectare	-73	123	342
Gross Margin per Forage Acre	-30	50	139

1. *Rearing Performance Data*:

	Low	Average	High
Ewes in Lamb	90%	93%	95%
Lambing Percentage	158%	172%	190%
Lambs born /100 ewes	142.2	160.0	180.5
Young Lamb Deaths	9%	7%	7%
Older Lamb Deaths	5%	5%	5%
Total Lamb Losses	14%	12%	12%
Lambs sold / 100 ewes put to ram	122	141	159

These performance figures are assumed for flocks of mature ewes, i.e. shearlings and older. Where ewe lambs or mainly shearlings are included in flock performance adjustment needs to be made. The breed will obviously have a large effect on lambing percentage, liveweight gains and carcase grades.

2. *Lamb Prices*. Prices for lambs sold for slaughter are based on the forecast for the 2014 season and assumes a continuation of the robust EU export market without restrictions.

An average market price of £1.66/kg liveweight (equivalent to £3.61/kg deadweight) has been assumed giving £64.74 per finished lamb at an average liveweight of 39kg.

The average budgeted price in the table above allows for 18% sold as stores. Store price is assumed at £48 per head. Low performance is £3.50 a lamb less, high £3.50 per lamb more for variations caused by differences in weights, time of marketing and proportion sold finished or retained as stores.

3. *Wool*: In recent years the wool price has improved. Reasonable, clean wool yields now give a small margin over the cost of shearing. Budget price assumed for upland flocks is £2.04 per ewe, based on a price of £1.20/kg at 1.7kg/ewe. Variations between flocks will occur due to ewe breed affecting wool quality and ewe size affecting weight of wool produced.

4. *Flock Depreciation:* (i.e. Market price of replacements less value of culls). It is assumed that 19% of the ewe flock is culled each year @ £42 each and that, allowing for 4% mortality, 23% are purchased or home-reared at £132 each. Rams: 1 per 45 ewes, 3.5 year life, purchased @ £480, sold @ £50. The net cost (flock depreciation) is £25 per ewe per year. *Cull ewe prices vary considerably depending on the weight and 'fleshiness' of the ewes. Cull values tend to be highly variable but remain high, partly at least through a strong, consistent demand from the UK ethnic sector. No other changes in flock valuation are assumed.*

5. *Concentrate Feeding*: Concentrate finishing of late season lambs has been common, but there has been a swing to sell as stores (for finishing on winter forage crops) rather than finish on high cost concentrates. Late season grass availability influences the store trade.

6. *Veterinary and Medicine:* includes allowance for wormer (ewes and lambs), vaccines, fly strike chemicals and foot treatments.

7. *Miscellaneous Costs:* include contract shearing @ £1.35/ewe, scanning £0.80/ewe and ewe and lamb tags £1.40/ewe (assuming slaughter batch tags are used), carcase disposal £0.72/ewe, straw £1.35/ewe, minerals and licks etc. £1.45/ewe, marketing, levy and transport £5.25/ewe.

8. *Forage Costs*: Based on *Low Input Pasture (£85/ha)* refer to *forage section, page* 85. Only variable costs are included and therefore overhead costs of forage production need to be considered. Similarly, bought in grass keep and forage may increase the forage costs over those shown.

Rearing Ewe Lambs

Purchasing ewe lambs and rearing over winter & summer for breeding

Sales:	£ Per Ewe
Sale Price / Transfer Value	138.00
Wool	1.80
Sub Total	139.80
Less Purchase Price / Transfer Value (2)	80.00
Losses & Culling (3)	3.80
Output per Ewe	**56.00**
Variable Costs:	
Vet and Med (4)..............................	7.00
Miscellaneous (5)...........................	3.27
Total Variable Costs (excluding Forage)	**10.27**
Gross Margin per Ewe, before	
deducting Forage Variable Costs	**45.73**
Forage Variable Costs (inc bought-in	
Forage and Keep) (6)	12.24
Gross Margin per Ewe	**33.49**
Stocking Rate (Ewe lambs per forage	
Hectare (acre))	12.5 (5.1)
Gross Margin per Forage Hectare	419
Gross Margin per Forage Acre	169

1. *System:* Involves rearing or purchasing ewe lambs suitable for further breeding. Animals are purchased / transferred in late summer / autumn, grazed and outwintered, grazed on in the following summer before sale / transfer out in the autumn (i.e. 12 month system). *The terminology for this system varies between regions; gimmers, thieves, shearlings and tegs all relate to the same age of female sheep.*

2. *Purchase Price*: Assumes better quality ewe lambs are acquired @ £80 per lamb.

3. *Losses and Culls:* 4% losses and 3% culled @ £60 (for meat as unsuitable for breeding).

4. *Veterinary and Medicine*: includes wormer, fly strike chemicals, vaccines and miscellaneous treatments.

5. *Miscellaneous Costs*: Shearing @ £1.35/head, minerals @ £1.60/head, carcase disposal @ £0.32/head. No marketing costs are included as it is assumed the ewes are retained for home use.

6. *Forage Costs*: Based on *Improved Permanent Pasture (£153/ha)* refer to *forage section, page* 85. Only variable costs are included and therefore overhead costs of forage production need to be considered. Similarly, bought in grass keep and forage may increase the forage costs over those shown.

Finishing Store Lambs

Purchasing store lambs and finishing late autumn & winter

	£ Per Lamb
Sales:	
Sale Price (1)	75.25
Less Purchase Price / Transfer In Value	52.00
Losses (2)	3.12
Output per Lamb	**20.13**
Variable Costs:	
Concentrates (3)	3.43
Vet and Med (4)..	2.90
Miscellaneous (5)...	5.75
Total Variable Costs (excluding Forage)	**12.08**
Gross Margin per Lamb, before	
deducting Forage Variable Costs	**8.06**
Forage Variable Costs (inc bought-in	
Forage and Keep) (6)	6.80
Gross Margin per Lamb	**1.25**
Stocking Rate (lambs per forage	
Hectare (acre))	28 (11.3)
Gross Margin per Forage Hectare	35
Gross Margin per Forage Acre	14

System: lambs are batch bought in the autumn at or shortly after weaning in September or October, then drawn out and sold as they are ready in smaller groups from then through to March the following year.

1. *Sales*: Assumes 43kg liveweight @ £1.75/kg.

2. *Losses*: assumed @ 6%.

3. *Concentrates:* 14kg per lamb @ £245 per tonne

4. *Veterinary and Medicine*: Allows for wormer and scab injection, clostridial vaccines and miscellaneous treatments.

5. *Miscellaneous*: Including transport, marketing, minerals, carcase disposal.

6. *Forage Costs*: Based on *Low Input Permanent Pasture (£85/ha)* and *Stubble Turnips* refer to *forage* section, page 85. Only variable costs are included and therefore overhead costs of forage production need to be considered. Similarly, bought in grass keep and forage may increase the forage costs over those shown.

GRAZING AND REARING CHARGES: CATTLE AND SHEEP

Grazing charges vary greatly according to the quality of the pasture, access, fencing and infrastructure. Local supply and demand also affect the value of grazing charges. The following figures are typical (estimated for 2014/15):

Summer Grazing (per head per week)

Store Cattle and in-calf heifers over 21 months, dry cows, and fattening bullocks over 18 months...........................	£2.50 - £3.50
Heifers and Steers, 12-21 months	£2.50 - £3.50
6-12 months Cattle	£1.50 - £2.50
Cattle of mixed ages	£1.50 - £3.00
Ewes (with lambs)......................................	£0.55 - £0.85

Winter Grazing (per head per week)

'Strong' Cattle	£2.25 - £3.50
Heifers	£2.00 - £3.00
Sheep...	£0.35 - £0.50

Note: the above figures assume the farmer on whose land the livestock are present does all the fencing and shepherding. Where the owner of the stock does the fencing, shepherding, etc., the figures may be halved, or be even less depending on local demand.

Grass Keep

Most typically around £100-£175 per ha (£40-£70/acre), with the best £185-£275 per ha (£75-£110/acre) and lower quality keep making £62-£90 per ha (£25-£36/acre).

These figures are highly variable, especially between one part of the country and another, and even between one parish and another. The charge can be very high where the pasture is good, the supply scarce and the demand strong. Good fencing, electricity supply, mains water etc. adds a premium to grass keep as does the quality of grassland and any licensor fertiliser applications. Grazing may be offered to livestock keepers at very little or no charge where the need for maintenance of grassland is the driving factor (e.g. amenity value, requirement to cross comply or meet agri-environment scheme agreements, value of cattle and sheep to 'clean-up' pasture or to provide beneficial mixed grazing). The length of grazing period offered will also influence the premium of grass keep (e.g. grazing until 30th September or until 31st December) as will permission to take a grass crop from the land (hay, haylage, silage).

The Nitrate Vulnerable Zone (NVZ) rules in England mean that demand for grass keep is high in some areas, especially where dairy enterprises are commonplace. The additional acreage helps some producers to keep within their livestock manure loading limit.

Winter Keep (Cattle per head per week)

Grazing + 9 kg hay and some straw....................	£9.50
Full winter housing in yards	£9.50 - £12.50
Calf rearing for beef	£12.00 - £15.00

A typical rental for labour, buildings and maintenance diet would be £9.50 per head per week. These rates apply where feed to achieve maintenance plus some growth is supplied plus labour and buildings and bedding where applicable. A typical rental for labour, buildings and a maintenance diet would be £7.50 per head per week. In recent years the cost of bedding (usually straw) has influenced the final values of winter keeping cattle.

Heifer Rearing Charges

There have historically been two types of arrangement:

1. Farmer X sells calf to a Rearer at agreed price; the calf is then Rearer's responsibility and he pays for all expenses and bears any losses. Farmer X has first option on heifers, which he buys back two months before calving. Approximate price: £1,200 above cost of calf for Holstein Friesians. Rearer fetches calf; Farmer X supplies transport for heifer. *This system is now less common due to the increasing popularity and general transparency of option 2 below.*

2. Farmer X retains ownership of calf, but sends it to a specialist rearer. Approximate rearer charges range from £0.60 to £1.20 per head per day for winter rearing and £1.00 to £1.30 per head per day for summer rearing. Charges vary depending upon cattle, system and location. Newer agreements often include a fixed incentive payment to the Rearer if the cattle have met specification at the end of the rearing period. This is usually defined in terms of final liveweight and the level of heifers in-calf. A typical fixed fee incentive payment would be £50 per head.

   Usually the owner of the cattle is responsible for transport costs and the choice and cost of vaccine programmes. The cost of semen for artificial insemination of the heifers is also usually incurred by the owner and paid for over and above the standard rearing charge. The rearer is responsible for all standard rearing costs including for normal veterinary services and worming etc. and any animal losses over an agreed tolerance level. *Model agreements are available from industry associations and advisors.*

Contract rearing on behalf of a third party may appeal to some producers who wish to reduce borrowing exposure and / or lower capital investment in a business. A well laid out contract rearing arrangement will also provide greater cost and income clarity to both the rearer and owner and therefore reduce the risk exposure to both businesses. It also enables each business to focus and specialise to achieve optimum performance without being distracted by other enterprises. Biosecurity issues are becoming increasingly paramount where an agreement is set up. In many cases the owner of heifers will require exclusive occupancy of a rearer's farm without cattle owned by the rearer or others being present. The Bovine TB movement rules must be considered by parties entering into heifer rearing agreements including the need for pre-movement TB testing between holdings.

RED DEER

A. *Breeding and Finishing*	Per 100 Hinds
Sales:	£
44 Stags (15-18 months) : 55kg dw @ £5.20/kg..................	12,584
34 Hinds (15-18 months) : 45kg dw @ £5.20/kg	7,956
8 Cull Hinds @ £150...	1,200
1 Cull Stag @ £100...	100
Less Replacements: 8 hinds @ £350 & 1 stag @ £600	3,400
Output	**18,440**
Variable Costs:	
Concentrates @ 4.0 tonnes @ £225/tonne.............................	900
Vet and Med...	494
Miscellaneous..	408
Total Variable Costs	**1,802**
Gross Margin before deducting Forage Costs	**16,638**
Forage Variable Costs (5.5 Hinds per hectare @ £211/ha).............	3,836
Gross Margin per 100 Hinds..	**12,802**
Gross Margin per Forage hectare (5.5 hinds/ha)........................	704
Gross Margin per Forage acre (2.2 hinds/ac)...............................	285

Lowland systems assumed. Hind replacements home-reared in systems A and B.

Herd Life: hinds, 12 years; stags, 6 years; 33 hinds per stag. Calves reared per 100 hinds: 90. Purchase price of breeding stock (good quality): hinds £350 plus, yearling hinds £275 plus, stags £500 plus.

B. *Breeding and Selling Store Calves*	Per 100 Hinds
Sales:	£
45 Stag Calves @ £150/head (45 kg liveweight)....................	6,750
35 Hind Calves @ £150/head (40 kg liveweight)..................	5,250
8 Cull Hinds @ £150...	1,200
1 Cull Stag @ £100...	100
Less Replacements: 8 hinds @ £350 & 1 stag @ £600	3,400
Output	**9,900**
Variable Costs:	
Concentrates @ 1.3 tonnes @ £225/tonne.............................	293
Vet and Med...	285
Miscellaneous..	204
Total Variable Costs	**782**
Gross Margin before deducting Forage Costs.............................	**9,119**
Forage Variable Costs (6.5 Hinds per hectare @ £153/ha).............	2,353
Gross Margin per 100 Hinds..	**6,765**
Gross Margin per Forage hectare (6.5 hinds/ha)........................	440
Gross Margin per Forage acre (2.6 hinds/ac)...............................	178

C. Finishing Stag Calves

	Per 200 Stags
Sales:	£
195 Stags (15-18 months) : 55kg dw @ £5.20/kg.................	55,770
Less Purchases : 200 @ £150 per head...	30,000
Output	**25,770**
Variable Costs:	
Concentrates @ 12.0 tonnes @ £225/tonne...........................	2,700
Vet and Med...	612
Miscellaneous...	995
Total Variable Costs	**4,307**
Gross Margin before deducting Forage Costs............................	**21,463**
Forage Variable Costs (11.0 Stags per hectare @ £211/ha)............	3,836
Gross Margin per 200 Stags..	**17,627**
Gross Margin per Forage hectare (11 stags/ha)..........................	969
Gross Margin per Forage acre (4.5 stags/ac).............................	392

The venison price reflects projected sales for 2015 to wholesale buyers and the higher prices being paid for farmed venison by supermarkets. Higher prices will be obtained for direct sales to consumers (e.g. farm shops and farmers' markets) and caterers, but extra costs will normally be incurred.

D. Deer Park

	Per 300 Hinds
Sales:	£
120 Stags (15-18 months) : 55kg dw @ £2.80/kg.................	18,480
110 Hinds (15-18 months) : 50kg dw @ £2.80/kg.................	15,400
25 Cull Hinds @ £150..	3,750
5 Live Stag Sales @ £1,000.......................................	5,000
Less Replacements: 25 hinds @ £350 & 2 stag @ £600	9,950
Output	**32,680**
Variable Costs:	
Concentrates @ 12.0 tonnes @ £225/tonne...........................	2,700
Vet and Med...	510
Miscellaneous...	306
Total Variable Costs	**3,516**
Gross Margin before deducting Forage Costs	**29,164**
Forage Variable Costs (3.0 Hinds per hectare @ £85/ha)................	8,537
Gross Margin per 300 Hinds...	**20,627**
Gross Margin per Forage hectare (3 hinds/ha)...........................	206
Gross Margin per Forage acre (1.2 hinds/ac).............................	83

Sales are based on skin-on carcases bought by a game dealer/butcher. Forage costs Refer to *Forage* on page 85.

Sources of further information: The British Deer Farmers Association, PO Box 7522, Matlock, DE4 9BR. Tel: 08456 344 758 www.bdfa.co.uk

Acknowledgement: Thanks to – John Fletcher BVMS, PhD, Hon FRCVS, ARAgS

HORSES: LIVERY

The horse industry is now reported to be the second biggest employer in the rural economy. Prior to the economic downturn it was also one of the fastest growing. Over the last 5 years the horse population has declined from its peak. Horse owners have tended to adopt spending reduction behaviours – looking for cheaper services such as DIY instead of part livery. Even so a premium segment of the market also persists, with owners of high disposable income seeking high quality services and facilities. Although there are other equine enterprises that farm businesses can operate, by far the most common is providing accommodation for horses; i.e. livery. There are many different forms of livery and the charges, therefore, vary widely also. This is apart from the effects of local supply and demand, which can lead to large price differences from one area to another. However, three fairly standard forms are offered on farms:

Grass Livery. Keep at grass, preferably with shelter, water supply and secure area to keep tack and store feed. Some grass livery will provide an exercise arena and off-road riding. Charges average £30 per week; range £20-£50.

DIY Livery. The owner still has full care of the horse but has the facilities of a stable, grazing, and in some cases an all-weather exercise arena. The owner is responsible for mucking out, turning out, grooming, exercising and all vet./med. care and the cost of all feed and bedding. Charges average £40 per week; range £25-£55.

DIY Plus Livery. As the above, except that the yard manager is responsible for certain tasks, such as turning out and feeding. Charges average £52 per week; range £35-£70.

In addition there is *Full Livery*. The yard supplies a complete service to the horse owner including tasks such as grooming and exercise. Services provided by the yard may be fitted to the needs of a horse/owner. Few farm-based liveries would offer such a high level of management unless there is equine expertise in the family. Full livery charges average £120 per week; with a range of £80-£180.

The above are only guidelines. There is a wide variation both within, and between regions.

Other Costs:

Grazing. Variable costs will average some £60 per horse per year. Average stocking rates are 0·8 ha (2 acres) for the first horse and 0·4 ha (1 acre) for each horse after.

Hay. Average price £5.00 per conventional bale (approximately 20kg) (range £3-£7.00), depending on the season. It has to be good quality. Average consumption is one to two bales per horse per week; less in the summer depending on the grass quality/quantity and the work of the horse. Some horses now have haylage; more expensive, dust free and higher fibre and energy/protein levels; less required per head.

Concentrate Feed. Can range from almost nil to 3.0-4.0kg per day depending, amongst other factors, on breed, size and intensity of work. Compound feed 35 to 50p per kg.

Bedding. Averages around £12 per stabled horse per week, with some horses stabled year round and others having significant turnout in the summer, which reduces bedding cost. Typical cost £300-£400 per year. Straw might cost only half as much; however, more expensive, but preferable, alternatives (such as wood shavings, shredded paper and hemp fibre) are now increasingly being used.

Vet. and Med. Averages approximately £185 per horse per year. Some yards include worming of the horse in the livery cost.

Rates. Livery is a non-agricultural use, and therefore any buildings being used for the enterprise are liable to business rates.

The supply of livery yards appears to be increasing, from both farms diversifying and other yards setting up. Filling a yard is, consequently, becoming more difficult. The level of service and facilities expected by customers has increased. There is a trend towards greater professionalism in the running and management of livery yards. Livery contracts should be exchanged showing clearly the responsibilities of each party. Comprehensive third party insurance is also important.

To be successful, a livery enterprise needs higher quality facilities than farm livestock. To the owner the horse can be anything from a highly trained athlete to a family pet. Horses are expensive: even modest quality horses cost between £1,500 and £3,000. Good customer relations and an effective security system (including burglar and fire alarms) are crucial to success, as is good market research and effective advertising. Ensuring prompt payment of livery fees is another issue, this can be helped by payment in advance or by direct debit.

A full livery yard will require stables, a secure room to store tack, a vermin-proof hard feed store, storage for hay and bedding, a muck heap, a riding arena and parking provision with room for horse boxes. Planning permission is required for the conversion of an existing building to stabling or the erection of new, purpose-built stables. Permission is also required for construction of an all-weather arena used for training horses and exercising them in bad weather. Hay and straw should be stored away from the stables and downwind of them to minimise the fire risk. A hard standing area with a water supply and good drainage should be provided for grooming and washing down the horses.

Good ventilation in the stables is crucial as horses are prone to respiratory diseases caused by spores and dust. Provision should be made for owners to soak hay in clean water before feeding it, to reduce respiratory problems.

Fences must be sound and free of protruding nails, wire etc. Ideally fields should be fenced using post and rail, but this is expensive. Barbed wire should be avoided wherever possible or should be 'protected' with an offset electrified fence. Fields should be divided into smaller paddocks to reduce the possibility of fighting between incompatible horses and to separate mares and geldings. Paddocks may be divided using two or more strands of electrified tape or rope but wire is not advisable as it is not easily visible to the horse.

Off-road riding opportunities on the farm are a real asset. The farmer may provide riding trails, a jumping paddock, or a cross country course. An all-weather ménage for exercising horses, possibly with floodlighting, is highly desirable, and some livery yards have horse walkers too. Good facilities can be rented out to individuals or organisations such as pony clubs. It is sometimes possible to link up with nearby farms to increase the length of riding tracks available.

Construction Costs. The cost of conversion of existing buildings will depend on their quality; prefabricated hardwood and steel internal stable partitions can be purchased from upwards of £1000 per stable, depending on size and specification. Free standing timber stables cost between £1,000 and £2,000 (plus base), depending on size and quality. As horses are fairly destructive animals (they both kick and chew) better quality stables will often prove more economic in the long run. All weather arenas (20 metres by 40 metres) cost between £20,000 and £50,000; construction is a specialist job as good drainage is essential; a badly constructed arena is worthless.

Contact: Further financial information on horse enterprises, including riding schools and equestrian centres, is available in 'Equine Business Guide', 5th Edition, 2005, edited by Richard Bacon, Warwickshire College; Tel. 01926 318319.

WILD BOAR

Wild Boar is farmed in the UK on about 50 farms, with a population of roughly 1,750 sows. Wild Boar come under the Dangerous Wild Animals Act and farms must be licensed by the Local Authority. The cost of a licence varies greatly between authorities and ranges anywhere from £150 - £700 plus veterinary inspection fees. These have to be renewed annually following a farm inspection with renewal fees at a lower rate. Enclosures must be secure with strong fencing: a minimum height of at least 1.8 metres and most authorities require 30-80cm below ground plus an additional strand of electric fence inside the main fence. The estimated minimum cost of fencing using approved contractors is from £13.50 per metre erected plus the hire of a digger.

Wild Boar live outdoors in groups of up to 10 sows per boar. Large arcs are suitable for a group of gestating sows, or sows running with maturing boarlets. About a hectare would be needed for 5 sows and a boar. They forage but need feeding concentrate and root crops. Gilts mature at 18 months. Farmed sows can give two litters in most years. Young sows produce 2 to 3 boarlets and mature sows 6 to 9. A well-run enterprise should average 7 boarlets per sow per year raised to maturity. Wild boar can live from 12 to 15 years, but in a commercial herd the sows are usually culled at 7 to 8 years. Wild boar take 9 to 18 months to reach a slaughter weight of 75-85 kg. This produces a 45-50 kg carcase.

Capital Costs: Housing and fencing £4,200 per hectare (*£1,700 per acre*); pure-bred adult boar £500-£700; pure-bred in pig sow £350-£500. Labour requirements are low, owing to the 'hands off' nature of wild boar management. One person should manage a herd of 30-40 sows plus fatteners.

In spite of the demand for wild boar meat, there is no organised marketing system and producers develop their own outlets. There are some wholesale butchers and game dealers who will take whole carcases, but many producers organise their own processing and arrange their own retailing.

Finished Boarlets per Sow per Year	7 (6 - 9)
Finished Carcase Weight (over 15 months)	45 - 50 kg
Price per kg deadweight	£4.00 - £6.00
Sales:	£
Meat sales per Sow per Year	1,575
Less Depreciation per Sow per Year (1)	52
Output per Sow	**1,523**
Variable Costs:	
Concentrates sow (2)	337
fatteners (150kg each at £300/t)	315
Other Feed	180
Bedding	40
Vet, Med and Licence	100
Miscellaneous (inc. Water and Electricity)	20
Total Variable Costs per Sow	**992**
Gross Margin per Sow	**531**
Gross Margin per Hectare (5 Sows/Ha)	**2,657**

1. Cost of sow £425, cull value £200, active herd life 5 years, plus share of boar and 5% mortality
2. Including share of boar
3. Bought-in waste vegetables

GOAT DAIRYING

Performance Level	Low	Average	High
Milk Yield (litres) per Goat (1)	500	800	1,000
Sales:	£	£	£
Milk Value (2)....................................	325.0	520.0	650.0
Value of Kids (3)...............................	2.8	3.6	3.6
Less Livestock Depreciation (4)..................	23.9	23.9	23.9
Output per doe	**303.9**	**499.7**	**629.7**
Variable Costs:			
Concentrates (5)...................................	110.5	176.8	221.0
Miscellaneous (inc. Vet and Med).......	70.0	70.0	70.0
Total Variable Costs	**180.5**	**246.8**	**291.0**
Gross Margin per Doe, before	**123.4**	**252.9**	**338.7**
deducting Forage Variable Costs			
Forage Variable Costs (6)	25.1	40.1	50.1
Gross Margin per Doe	**98.4**	**212.9**	**288.6**
Stocking Rate (Goats per Forage Hectare			
(acre) - zero-grazed system).................	10.0 (4.0)	12.0 (4.9)	15.0 (6.1)
Gross Margin per Forage Hectare...............	984	2,554	4,329
Gross Margin per Forage Acre....................	398	1,034	1,752

1. *Yield:* Per 300 day lactation, kidding each year. Autumn kidders tend to yield less.

2. *Price:* 65p per litre; 60p to 70p (+) with the higher prices being in the winter months (November to February) and the lower end of the range in the summer. 12.5% solids delivered.

3. *Kid(s):* Prolificacy relates to age, breed, seasonality and feed level. Assumptions: low 140%; average and high 180%. There is very little trade in kids for meat (£2 per kid assumed).

4. *Culls and Replacements:* Replacements at £180/head; culls £35 to £45, average life 6 years. Bucks: 1 per 40-50 does. Does normally mate in autumn; gestation 150 days; young goats can be mated from 6 months.

5. *Concentrates:* Average 0.85kg concentrate per litre (higher for 1,000 litre producers), at £260 per tonne.

6. *Forage:* Average 0.5 kg DM forage per litre at £116 per tonne DM (Refer to Forage Section on page 85). Goats can be grazed but are normally storage fed to avoid problems with worms, fencing, milk taints and pneumonia. Farmers able to produce maize silage will have a better forage conversion ratio.

7. *Miscellaneous:* Bedding £25, vet and med. £25 (includes treatment for out-of-season breeding, vaccination against Johnes), sundries £20.

9. *Labour:* 1 full-time person per 150 to 200 goats, dependent on technology employed.

10. *Markets:* Herd sizes in the UK range from 50 to 3,000 milking does. Average herd size is growing as established producers expand with the market at about 15% average annual growth. Successful businesses have been built on producer processing and retailing, as bulk purchasers of goats' milk are few and far between. Prolificacy and technical improvements allow higher annual growth than the market and there is a cycle in milk and stock prices.

SHEEP DAIRYING

Performance Level	Low	Average	High
Milk Yield (litres) per Ewe per Year	225	375	450
Sales:	£	£	£
Milk Value (1).....................................	236	394	473
Value of Lambs (2).............................	93	93	93
Wool..	2	2	2
Less Livestock Depreciation	22	22	22
Output per Ewe	**310**	**467**	**546**
Variable Costs:			
Concentrates (4)...................................		217	
Miscellaneous (inc. Vet and Med).......		19	
Total Variable Costs (excluding forage)		**236**	
Gross Margin per Ewe, before deducting Forage Variable Costs	**73**	**231**	**309**
Forage Variable Costs...........................		19.2	
Gross Margin per Ewe	**54**	**212**	**290**
Stocking Rate (Ewes with Lambs per forage Hectare (acre))....................................		11 (4.5)	
Gross Margin per Hectare	595	2,327	3,193

1. Price: 1.05p per litre at farm gate (range from 100p-110p per litre).

2. *Lambing %:* 175%. Assume a 300 Friesland ewe flock. Retain 60 ewe lambs for flock replacements. Sell 390 finished lambs reared from 2 days old (inc. 15% mortality) at £60. If meat-type terminal sires used then cross-bred lamb values increase to £80.

3. *Cull ewes:* Assumed 18% culled at £50.00 per head (average, including mortality).

4. *Concentrates:* Milking ewes: 200 days at 1.5 kg/head/day, 100 days at 0.5 kg/head/day; cost £275-300 /tonne. Ewe lamb replacements and artificially reared finished lambs at £75/head.

5. *Forage costs:* Quality silage: 1 tonne per milking ewe (or hay equivalent). Grazing: early grass in March/April; good grazing on leys or pasture; similar for dry stock and lambs. For details on *forage* refer to page 85.

   Fixed Costs per Ewe: Labour (paid) £84; Power and Machinery £26; Property Costs £15; Other £15; Total, excluding Finance and Rent, £140.

   Capital Costs of Equipment: Complete milking unit for 300 ewes (including yokes, bulk tank, dairy equipment, installation): £12,500-£25,500. A small 50 ewe unit can be put together for £10,000. Any building works would be additional to the above costs.

Acknowledgements: thanks to - Anthony Hyde, FRICS, FBIAC, FRAgS.

ANGORA GOATS

Angora goats produce mohair; angora rabbits produce angora; cashgora is produced by angora cross dairy goats; cashmere is produced by improved feral goats (valuable 'down' has to be separated from guard hairs; thus, with cashmere production, 'yield of down' must not be confused with 'weight of clip' as percentage down is low and can vary widely). Goat meat is sometimes called 'chevon'.

The UK angora goat population is thought to have reduced to about 1,000 animals which produce an estimated annual clip of 5 tonnes. The figures below are for a commercial enterprise. There is a strong demand for angora goats from small holders and smaller farmers which is making stock sales buoyant. Many UK angora flocks are kept on a semi-commercial or hobby basis, in which case different criteria may apply – does retained longer, mortality rates lower, doe/buck ratio different. Currently (2014) the world price of mohair is buoyant but adversely affected by the South African Rand:US dollar exchange rate. There is a world shortage of mohair. The figures used in the calculations are based on prices in 2014. Much of the UK clip is exported by the producers' co-operative, British Mohair Marketing, to South Africa where it is graded and sold through the Cape Mohair auctions. The rest of the UK annual clip is processed for other enterprises in UK and for hand spinning where higher prices can be achieved.

Performance:	Per Doe
Kids per Doe per Year (1)	1.5
Fibre: Doe/Buck, 2 clips, 2.5 & 4kg/clip respectively (2)	5.3 kg
Kids (1.5), first and second clips (3)	5.0 kg
Wethers/Replacement Does (0.95), third clip (3)	3.3 kg

Fibre Sales per doe:	£
Doe/Buck: 5.3kg @ £8.50/kg (3)	45.2
Kids: 5.0kg @ £12.0/kg (3)	59.4
Wethers/Replacements: 3.3kg @ £9.2/kg (3)	30.6
Stock Sales:	
0.6 female kids sold for breeding @ £200 each (1)(4)	110.0
Wethers: 0.8 males sold for meat @ £50 each (1)(4)	37.5
Culls: 0.14 does @ £50 each (1)(4)	7.3
Skin Sales:	8.9
Less Replacements (4)	30.9
Output per Doe	**268.0**

Variable Costs:	
Concentrates (6)	60.4
Vet and Med (7)	8.2
Miscellaneous (8)	18.4
Total Variable Costs per Doe	**87.0**
Gross Margin per Doe before Forage Costs	**181.0**
Forage Variable Costs (9)	31.9
Gross Margin per Doe	**149.2**
Gross Margin per Forage hectare	716.0
Gross Margin per Forage acre	290

Angora goats require more management than sheep. Fencing requirements are similar but housing costs rather higher. Margins are particularly sensitive to the value and number of breeding stock sold, yield and value of fibre, kidding percentage and meat values. There is a market for meat from older animals but no reliable market has yet been developed specifically for younger animals. Angoras are probably most successfully run as a subsidiary enterprise on a farm rather than a stand-alone operation.

1. 1.5 kids born alive per doe mated; 2% mortality to each clip. Of 0.7 surviving doe kids, the majority (0.5) are sold for breeding, the remainder (0.2) are retained for replacements. Culls (0.15) and casualties are equal to the number of replacements (unless the flock size is changing). Progeny are sold after 2 clips for breeding or after 3 clips for meat. Stock may be retained for further shearing. This has become more common, as the demand for breeding stock is small, fibre quality has improved and there is little market for meat.

2. The data for Breeding Does includes output and inputs for breeding bucks. Assumes 25 does to one buck.

3. Angora goats are usually clipped twice a year. Yield increases over first four clips, but quality decreases with age. Prices can be volatile, being dependent on fashion and on the world market dominated by South Africa and Texas. Demand and prices are highest for the high quality kid fibre <25 microns in diameter.

The following yields and prices have been used:-

Clip 1 = 1.2 kg at £12.00 per kg; clip 2 = 2.1 kg at £12.00 per kg; clip 3 = 3.5 kg at £9.20 per kg. Adult doe: 2.5 kg, adult buck 4.0 kg at £8.50 per kg.

British Mohair Marketing arranges a collection once a year, currently in September. Since 2010, the entire collected clip has been containerised and shipped to South Africa where it has been sold by auction by Cape Mohair Ltd. The prices thus achieved were considerably better than those previously attained in the UK and easily covered the increased handling expenses. Membership of BMM costs £30 and there is a handling/marketing levy of £1.10/kg. (Some producers improve their return by processing and using the fibre themselves or selling to local spinners. Commercial processing costs are significant: combing about £3.50 per kg and spinning about £20 per kg).

4. *Stock sales.* Breeding stock in commercial flocks are culled after seven years on average. Subsequent shearing stock culled after a further 4 clips. Value of all cull stock: £50 each. Depending on quality, the skin can be worth £10 before curing or up to £120 after curing. Replacement costs: does, £200; bucks, £400. Shearing stock, £20 (as transfer from breeding enterprise). Show quality stock command a premium.

5. *Skin Sales:* From cull does and males sold for meat @ £10.00

6. *Concentrates.* Quantities: Kids - 50 kg to clip 2, 15 kg to clip 3; Adults - breeding adults 90 kg per year, shearlings 40 kg per year.

7. *Veterinary* costs can be high and include vaccinations, worming & foot trimming. Membership of disease control schemes (MV/CAE) or Scrapie monitoring will be extra.

8. *Miscellaneous* costs include £2.50 to £3.50 per shearing per head (it may be more) and bedding materials.

9. *Forage:* 4.8 does per hectare at £153 per hectare (grass), refer to *forage* on page 85.

Contact: *British Angora Goat Society*: www.britishangoragoats.org.uk British Mohair Marketing: www.mohairmarketing.org.uk

Acknowledgements: thanks to - Stephen Whitley, Corrymoor Angoras, Stockland, Honiton, Devon EX14 9DY socks@corrymoor.com www.corrymoor.com

OSTRICHES

Introduction

Ostrich production in the UK is 20 years old. Production is limited to a few small farmers, working individually, selling most meat through farmers' markets and restaurants. There is minimal processing infrastructure in the UK. Slaughter is carried out under contract in dedicated ostrich plants and red meat slaughter plants with a ratite (flightless bird) license.

Ostriches are produced primarily for meat, with their skins (for leather), fat and feathers also providing revenue potential. Skins are generally sold in minimum numbers of 200 so it can require long-term storage to build up sufficient numbers.

Adult breeding stock are normally kept in trios of one male and two females, but pairs and colonies are not unusual. A trio requires about 0.2 ha (0.5 acre) well drained land and must be able to run. A stout hedge or smooth wire fence of 1.7 metres high should surround the enclosure. Adult birds need shelter from wind and rain, and a dry floor on which to sleep. Domesticated ostrich are generally docile and easily handled. There are two systems costed here, the production of chicks from trios, and fattening the chicks.

Production

Laying Bird Trios

Performance Level	Low	Medium	High
Eggs – *per hen per year*	45	60	70
Hatching - %	65%	75%	85%
Surviving Chicks - %	50%	70%	85%
Total Chicks per hen	15	32	51
Financial Data per Trio			
Sales:			
Chicks Per Year	29	63	101
Chick Income (1)	453	977	1,568
Output per Trio	**453**	**977**	**1,568**
Variable Costs:			
Concentrates (2).....................................	598	832	962
Miscellaneious (3)..............................	34	34	34
Bird Depreciation (4)..........................	83	83	83
Total Variable Costs	**715**	**949**	**1,079**
Gross Margin per Trio	**-262**	**27**	**488**
Stocking Rate 5 Trios per hectare			
Gross Margin per Ha	**-1,310**	**136**	**2,442**

Notes:

1. *Chick Income:* Chicks sold out at £15.50 per head

2. *Concentrate feed:* £260/tonne. Low production birds eat 2.4 tonnes per trio, average = 3.2 and high production birds 3.7 tonnes/trio

3. *Miscellaneous:* includes vet & med., forage etc.

4. *Bird Depreciation costs:* replacement for a trio £1,450 over 15 year's productivity less £200 cull value

Historically, skin was the ostrich's primary product. Now, meat is the highest value, especially if marketed into the restaurant sector. This clearly requires marketing expertise. Doubling meat yields and halving the time to reach slaughter transforms the economics as is shown below. Many systems involve a high cost building and fencing layout which should be taken into consideration with the economics of the gross margins shown here.

Slaughter Birds

Performance Level	Low	Average	High
Days to Slaughter	425	300	220
Sales:	£	£	£
Meat: (1)...	300	350	400
Value of Skin (2)................................	52	52	52
Less Day Old Chick (3)..............................	16	16	16
Output per Bird	**337**	**387**	**437**
Variable Costs:			
Concentrates (4)....................................	204	185	109
Other Rearing Costs (5).......................	107	88	58
Slaughter, Processing etc.	77	77	77
Marketing	5	5	5
Total Variable Costs	**393**	**356**	**250**
Gross Margin per Bird	**-57**	**31**	**187**
Gross Margin per year per bird	**-49**	**38**	**310**
Stocking Rate 5 birds per hectare			
Gross Margin per Ha	**-244**	**188**	**1,551**

Notes:

1. *Meat:* £9/kg, 30kg, 35kg and 40kg meat for low to high performance levels.

2. *£52 per hide,*

3. *Chicks* bought in at £15.50 each (see schedule above) but varies from £10 to £22

4. *Concentrates:* Price of feed rises as performance rises (£260, £340 and £390/t) but consumption per bird falls from 2kg/day to 1.12kg/day.

5. *Other Costs:* includes depreciation of site, vet. & med. and miscellaneous

Contact: British Domesticated Ostrich Association (BDOA), 33 Eden Grange, Little Corby, Carlisle, CA4 8QW. (Tel.: 01228 562 946); www.ostrich.org.uk

CAMELIDS

Llamas, alpacas, guanacos and vicunas are collectively known as South American Camelids. Originally they all came from Central America. They are all members of the same family and are related to camels. Camelids are herd animals and should not be kept in isolation but will live happily with other animals.

Llamas

The llama is the largest of the Camelids, weighing up to 180kg (400lbs) and standing 1.25m (4ft) at shoulder height. Llamas are strong animals traditionally used as pack animals and kept in the UK for trekking or pets. They have a life span of 15-20 years. They produce offspring for 10-15 years.

Llamas can be kept at stocking rates of 10-12/ha (4-5/acre). They are generally hardy animals but benefit from an open fronted shelter. They eat grass and hay, with occasional supplements. They can be bought from a few hundred pounds.

Alpacas

Alpacas are smaller with a shoulder height of 1m (3ft) and weigh around 70kg (155lb). They produce an outstanding quality fleece. Their fibres are very fine and exceptionally strong. An annual shearing will produce an average fleece of 0.7 to 4.5kg. The saddle or prime fleece part of the shearing will, when skirted (primary clean), sell to trade processors for;

- Baby Alpaca £8 per kg coloured, £12/kg white (21 micron or below)
- Fine Alpaca £5 per kg coloured, £8 per kg white (22-26 micron)
- Coarse Alpaca £0.40 - £1.00 per kg (27+ micron)
- Retail prices are substantially higher, typically £16-35 per kg

Alpacas require shearing annually with Huacaya (95% of UK alpacas) having a crimpy staple style suitable mostly for knitting yarms and Suri with longer curly locks like a Wensleydale sheep suitable for most woven cloth and some knitting.

Alpacas should be kept at 12–20 per hectare (5-8/acre). They are hardy animals well suited to the UK climate, but require shelter. They graze all year, with additional hay and a daily mineral supplement for breeding stock. Their feed and maintenance costs are similar to that of lowland sheep however they so no suffer from foot rot and are unlikely to be fly struck as they are clean under the tail and do not require tail trimming.

An alpaca can cost anything from £200 for non-breeding stock and £500 to £10,000 for female breeding stock. Fibre producing wethers typically cost £200 for coloured rising to £500 for white. Price will vary according to genetics, age, fertility, fibre quality and colour. The alpaca gestation period is 11-12 months.

The earning potential of an Alpaca is dictated by the quality of its fleece and through breeding. The UK alpaca meat market remains small and is generally associated with other on-farm meat products. Typical terminal prices are £60-£75 per live animal. Animals with low quality fleeces may have a value as pets, flock guards or tourist attractions. Alpaca fleece is a luxury fibre thus only the highest quality fleeces and stock command good prices.

Breeding and Fleece Production (per alpaca)

Performance Level	Average	High
	£	£
Fleece Weight (Kg)	1.70	2.00
Fleece Sales (1)	12	18
Progeny Sales (2)	371	421
Less Depreciation and Purchases	257	257
Output	**126**	**182**
Variable Costs:		
Feed Supplement Costs (3)	30	30
Vet & Med	25	25
Shearing Costs	12	12
Miscellaneious Costs	15	15
Total Variable Costs (excl. forage)	**82**	**82**
Gross Margin per Alpaca, before		
deducting Forage Variable Costs	45	100
Forage Variable Costs	10	10
Purchased Hay (4)	48	48
Gross Margin per Alpaca	**-14**	**42**
Alpcas per hectare	15 (6.1)	15 (6.1)
Gross Margin per Forage Hectare (Acre)	**-203** *(-82)*	**631** *(255)*

Notes:

1. *Fleece Sales:* Average performance fleece price £7.00/ kg. High performance fleece price £9.00/ kg.

2. *Progeny Sales:* Non breeding stock sold at £250/hd, Breeding geldings sold at £750/hd, 25% breeding stock at average performance level, 35% at high performance level.

3. *Feed Costs:* 65g per day at £1.25 per kg.

4. *Bulk Feed:* 1 small hay bale per month

GRAZING LIVESTOCK UNITS (GLU)

Dairy cows	1.00	Lowland ewes	0.11
Beef cows (excl. calf)	0.75	Upland ewes	0.08
Heifers in calf (rearing)	0.80	Hill ewes	0.06
Bulls	0.65	Breeding ewe hoggets:	
		½ to 1 year	0.06
Other cattle (excl. intensive beef):		Other sheep, over 1 year	0.08
0-1 year old	0.34	Store lambs, under 1 year	0.04
1-2 years old	0.65	Rams	0.08
2 years old and over	0.80		
Breeding sows	0.44	Broilers	0.0017
Gilts in pig	0.20	Other table chicken	0.004
Maiden gilts	0.18	Turkeys	0.005
Boars	0.35	Ducks, geese, other poultry	0.003
Other pigs	0.17	Horses	0.80
Cocks, hens, pullets in lay	0.017	Milch goats	0.16
Pullets, 1 week to point of lay	0.003	Other goats	0.11

Source: as advised by DEFRA for the Farm Business Survey.

1. *Total livestock units on a farm* should be calculated by multiplying the above ratios by the monthly livestock numbers averaged over the whole year.

2. *The ratios are based on feed requirements.* Strictly speaking, when calculating stocking density, allowances should also be made for differences in output (e.g. milk yield per cow or liveweight gain per head), breed (e.g. Friesians v. Jerseys) and quantities of non-forage feed consumed.

FORAGE VARIABLE COSTS

Grassland	1-2 year Ley		Intensive 3-5 year Ley		Long Term Ley		Improved Permanent Pasture		Low Input Pasture	
Yield t/ha *(ac)*	50	*(20)*	47	*(19)*	42	*(17)*	35	*(14)*	25	*(10)*
Years Ley	2		4		7		-		-	
Kg/Ha *(units/acre)*										
N	250	*(199)*	200	*(159)*	150	*(120)*	100	*(80)*	50	*(40)*
P	35	*(28)*	33	*(26)*	29	*(23)*	25	*(20)*	18	*(14)*
K	120	*(96)*	113	*(90)*	101	*(80)*	84	*(67)*	60	*(48)*
Costs £/Ha *(£/ac)*										
Seed *per year*	69	*(28)*	35	*(14)*	22	*(9)*	15	*(6)*	3	*(1)*
Fertiliser	268	*(109)*	225	*(91)*	179	*(72)*	130	*(53)*	76	*(31)*
Sprays	17	*(7)*	13	*(5)*	10	*(4)*	8	*(3)*	6	*(2)*
Total £/Ha/Yr	354	*(143)*	272	*(110)*	211	*(85)*	153	*(62)*	85	*(35)*
cost £/t fresh weight	7.08		5.80		5.02		4.37		3.41	

Other Forages	Maize	Clover Ley	Kale	Swedes
Yield t/ha (t/acre)	40 *(16)*	40 (16)	45 (18)	70 (28)
Seed	175 (71)	28 (12)	56 (23)	172 (70)
Fertiliser	111 (45)	37 (15)	145 (59)	138 (56)
Sprays	50 (20)	18 (7)	50 (20)	54 (22)
Total	336 (136)	83 (34)	251 (102)	364 (148)
Cost £/t fresh weight	8.40	2.08	5.58	5.20
	Fodder Beet	Forage Rape	Maincrop Turnips	Stubble Turnips
Yield t/ha (t/acre)	70 (28)	35 (14)	65 (26)	35 (14)
Seed	133 (54)	24 (10)	57 (23)	20 (8)
Fertiliser	191 (78)	106 (43)	138 (56)	116 (47)
Sprays	159 (64)	25 (10)	52 (21)	27 (11)
Total	483 (196)	155 (63)	247 (100)	162 (66)
Cost £/t fresh weight	6.91	4.42	3.80	4.64

Notes

1. An appropriate combination of these forage gross margins is used to calculate the forage costs of all the grazing livestock margins throughout the book. In fact, for simplicity, only the grass, maize and stubble turnips are used. Each livestock gross margin explains which forage crops are used.

2. *Seed costs* vary according to the proportion of permanent pasture and length of leys.

3. *Fertiliser* is assumed to come partially from manure as well as bagged fertiliser. It is often less on permanent pasture, depending on management style which also affects stocking rates and productive levels per animal.

4. Contract work on maize, silage and cultivations: Refer to Page195.

5. Standing maize crops are typically sold for £750 to £920/ha (£300-370/acre) but can be over £1,000/ha (£400/acre), depending on the potential yield of the crop and local supply and demand which has become volatile with local demand from anaerobic digestion plants.

6. Labour: forage and conservation labour, pages 172

7. Conservation machinery: page 189.

Whole Crop (feed wheat). Variable costs are as for combined crop (page 5) plus contract harvesting and clamping at £160 per ha (£64.7/ac.). Fresh yield averages 27.5 tonnes per ha (11 t/ac.) harvested in late June at 35% dry matter. Urea treatment (for higher dry matter) for whole-crop alkalage: £7.60/treated tonne. For urea treated grain, add £15.50 per tonne. Standing wheat auctions for about £1,000 per hectare (£400/acre). This is based on 8.5t/ha at £150, opportunity cost of harvesting as grain less costs.

Plastic wrap for bagged silage = £4.60/ round bale (120cm).

Net wrap for bales = £0.53/round bale.

TOTAL COSTS OF PRESERVED FORAGE

Cost of Preserved Forage	Clamped Grass Silage	Wrapped Grass Silage	Hay	Clamped Maize
Variable Costs £/Ha	272	272	272	336
Mowing		30	30	
Turning		16	32	
Raking		16	16	
Harvesting & Clamping	304	-	-	168
Drilling	8	8	8	44
Land Preparation	28	28	28	111
Fertilising & Spraying	31	31	31	31
Land Rent *	250	250	250	250
Land based Costs £/Ha	893	651	667	940
Less Basic payment *	187	187	187	187
Total Costs £/fresh t	16.80	11.04	11.42	17.92
Fresh DM	18%	18%	18%	30%
Preserved DM	25%	30%	85%	30%
Sub-total £/t Preserved	23.33	18.40	53.94	17.92
Baling £/bale	0	2.75	2.75	
Wrap £/bale	0.0	4.25	0	
sheet £/t	1.00			1.00
Bale Weight	1000	600	400	
Total Costs £/t Preserved	**24.33**	**30.07**	**60.81**	**18.92**

Notes:

1. *Variable Costs:* Linked to previous schedule, grass silage using 'Intensive 3-5 year'.

2. *Operational Costs:* Taken from contractor's charges, page 195, land preparation and drilling divided by length of rotation.

3. For simplicity, all costs are charged to the forage, despite possible late season grazing.

4. * Both land rent and the Basic Payment Scheme costs and incomes are included in this schedule. Depending on its use, will depend on whether you should include it in your costings. But if one is in, the other should be in most cases.

Sale Value of hay and (far less common because of its bulk) silage vary widely according to the region and season (supply/demand situation), quality and time of year:

a. *Hay* (pick-up baled) has an average ex-farm sale value of £60 to £120 per tonne, average £70. Seed hay £100 to £110 per tonne and £70-£90 per tonne for meadow hay; prices are higher in the west than the east and more after a dry summer (giving low yields of grass). Prices tend to be higher for horses as quality is higher. Big bale hay is £20 to £30/tonne cheaper.

b. *Grass silage* is typically about £36 a tonne delivered (higher when forage is very short in an area and *vice versa*), maize silage approx. £32 a tonne.

Relative Costs of Grazing, Conserved Grass, etc.

	£/t Fresh Weight	Yield DM tonnes/ha (acre)		Cost per tonne DM (£)	MJ per kg DM	Pence per MJ of ME in DM
Grazed Grass	9.57	7.6	(3.1)	£53	12.8	0.42
Grass Silage	24.33	7.6	(3.1)	£97	10.9	0.89
Big Bale Silage	30.07	7.6	(3.1)	£100	10.8	0.93
Hay	60.81	7.6	(3.1)	£72	8.8	0.81
Kale (direct drilled)	16.69	6.8	(2.7)	£111	11	1.01
Forage Turnips (d.d.)	11.50	6.8	(2.8)	£109	10.2	1.07
Brewer's Grains	50	-		£208	11.7	1.78
Concentrates	230	-		£267	12.8	2.09

1. *In interpreting the above figures* for use in planning feed use on farm, it is important to remember that own land, labour and capital for equipment are included here for home-produced fodder but not for purchased feed, and much more storage is required

2. *The consumption of fodder* is limited by its bulk although this very much depends upon its quality/digestibility.

3. *The cost of forage* will vary enormously depending on growing conditions, soil fertility and type, intensity of farming practice and management ability.

FODDER CROPS, GRASSES, CLOVERS AND ENVIRONMENTAL SEEDS

Seed Prices (for 2015) and Seed Rates

Crop	Price £/Kg	Seed Rate Kg/Ha	Cost £/Ha
Grass Leys			
1 year Westerwolds	£2.40 - 3.42	35-55	84 - 153
2 year leys	£2.50	35	85
3-4 year leys	£3.85	35	135
4-6 year leys	£4.10	35	145
Long-term ley	£4.40	37.5	165
Permanent Grass	£4.90	32.5	160
Drought Resistant	£6.00-7.15	32.5-35	195-250
Mixed and Clover Leys			
White Clover ley	£4.00 – 5.33	30	120
Red Clover ley	£3.80 – 2.70	30-55	115 - 150
Timothy/M. Fescue ley	£4.68	31	145

Crop	Price £/Kg	Seed Rate Kg/Ha	Cost £/Ha
Fodder Crops			
Fodder Kale	£9.80-13.50	5	49-68
Swedes	£42	Precision drill 0.7	30
		seed drill 4.00	168
Stubble Turnips	£3.60	3.75 kg drilled,	13.5
		5.0 kg broadcast	18
Maincrop Turnips	£11.25	3.75 kg drilled,	42
		5.0 kg broadcast	56
Rape	£2.80	10	28
Rape/Kale hybrid	£8.00	7.50	60
Mustard	£2.00	20	40
Rape and Turnip mix	£5.00/kg mix	1.25 kg rape	
		3.75 kg turnips	17
Kale, Swede & Turnips	£14.50/kg mix	1.5 kg kale,	
		0.5 kg swede	
		1.75 kg turnips	55
Cover Mixes, Environmental and Equine			
Game Cover mixture	£4.08	25	102
Game Maize	£3.50	27.5	98
Forage Maize: Silage			148
Vetch	£1.55	75	116
Quinoa & Kale mix	£10.0	7.5	75
Field Corner mixture	£12.70	25	317
Horse grazing	£4.85	35	171
Gallop mixture	£3.80	125	478
Individual Varieties			
Westerwold Ryegrass	£2.40	35	84
Italian Ryegrass	£2.50	35	88
Perennial Ryegrass	£4.50	25 to 40	112 - 180
Hybrid Ryegrass	£3.70	35	130
Cocksfoot	£4.20	20 to 25	84 - 105
Red Clover ley	£7.80	15	118
White Clover ley	£8.90	7	62
Timothy	£4.80		
Meadow Fescue	£6.20		
Sweet Vernal	£60.00		
Reed Canary Grass	£18.00	7.5	135
Lucerne	£5.90 (inoculated)	20	118
Sainfoin	£2.66	87	232
Millet	£2.40	25	60
Sunflower	£4.40	25	110
Sorghum	£3.70	20	72

Acknowledgement: Particular thanks to - Cotswold Seeds 0800 252 211

3.   PIGS, POULTRY, TROUT, RABBIT

PIGS

Breeding and Rearing *(to 35kg liveweight)*

Performance Level	Average		High	
	per sow	per pig	per sow	per pig
	£	£	£	£
Weaners: (ave) 23.2 (1) @ £57 (3)...........	1324	57.00		
(high) 26.2 (2) @ £57 (3).........			1493	57.00
Less Livestock Depreciation (4)...............	62	2.57	76	2.80
Output	1262	54.43	1417	54.20
Variable Costs:				
Food (5)..	744	30.75	731	27.09
Miscellaneous (6).............................	107	4.42	115	4.26
Total Variable Costs	851	35.17	846	31.35
Gross Margin (per year)	**411**	**19.26**	**571**	**22.85**

1. *Weaners per sow:* - average: 10.0 weaned per litter, 2.30 litters per year, 4% rearing losses = 23.2 weaners sold per sow per year. Productivity is generally improving in the UK pig sector.

2. *Weaners per sow:* - high: 11.5 weaned per litter, 2.35 litters per year, 3% rearing losses = 26.2 weaners sold per sow per year. For Outdoor Breeding performance figures see page 94.

3. *Price:* assumed pig cycle average. (See General Prices on page 92). Prices for 35kg weaners have varied from £15 to £60 during the past decade. Prices are currently reasonably firm in line with finished pig prices. Values between £55 and £60 per head are forecast to persist for the next 12 months.

4. *Average livestock depreciation* assumes an in-pig gilt purchase price of £210, a cull value per sow of £115 and a 52% replacement rate (i.e. approximately 4.5 litters per sow life). Sow mortality 4%. Boars (1 per 24 sows) purchased at £750 (40% a year replacement), sold at £110. 'High' compared with 'Average': higher gilt purchase prices, higher replacement rate and slightly fewer sows per boar assumed.

5. *Food:* total food per sow of 2.61 tonnes breaks down as:

	Tonnes	Value £/t	Total Cost
Sow	1.35	255	344
Boar	0.05	255	13
Weaner feed	1.21	320	387
Total	**2.61**	**285**	**744**

High performance: lower sow feed but extra piglet rearing feed for additional weaners. Piglets weaned at average 3.75 weeks, 7.5kg weight.

6. *Miscellaneous Average:* vet. and med. £41, transport £12, straw and bedding £15, miscellaneous £18, electricity and gas £13, and water £8.

7. *Direct Labour Cost* per sow: average £180, good £145; per weaner: average £7.40, good £5.30.   This figure does not include labour used for 'overhead' activities – repairs etc. For further fixed costs information see page 216.

8. *Building Costs:* see page 226.

Feeding (from 35 kg liveweight): per pig

Average Performance	Pork £	Cutter £	Bacon £
Sale Value	97.10	113.90	128.80
Less Weaner Cost (1)	57.00	57.00	57.00
Mortality Charge	1.50	1.60	1.70
Output	38.60	55.30	70.10
Variable Costs:			
Food	32.80	42.60	51.90
Miscellaneous	7.00	7.50	8.00
Total Variable Costs	39.80	50.10	59.90
Gross Margin	**-1.20**	**5.20**	**10.20**
Liveweight (kg)	80	93	105
Deadweight (kg)	58.5	69	79
Killing Out %	73%	74%	75%
Price per Deadweight (p)	166	165	163
Price per Liveweight (p)	121.4	122.4	122.6
Food Conversion Rate	2.65	2.72	2.80
Food per Pig (kg)	119	158	196
Average Cost of Food per tonne (£) (2)	£275	£270	£265
Food Cost per Kg l/w Gain (p)	72.88	73.44	74.20
Liveweight Gain per Day (kg)	0.73	0.76	0.79
Feeding Period (weeks)	8.8	10.9	12.7
Mortality (%)	2.6	2.8	3.0
Direct Labour Costs per Pig (£)	4.60	5.70	6.60

High Performance (same pig price)			
Food Conversion Rate	2.52	2.58	2.65
Food per Pig (kg)	113	150	186
Food Cost per Pig (£5/t less than ave.)	30.62	39.65	48.23
Food Cost per Kg l/w Gain (p)	68.04	68.37	68.90
Gross Margin per Pig	**2.30**	**9.50**	**16.30**
Direct Labour Costs per Pig	3.60	4.40	5.10

1. *Weaner cost* assumes on farm transfer. If purchased (i.e., feeding only) transport and purchasing costs have to be added: these are very variable but average about £2.00 per weaner.

2. *Average of home-mixed and purchased compounds:* There can be big variations in feed costs per tonne between farms, according to whether the food is purchased as compounds or home-mixed, bought in bulk or in bags, size of unit, etc.

3. *Labour:* see page 172.

4. *Building Costs:* see page 230.

5. *Sensitivity Analysis.* The effect of changes in important variables are as follows:

Change in Gross Margin (£)	Porker	Cutter	Baconer
Price: 5p per kg dw difference 2.93		3.45	3.95
Food Cost per tonne: £10 difference 1.19		1.58	1.96
Food Conversion Rate: 0.1 difference . . . 1.24		1.57	1.86

Combined Breeding, Rearing, and Feeding: per pig

	Pork £		Cutter £		Bacon £	
Performance Level*	Ave.	High	Ave.	High	Ave.	High
Sale Value	97.10	98.30	113.90	113.90	128.80	128.80
Sow and Boar Deprcn	2.57	2.80	2.57	2.80	2.57	2.80
Mortality Charge	1.50	1.40	1.60	1.50	1.70	1.60
Output	**93.03**	**94.10**	**109.73**	**109.60**	**124.53**	**124.40**
Food	63.55	57.69	73.35	66.79	82.65	75.29
Miscellaneous	11.42	11.26	11.92	11.76	12.42	12.26
Total Variable Costs	**74.97**	**68.95**	**85.27**	**78.55**	**95.07**	**87.55**
Gross Margin per Pig	**18.06**	**25.15**	**24.46**	**31.05**	**29.46**	**36.85**
Gross Margin per Sow	**437**	**679**	**592**	**838**	**713**	**995**
Labour Costs per Pig	14.27	10.53	15.37	11.33	16.27	12.03
Labour Costs per Sow	345	284	372	306	394	325

*   Performance levels refer to breeding and rearing differences as on the previous 2 pages and, for feeding, differences in food conversion rate, food costs and labour cost only.

Prices - General

Pig prices are notoriously difficult to predict. Over the last four years the GB average pig price (DAPP Eurospec) has ranged from 100p per kg deadweight to almost 170ppkg. The vast majority of UK pigs are taken to baconer weight. The level shown in the finisher margins for baconers above, of 163p, is an estimated average for late 2014 through 2015. This is slightly lower than at the time of writing. The strengthening of Sterling could place UK pig prices under pressure.

Further Performance Data

Source: 'BPEX Yearbook 2013-2014' (data for the year ended December 2013).

| | Performance Level | | |
All Breeding	Average	Top Third*	Top 10%*
Sow replacements (%)	53.3	54.3	57.4
Sow sales and deaths (%)	52.4	55.7	59.0
Sow mortality (%)	4.6	4.1	5.4
Litters per sow per year	2.29	2.35	2.40
Pigs reared per litter	10.3	11.2	11.9
Pigs reared per sow per year	23.5	26.4	28.6
Weight of pigs produced (kg)	7.2	7.3	7.2
Average weaning age (days)	26.4	26.4	26.3
Sow feed per sow per year (tonnes)	1.53	1.42	1.48
Feed per pig reared (kg)	66	54	53
Sow feed cost per tonne (£)	238	243	245
Sow feed cost per sow per year (£)	356	352	359
Feed cost per pig reared (£)	15.44	13.15	12.74

* selected on basis of pigs reared per sow per year.

Rearing	Average	Top Third*	Top 10%*
Weight of pigs at start (kg)	7.2	7.3	7.4
Weight of pigs produced (kg)	31.5	29.8	28.3
Mortality (%)	4.0	3.8	3.0
Feed conversion ratio	1.84	1.63	1.45
Daily Gain (g)	479	515	486
Feed cost per tonne (£)	352	324	308
Feed cost per kg gain (p)	65.2	52.3	44.5
Feed cost per pig reared (£)	14.13	11.32	7.80
Feeding	Average	Top Third*	Top 10%*
Weight of pigs at start (kg)	38.9	36.5	32.5
Weight of pigs produced (kg)	99.9	102.0	99.0
Mortality (%)	3.1	2.7	2.3
Feed conversion ratio	2.83	2.59	2.41
Daily Gain (g)	787	821	842
Feed cost per tonne (£)	248	222	209
Feed cost per kg gain (£)	68.1	53.6	45.6
Feed cost per pig reared (£)	40.41	35.06	30.15

* selected on basis of feed cost per kg liveweight gain.

Feed conversion ratio for rearing and feeding combined, from 7.5kg to 105kg liveweight is approximately 2.54.

Outdoor v Indoor Performance

Breeding	Outdoor	Indoor
Sow replacements (%).....................................	52.9	53.0
Sow sales and deaths (%)..............................	46.7	55.4
Sow mortality (%)...	3.4	5.2
Litters per sow per year.................................	2.27	2.30
Pigs reared per litter.......................................	9.6	10.8
Pigs reared per sow per year.........................	21.7	24.9
Weight of pigs produced (kg).......................	7.0	7.3
Average weaning age (days).........................	25.8	26.9
Sow feed per sow per year (tonnes)..............	1.60	1.48
Feed per pig reared (kg)................................	76	50
Sow feed cost per tonne (£)...........................	227	212
Sow feed cost per sow per year (£)	368	259
Feed cost per pig reared (£)...........................	17.63	10.60

1. *Stocking Rate for outdoor pigs* is mainly between 12 and 25 per hectare (5 and 10 per acre), 20 (8) being the most common. Good drainage is essential. A low rainfall and mild climate are also highly desirable. In 2003, MLC's Agrosoft puts the cost of establishing a sow herd on a greenfield site at £1,800 per sow place for an indoor unit and about £600 per sow place for an outdoor unit.

2. *Data on the split* of indoor and outdoor herds is hard to come by. However, it is probable that well over a third of the UK breeding sow herd is now kept outdoors. A somewhat smaller proportion (probably <10%) of pigs are finished outdoors.

   Further costing information can be found in 'Pig Production in England 2012-13' produced by Askham Bryan College, York on behalf of Rural Business Research. See www.ruralbusinessresearch.co.uk

Acknowledgement: The main data source for the margins within the Pigs section is the BPEX Yearbook 2013-2014 (AHDB), but the pig and feed prices are the author's responsibility.

EGG PRODUCTION

Brown egg layers; 55 week laying period, 2 week changeover period. This reflects current commercial practice

Level of Performance	Enriched Cages				Free Range	
	Average		High		Average	
	per bird	per doz eggs	per bird	per doz eggs	per bird	per doz eggs
	£	p	£	p	£	p
Egg Returns.....................	19.76	76.0	20.90	76.0	26.25	105.0
Less Livestock Deprcn.....	3.76	14.5	3.77	13.7	3.91	15.6
Output	**16.00**	**61.5**	**17.13**	**62.3**	**22.34**	**89.4**
Variable Costs:						
Food............................	12.42	47.8	12.42	45.2	13.50	54.0
Miscellaneous.............	0.41	1.6	0.41	1.5	0.82	3.3
Total Variable Costs	**12.83**	**49.4**	**12.83**	**46.7**	**14.32**	**57.3**
Gross Margin	**3.17**	**12.2**	**4.30**	**15.6**	**8.02**	**32.1**

1. *Hen-housed data* are used throughout, i.e. the total costs and returns are divided by the number of birds housed at the commencement of the laying period. IPPC permit charges have not been included. *Large variations* in input costs and returns occur.

Cage Production
2. *Yields assumed* per bird per year are:
    - Average............... 312 (26 dozen)
    - High................. 330 (27.50 dozen)

3. *The price* used, 76p per dozen, includes all quantity and quality bonuses. If sold direct (to local shop, add 35p/doz., if sold to consumers (farm-gate) add 65p/doz.

4. *Livestock Depreciation* - average point of lay pullet is priced at £4.05 (16/17 weeks).

5. *Feed* is 45kg per bird at £285 per tonne. Feed cost is dependent on breed, housing and environmental conditions, quantity purchased and type of ration.

6. *Miscellaneous Costs:* refers to variable costs: water, medication and veterinary, electricity and bird insurance.

7. *Other Costs:* include repairs and maintenance, vehicle costs, administration, general insurance and clean-down between batches. These come to around 65p per bird in total. In addition, there are labour costs and housing costs (see below).

8. *Direct Labour Costs:* average £1.65 per bird. See page 186.

9. *Housing Costs:* see page 231. Deadstock depreciation averages about £2.90 per caged bird. Deadstock depreciation is calculated over 57 weeks (55 week laying period plus 2 weeks clean out).

10. *Stocking density:* 750cm^2/bird (13.3 birds/m^2) in enriched cage systems.

Free Range Production
11. *Egg yields:* 300 (25 dozen) and average price: 105.0p per dozen.

12. *Quantity of feed used* = 50 kg. Price £285 per tonne.

13. *Livestock Depreciation* - the average point a lay pullet is priced at £4.20 (16/17 weeks).

14. *Miscellaneous Costs:* see 'Cage Production' notes above for details. Other Costs in this case are likely to be around 90-100p per hen.

15. *Direct Labour Costs:* average £3.00 per bird, dependent on degree of automation.

16. *Stocking density in house:* 1,111 cm² /bird (9 birds per m²) up from 855cm²/bird (11.7 birds/m²) since Jan 2012, stocking in multi-tier systems can be higher, if appropriate use is made of the height of the building. *Stocking density outside the house*; regulations allow 2,500 birds/ha (1,000/acre). Freedom Foods and the Lion Code allow 2,000 birds/ha (810/acre).

REARING PULLETS

Average per bird reared

	£
Value of 16/17 weeks old bird...	4.10
Less Chicks (1) @ 71p (inc. 3% mort. and levy)...............................	0.71
Output	**3.39**
Variable Costs:	
Food: 6.35 kg @ £260 per tonne....................................	1.65
Miscellaneous (2)...	0.87
Total Variable Costs	**2.52**
Gross Margin	**0.87**

1. *Chick Value:* Assumes 3 per cent mortality.
2. *Miscellaneous:* Excluding transport (26p), but including full vaccination costs.
3. *Labour (40p);* deadstock depreciation (40p).

TABLE POULTRY

A **Broilers** (per bird sold at 41 days)	p
Returns: 2.2 kg per bird @ 92.0p per kg lw......................................	202.4
Less Cost of Chick..	37.5
Output	**164.9**
Variable Costs:	
Food: 4 kg @ £325 per tonne..	130.0
Miscellaneous..	18.0
Total Variable Costs	**148.0**
Gross Margin	**16.90**

1. *Building depreciation* cost approximately 7.5p per bird sold. For capital costs of housing: see page 231.
2. *Labour*: 6.0p, excluding catching and cleaning out (5.0p) but includes management; see page 186.
3. *Stocking density*: 38kg/m², 263cm²/kg
4. O.R. = Oven Ready

B All Year Round Turkey (per bird at 20 weeks, sexed stags)

	£
Returns: 14 kg per bird @ £2.70 per kg L.Wt.	37.8
Less Cost of Poult...	2.1
Output	**35.8**
Variable Costs:	
Food: 50 kg @ £290 per tonne..	14.5
Miscellaneous..	5.3
Total Variable Costs	**19.8**
Gross Margin	**16.0**

1. 10% *mortality* allowed in cost of poult figures.

2. *Rearing turkeys* all the year round now tends to be just in the hands of a few large and vertically integrated companies. Imports have outcompeted many small operators.

C Christmas Turkey (Traditional Farm Fresh - indoor reared)

	Light	Medium	Heavy
	£	£	£
Returns per bird sold......................................	42.90	48.40	69.44
Less Cost of Poult..	5.00	5.00	4.15
Output	**37.90**	**43.40**	**65.29**
Variable Costs:			
Food..	7.81	9.86	10.61
Miscellaneous..	13.60	14.00	14.60
Total Variable Costs	**21.41**	**23.86**	**25.21**
Gross Margin	**16.49**	**19.55**	**40.08**
Killing Age (weeks)..	18	22	22
Live Weight (kg)...	6.6	8.0	12.4
Oven Ready Weight (kg).................................	5.4	6.6	10.2
Food Conversion...	3.2	3.4	2.4
Food per Bird (kg)...	20.8	27.0	29.5
Food Cost per tonne..	£375	£365	£360

1. *Mortality*: 7, 8 and 10% mortality allowed for in cost of poult figures for light, medium and heavy weights respectively.

2. Performance Categories:

    a.   Light and medium = slow growing sexed hens.

    b.   Heavy = stags (as hatched).

3. *Liveweight Price per kilogram*: small £6.42p/kg, medium £6.02 p/kg, large £5.54p/kg

4. Miscellaneous costs include processing (inc. plucking and eviscerating) and marketing

Note: With both turkey enterprises, considerable variations will occur between individual strains and because of different production systems and feeding regimes. Free range systems for example will show higher costs and returns. The figures should therefore be used only as rough guidelines.

D Large roaster chickens (per bird sold at 12 weeks; Christmas - males only)

	£
Returns: 4.8 kg per bird @ £3.45 per kg O.R.	16.56
Less Cost of Chick...	0.84
Output	**15.72**
Variable Costs:	
Food: 14.3 kg @ £315 per tonne..	4.50
Miscellaneous..	1.70
Total Variable Costs	**6.20**
Gross Margin	**9.52**

10% mortality allowed for in cost of chick figures.

E Ducks (Pekin type) (per bird sold at 7 weeks)

	£
Returns: 2.3 kg per bird @ £3.55 per kg O.R..................................	8.17
Less Cost of Duckling..	0.63
Output	**7.54**
Variable Costs:	
Food: 11.3 kg @ £280 per tonne..	3.16
Miscellaneous..	2.35
Total Variable Costs	**5.51**
Gross Margin	**2.02**

Day-old costs allow for 10% mortality. There are very few indoor duck farmers left in the UK operating to this system, but they are large-scale.

F Geese (Traditional Farm Fresh - free range and dry plucked)

	£
Returns: 6.5 kg per bird @ £10.50 per kg O.R.................................	68.25
Less Cost of Gosling..	6.50
Output	**61.75**
Variable Costs:	
Food: 56 kg @ £294.285714285714 per tonne.............................	16.48
Miscellaneous..	12.80
Total Variable Costs	**29.28**
Gross Margin	**32.47**

1. *Day-old costs:* allow for 6% mortality.

2. 16.5kg feed wheat at £155/t and 40kg goose concentrate at £350/t

3. Farm gate output values used

4. *Miscellaneous costs* include processing / marketing

Acknowledgement: The figures in the poultry section are provided by John Newton, ADAS, Pendeford House, Wobaston Road, Wolverhampton.

RAINBOW TROUT (FRESHWATER)

	£ per tonne of fish
Returns: 1 tonne of fish @ £2.25 per kg...	2,250
Less 4000 fingerlings @ 8.0p each..	320
Output	**1,930**
Variable Costs:	
Food: 1 tonne @ £1350 per tonne...	1,350
Vet and med;..	150
Miscellaneous...	80
Total Variable Costs	**1,580**
Gross Margin	**350**

1.   Fish growing to 350g from fingerlings at 4.5g.

2.   Prices are estimated ex-farm to processor or wholesaler for portion sized (c.500g) freshwater rainbow trout. Higher prices of up to £4.20 per kg can be achieved by selling direct to retailers, caterers and consumers at, say farmers markets, but significant additional costs are associated with such sales.

3.   Fingerlings price: varies according to quantity ordered and time of year.

4.   Average feeding period, 10 months. Mortality, from fingerling to market size, 15%. Food conversion ratio 1.1:1, having a very low maintenance requirement. The price for fish food is for a pigmented high oil expanded pellet. It is a guide price as different diets and formulations will retail at different prices and at different economies of scale depending upon volume purchased.

5.   Current capital costs for construction of earth pond unit approximately £90 per cubic metre, to include buildings, holding systems and installation of water supply and services, but excluding land.

6.   Labour requirement: the basic norm has in the past been 1 man per 50 tonnes of fish produced per annum on a table fish farm, but to remain competitive farmers now need to produce at least 150 tonnes per annum of table fish per man.

The figures given are illustrative and don't reflect the complexities of trout farming. Trout farming varies in the UK from Cage Farming in Scottish lochs (freshwater and marine) to 'traditional' flow through earth/pond/concrete raceway river farming. Trout farming also encompasses both the table and restocking sectors, prices given above relate to the sale of fish for the table market. As such feed costs, conversion rates etc. do vary which obviously has an effect on the costings for the enterprise. Differences in water temperature will also impact significantly on food conversion ratios, growth rates etc.

Acknowledgement*:* thanks to - British Trout Association, The Rural Centre, West Mains, Ingliston, Edinburgh, EH28 8NZ. Tel: 0131 472 4080 www.britishtrout.co.uk

MEAT RABBITS

The consumption of rabbit meat in the UK is low, much of which is imported. There are few buyers and processors of meat rabbits in the UK but they do not cover all parts of the country. It is important that prospective producers research the market. An individual producer may develop local markets. The demand for rabbit meat is seasonal - more is eaten in winter than summer, which can pose marketing problems. Producers often adjust their production by 15 to 20% in summer to allow for this.

Intensive commercial rabbit production requires planning permission and building regulation approval from the Local Authority. The construction or conversion of a building to house rabbits is the main expenditure and must be done in accordance with Defra's Welfare Code. Housing can be fully environment controlled to give good feed conversion rates and better winter conditions for both stock and personnel, or be natural environment, which has lower capital and running costs and possibly keeps animals healthier.

A non-cage system incorporates large movable lightweight aluminium and plastic runs which are moved frequently allowing the rabbits to graze naturally minimizing the amount of dry feed required. Typical runs are 8.5m x 4.5m with a 30-year life. Each run has an integral water supply and gives shelter against wind, rain and the sun and each doe has a nesting box. The set up cost of a 250 doe rabbit farm using this method is in the order of £29,100 plus VAT.

	£	£
	Per Doe	Per 300 Does
Finished Young per Doe per Year.............................	46	
Live Weight Each (at 12 weeks)................................	2.6	
Price per kg to processor...	1.8	
Sales:	£	
Meat sales per Doe per Year.......................................	215	
Sales of pelts(1)	18	
Less Depreciation per Doe (incl.Buck) per Year (2).......	4.0	
Output	**230**	**68,907**
Variable Costs:		
Feed (doe & Progeny) (3)................................	87	
Bedding...	2	
Vet and Med	4	
Miscellaneous	4	
Total Variable Costs	**97**	**29,169**
Gross Margin	**132**	**39,738**

1. A further income stream can be developed for pelts currently 80p (assume 50% sold) and fallen stock for reptile food.

2. Depreciation – Doe £3.60 (incl.10% mortality), Buck £0.39 per doe (incl. 10% mortality) Average 1 buck per 10 does. Does are kept for 2 years, bucks for 3 years. purchased at £10, culled for £2 each.

3. Feed conversion 4:1 includes doe, progeny and 10% of buck.

Meat rabbits require a lot of maintenance. Health, hygiene and good stockmanship are crucial. One full time person can look after 250 – 300 does and their progeny. New Zealand White or Californian stock are used. Young does are bought in at 12 weeks and mated at 16-20 weeks. Bucks are bought at 16 weeks and first mated at 20 weeks. A ratio of one buck to 10-20 does is recommended. Gestation is 31 days. Average litter size is 8-9, of which 6-7 should be successfully fattened. Re-mating can be immediately post-partum or up to 6 weeks afterwards; the average is about 21 days. A doe can have a useful life of 10-12 litters over 18 months; less productive animals may be culled sooner. A mortality rate of up to 12.5% can be expected.

Young rabbits are weaned at 35-42 days at about 1.1-1.4 kg and then fed *ad-lib* until they are ready for marketing at about 2.6kg liveweight at 11-13 weeks. Food conversion rate, including the doe's feed and a share of the buck's is around 4:1. A doe should produce around 46 meat rabbits each year.

Acknowledgements: Thanks to – T & S Rabbits, part of T & S Nurseries and the Abbey Vineyard Group.

4.   RENEWABLE ENERGY

GENERAL

The renewable energy sector presents a business opportunity for many farmers but is not a guaranteed profit for everybody. It depends on individual circumstances and often on decisions made right at the start. Some farmers have made good money from it, others are breaking even, and others have lost sums of capital. Correct investment appraisal is necessary for renewable energy projects just with any other. Land is fundamental to the renewable energy sector; it is capital intensive and requires an entrepreneurial approach to its implementation. Agriculture is therefore a natural partner for the sector.

Renewable energy is a relatively novel concept in industrial terms even though all technologies are not new and are well understood. Wind power and wood heating clearly have long histories, as has anaerobic digestion having been harnessed by man for centuries. Even biofuels were available for the Second World War and second generation biofuels, whilst well understood are simply prohibitively expensive. What is new is the increasing focus on these technologies as a means to combating climate change.

The Renewable Energy industry is developing in response to incentives to cut the emissions of climate changing greenhouse gases (GHGs) as a result of human activities. The main GHGs are:

- Carbon Dioxide (CO_2), which accounts for up to a quarter of the greenhouse gas effect

- Methane (CH_4) accounts for between 4% and 9% of the effect but is about 25 times more potent by volume than carbon dioxide

- Nitrous Oxide, which, whilst very low in concentration in the atmosphere, is about 300 times more potent than carbon dioxide

In 2012, human activity in the UK accounted (provisionally) for 575.4 million tonnes of GHG emissions (CO_2 equivalent), 3.3% up from 556.7mt in 2011. Agriculture accounted for 56.6mt CO_2 equivalent, most of which comes from the enteric fermentation of ruminating animals (methane) and the use of (and manufacture) nitrogen fertilisers (nitrous oxides).

UK GHG Emissions 2012 (measured in million tonnes of CO_2 equivalence)

	GHG Total	Carbon Dioxide	Methane	Nitrous Oxide	Others
UK	**575**	474	50.6	36	14.7
UK percentage		82%	8.8%	6.3%	3.0%
UK Agriculture	**56.6**	4.1	22.2	30.3	0.0
Percentage	**9.8%**	0.9%	44%	84%	0%
GWP[1]		1	21	310	

1.   *GWP is the Global Warming Potential over 100 years relative to 1 tonne CO_2 Figures from DECC.*

Agriculture, being a user of natural resources (such as land) will intrinsically have an environmental footprint. Crops have been considered sequesters of carbon and animals producers. The carbon-economics is not so simple though as accounting for the carbon costs of inputs often reduce the percentage carbon saving, even if raising the overall savings (through higher yield for example). Thus, different crops and technologies have differing GHG benefits and costs.

RENEWABLE ENERGY POLICY

Renewable Energy is a government led industry. It is only viable in its current model with subsidies and incentives. Policy is therefore more critical than other sectors less reliant on subsidies.

The EU's 2008 Climate Change Package became the 2009 Renewables Energy Directive (RED). It aims to ensure the EU will achieve its self-set 2020 climate change targets by setting binding targets:

- a 20% reduction in greenhouse gas emissions,
- a 20% improvement in energy efficiency, and
- a 20% share for renewables in the EU energy mix (the UK national target is 15%)
- of this target, biofuels and electricity should account for 10% of the EU's transport fuel consumption.

The UK 2008 Climate Change Act set legally binding targets for government, to steer it to achieve an 80% reduction of GHG emissions by 2050. It does this through additional targets; a 26% reduction of CO_2 emissions by 2020 and capped emissions over 5 year periods, 3 budget periods set at a time. Published in July 2009 was the Renewable Energy Strategy which set out how the UK plans to meet its target of delivering 15% of UK energy by 2020.

In 2011, a coalition of agricultural industry partners launched the Greenhouse Gas Action Plan, to meet the climate change challenge without compromising production. In 2012, the same coalition demonstrated to Government (The Committee on Climate Change) the industry's voluntary actions to address its GHG emissions by 2018. This action needs to be robust to stave off policy intervention. Defra published a review of progress in reducing greenhouse gas emissions from English Agriculture in November 2012.

The Renewables Obligation (RO)

The primary mechanism for encouraging electricity supply from renewable sources in the UK is the Renewables Obligation (RO). Renewables Obligation Certificates (ROCs) are issued to registered electricity generators for producing electricity from renewable sources at between ¼ and 2 per megawatt hour (MWh) depending on the generation type. This so called 'ROC banding' was introduced in April 2009.

Renewables Obligation Target, ROC Value and Non-Compliance Penalty

Year*	Renewables Obligation Target (GB) (ROCs per 100MW)	Non-compliance Penalty per MWh (buy-out price)	Average Value of ROCs
2010/11	10.4	£36.99	£48.10
2011/12	11.4	£38.69	£50.94
2012/13	12.4	£40.71	£45.19
2013/14	13.4	£42.02	£44.09
2014/15	14.4	£43.30	£41.31
2015/16	15.4		Market Price

ROCs are required by registered electricity suppliers to offset their annual RO target (an annually rising target of ROCs per 100MW of use). If they do not have sufficient ROCs to meet their target, they are charged £30/MWh for the difference (index linked to 2002/03 making £43.30 in 2014/15). This money is re-circulated equally to all certificates after each year-end, meaning ROCs are worth more than their face value, especially if there is lots of non-compliance. Thus ROCs have a market value; their average price to the year July 2014 was £41.31/ROC. Electricity suppliers can fulfil their RO by purchasing ROCs from other generators. Farmers generating renewable electricity can sell the ROCs, having no obligation to keep them.

The introduction of 'ROC banding' meant some renewable electricity generation types 'earn' more ROCs per MWh than others as the next table illustrates. Micro generators (generating less than 50kw) are not eligible for ROCs.

Number of ROCS per MWh depending on Generation Type for England & Wales

Generation types	ROCs per MWh		
(non-exhaustive list)	*2014/15*	*2015/6*	*2016/17*
Onshore wind	0.9	0.9	0.9
Hydro-electric	0.7	0.7	0.7
Energy from waste with CHP	1.0	1.0	1.0
Dedicated biomass	1.5	1.5	1.4
Anaerobic digestion	2.0	1.9	1.8
Dedicated energy crops	2.0	1.9	1.8
Dedicated biomass with CHP	2.0	1.9	1.8
Dedicated energy crops with CHP	2.0	1.9	1.8
Solar photovoltaic building mount	1.6	1.5	1.4
Solar photovoltaic ground mounted	1.4	1.3	1.2
Geothermal	2.0	1.9	1.8

Feed-in Tariffs (FIT)

Designed to facilitate the administration and subsidy receipts of small-scale electricity generators, the Feed in Tariffs encourage the production of renewable electricity at levels up to 5MW capacity. This is equivalent to a rather large offshore turbine or a very large anaerobic digestion plant. Almost all farm-scale renewable energy schemes would therefore fit within the FIT scheme. The Tariffs work as follows:

- A renewable electricity generator receives a fixed payment for each kWh electricity generated; the 'Generation Tariff'. This is set at different levels depending on technology type, installation size and start date (see below).

- The 'Export Tariff', a guaranteed market payment is available if required for its export to the wider market of 4.77 p/kWh (to October 2014), less for existing installations.

- Generators can opt out of the Export Tariff by either selling electricity directly to an electricity consumer or making use of the electricity themselves (entirely or partially).

- The FIT payments are made by the registered Electricity Suppliers, the cost of which is redistributed among all suppliers in a pro-rata manner.

- Generators with capacity below 50kW (known as micro-generators) are eligible for FIT, whilst installations between 50kW and 5MW have the option to choose between FIT and the RO but cannot claim both.

This was implemented in April 2010. Generation Tariff rates for photo voltaic and wind technologies reduce most years for new claimants as technology becomes cheaper.

Generation and Export Tariffs are index linked once commissioned. Tariffs are guaranteed for 20 years (25 for solar PV if installed before 1 August 2012).

Generation Tariffs for FITs for New Installations

Generation Technology	Scale	Generation Tariff p/kWh From 1 April 2014 March 2015 ⅄
Anaerobic Digestion	< 250kW	12.46
	250 - 500kW	11.52
	> 500kW	9.49
Hydro	< 15kW	21.12
	15-100kW	19.72
	100kW – 500kW	15.59
	500kW-2MW	12.18
	2-5MW	3.32
Photo Voltaic *	< 4kW	14.38, 12.94, 6.38
	4kW - 10kW	13.03, 11.73, 6.38
	10kW - 50kW	12.13, 10.92, 6.38
	50kW - 150kW	10.34, 9.31, 6.38
	150kW - 250kW	9.89, 8.90, 6.38
	250kW - 5MW	6.38
	Stand Alone **	6.38
Wind	< 1.5kW	17.78
	1.5kW - 15kW	17.78
	15kW - 100kW	17.78
	100kW - 500kW	14.82
	500kW - 1.5MW	8.04
	> 1.5MW	3.41
RO Migrated Installations		10.49
Export Tariff *of new installations*		4.77

⅄ *Apart from Photovoltaic which is to 1 Oct 2014.*

* *If electricity supplies a building with an Energy Performance Certificate of A to D, higher rate is payable, if multiple installations, middle band, if neither of the above, lower band.*

** *Stand Alone Systems are not attached to a building and not wired to provide electricity to an occupied building.*

The Renewable Heat Incentive (RHI)

Heat accounts for approaching half of all energy used in the UK. Government's target for 2020 is that 12% of this will come from renewable sources. The value of heat is low (possibly 1-2p/kWh thermal energy depending on local market) which rarely justifies the capital expenditure in the UK of harnessing heat or generating it from a renewable source. The RHI is designed to change this (in GB). Phase 1 was in July 2011, for non-domestic installations, the second is for domestic installations, launched in April 2014. Payments shown in the table are irrespective of installation capacity and are available until 31 March 2015. The Renewable Heat Premium Payment (RHPP) scheme that was launched with it for domestic installations in 2011 is now closed. Householders can now apply for the domestic RHI scheme.

The RHI metered payments began for residential installations in April 2014. All tariffs are paid for 20 years to eligible technologies that have been installed since 15 July 2009 for each kWh of renewable heat generated from biomass boilers, solar thermal, ground or water source heat pumps, on site biogas consumption, deep geothermal, energy from municipal wastes or injection of biomethane into the grid. Payments are index linked. The RHI is being administered by OFGEM. The domestic RHI will pay the following tariffs per unit of heat generated for seven years:

Levels of support for the Domestic Renewable Heat Incentive

Generation Technology	Domestic Tariff p/kWh Rates to March 2015
Air-source heat pumps	7.3
Ground and water-source heat pumps	18.8
Biomass-only boilers and biomass pellet stoves with integrated boilers	12.2
Solar thermal panels (flat plate and evacuated tube for hot water only)	19.2

Levels of Support for RHI for Non Domestic Installations

Tariff name	Eligible technology	Eligible sizes	Tariff rate (p/kWh)*
Small biomass	Solid biomass; Municipal Solid Waste (inc. CHP)	< 200 kWth	Tier 1: 8.4
			Tier 2: 2.2
Medium biomass		200 - 1000 kWth	Tier 1: 5.1
			Tier 2: 2.2
Large biomass		>= 1000 kWth	2.0
Solid Biomass CHP	combustion		4.1
Air Source	Heat Pumps	all sizes	2.5
Deep Geothermal			5.0
Ground source	Ground and Water-source heat pumps;	Tier 1	8.7
		Tier 2	2.6
Solar thermal		Less than 200 kWth	10
Biomethane	Injection	all sizes	7.5
Biogas	Biogas combustion	under 200 kWth	7.5
		200-600kWth	5.9
		Over 600kWth	2.2

* Tier Break is: installed capacity x 1,314 peak load hours (15% rating), i.e.: kWth x 1,314

The Renewable Transport Fuel Obligation (RTFO) and Fuel Excise Duty

The RTFO started in 2008. For every litre of biofuel that excise duty is paid on, a Renewable Transport Fuel Certificate (RTFC) is issued. Companies supplying at least 450,000 litres of any road fuel to the UK market annually (about 14 companies) must participate by incorporating a proportion of biofuel into their sales, buying RTFCs from another biofuel provider or paying a 'buy-out' penalty (fine) of 30p/l (index linked). As a compelling incentive, the 'buy-out fund' generated is redistributed equally to every RTFC issued by the year-end. This means that the further away the UK is from hitting the annual target, the greater the incentive to incorporate as RTFC values rise. These subsidies are essential to make the industry viable, without them there would be no biofuel industry. The required proportion of biofuels to incorporate is 5%.

Biofuels have the same duty payable as mineral fuels for most producers. A 100% duty exemption for small scale biofuel producers of up to 2,500l biofuel per year (notionally sufficient for home use) remains in place. The RTFO includes sustainability criteria of the Renewable Energy Directive (refer to page 103). The criteria include minimum carbon savings requirements. Greater rewards are now also available for fuel generated from waste materials.

Fuel Excise Duty:	*to May 2015*
Petrol, Diesel *ppl*	57.95
Bioethanol and biodiesel *ppl*	57.95
Rebated gas oil (red diesel) *ppl*	11.14
Biodiesel for non-road use *ppl*	11.14
Natural Gas (inc. biogas) *p/kg*	24.70

These figures are before VAT. Pump prices include VAT (20%)

BIOMASS FOR POWER

This section covers crops that are grown to be burnt directly to produce heat and/or electricity. The plant material is pelleted, chipped, or baled and is generally either used in boilers in dedicated biomass power stations, or mixed with coal for co-firing in conventional power stations. Biomass includes short rotation coppice, Miscanthus, straw, canary reed grass and switch grass as well as forest residues.

Previous Editions of this book have included estimates of planting including fencing, land preparation and plants themselves. It has come to £2,747 and £2,647 for Short Rotation Coppice and Miscanthus respectively before 50% planting grants. However the planting grant (Energy Crops Scheme) is no longer available and minimal panting will be taking place as a result. If it is replaced for 2016, the new details will appear here.

Short Rotation Coppice

Short Rotation Coppice (SRC) is a fast growing willow (or occasionally poplar) that when chipped and dried is used as a fuel for heat or power generation. SRC willow needs ample moisture but grows on any cultivated land. Planting is in the spring using un-rooted cuttings at a rate of 15,000/ha. Rabbit (or deer) fencing may be necessary. Crops are usually harvested on a 3 year cycle, although 2 and 4-year cycles are practiced depending on conditions. Crops should last 20 years. Most growers apply some fertiliser post-harvest, 60 kg/ha N is sufficient. Sewage sludge is commonly used as are animal manures.

The harvested crop is stored as billets or chips, increasing density and improving transport efficiency but adding to costs. Pellets flow better in automated fuel-feed systems and are preferred for co-firing (with coal) as the willow has been milled prior to pelleting easing the load on the generator's mills. Pellets command a premium price over billets (6-8 inch lengths) and chips. SRC wood chip sells for around £65/odt (oven dried tonne) delivered, and, depending on contractual details, the consumer may organise delivery to the furnace. The first harvest should yield 10-20odt/ha, subsequent ones 20-25odt/ha.

Annual Net Returns: Output 25 odt/ha at £65 every third year; £511/year (accounting for gradual yield increase). Harvesting £355/ha plus £50 fuel, transport and handling £11/tonne harvested. Planting costs (including fencing etc.) have been spread over the forecast period of the crop and include the 50% planting grant previously mentioned. Use the Amortisation Table in section VIII. SRC land is eligible for the Single Payment.

SRC Gross Margin (gross margin per year, based on harvest every third)

Production level	Low	Average	High
Yield: tonnes per ha (tons per acre)	7.00 (2.8)	8.00 (3.2)	9.00 (3.6)
	£	£	£
Output	455 (184)	520 (211)	585 (237)
Variable Costs:			
Establishment		65 (26)	
Fertiliser/spray...........................		21 (9)	
Harvest.....................................		118 (48)	
Cart, stack	44 (18)	50 (20)	56 (23)
Transport & Handling..................	78 (32)	90 (36)	101 (41)
Total Variable Costs		344 (139)	
Gross Margin per ha (acre)	**128** (52)	**176** (71)	**223** (90)

Establishment costs of £2,747/ha (£1,112/ac) including fencing (£1127/ha) less the 50% establishment grant mentioned above shared between 21 years.

Miscanthus (Elephant Grass)

Miscanthus is a perennial grass crop lasting 20 years grown for energy and fibre. It is harvested annually with conventional farm machinery. After treatment, Miscanthus can be used as animal bedding, paper making biopolymer manufacture or to produce bio-degradable products, such as plant pots. Miscanthus is grown throughout the UK. It is propagated from rhizomes. A mature crop suppresses weeds. There are no significant pathogens or pests in the UK so agro-chemical use is minimal

Miscanthus Gross Margin

Production level	Low	Average	High
Yield: tonnes per ha (tons per acre)	10.00 (4.1)	12.00 (4.9)	14.00 (5.7)
	£	£	£
Output	550 (223)	660 (267)	770 (312)
Variable Costs:			
Establishment		63 (26)	
Fertiliser/spray...........................		21 (9)	
Harvest....................................		79 (32)	
Bale		164 (66)	
Cart, stack	42 (17)	50 (20)	58 (24)
Transport & Handling...................	120 (49)	144 (58)	168 (68)
Total Variable Costs	489 (198)	521 (211)	553 (224)
Gross Margin per ha (acre)	**61** (78)	**139** (56)	**217** (167)

Yield accounts for average over 21 years

Establishment costs of £2,647/ha (£1,072/ac) including fencing (£1127/ha) shared between 21 years.

Fertiliser requirement is low. Research suggests the mature crop removes 7kg P and 100kg K/ha/year. The plant being deep rooted may access minerals from deeper than most other crops. Sewage sludge is an ideal fertiliser. The Miscanthus gross margin below has a small cost for imported slurry, biosolids or other organic manure.

The crop shoots in April, and grows to 4 metres by September. Stems desiccate to 50% moisture during winter. The canes are harvested in February-March. The harvest method depends on end use. For energy the crop is cut with a mower conditioner or modified forage harvester at 35% moisture and then baled 10 days later into 550-700kg Hesston bales at 16% moisture, the contractual benchmark moisture level. For other end uses a standard maize harvester can be used.

The price for Miscanthus ranges from £45 to £75 with £60 fairly standard for energy crop contracts. Note most contracts now use fresh harvested weight (normally 16% moisture) rather than the former 'oven dried tonnes'.

In year 1, 50 to 60% of the mature yield is obtained. Recent precision planting machinery improvements facilitate evenly established crops, offering greater fresh weight yields of on light land 9 – 12t/ha and on medium to heavy land 12 – 18 t/ha.

Small on-farm boilers, to produce heat and energy, have been developed which offer potential for Miscanthus growers. This will be fuelled by the Renewable Heat Initiative (see page 105). Planting and establishment costs are in the region of £3,000 per hectare including fencing. Some agro-chemicals will probably be required in the first 2 years. In the UK there is a 50% establishment grant for all costs in the first 2 years.

Acknowledgement: thanks to – Andrew Riche, Rothamsted Research.

ANAEROBIC DIGESTION

Anaerobic Digestion (AD) is the digestion of non-woody organic material in the absence of oxygen by micro-organisms to produce biogas (a mixture of *circa* 40% carbon dioxide CO_2 and *circa* 60% methane CH_4) and digestate (a soil conditioner). It works in the same way as a very large rumen. The biogas is collected and normally used in a combined heat and power (CHP) generator to produce heat and electricity for use or sale. The biogas can also be purified by removing the CO_2 and contaminant gasses (less than 1%) making biomethane and compressed for use as road fuel or in place of natural gas. AD is a natural process and is well understood by mankind having been harnessed for many years.

An extensive range of feedstock can be used. Livestock manure is cheap with high levels of micro-organisms but has a low biogas yield and not commercially viable as the sole feedstock. Energy crops such as maize silage offer high yields and are commonly used in AD business models but are expensive feedstocks so add substantially to operating costs. Non-farm waste streams from food processing companies or separated kitchen wastes offer a high return, with potential to earn revenue from gate fees. Regulatory controls and 'front-end' processing requirements are far greater when importing others' waste streams though, especially if animal by-products are likely to be included pushing up capital costs and changing the business model substantially.

There are several types of AD plant, all suited to different situations and feedstocks. The rate of turnover of digestate is controlled by the rate at which feedstock enters the digester less the small (usually 3-10%) fall in volume from the production of biogas. Depending on feedstock and system used, digestion can take as little as a week up to 2 months in some circumstances.

Example On-Farm Feedstocks for Anaerobic Digestion

Feedstock	Biogas Yield m³/t feedstock	Value of Biogas £/t feedstock*
Cattle/pig slurry	15 – 25	5.20 – 8.80
Poultry manure	30 – 100	10.50 – 35.00
Maize silage	190 – 220	66.00 – 77.00
Grass silage	150 – 200	53.00 – 70.00
Whole crop wheat	185	65
Maize grain	560	196
Rolled wheat grain	600	210
Crude glycerine	580 – 1,000	200 – 350
Rape meal	620	217
Fats	Up to 1,200	up to 420

* *11.52p/kWh Generation Tariff, 4.77p/kWh Export Tariff, 1p/kWh heat*

Policy

When biogas is used to generate electricity, it can be sold with Feed in Tariffs or 2 ROCs can be claimed per MWhe (Mega Watt hour of electricity) as part of the Renewables Obligation. Biomethane for road transport is technically eligible for RTFCs (see Biofuels section above) or the RHI. AD also benefits indirectly from the Landfill Directive by diverting waste from landfill to uses such as AD. AD does not facilitate NVZ implementation regulations but has been a favoured renewable energy of the Government.

Economics

The two major costs associated with AD are usually the capital set up and feedstock (if home grown or purchased feed is used). Operating and maintenance costs such as insurance, labour and utilities are usually comparatively low. An average size plant

(2,500m^3 digester and 490kW CHP generator) would cost in the region of £1.7-2.25 million to build and commission. Depending on feedstock, temperature and other settings, this size plant could digest in the region of 20,000 tonnes of feedstock per year with a 45 day retention time (spent in the digester) or 30,000t with a 30 day retention period.

Revenue from this system digesting 20,000 tonnes using the assumptions from the table above, an average gas yield per tonne of feedstock of 100m^3/tonne and an efficiency of 90% gas conversion would return income before costs and without gate fees of about £700,000 with FITs.

LIQUID BIOFUELS

Liquid biofuels are road transport fuels produced from organic materials, including farm crops. *Biodiesel* is produced from oilseeds such as oilseed rape, soybeans and palm and is a replacement for mineral diesel. *Bioethanol* is a petrol replacement, produced from starch/sugar-based crops including wheat, maize and sugar beet or cane. There are other fuels such as *biobutanol* that are not widely used in the UK.

Biofuels from cellulosic (woody) feedstock is possible referred to as 'second generation' biofuels. This would enable a higher energy return per hectare and the opportunity to process household, manufacturing and agricultural organic 'wastes'. Its production is not financially viable so may be some years from large-scale commercial production. It also requires substantially more energy in the processing to release the energy from cellulose.

Supply

About 40 million tonnes of road fuel is used in the UK (diesel exceeding petrol use by about 55:45). To meet the RTFO target, about 2m tonnes of biofuel are required (5%). The RTFO does not differentiate between biofuels so one may dominate the market. Splitting the market proportionately would require roughly 1.1 million tonnes of biodiesel and 900,000 tonnes bioethanol. This would need 2.6m tonnes OSR or equivalent feedstock (at 42% extraction) covering 800,000 hectares (at 3.25t/ha) and 3m tonnes of wheat (or equivalent feedstock) covering 353 thousand hectares (at 8.5t/ha).

Farmers' options on whether to grow a crop to supply a biofuel facility are determined simply by price and contractual terms. As crops used in biofuel production are, in the most part, mainstream crops that could also be sold to other consumers, the processor that bids the farmer the best deal ought to win the contract. Clearly headline price is important, but also other contractual details including the risk of rejection or cost of claims, turnaround times etc. should be considered. There are therefore no farm-level gross margins for biofuel crops.

SOLAR POWER

Solar Photovoltaic (PV)

Solar PV panels generate electricity through the direct conversion of daylight. Panels can either be roof mounted, free-standing or integrated as a form of building material though solar slates, tiles or glass laminates.

Supply and installation costs for a 1kWe capacity system start at around £6,000, ranging up to £16,000 for a 4kWe capacity system; £4,000/kW and considerably lower for larger arrays. Capital and installation costs have fallen sharply recently following the reduced FIT rates. Little maintenance is required. There are companies that will 'rent' your barn roof for installation of solar PV if you did not wish to invest in equipment yourself. Terms vary but typically offer the electricity generated as rent whilst they keep the FITs.

Approximately 7-8m^2 of PV panels is required to generate 1kW of electricity. A typical panel weighs 13kg per m^2 so additional roof support may be required. Panels should last for 25 years although electricity inverters might need replacing after 5 -10 years.

For optimum results, modules should be south facing at an angle of 30-40 degrees and un-shadowed by trees or surrounding buildings. Productivity varies across the UK with levels between 1100 kWh per m^2 in the South West, to 800 kWh per m^2 in Scotland. Modules that face East or West will drop in efficiency to 85%.

In England and Scotland most private PV installations do not require planning permission, unless the building is of conservation status, is in a designated area or is a large free standing system. Wales and Northern Ireland will need to seek planning permission from their local planning authority.

Solar Thermal

Solar thermal systems use the sun's energy to warm water through using either evacuated tubes or flat plate collectors fitted to a roof. A conventional or immersion boiler is then used to heat the water further.

Costs of a typical water heating system are £3,000 to £7,000. Most systems come with a 5-10 year warranty and require little maintenance. Savings are modest; the average system can provide one third of water needs, reducing heating bills by approximately £80-£140 per year.

In England most systems will not require planning permission unless the building is listed or within a designated area. Wales, Scotland and Northern Ireland will need to contact their local planning authority.

HYDRO POWER

The UK has about 1,650MW hydro-electricity capacity, and generates 40% of renewable electricity in the UK. Most of this is from large (10-100 MW) schemes that have been built over the last 40 years. Viable sites vary from around 5kW to a few MW. Typically power output is more constant for hydro than wind or solar power but it is equally unpredictable; electricity generation is not aligned with electricity requirement.

Hydro, like other renewable energy projects is capital loaded, expensive to install but cheap to operate and can have a very long life. Installation costs of around £3,000 to £6,000 per kWe for small hydroelectric systems are typical, but are very site dependant. Operational costs are low, generally 1-2% of capital setup. Capital cost and electrical capacity depend largely on the following:

- *The head (maximum vertical fall) of water:* The higher the head, the smaller the flow required to generate the same amount of electricity. Smaller flow means smaller pipe and turbine. High head is over 50 metres drop, medium head 10 to 50 metres and less than 10m is low head.

- *The flow rate of water* is determined by the catchment size, amount of rainfall and the proportion of flow abstracted. The latter is determined by the environmental sensitivity of the river. Flow for small schemes is measured in litres per second.

- *Project size:* The cost of construction per kW falls as capacity rises; smallest projects take longest to repay the investment. Access affects costs. Costs for obtaining planning permission, abstraction and impoundment licenses and detailed design and specification of the equipment are similar for a 5kW scheme or a 30kW scheme.

- *Construction management:* Projects can be contracted to a single turnkey contractor to undertake design, specification, procurement and construction work, requiring little input from the landowner but is dearer. Many landowners oversee the project management which with some specialist input, costs can be greatly reduced.

- *Grid connection:* The capacity of the grid can be a major limitation, with upgrade of grid connection lines being expensive, particularly so in more rural or remote areas.

- *Development companies* take on a complete project and pay a rent to the landowner, typically 5% to 20% of income. Schemes of interest to such companies are usually at least 100 kW. There is significant competition for larger schemes.

Typical costs of example projects:

- 5kW medium to low head scheme, by civil contractors with specialist hydro input. Annual generation 14 MWh. Cost around £80,000

- 15 kW very high head. Landowner undertook project management and most civils and pipe-laying works. Annual generation 45 MWh. Cost around £52,000

- 30 kW high head scheme. Managed by landowners using local contractors. Annual generation around 110 MWh. Cost around £77,000

- 100 kW scheme medium head, managed by the landowner with significant time input. Annual generation around 450 MWh. Cost around £410,000

- 300 kW scheme high head. Contractors led constructor with specialists. Annual generation around 1,200 MWh. Cost around £1,330,000

WIND TURBINES

There are currently 4,944 operational wind turbines spread across 635 wind farms throughout the UK (July 2014) (renewableuk.com). Small scale turbines can have capacities of as little as 100 watts (W) up to models of 3 megawatts (MW) and 6MW for offshore turbines. Wind farms are becoming larger; the average size a decade ago was 7MW and is now 20MW, albeit with considerable offshore wind farm growth. The average onshore turbine has 1.65MW capacity with the average wind farm over 10MW.

Wind turbines in good locations produce energy equivalent to their rated capacity for around 30% of the year. For example: for a turbine rated at 40kW this calculates as 40kW x 30% x 8760 (hours in a year) = 105,120 kWh per year (105.12MWh). If this electricity is sold at 22.55p/kWh (17.78p Generation Tariff + 4.77p Export Tariff) with FITs, then a return of £23,700 per year is achieved.

Typical costs for a range of turbine capacities are in the region of the following table. Good quality constructions should have an operational life of 20 years.

Guideline Figures for Capital and Revenue of Wind Turbines

Capacity	Capital	Annual	Revenue/yr using
kW	Cost	Output (kWh)	FIT*
5.0	22,000	13,100	£4,260
11	75,000	28,900	£9,400
75	220,000	197,000	£58,900
250	710,000	657,000	£164,900
800	1,200,000	2,100,000	£312,900

* Relevant FIT price as in FIT Table on page 105.

The land surrounding a wind turbine is usually un-affected, apart from access required up to the base of the tower. A minimum average wind speed of 5 meters per second (m/s) is required; they operate at their rated capacity at 11-15m/s. Many turbines have automatic shut-down mechanisms when wind speeds exceed about 25m/s to avoid damage. Selection of the correct turbine technology and size is important.

Planning permission is required and consultation with neighbours and stakeholders for all scale turbines. Wind farms (multiple large turbines) are built in association with developers as the costs and expertise required planning and preparing them is very high. Many schemes are operated by developers with land rented to them by the land owner for 20 years. In this situation, a rent will be payable to the landowner, usually at about 2-4% of income (£5,000 to £7,000 per mast per year is not uncommon plus similar construction access fees). Access to the turbines must be possible, but land between the turbines can be farmed normally. Other benefits like road improvements may also be included. An option to develop a site could be worth £1,000 to £5,000 per year. Beware the 'small-print' and make sure you understand it all before signing.

An 11kW turbine will have a hub (mast) height of 15 to 18 metres, blade diameter of 9 metres and a 63m³ swept area. Tip height will be up to 22.5m. A large (800kW) wind turbine has a standard hub height of 76m, a height at the maximum blade position of 102m, and a blade diameter of 53m. The area of wind captured by this size blade is 0.88ha.

5.   OTHER ENTERPRISES

MUSHROOMS

The mushroom industry has shrunk considerably during the past few years. Several businesses of all sizes and locations have ceased production and few new growers have entered the business. Less than 75 firms remain in production. Those that remain are either highly efficient enterprises with strong links to supermarkets or small low cost family-run businesses selling largely to wholesalers. The reasons for this are static consumption levels and fierce competition from imports. There are a few organic mushroom producers who sell at a premium.

There have also been changes in production methods. Traditionally, most growers used Phase 1 compost, which was pasteurised and spawn-ran on the premises, to fill moveable trays or shelves in growing rooms. Now, the most prevalent system (70% of growers) use purchased Phase 2 compost (pasteurised, with spawn added). This is supplied in shrink-wrapped blocks, plastic bags or in bulk. Phase 3 compost (fully spawn-run) in blocks or bags is used by some growers. Organic Phase 2 and Phase 3 compost is also available.

Type of Compost Used	Phase 2	Phase 3
	per tonne compost	
Mushroom Yield/tonne compost	250 kg	300 kg
	£	£
Mushroom Price/kg	1.85	1.85
Spent Compost/tonne	2.10	2.10
Output	**464.6**	**557.1**
Variable Costs:		
Compost (incl. delivery)	96.0	136.0
Casing	15.5	15.5
Operations & growing labour at 6.6p/kg	16.5	19.8
Supervision & picking labour at 49p/kg	122.5	147.0
Packing materials at 22p/kg	55.0	66.0
Packing labour at 11p/kg	27.5	33.0
Energy costs at 11p/kg	27.5	33.0
Other costs at 15p/kg	37.5	45.0
Total Variable Costs	**398.0**	**495.3**
Margin / tonne compost	**66.6**	**61.8**
Variable Costs / kg mushrooms	1.59	1.65
Margin / kg mushrooms	0.27	0.21

Output: Growers using Phase 2 compost will fill on an 8-week cycle and produce 6.5 crops per year. Phase 3 compost can be filled on a 6-week cycle and allows 8.5 crops per year. Yields are expressed as kg per square metre of bed or kg per tonne of compost. Commercial yields are 25-35kg/m^2 of bed area per crop (250-350kg per tonne of compost) using Phase 2 or 3 compost, but only 18-20kg/ m^2 (180-200kg/tonne of compost) using Phase 1. Phase 1 compost costs £25/tonne, Phase 2 £85/tonne and Phase 3 £125/tonne plus delivery which can add £6-15/tonne, depending on distance and size of load.

Labour costs: All labour is included but labour for growing, if not picking and packing, could be regular. If Phase 2 or 3 compost is used, labour for growing amounts to around 10% of all labour costs while picking is 75% and packing 15%. Using Phase 1 compost labour cost for growing is significantly greater, perhaps 40p/kg or 40% of total labour, but the initial compost is cheaper.

Prices: Mushroom prices are in the range of £2.00/kg supplied to a supermarket to £1.00 or less sold on the wholesale market. Small growers marketing through a producer organisation would get around £1.60/kg delivered. At present 60% of the crop is sold by growers direct to supermarkets. Prices can be volatile and oversupply can lead to mushrooms being sold at a loss. Imports now account for 65% of all mushrooms sold in the UK, and 60% of the value of sales. Almost all imports are from the Netherlands and the Republic of Ireland.

Returns: The data suggest that ex-farm it costs £1.54 to produce 1kg of mushrooms using Phase 2 compost and £1.60 using Phase 3 compost. This does not take into account management or finance costs. The yield of the crop and the number of cycles each year are, of course, crucial.

Establishment Costs: A mushroom farm using Phase 2 compost on an 8-week cycle would require 8 rooms each with a 200sq m capacity. A farm using Phase 3 compost on a 6-week cycle would need 6 rooms of 200sq m capacity. In both cases one growing room would be filled each week using 20 tonnes of compost. To set up such a production system would require a capital investment of £200,000-£300,000 for the rooms, trays or shelves, heating and cooling systems, packing area, hard standings and equipment. If Phase 1 compost is used then buildings and equipment for composting, peak heating and spawning are also required.

COARSE FISHING

In excess of 1.5 million people regularly coarse fish in the UK and numbers are rising. It is a freshwater method of line fishing usually from the banks of a watercourse. Coarse fish species include Rudd, Roach, Bream, Barbel, Tench, Chub, Perch, Pike, Carp, exclude sea species and 'game' fish like salmon and trout (usually caught by 'fly fishing'). Coarse fish are returned to the water after catching and weighing. Facilities can be rivers, streams, canals, lakes, ponds and even drains. The close season for coarse fishing is 15th March to 15th June although most canals and still waters are exempt from the close season. Anyone fishing must have a rod licence (available from the Environment Agency).

Fishing permit prices vary depending on the location, quality of the fishing, species etc. They will be higher if the water is actively managed to attract more or certain fish species. Maintenance and landscaping of the water banks will add a premium to a facility as will secure car parking and easy access to fishing pegs (platforms). Typically permits cost:

- Half-Day Ticket (per rod)   £4.00 to £7.00
- Full-Day Ticket (per rod)   £5.00 to £13.00
- Season Ticket (per rod)   £50.00 to £180

Typical Net Margin for Coarse Fishing Lake, Labour excluded

1 Hectare (2.4 acre) Lake	**per peg**	**per Lake**
	£	**£**
Fishing Permits	1,300	13,000
Fish Sales	80	800
Output	**1,380**	**13,800**
Costs		
Peg Capital	45	450
Peg Maintenance	10	100
Fish Restocking	20	200
Feed Feed	150	1,500
Plants and Ground Maint.	40	400
Total Variable Costs	**265**	**2,650**
Gross Margin per ha (acre)	**1,035**	**10,350**

Ponds and lakes can be initially stocked costing around £5,000 for a 1 hectare lake. Pegs should be spaced at no less than 25m apart (dictating income potential). Ponds and lakes can be initially stocked or routinely restocked. A 2 acre carp lake would cost around £5,000 to stock with annual feeding costs of £1,500. Plants and other costs would total around £3,000 initially and will then need maintaining.

The larger the fish the higher the price that can be charged therefore the smaller fish can be routinely removed and sold. The total income from a two acre managed lake would be in the region of £10-15,000. Further diversifying into accommodation (log cabins) on a two acre lake stocked with 30lb carp could demand up to £1,000 per week for 4 anglers. Labour could become significant to manage the permits, stock and landscape.

LOG CABINS

A renewed interest in British short breaks and holidays has lead to a popularity surge of 'alternative' accommodation over the more traditional cottage rentals or caravan and camping. There are examples where log cabin rentals for tourism and leisure purposes have been extremely successful as farm diversification projects. As with any tourism and leisure based enterprise, location is everything and will determine the success (or failure) of the proposal. It will also determine the rental income and occupancy that can be achieved. There may also be potential for using log cabins as a substitute for 'permanent', traditional buildings for office, storage facilities etc.

Full planning permission will be required before the construction of any log cabin. It is recommended that professional support is sought in this respect prior to any expenditure on equipment / groundwork.

Build Costs

Prices for cabins vary considerably, primarily linked to the size and finish (quality) of the final build and the cost of routing any mains services. The figures below are a guide to log cabin purchase and build costs, but excluding fixtures and fittings which may add £85.00 to £125.00 of additional cost per m^2. Costs in routing mains services to the cabins will be greatly dependant on remoteness, topography, environmental restrictions etc and the extent of supplies required (bottled gas and septic tanks can be used in place of mains gas and sewage):

'Fishing' Log Cabin	$30m^2$ floor space plus sleeping 'loft'	£10,000 - £40,000
'Holiday let' Log Cabin	$60m^2$ floor space with 2 bedrooms	£20,500 - £52,500

For cabins larger than the examples above, add £250.00 to £300.00 per m^2 for every m^2 over and above the sizes stated

Rental Potential

Good occupancy rates of the cabins will be paramount to the viability of any investment. Annual occupancy rates will vary depending on location, seasonality of local attractions and level of discount given in the 'off' season. Rental incomes again vary considerably, but typically range from £250 to £1,100 per week, with the higher incomes being achieved where the cabins are located in more desirable locations i.e. near to areas popular for fly and course fishing, mountain biking, walking, coastal activities, tourist attractions etc. Single night stays and short breaks often command a higher income pro rata than weekly lets. The faltering economy has led to reductions in the more 'typical' tariff rate ranges as businesses realise the importance of maintaining occupancy levels.

GAME SHOOTING

Game shooting is an increasingly popular activity. It refers to the shooting of game species which include both feathered and fur animals. The most common birds shot in the UK include pheasant, partridge, duck, woodcock, snipe and grouse. Most feathered game are reared in captivity and then released but wild populations can be enhanced by different management techniques. There are strict and differing shooting seasons for different species, both game and pests.

'Driven' game shooting is the most popular method of game shooting in the UK whereby game birds are 'flighted' towards a standing line of guns. The quality and type of driven shoot varies according to landscape and management factors as well as the number of birds present. These variances also have a major impact on the cost of partaking in a shoot.

	per bird	per Gun	per Shoot Day	per Season
		25 birds	8 guns	10 shoots
	£	£	£	£
Charge for Gun	32.00	800	6,400	64,000
Other charges				1,500
Output	32	800	6,400	65,500
Costs				
Bird Placing (1)...............	12.00	300	2,400	24,000
Bird Feed	2.00	50	400	4,000
Hospitality		75	600	6,000
Beaters & Pickers (2).........		80	640	6,400
Ground Maint. Costs			*850*	8,500
Capital depreciation (3)				4,000
Gamekeeper (4)...............			*800*	8,000
Attributable Costs	14.00	505	5,690	60,900
Net Margin	4	89	710	4,600

1. *Birds at £4/head. Many more are placed than shot, this example is 3-fold.*
2. *15 beaters per shoot and pickers*
3. *Bird pens, feeders, water, etc.*
4. *Half time wage. May include imputed costs.*

As a rough guide, a 200 bird day driven shoot will cost in the range of £800 per gun (participant), at £32 per bird. A driven shoot normally has 7 to 9 guns with up to 8 'drives' in a day.

The expensive nature of most driven game shoots is required by the amount of work and cost involved in running a shoot (buying birds, feeding, structural equipment costs, game plot establishment, game keeper and beater's costs, shoot day hospitality etc) and so margins may be small given the investment required.

Further information: British Association for Shooting and Conservation – www.basc.org.uk

TURF

The market for turf had shrunk as a result of the downturn in the home building industry, but is now improving again in line with the rest of the economy. Competition remians strong, particularly among the producers of general contract grade turf. The market is predominantly supplied with seed sown turf or cultivated lawn turf. Pasture turf is still available in some areas, but its importance is small and declining. Suitable pasture for turf lifting is scarce and it can be cheaper to grow cultivated turf than treat and prepare existing pasture. Special seed mixtures and cultivation techniques produce a range of types of turfgrass that can be matched to particular sites and uses. The Turfgrass Growers Association (TGA) has quality standards. It is estimated that there are around 16,000 ha (*40,000 acres*) of turfgrass grown in the UK. Although several turfgrass companies were originally set up by farmers, the production is now in the hands of specialist turf growers but there are also farmers who use turf as part of their agricultural rotation.

Selling existing pasture turf to a turf company

This is the traditional option but it now represents very little of the turf market. Minimum 5-6 year ley/pasture generally needed for spring or autumn lifting, 8-10 year grass is better for summer cutting.

Payment varies between £750-£1,500 per hectare (£300-£600 per acre), but mainly £900-£1,200 per ha (£360-£480 per acre). There is usually an initial payment plus further payments as turf is lifted. There may be a penalty clause if lifting delays prevent subsequent timely drilling. Lifting can take from two months to a year. It can be done at any time of year except when there is snow or frost on the ground. The turf company sprays against broadleaved weeds, fertilises and mows before lifting; the farmer may do these tasks, for payment. He may graze the land, for a rent, if lifting is delayed.

The effect on the land is not detrimental, the amount of topsoil removal is not much greater than other root crops; some say there are benefits (removal of accumulated pests, etc. in the top half inch of grass, roots and topsoil). Some local authorities require planning consent for turf harvesting. In some instances it has been refused on the grounds that pasture turf is not an agricultural crop. Cultivated turf, however, is deemed to be an agricultural crop. On tenanted land landlord's permission is necessary to cut pasture turf.

Farmer cutting, lifting and selling pasture turf himself

This is extremely uncommon. The turf must be treated, as in option 1. A small turf cutting machine can be hired for £65 a day. This slices off the turf which must then be cut into lengths and picked up by hand. It is slow going even in good conditions. Wastage is commonly 10-20% of the area. It is possible to hire a machine which cuts and picks up the turf but the charge will be considerably more.

Renting land to a turf company for production of cultivated turf

Turf companies rent land for turfgrass production. Typically the land is rented on a per crop basis and one or two crops grown. A turf crop usually takes 12 to 18 months from preparation to harvest but autumn sown crops may be harvested within 12 months. Rent levels depend on the quality of the land, the provision of irrigation and the profitability of competing agricultural enterprises. Currently rents are in the order of £700-£1,300 per hectare per crop (£280-£525 per acre) or £525-£780 per ha per year (£210-£315 per acre).

Cultivated turf production

Important features: good root structure, number and type of weeds, level, well-drained, stone-free land; good access. Turf has a short life once cut and stacked - a maximum 1 to 2 days in summer, 3 to 4 days in winter, depending on temperature. On their own land turf producers can grow turf continuously, taking a crop every 18 months to two years on average. On rented land (as in option 3), they take one or two crops and move on. Usually they produce a quick growing turf on rented land and cultivate more specialist and slower growing turf on their own. A high level of agronomic expertise and considerable investment in machinery are needed and labour requirements are heavy. A high degree of marketing expertise is essential. While the bulk of the trade goes into general landscaping or garden centres there is an increase in the number of contracts where the quality and type of turf is specified. It is estimated that a turf farm would need to be 150-200 hectares (400-500 acres) or more in size to be viable – in order to justify the machinery and equipment necessary and to produce a succession of turf for the market. There are significant economies of scale. The cost of specialist machinery for turf production can be £350,000. The new one-man harvesting machine costs in the order of £120,000-£200,000 but significantly reduces labour costs.

Costs and Returns

Variable Costs plus Rent:	£/ha	(£/ac)
Seed	750-1,100	(300-445)
Fertiliser	350-700	(140-280)
Herbicide	90-150	(35-60)
Fungicide	100-210	(40-85)
Rent (for 15 months)	700-1,300	(385-525)
Total Costs	1,990-3,510	(805-1,400)

It may be necessary to irrigate and on occasions use netting to grow the grass for certain sites.

Labour: Special seed bed preparation (including subsoiling and stone burying), regular mowing (twice a week May/June), picking up clippings, harvesting (2 men on harvester plus one loading lorry) between 0.2-0.4 hectares per day (0.5-1.0 acre). The new one-man harvester can do 2 ha (5 acres) a day.

Total costs of the order of £5,000-£7,500 per ha (£2,000-£3,037 per acre), approximately 50-75p per square metre.

Value of Turf (on the field)

	per m^2	per sq. yd.	per ha*	per acre*
Pasture turf	38-43p	32-36p	£3,420-£3,850	£1,380-£1,570
Hardwearing, domestic general contract	70-95p	58-79p	£6,300-£8,550	£2,550-£3,460
Football, hockey, prestige landscape	115-145p	95-120p	£10,260-£12,825	£4,150-£5,200
High quality/specialist**	190-475p	160-405p	£17,100-£42,750	£6,910-£17,290

* assuming 90% recovery, but some producers work on 85%.

** for some contracts the price may be higher.

Delivery charges 45-55p per m^2 for a full lorry load. Higher for smaller deliveries.

Acknowledgements: Turfgrass Growers Association, PVGA House, Nottingham Road, Lincolnshire, LN11 0WB. Telephone: 01507 607722. www.turfgrass.co.uk. *Robert Laycock,* Littlegarth, Low Street, Lastingham, North Yorkshire, YO62 6TJ. Telephone: 01751 417191. www.robertlaycock.co.uk.

GOLF

Despite the UK economy coming out of recession, the game of golf is slow to recover. Most clubs continue to struggle to survive although there are some glimmers of hope for the future. The number of bankruptcies has slowed with the most vulnerable clubs already having failed. The sale price of courses continues to be relatively depressed since bottom line profits have not really improved. Clubs bought by overseas investors as 'bargains' have seen further falls in revenues which has scared off a number of potential new investors.

Golf is also suffering from longer-term problems than just lower disposable incomes caused by the economic downturn. The game suffers from a 'staid' image that is at odds with the demand for high-adrenalin sports from the younger generation. Also, the length of time required for a round of golf does not fit well with the commitments of modern life. Therefore it looks as though golf will continue to struggle financially for years to come although there is a slight increase in the number of youngsters taking up the sport. Clubs have become more family orientated in an attempt to stop the loss in members and attract new membership with many clubs are now offering a variety of ways to pay memberships in an attempt to retain members. But the age bracket of those playing continues to rise and the spend per head at the clubs continues to fall in real terms.

Relatively high agricultural land prices mean that it is virtually impossible to generate a profit on a stand-alone golf site. Driving range development has also virtually stopped with a declining marketplace and less practice taking place. Anyone considering development is well advised to resolve their financing in principle before entering the design / development phase. In many cases the planning system has failed to identify sites for new golf developments within the Local Plans. These have failed to address the re-use of courses which have become redundant.

There are no known locations left where there is proven demand. In our experience, the old guidelines of 1 course per 18,000 people no longer apply and should be revised to 1:30,000. For those who are interested in development the following guidelines may help but the best advice is to check that there really is a market before starting to even think about development.

Type of Facility and Costs

*   18-hole 6,400 metre (7,000 yard) course: 70-80 ha (*170-195 acres*) including Clubhouse and Pro Shop (600 sq. metres), parking, proper access and maintenance buildings. *The course will take between 1 and 2 years to construct, and will cost £2.5m-£3.5m according to drainage, earthmoving and irrigation, but excluding green keepers building and machinery. A Clubhouse (600 sq. metres) will cost from £850,000 to £2.5m fitted out. A full inventory of new machinery for an 18-hole course will cost £550,000*

*   9-hole course: 35-40 ha (*84-95 acres*). *Cost: £800,000-£1.2m*

*   9-hole Par 3 course: 7 ha (*17 acres*). *Cost: £600,000-£900,000*

*   6-hole Par 3 or 4 course: 14 ha (*34 acres*). *Cost: £500,000-£800,000*

*   Driving range: 4 ha (*10 acres*). *Cost: £250,000-£800,000, to include offices, storage, equipment, fencing and floodlighting*

*   Pitch and putt course: 1.5 ha (*4 acres*).

Using own labour may reduce costs by around a third but it is very risky in terms of resultant course quality. Anything involving plastics such as irrigation supplies will have seen rises in prices but labour rates have fallen. It is crucial to obtain professional advice at the outset for investment appraisal, feasibility study and a business plan. Before starting design work it would be wise to commission a Feasibility Study which need only cost £10-

15,000 to check that there really is a demonstrable business case on which finance can be raised.

Type of business organisation

To sell land with planning permission: The cost of development of an average new course will be significantly more than the value of the facility when it is complete. There is currently no premium over agricultural value unless the situation or planning consent offers something exceptional. The cost of obtaining permission depends on the sensitivity of the site but it would seldom cost less than £200,000 including design, environment impact study and Local Authority fees.

To let land to a developer/operator: Assuming the latter pays for constructing the course, a long lease will be required. Rental levels will depend on the expected profitability of the facility but currently, in our experience, leases remain around £40-60,000 for an 18-hole course.

To form a joint company with a developer/operator: This obviously means the farmer shares in the success or failure. The land would be all or part of the farmer's equity. There are no known active developers in this market at present

To develop and operate the course himself: the farmer would need good knowledge of golf and exceptional management ability besides access to substantial capital.

Returns

Few courses or clubs are now profitable with many struggling to break even. Bankable rates of return on new courses are extremely rare. Associated residential or other development could make developments profitable, but planning permission for such developments is very difficult.

Acknowledgement: *International Design Group* Studio 5.17, The Paintworks, Bath Road, Bristol BS4 3EH. Telephone: 0117 316 0591. www.idgplanet.com

BED AND BREAKFAST

The person running bed and breakfast should enjoy meeting people, have good social skills and be prepared to work unusual hours. In a crowded market, and with rising customer expectations, the standard of the product and service is critical. Farms must provide a standard of accommodation equal to that found in hotels. This will involve some refurbishment; both before starting the enterprise, to upgrade existing B&B to rising standards and ongoing repair of wear and tear.

It is vital to know the planning, legislative and financial requirements involved in B&B. Details are available from VisitBritain in the *'The Pink Booklet' - a practical guide to legislation for accommodation providers'*. This is available online at www.accommodationknowhow.co.uk/. Advice is also provided by National Tourist Boards of England, Scotland and Wales and Regional Tourist Boards.

Marketing is important. Some establishments produce a brochure or card giving details of the B&B, its location, facilities, and quality standards rating. New routes to customers have been opened up recently by of 'peer-to-peer' renting websites such as Airbnb. To join a marketing organisation the B&B should have a Quality Assurance Standard rating. These are awarded either by the official National Tourist Board inspectorate (which in England is Quality in Tourism), or the AA. The rating is at one of five levels, expressed as stars.

As there is considerable competition it is useful for the enterprise to offer something special or different such as accommodation for visitors' horses, a welcome for pets, or access to view the working farm. Establishments that can accommodate bigger parties are gaining in popularity. The number of B&Bs offering an evening meal has declined in recent years, but providing locally grown produce can be a draw.

Prices that can be charged reflect the quality of accommodation and location but cannot be far out of line with other local B&Bs and hotels. Prices can also vary depending on length of stay and time of year. The price range for one person per night ranges from £30 to over £150 on the basis of two adults sharing a room. A higher rate per person usually applies for single occupancy. There are regional differences with higher prices generally being charged in the south and east.

The range of B&B facilities has become enormous in the last decade. Decide the marketplace that suits you by identifying your selling point. Is it low cost, luxury, access to a working farm, family comfort etc.? Prepare the B&B enterprise, target your marketing and price the rooms accordingly to meet that marketplace.

Receipts from the enterprise can be calculated as follows: If the B&B is open for 40 weeks of the year at £40 per person per night, given a 60% occupancy rate the gross return per bed place will be around £6,720. Most farmhouse B&Bs have 4-6 bed spaces, which would generate a gross return of between £27,000 to £40,000 p.a.

Costs vary considerably: As every farmhouse B&B is different and some costs are difficult to apportion between guests and family, the following provides some pointers. Variable costs are food, electricity, heating, laundry, cleaning materials and additional help. There will also be regular redecoration costs, repairs, and replacement and renewal of glassware, china, cutlery, towels and bed linen. Variable costs if no non-family labour is used average about 20% of the nightly charge. If casual labour has to be included variable costs rise to 30-35% of the nightly charge.

Fixed costs include insurance, business rates (if they apply), membership of marketing organisations, regular advertising, repayments on loans taken out for building and equipment and regular labour; they are likely to average 30-35% of charges.

Contact: Farm Stay UK, Tel: 02476 696 909. www.farmstay.co.uk, *VisitBritain,*.Tel: 020 8846 9000. www.visitbritain.org. *Quality in Tourism*, Tel: 0845 300 6996. www.qualityintourism.com.

CHRISTMAS TREES

About 7 million real Christmas trees are sold a year in the UK; this figure has reduced as the quality of artificial trees has improved. Most real trees sold are UK produced, although some imports come chiefly from Scandinavia. Eight years ago 80% were Norway Spruce, but this is now less than 20%, with Nordman Fir, which retains its needles longer, at two-thirds (95% in urban areas) and Fraser Fir, a US favourite, 10%. The most popular sizes are between 5 to 7 feet.

There are 400 British growers across all parts of the country, with plantations ranging from less than one hectare to 1,000 ha. It is estimated that there are 60 million trees being grown, covering 25,000 ha. The average grower sells 6 to 7,000 a year from about 20 ha. The majority of sales are through big garden centres, which require a uniform tree, netted and palletised, but there are successful 'choose and cut' operations and the enterprise works well on a farm with a farm shop. Internet sales are growing. Producers need to sell 10,000 to 15,000 a year to justify buying machinery to assist in cultivation

The enterprise is slow to make a return. Nordman and Fraser Firs are typically harvested in years 7 to 9. The quicker-growing Norway Spruce is harvested in years 5 to 7. This makes the enterprise vulnerable to changing market conditions. About 30% of the crop is harvested in the first harvesting year, 40% in the second, 30% in the third. All species need a well-drained site free from late frosts, with good access. As with any crop, the better the land, the better the crop.

	Nordman Fir	
	£/ha	(£/ac)
4700 5 to 7 foot trees per ha @ price of . .	£4.00 - 5.00 / ft	
Output (average)	126,900	(51,356)
Variable Costs:*		
Plants	4,200	(1,700)
Planting	1,020	(413)
Fertiliser	387	(157)
Weed control	1,925	(779)
Pesticides	830	(336)
Pruning and shaping	5,005	(2,025)
Harvesting	4,675	(1,892)
Marketing	12,690	(5,136)
Total Variable Costs	30,732	(12,437)
Gross Margin (whole period)	96,168	(38,919)
Gross Margin per year over 8 & 6 years	**12,021**	**(4,865)**

1. *Labour* assumed to be casuals.

2. *Establishment*: Rabbit fencing (£4-£5 per m) is necessary and possibly deer fencing (£6-£8 per m). Spacing is possible from 60cm x 60cm to 1.8m x 1.8m, but 1.2m x 1.2m gives 5,500 plants per ha allowing for land loss for headlands, access, etc. Losses of 5 to 10% in the first year means 300-500 replacements are needed in second year. Norway Spruce transplants 25p-40p each, Nordman Fir 50-90p. Planting, by hand or machine, 15-20p/per plant.

3. *Variable Inputs:*

    Fertiliser in a split top dressing of 350 kg/ha 12:11:18 + Mg and TE in late March and mid-September.

Herbicides for weed control: residual herbicide, as cereals, in first year; subsequently an over-spray in October/November plus spot weeding until the canopy closes over. Weed control costs are likely to be 35p per plant over the life of the tree.

Pesticides: aphicide once a year for Nordman Fir (three times a year for Norway Spruce) at £35 per ha per application. Acaricide from year 3 to harvest: £110 for Nordman Fir (£200 per ha per year for Norway Spruce),

4. *Pruning and Shaping*: This is essential to produce the shape of tree the market demands. Nordman Fir: basal pruning in year 3 or 4 at 20p per tree plus shaping in the same year at 16p per tree and bud-rubbing every year except harvest at 5-10p per tree per year. Norway Spruce: shaping 17p per tree per year from year 3 or 4.

5. *Harvesting:* Done over 3 to 6 weeks, for dispatch Nov 20th to Dec 12th. A full-time person is needed per 3,000 trees sold, or one person per week per 400-500 trees. Cost: Norway Spruce 70-90p per tree, Nordman Fir 75-100p. Norway Spruce may be dipped or sprayed to reduce needle drop. Marketing costs around 10% of output.

6. *Machinery:* Inter-row plantation tractors £15,000-£65,000; stump clearing machines £7,000-£25,000; palletiser £13,000-£14,000; mist blowers £8,000-£10,000; hydraulic netting funnel £8,000-£10,000; manual netting funnel £175.

7. *Labour:* Planting and pruning can be done in January/February and tagging for height and quality in October/November. Thus it fits in well with combinable cropping.

The gross margins given are high, but these will only be achieved by a high level of expertise and commitment and the long period before any return is obtained must also be stressed, together with the risk this entails.

Acknowledgement: Thanks to - British Christmas Tree Growers Association, Tel: 01473 210519 www.bctga.co.uk.

OTHER DIVERSIFICATION

Well calculated diversification is to be encouraged. Non-agricultural enterprises managed in conjunction with the farming operation can offer several benefits to the business. These include:

- Spreading risks of returns; if the economics of agricultural production declines, revenue from non-commodity based enterprises may boost business income.

- Resource efficiency; most farm systems have quieter and busier periods for staff and management which may be switched into other roles for examples.

- Increased profit.

Any new enterprise will have its own risks associated with it. These must be clearly and objectively calculated (this will be a requirement if borrowed money is necessary). Each resource employed will have its own opportunity cost (what could it be earning if it was not being used for this new venture?). Cash (return on capital) is the obvious one, what could it earn in a high interest account? Labour is less straight forward. For example, a B&B might require minimal new capital under some circumstances, but tie somebody to the house at key times of the day, restricting other employment opportunities.

Before a major investment or change in business structure to incorporate new diversifications, business plans and market research to assess the income potential are needed. Most new enterprises require new skills (such as different production systems, new marketing and sales techniques). These take time and dedication to acquire. Developing new ideas and expanding a novel business venture can be exciting and time consuming; maintaining sufficient management time on the existing farm business is a common problem.

Nevertheless, many ventures exist where entrepreneurial skills have achieved notable success. Conversion of surplus farm buildings, for offices, workshops, retail and storage, has been the primary farm diversification activity up to date. A DEFRA survey found that 51% of farms had diversified activity in 2008/09, but if letting farm buildings is stripped out the percentage of diversified farms falls to 28%. It also shows that arable farms tend to be more diversified than livestock and farms in the South East are more diversified than elsewhere in the UK. Diversified enterprises might have a different VAT and taxation treatment. Check in advance with your accountant.

Some 'diversification' enterprises have been included above. There are many others, such as;

Novel Crops/Livestock
- Herbs
- Carp and Crayfish
- Quails
- Snails & Worms
- Maggots

Barn Conversions
- Business Lets
- Dwelling Let

Sporting
- Fisheries
- Stalking
- Clay Pigeon Shooting

Horses
- Riding School
- Trekking

Adventure Games
- Motor Sports
- Go-carting

Tourism
- Caravans / Camping
- Glamping
- Holiday Cottages

Vertical integration
- Yoghurt / Ice cream
- Meat sales
- Farm Shop

Many of these have been taken to new levels in recent years, for example the farm shop has moved on substantially from where it was 10 years ago and is now a vibrant and growing industry for high-end shoppers in market towns and motorway service stations. Other services as well as sale of fresh produce are being provided. Camping has given rise to Glamping, again focussing at the more affluent end of the market keen on luxury and service.

6.   FORESTRY

ESTABLISHMENT COSTS (BEFORE GRANT)

Unit Cost of Operations

Year/s	Operation	Cost (£)
1.	Trees for planting	
	(i) Bare rooted:	
	Conifers	220-350 per 1,000
	Broadleaves	250-400 per 1,000
	(ii) Rooted in small peat blocks:	
	Conifers	270-355 per 1,000
	Broadleaves	330-430 per 1,000
1.	Tree Protection	
	(i) Fencing (materials and erection)	
	Rabbit	4.20-6.00 per metre
	Stock	4.15-5.15 per metre
	Deer	5.00-6.50 per metre
	Deer and Rabbit	6.50-8.00 per metre
	Split post and rail	5·50-8.50 per metre
	(ii) Tree guards/shelters	
	Spiral and canes (750mm)	35-45 per 100
	Plastic tubes (1,200mm)	100-135 per 100
	Stakes	50-70 per 100
1.	Spot spraying	45-70 per 1,000 trees
1.	Hand planting	
	Conifers	200-240 per 1,000 trees
	Broadleaves *	300-600 per 1,000 trees
	Machine planting (loams and sand based on	
	2,250 plants per ha)	225-450 per ha
2-3.	Replacing dead trees **	
	Operation	110-200 per ha
	Plant supply	90-150 per ha
1-4.	Weeding per operation	
	Herbicide ***	70-130 per ha weeded
2.	Inter-row mowing	70-200 per ha

Costs specific to location			Upland	Lowland
1.	Ground Preparation:	ploughing	132-209 per ha	66- 99 per ha
		mounding	275-385 per ha	275-385 per ha
1.	Drainage		88-110 per ha	—
1.	Fertilising		132-297 per ha	—

*   Includes cost of erecting guards/shelters.

**   Replacing dead trees (beating up) may be necessary, once in the second year and again in the third year. Costs depend on number of trees.

*** Up to 2 weeding operations may be necessary in each of the first 4 years in extreme situations. Costs are inclusive of materials.

Access roads may need to be constructed and can typically cost between £13,500 and £33,000 per kilometre (£21,700 to £53,000 per mile) depending on availability of road stone and the number of culverts and bridges required.

Total Establishment Costs up to Year 3

1. *Conifer—Lowland Sites:* On a fairly typical lowland site, requiring little or no clearing or draining, the approximate cost before grant of establishing a conifer plantation would be in the range of £2,000-£4,000 per hectare. Up to 8 separate weeding operations may be required.

2. *Conifer—Upland Sites:* Establishing a similar conifer plantation on an upland site could cost £1,800 to £3,800 per hectare. Normally some form of site preparation and drainage is required but only one weeding operation may be necessary. Overall costs tend to be £110-£270 per hectare less than on lowland sites.

3. *Hardwoods:* Costs of establishing hardwood plantations are highly dependent on the fencing and/or tree protection required. If tubes are needed the overall costs will be influenced by the number of plants per hectare. Costs could be in the range of £4,000-£8,000 per hectare. Site conditions normally mean that hardwoods being grown for timber production are restricted to lowland sites.

4. *Farm Woodlands:* Establishment costs for farm woodlands may be lower than those indicated for hardwoods in (3) above if lower planting densities are used; costs of about £6,000 per ha for woods under 3 ha and £5,000 per ha for woods of 3 to 10 ha would be typical. However it should be noted planting at lower densities may increase maintenance cost and will lead to production of lower quality material.

5. *Size Factor:* Savings in fencing and other economies of scale may reduce average costs per ha by 10 to 20% where large plantations are being established.

6. *Method of Establishment:* A range of organisations and individuals undertake forestry contracting work and competitive tendering can help to control costs.

    The costs of establishment given above, and those for maintenance given below, are estimates for England. Costs in Scotland tend to be lower.

Re-Stocking Costs

Once trees on a site have been felled, the Forestry Commission usually requires the site to be restocked as a condition of awarding a felling licence. This can be done by replanting or through natural regeneration, leaving a proportion of the trees standing and using seed from these trees to re-stock. Minimal site preparation is usually required for natural regeneration although ongoing maintenance will be required to encourage a viable crop. Re-stocking a clear felled area would incur similar costs to those above. Grants similar to the now closed Woodland Regeneration Grant may be available in future to contribute towards restocking costs where native trees are being planted.

MAINTENANCE COSTS

Once trees have been established they normally require some maintenance and management work each year. For trees being grown primarily for timber production on a large scale, operations required may include ride and fence maintenance, pest control, fire protection, management fee and insurance premiums. Costs are normally £40-£80 per ha per annum depending on the size of the plantation and the complexity of management. In upland areas, fertiliser is occasionally applied once or more times in the first 20 years of the tree's life depending on the quality of the site. Estimated cost of £110-£275 per ha, depending on elements applied. For trees being grown for sporting and amenity purposes, annual maintenance costs are likely to be less and may range up to about £11 per ha.

A brashing operation which involves removing branches up to two metres may be required for access reasons as the crop matures. Opening up inspection racks over 5-10% of the crop may cost £44-£77 per ha. Brashing 40-50% of the crop costs £180-£400 per ha.

PRODUCTION

Production is usually measured in terms of cubic metres (m³) of marketable timber per hectare and will vary according to the quality of the site, species planted and thinning policy. Sites in lowland Britain planted to conifers typically produce an average of 12 to 18 m³ of timber per ha per year over the rotation as a whole and would accordingly be assessed as falling in yield classes 12 to 18. Under traditional management systems, thinning begins 18 to 25 years after planting and is repeated at intervals of approximately 5 years until a conifer wood is clear-felled at between 40 and 60 years, or a broadleaf wood at 80-120 years. Approximately 40-45% of total production will be from thinnings. Broadleaves typically produce an average of between 4 and 8 m³ of timber per hectare per year and fall in yield classes 4 to 8.

Prior to a thinning sale the trees normally have to be marked and measured at an estimated cost of 75p - £1 per m³, which is equivalent to £175-£300 per hectare depending on species, crop density and age. For a clear-felling sale the cost can range from £300 to £400 per ha, or about £1.50 per m³ where a full tariff applies, i.e. where each tree is counted and sample measurements of individual trees are taken. These costs associated with mensuration and marking can vary significantly and will correlate to the value of the crop to be harvested.

Felling permission is required when more than 5m³ are to be removed in one calendar quarter. This requires an application to the Forestry Commission for a Felling Licence which will vary in complexity depending on the size and variety of the woodland. A felling licence must be obtained from the Forestry Commission before any felling takes place, unless a Forest Management Plan has already been approved by them. Grants are expected to be available for preparing a Forest Management Plan (which covers a 20 year period and provides 10 years of consent for an agreed felling programme) under the new grant scheme launching in autumn 2014.

PRICES

Prices for standing timber are extremely variable, depending on species, tree size and quality; ease of extraction from site; geographical location (nearness to end user); quantity being sold; world market prices and effectiveness of marketing method used. The use of wood for energy generation continues to provide a market for poorer quality hardwood, conifer logs and forest residues.

Conifers

Coniferous Standing Sales Price for Great Britain from the Forest Enterprise Estate

Year to:	Average Price (Per m³ Overbark)		Fisher (5 yearly ave)	
	Nominal Terms (£)	Real Terms (2011 price in £)	Nominal Terms	Real Terms (2011 Price)
31-Mar-05	6.13	7.23	44.8	52.8
31-Mar-06	7.25	8.39	51.6	59.7
31-Mar-07	7.97	8.97	57.2	64.4
31-Mar-08	12.48	13.71	89.6	98.4
31-Mar-09	9.15	9.77	64.0	68.3
31-Mar-10	9.61	9.99	67.5	70.2
31-Mar-11	13.7	13.88	93.5	94.7
31-Mar-12	14.1	13.96	97.5	96.6
31-Mar-13	13.29	13.01	91.3	89.4
31-Mar-14	15.62	15.03	105.5	101.5

Source: Forestry Commission: Timber Price Indices. March 2014.

Fisher 5 yearly index corrects distortions in size mix enabling different years to be compared on the basis of a consistent tree size. In order to ensure this base size mix remains relevant over time it is updated every 5 years. The current base year is 2011. *Real Terms* accounts for the effects of general inflation

Hardwoods

The hardwood trade is very complex. Merchants normally assess and value all but the smallest trees on a stem by stem basis. Actual prices fetched can show considerable variation depending on species, size, form, quality and marketing expertise of the seller. Felling usually takes place in the winter months.

Some indicative prices for hardwoods are given below, but it is important to note that actual prices fetched can vary quite widely. Wood quality is particularly important in determining prices.

Harvesting stage	Tree size range (m³)	Price range £ per m³ standing	Possible use
First Thinnings	<0.13	0-16	Firewood, board products and pulp wood. Poles for refineries and turnery.
Subsequent Thinnings	0.13-0.3	5-20	Smaller sizes and lower quality
	0.3-0.6	8-25	material may go for fencing or
	0.6 -1.0	10-70	for use in the mining industry.
Clearfellings	1.0-2.0	15-120	Trees over 30 cm in diameter and of better quality may go for planking, furniture or joinery.
	2+	25-250	High quality material may go for veneers and can fetch between £150 and £300 per m³ depending on species and specifications.

Prices for Oak, Sycamore, Cherry and Elm tend to be significantly higher than for Beech, which seldom exceeds about £45 per m³ standing, even for stands containing significant volumes of first quality planking.

TIMBER MARKETING

In-house marketing by the owner or agent can be cost effective but only if they have detailed, up-to-date knowledge of timber buyers in the market place. The alternative is marketing through a forestry manager or management company.

Sales can take place of either standing timber or felled timber at roadside. Standing sales place felling and extraction costs on the purchaser who will usually pay for the timber on an outturn basis. These types of sales suit thinning and lower quality material. Roadside sales require the owner to pay for trees to be felled and extracted to a collection point where they can be accurately measured and inspected by potential purchasers. These types of sales are generally suitable for higher value timber.

Nationwide electronic sales of timber by auction and tender are now available for all types and quantities of timber.

MARKET VALUE OF ESTABLISHED PLANTATIONS AND WOODS

The value of woods depends on many factors, such as location, access, species, age and soil type. The table below gives an indication of the range of current market values of commercial woodlands of different ages, based on recent market sales.

From years 20 to 25 onwards, prices of commercial woods will also be increasingly influenced by the quantity of merchantable timber they contain. Depending on the time of clear-felling, the timber may be worth between £900 to £6,000 per hectare (£360 to £2,500 per acre).

Relatively small woods or those with high amenity or Ancient Woodland status often command a premium over prices for commercial woodlands as can those that are freehold with minerals or sporting rights; this is particularly in southern England. Conversely conservation designation can restrict value due to a perception of preventing economic forest management; however this need not be the case. Recent sales of predominately broadleaved woodlands of amenity type range from £10,000 per ha to £20,000 per ha with exceptional woodlands exceeding this by over 20%. The value of woods containing mature hardwoods will depend on the quality and value of the timber they contain and the quality of access.

Market Value of Commercial Sitka Spruce Woodlands

Age of Commercial Woods and Plantations	Price Range for crop and land	
	£/ha	£/acre
0-5 years	1,000-2500	(400-1000)
6-10 years	2,000-2,800	(800-1,200)
11-15 years	2,500-3,900	(1,000-1,600)
16-20 years	3,000-4,900	(1,200-2,000)
21-25 years	3,500-6,500	(1,400-2,600)

WOODLAND GRANTS

Each part of the UK has its own woodland grant scheme funded via the Rural Development Programme (RDP) and administered by the Forestry Commission. The current 7 year RDP funding round ends in 2014 and consequently the grant schemes in England, Scotland, and Wales are largely closed, pending the start of the new funding round in 2015. The Details of all the schemes are on the Forestry Commission's website (www.forestry.gov.uk).

English Woodland Grant Scheme

The English Woodland Grant Scheme (EWGS) was the Forestry Commission's suite of grants designed to develop public and environmental benefits from England's woods. EWGS is closed to applications from September 2014 and details of the new scheme (New Environmental Land Management Scheme or NELMS) are expected in the autumn of 2014 though at the time of going to print details had yet to be released. NELMS is expected to launch over the winter of 2015/16, with new schemes starting from 2016. In order to be eligible for NELMS, woodlands will still need to be registered on the Rural Land Register and the owner must hold a Single Business Identifier. In addition, woodlands will have to have an approved management plan in place.

There were six components of the EWGS and in the absence of any details on NELMS these are repeated below, for reference only, on the basis they are likely to be resurrected in some form under NELMS:

1. *Woodland Management Planning Grant:* was a contribution towards the cost of producing plans for existing woodlands which meet the UK Forestry Standard. Rates

of grant contribution were £20 per hectare for the first 100 hectares and £10 thereafter. A minimum payment of £1,000 for plans covering more than 3 hectares.

2. *Woodland Assessment Grant:* was a contribution towards the costs of obtaining additional information about a woodland in relation to ecology, landscape, historic and heritage assessments, and to determine stakeholder interests. Grant varied from £2.80 per ha - £5.60 per ha with a minimum payment of £300.

3. *Woodland Management Grant:* was paid for providing public benefits and to undertake sustainable woodland management. Potentially eligible activities included public access; maintaining boundaries; protecting archaeological features; management of old wood habitat and open space; soil and ground water protection; controlling non-native species; pest control; woodland health and monitoring sustainability. The grant was £30 per hectare per year.

4. *Woodland Regeneration Grant:* was a contribution towards the cost of regenerating woodland after felling. The aim was to promote the replanting of felled woodland whilst changing woodland types for increased biodiversity or public benefit. This grant will not provide support if the area of broadleaved woodland is diminished. Grant rates depend on the type of wood being felled and the type of wood which replaced it:

Type of woodland site	Type of woodland being regenerated	Grant (£/ha)
Ancient Woodland Site	Native Woodland	1,750
Ancient Woodland Site	Non-Native Woodland	0
Non-Ancient Woodland Site	Native Woodland	1,000
Non-Ancient Woodland Site	Non-Native Woodland	500

5. *Woodland Improvement Grant (WIG):* was a contribution towards the cost of work to improve the quality of woodland for social, environmental, and economic benefits. The rate of grant was set between 50% - 80% of standard costs. The focus was on improving access, biodiversity, and protecting SSSIs (Sites of Special Scientific Interest). FC regions may vary the rate of contributions or set priority areas to reflect regional and national strategies (e.g. red squirrel protection).

The relatively new national *Woodfuel Woodland Improvement Grant* funded mensuration and access works based more on receipted invoices rather than FC standard costs. This paid 60% towards works in undermanaged and inaccessible woodlands.

An agreed Woodland Management Plan is required for the Woodfuel WIG and generally required for other WIG funding on woodlands over 30ha.

6. *Woodland Creation Grant:* aided the establishment of new woodlands from 0.25ha upwards. The standard rates were as below.

Woodland category	£/ha
Broadleaved	2,800
Conifer	2,100

If the woodland meets with specific priorities there were additional contributions to this base level of grant available. The categories of this are shown below.

Additional Contribution	£/ha
Delivering Key Priorities	2,000
Delivering Other Priorities	1,000

These key priorities included: improving water quality and mitigating flood risk; enhancements to biodiversity; and offering public access (dependent upon demand). Other Priorities included woodlands near to people and new productive woodland.

For example a broadleaved woodland within a *Woodlands for Water* target area would have been eligible for £4800/ha. Payment of the grant is made 80% on the completion of the work, with the final 20% payable after 5 years as long as the plantation is maintained.

Planting on Agricultural Land: Annual payments were available under the Farm Woodland Payment for converting agricultural land to woodland (similar to the old FWPS). Payments were for 15 years where new woodland comprised more than 50% broadleaved species, and 10 years where the percentage of broadleaves was less than 50% (or fast growing broadleaved species such as poplar). Payment rates depended on the agricultural land use category being converted to woodland.

Historical payments available under the Farm Woodland Payment

Agricultural Land Category	Annual payment (£ per ha)
Arable Land in the Lowlands.................	300
Other improved land in the Lowlands....	200
Unimproved or land in the Uplands.......	60
Non-farmer...	Capped €150 (or one of above rates if lower)

Landowners who were eligible for the Farm Woodland Payment could also continue to claim Single Payment on the same land if planted after 2009.

Forestry grants are currently in a state of flux but details of NELMS will be posted on the Forestry Commission website (www.forestry.gov.uk) as they are released. Early discussions with one of the Forestry Commission Conservancy offices is advised if you are planning significant work or want to fully utilise future grant funding. Alternatively your forestry agent should be able to provide an up to date summary of what funding is appropriate and available.

CARBON FUNDING

The Forestry Commission will not fund applications for new woodland creation that include carbon co-funding if there is any link between the proposals and use of the term 'offsetting'. It will, however, allow co-funding provided certain criteria are met and appropriate language is used. This has been formalised with the Forestry Commission's Woodland Carbon Code which new plantations can be registered with to verify their CO_2 sequestration and allow it to be marketed as a potentially valuable asset to be sold or reported in the short or longer term. Carbon is currently being valued at around £5-10 per tonne however the Department of Energy and Climate Change predict values to reach £10 per tonne minimum by 2015 even on the lowest scenario. A typical broadleaved planting on a no-thin option may sequester over 500 tonnes of carbon per hectare over 60 years (http://www.forestry.gov.uk/carboncode).

WOODLAND TAXATION

Income from commercial woodlands is not subject to income tax, and tax relief cannot be claimed for the cost of establishing new woodlands. In general EWGS grants are tax free but annual Farm Woodland Payments are regarded as compensation for agricultural income forgone and are liable to income tax. The sale of timber does not attract capital gains tax, although the disposal of the underlying land may give rise to an assessment.

Woodlands which are managed commercially or which are ancillary to a farming business may be eligible for either business property relief or agricultural property relief respectively, for inheritance tax purposes, if owned for more than two years.

Acknowledgement: The above estimates are based on information supplied by Justin Mumford FICFor CEnv of Lockhart Garratt Ltd (Tel: 01536 408 840).

7.   ORGANIC FARMING

The Organic Sector:

The total organic land area fell in the UK in 2013 by 4% and has fallen 18% since 2010. All organic livestock numbers also fell in 2013 apart from a small rise in poultry.

Throughout 2013, 3.3% of UK agricultural land (excluding common grazing) was in organic production. The number of organic producers fell by 6.4% for the fifth consecutive year to 3,918 (4,281) holdings. In 2013 the area (in thousand hectares) devoted to organic production was as follows:

Area in '000 Hectares	Fully Organic	In conversion	Total	% of Agric. Area	of UK Organic Area	% of UK Organic Producers
England	302	14	316	3.5	55.0	66
Wales	100	2	102	6.5	17.7	20
Scotland	140	8	148	2.6	25.7	10
N. Ireland	9	0	9	0.9	1.6	4
Area in hectares						
2013	550,999	24,350	575,349	3.3		
2012	573,406	32,223	605,629	3.6		
2011	619,073	36,914	655,987	3.8		
2010	667,551	50,794	718,345	4.0		
2009	619,268	119,441	738,709	3.7		
2008	594,413	149,103	743,516	3.6		

The 5-year decline in organic food production in the UK has been led by a sharp fall in demand for organic goods in the UK. Organic food and drink sales have fallen by 33% since their peak in 2008 despite sales of all 'ethical produce' having risen annually since 2007, despite the downturn (Food Statistics Pocketbook 2013). The premium for organic food is somewhat dearer than most other such product groups. However, anecdotal evidence suggests an upturn for organic goods in 2014/2015. It appears in the future, such goods are less likely to be purchased solely for being organic but to help support a 'story' of added-value, high-end goods.

Organic Prices

The table below gives an indication of prices comparing organic with conventional. Note it is not possible to simply change the prices or even gross margins in a farm system, the overhead structure would also change, probably considerably.

Farm Gate Prices (estimate for 2015)

	Organic	Conventional	Difference	
Feed Wheat	£215	£135	£80	60%
Milling Wheat	£235	£152	£83	55%
Feed Barley	£205	£125	£80	64%
Milling Oats	£200	£125	£75	60%
Beans	£275	£230	£45	20%
Finished Beef (R4L Steer)	£3.90/kg dw	£3.50	4p/kg	11%
Stores (lowland Suckler)	£1.95	£1.83	12p/kg	7%
Finished Lamb	£4.35/kg dw	£4.05	30p/kg	7%

Finished Pig	*2.65*	*1.65*	*£1.00*	*60%*
Milk	*37p/l*	*30.5p/l*	*6.5ppl*	*21%*
Eggs (medium)	*£1.75/doz*	*£0.77*	*£0.98/doz*	*127%*

A net 116,000 hectares of organic farm land (14% of all organic farmland) has been reverted to conventional production in 3 years primarily because of low organic premiums over conventional and lower demand. The allocation of resources in organic farming is more expensive per unit of output than conventional farming systems; for example yields per hectare or per unit of labour tend to be lower meaning land and labour costs per unit of product are increased. Higher sale prices (or greater subsidisation) are therefore necessary to make organic farming as financially viable.

Many hill and upland livestock farms have converted to organic production to receive the higher prices. With inputs already low, management changes need only be small. Similar factors have meant that a sizeable number of extensive lowland beef and sheep producers have also embraced organic production. This highlights an important fact that there is a large grey area of farming systems between 'totally organic' to 'totally un-organic'. Curiously, a very large proportion (over 50%) of land for herbaceous and ornamental crops (i.e. non-food crops) are organic and continues to rise.

Below are the land use estimates of producers of organic and in conversion crop areas and livestock numbers for the applicable years:

Organic Land Use according to Crop Type (UK)						*year on year*
'000 ha	*2009*	*2010*	*2011*	*2012*	*2013*	*% change*
Cereals	60.0	56.9	52.5	47.8	43.7	-8.6
Other arable crops	11.2	10.8	9.3	8.3	7.5	-9.6
Fruit & Nut	2.2	2.3	2.1	2.1	2.1	-3.5
Vegetables & Pots	18.9	17.9	15.7	12.2	11.3	-7.4
Herbs & Ornam.s	5.8	6.2	6.1	5.8	6.8	-17.2
Temporary pasture	126	124	116	106	98.9	-6.7
Permanent pasture	496	497	435	406	387	-4.7
Woodland	7.2	8.1	8.3	7.4	7.6	2.7
Unused Land	11.6	12.4	10.9	10.2	10.4	2.0
Total area ha	*739*	*718*	*656*	*605*	*575*	*-5.0*

Organic Livestock Numbers (UK)						*year on year*
'000 head	*2009*	*2010*	*2011*	*2012*	*2013*	*% change*
Cattle	*331.2*	*350.2*	*334.8*	*290.2*	*283*	*-2.4*
Sheep	*884.8*	*981.2*	*1,162*	*1,152*	*999*	*-13.3*
Pigs	*48.2*	*47.4*	*52.6*	*34.6*	*30*	*-12.9*
Poultry	*3,959*	*3,870*	*2,838*	*2,458*	*2,488*	*1.2*
Other Livestock	*3.3*	*4.5*	*5.0*	*4.1*	*4.0*	*-0.4*

Economics of Organic Farming

The economics of organic farming to the farmer depend primarily upon the:

- relative yield compared with conventional farming;
- price premium compared with conventional farming.

In the case of cereals, organic crop yields are typically between 60% and 70% of those of conventionally produced crops. Historically, much higher prices have compensated for this, in addition to the obvious saving in fertiliser and spray costs. Gross margins are often normally much higher as long as a good yield is achieved. There are also the wider whole farm effects to be considered, e.g., unless the farm already has a substantial percentage of its area down to leys this will probably have to be increased in order to maintain yields and this extra grass has to be utilised profitably – which is far from easy, and the extra capital requirements could be heavy.

There is also a two year 'conversion period' to undergo before full price premiums can be claimed. Also, in the case of vegetable crops, quality (in the sense of appearance) can be badly affected by pests and diseases. Survey data have indicated overall labour requirements to be 10-30% higher than on conventional farms, with machinery costs generally similar per hectare, making the cost per unit of output, rather higher.

A recent report by the Soil Association and Organic Research Centre (Organic Farming; how it Stacks Up 2013) identified that organic farming is more profitable than conventional in all sectors, especially upland beef and sheep. By not using some resources, such as some agrochemicals, organic farming systems require higher levels of other resources such as land and labour to produce the same output. Therefore the overall costs are structured very differently to 'conventional' farming.

Aid for Organic Farmers:

In England, support for organic farmers has been through the Organic Entry Level Stewardship (OELS) (see Section III). Existing schemes will be continued but no new ones will begin in 2015. This provided support for the two-year conversion period of £175/ha/year. Rates then dropped to a 'stewardship' level thereafter at £60/ha, double the 'mainstream' ELS rates. Similar schemes, but with different categories and payment rates, are available in Wales and in Scotland. Just as with all other Rural Development schemes, it is as yet unclear whether and how organic farming is to receive additional support in the new RDP. This will become clear in 2015 and schemes begin on 1 January 2016.

Further Information:

No gross margin data for organic enterprises are included in this section because a specialist publication is available on the subject: the '2014 Organic Farm Management Handbook', (10th Edition) by Nic Lampkin, Mark Measures and Susanne Padel, Organic Research Centre, Elm Farm, Newbury. Tel: 01488 658 298.

8.   SUMMARY OF GROSS MARGINS

This page summarises the key figures of the gross margins over the previous pages. There are well in excess of 100 gross margins in the Pocketbook and additional data for other enterprises too. They cannot all be directly compared on a like for like basis, as different resources are required in order to produce each one and some offer whole farm benefits beyond the gross margin. Some, for example require different resources such as higher quality land, more overheads in terms of machinery, labour, buildings or working capital than others. Management requirement varies from one enterprise to another. Others are subject to having a supply contract with the processor.

Summary of Arable Crop Gross Margins

Crop (£/Ha)	Price	Yield	Output	Variable Costs	Gross Margin
Winter Feed Wheat	£135	8.40	£1,134	£498	£636
Winter Milling Wheat	£152	7.75	£1,178	£552	£626
Spring Milling Wheat	£151	5.75	£868	£371	£497
Red Spring Wheat	£210	5.00	£1,050	£481	£569
First Feed Wheat	£135	8.82	£1,191	£488	£703
Second Feed Wheat	£135	7.90	£1,067	£542	£525
Winter Feed Barley	£125	6.90	£863	£396	£467
Winter Malting Barley	£142	6.00	£852	£360	£492
Spring Malting Barley	£152	5.45	£828	£302	£526
Winter Oats	£125	6.30	£788	£298	£490
Spring Oats	£125	5.50	£688	£246	£442
Winter Rape	£265	3.40	£901	£439	£462
Spring Rape	£265	2.00	£530	£293	£237
Spring Linseed	£286	1.75	£501	£229	£272
Winter Linseed	£286	2.30	£658	£311	£347
Winter Beans	£220	4.00	£880	£231	£649
Spring Beans	£230	3.70	£851	£233	£618
Blue Peas	£260	3.75	£975	£261	£714
Marofats	£330	3.40	£1,122	£403	£719
Vining Peas	£320	4.30	£1,376	£425	£951
Maincrop Potatoes	£123	45.00	£5,535	£3,201	£2,334
Early Potatoes	£200	23.00	£4,600	£2,173	£2,427
Sugarbeet	£29.51	70.00	£2,065	£1,264	£801

Summary of Arable Crop Gross Margins (Continued)

Crop (£/Ha)	Price	Yield	Output	Variable Costs	Gross Margin
Lupins	£215	3.00	£645	£276	£369
Rye	£145	6.20	£899	£359	£540
Triticale	£130	5.00	£650	£276	£374
Naked Oats	£183	5.50	£1,007	£286	£721
Durum Wheat	£185	6.20	£1,147	£350	£797
Borage	£3,300	0.40	£1,320	£291	£1,029
Crambe	£180	2.50	£450	£300	£150
Hemp	£160	7.50	£1,200	£443	£757
Grain Maize	£155	7.50	£1,163	£336	£827
Millet	£235	3.00	£705	£270	£435
Poppies	£590	2.00	£1,180	£339	£841
Soya	£400	2.50	£1,000	£276	£724
Sunflower	£315	2.00	£630	£305	£325
Itallian Ryegrass	£1,100	1.30	£1,430	£694	£736
Early Perennial Ryegrass	£1,200	1.20	£1,440	£674	£766
Intermediate Perennial	£1,300	1.20	£1,560	£674	£886
Late Perennial	£1,400	1.00	£1,400	£644	£756
Hybrid Ryegrass	£1,100	1.25	£1,375	£674	£701
Dry Bulb Onions	£140	41.00	£5,740	£1,741	£3,999
Cauliflower			£4,445	£3,409	£1,036
Calabrese			£3,765	£3,263	£502
Dessert Apples	525-895	15-55	7.8-49k	6.7-33k	1.1-16k
Culinary Apples	265-525	25-50	6.6-26K	7.9-22k	(1.3)-4.1k
Pears	475-685	15-30	7.1-21k	5.9-16K	1.2-4.9k
Raised Bed Strawberries	2.4-3.4k	18-23	45-78k	44-63k	1-15k
Everbearer Strawberries	2.5-3.3k	28-44	71-149k	69-115k	2-33k
Raspberries	5.3-7.1k	8-15	42-106k	41-77k	0.5-30k
Blackcurrants	£650	6.50	£4,225	£1,430	£2,795
Hops (£/kg)	£6.40	1500	£9,600	£5,820	£3,780
SRC /year	£65	8.0	£520	£344	£176
Miscanthus	£55	12.00	£660	£521	£139
Mushrooms £/t compost	£1.85	250	£465	£398	£67
Christmas Trees	£4.50/ft		£15,863	£3,842	£12,021

Summary of Livestock Gross Margins

Livestock		Output	Variable Costs	Gross Margin /Head	Gross margin £/Ha
Dairy					
Spring Calving Friesians	per Cow	£1,545	£491	£1,054	£2,530
Autumn Calving Friesian/Holsteins	per Cow	£2,048	£796	£1,252	£2,754
All-Year-Round Calving Holsteins	per Cow	£2,291	£1,021	£1,270	£2,794
Channel Island	per Cow	£1,818	£774	£1,044	£2,610
Friesian Followers	per Head	£1,187	£529	£659	£908
Channel Followers	per Head	£1,031	£463	£568	£987
Beef Cattle					
Bucket Reared Calf 3 month	per Calf	£151	£98	£53	
Bucket Reared Calf 6 month	per Calf	£261	£188	£73	
Spring calving lowland sucklers	per Cow	£286	£260	£26	£47
Autumn calving lowland sucklers	per Cow	£413	£321	£92	£151
Spring calving upland suckler	per Cow	£258	£247	£11	£18
Autumn calving upland sucklers	per Cow	£382	£323	£59	£74
Store Cattle Keeping Summer	per Head	£258	£64	£194	£1,115
Store Cattle Keeping Winter	per Head	£252	£162	£90	
Summer Store Finishers	per Head	£422	£190	£232	£695
Winter Store Finishers	per Head	£428	£303	£125	
Summer finished sucklers	per Head	£652	£225	£427	£1,368
Winter finished sucklers	per Head	£377	£283	£93	
Maize Finishing (dairy)	per Head	£772	£347	£425	
Maize Finishing (suckler)	per Head	£715	£303	£412	
Cereal Bull Beef (continental)	per Head	£656	£586	£71	
Cereal Bull Beef (dairy)	per Head	£761	£586	£175	
Sheep					
Lowland Spring Lamb	per Ewe	£81	£55	£26	£260
Upland Spring Lamb	per Ewe	£64	£49	£15	£123
Gimmering Ewe Lambs	per Ewe	£56	£23	£33	£419
Finishing Store Lambs	per Ewe	£20	£19	£1	£35

Summary of Livestock Gross Margins (Continued)

Livestock		Output	Variable Costs	Gross Margin /Head	Gross margin £/Ha
Pigs					
Weaners	per Sow	£1,262	£851	£411	
Pork	per Pig	£39	£40	-£1.20	
Cutter	per Pig	£55	£50	£5.20	
Bacon	per Pig	£70	£60	£10.20	
Combined Pork	per Pig	£93	£75	£18.06	
Combined Cutter	per Pig	£110	£85	£24.46	
Combined Bacon	per Pig	£125	£95	£29.46	
Poultry					
Enriched Caged Eggs	per Bird	£16.00	£12.83	£3.17	
Free Range Eggs	per Bird	£22.34	£14.32	£8.02	£16,042
Pullets	/Bird Reared	£3.39	£2.52	£0.87	
Broilers	p/Bird	165p	148p	17p	
All year turkey	£/Bird	£35.75	£19.80	£15.95	
Christmas Turkey	£/Bird	£43.40	£23.86	£19.55	
Large Roaster Chickens	£/Bird	£15.72	£6.20	£9.52	
Ducks	£/Bird	£7.54	£5.51	£2.02	
Geese	£/Bird	£61.75	£29.28	£32.47	
Other Livestock					
Breeding & Finishing Deer	/100 Hinds	£18,440	£5,638	£12,802	£704
Deer Calves	/100 Hinds	£9,900	£3,135	£6,765	£440
Finishing Stag Calves	/200 Hinds	£25,770	£8,143	£17,627	£969
Deer Park	/300 Hinds	£32,680	£12,053	£20,627	£206
Alpacas	Per head	£182	£140	£42	£631
Ostriches ~ Laying Trios	per Trio	£977	£27	£949	£136
Ostriches ~ Fatteners	per bird	£387	£356	£31	£188
Wild Boar	per Sow	£1,523	£992	£531	£2,657
Dairy Sheep	per Ewe	£467	£255	£212	£2,327
Dairy Goats	per Doe	£500	£287	£213	£2,554
Angora Goats	per Doe	£268	£119	£149	£716
Trout	/tonne Fish	£1,930	£1,580	£350	

III. GOVERNMENT SUPPORT

1. INTRODUCTION

Agricultural support to farmers and the rural economy is largely provided through the European Union's Common Agricultural Policy (CAP), and delivered in the UK by the devolved Governments of England, Wales, Scotland and Northern Ireland. The World Trade Organisation (WTO) provides a global tier in the hierarchy of agricultural (trade) policy. The Doha Round was intended to lead to an agreement that would have meant (amongst other things) the EU reducing barriers to imports (mainly tariffs and tariff quotas) which could have had the effect of reducing prices (of protected goods) for UK farmers and opening new markets for exports which could have raised them. Negotiations have stalled following several failures and agreements currently seem unachievable.

The CAP has two main budgets (or pillars). Pillar 1 includes the Single Payment Scheme (SPS) to 2014, Basic Payment Scheme (BPS) from 2015, which provides direct aid to farm businesses and also Market Support for agricultural produce – the latter once being the mainstay of CAP support, but now much reduced in importance. Pillar 2 is support through Rural Development and provides direct support to farmers and also to rural communities. In 2013 Pillar 1 will have amounted to approximately 75 per cent and 25 per cent for Pillar 2 to English farmers. Market support (which is not paid direct to farmers) is not included.

A new Basic Payment Scheme (BPS) replaces the Single Payment Scheme (SPS) from January 1st 2015. Transitional measures were put in place to allow the SPS to 2014. The last applications to the SPS were submitted in May 2014. Applicants must adhere to the rules of this scheme until 31st December 2014, after which the new BPS commences. As the new scheme builds on the use of 'entitlements', a concept first introduced for the SPS in 2005, we have given a summary of this scheme first. Details of the Basic Payment Scheme can be found in Section 3 below.

Details of the CAP mechanisms are given in the following paragraphs. In individual situations businesses should always check with the latest legislation and their devolved administrations' publications.

2. SINGLE PAYMENT SCHEME

Major reforms of Pillar 1 of the CAP were implemented for the most part, in January 2005 and will end at the end of 2014. In November 2005 a reform of the Sugar Regime was agreed including price cuts and compensation to farmers starting with the 2006 sugar beet crop. In 2007 a reform of the Fruit and Vegetable regime was agreed. These subsequent reforms have been incorporated into the SPS legislation and there have been some significant simplifications. The latest changes were in 2008 when the 'Health Check' of the CAP was agreed. This was not a radical reform.

SINGLE PAYMENT SCHEME BASICS

The major, essential change of the 2005 reforms was *decoupling*. This means that farm support is no longer linked to what is being produced on the farm during the year, i.e. to the crops being grown or the livestock kept. In most member states (including Wales, Scotland and NI), the 'Single Payment' (SP) (also referred to as the 'Single Farm Payment') is made according to the support received by each claimant during the three years 2000-2002 (the reference period). This is known as the 'historic system' of SP allocation. England opted for a system which moved the payment from being calculated on an 'historic' basis to a 'flat-rate' Regional Average Payment (RAP) per hectare over the period 2005 to 2012. This transition is now complete.

The English transition system shifted direct payment from a historic to regional average payment, with the proportions changing over an eight-years: starting mainly historic and changing annually to become entirely a flat rate regional average, as follows:

Transitional Percentages from Historic to Regional Component in English SPS

Year	2005	2006	2007	2008	2009	2010	2011	2012
% historic	90	85	70	55	40	25	10	0
% regional	10	15	30	45	60	75	90	100

The regional payments in England differ according to topography, with three types: lowland (or non-SDA), non-moorland severely disadvantaged areas (SDAs) and moorland SDA. Payments for the second of these are approximately 80% of those in the lowland and those for moorland about 14% (i.e. about a sixth of those in non-moorland SDAs). Since 2012, the claimants in each of these regions receive the same amount per hectare as any other in that region.

In order to receive SPS payment, recipients have to be farming 'eligible' land (see below). They must also satisfy 'cross-compliance' rules, which are in two parts: 'Statutory Management Requirements' (SMRs; directives, largely already in force, on public and plant health, animal welfare and the environment) and keeping the land in 'Good Agricultural and Environmental Condition' (GAEC). They apply to the entire holding. The rules in England include no cultivating, fertilising or spraying within two metres of the centre line of any hedge or ditch, no hedge cutting between 1st March and 31st July 2014 and providing a soil management plan. The area of permanent pasture in each region must be maintained (this is a government responsibility to monitor not an individual farmer responsibility). Refer to the legislation for detailed requirements.

OTHER SINGLE PAYMENT POINTS

The other important points are as follows:

- As the payments are calculated in euros the pound:euro exchange rate is important. The rate used is that prevailing on 30th September each year. For the first three years the rate was €1 = 68-69p. There was an increase in 2008 to 79p. In 2009 the rate jumped to €1=91p. It reduced in 2010 and 2011 to 86 – 87p. For 2012 the rate fell to 80p but rose again to 83.6p in 2013. At the time of writing the UK economy is improving and the Pound is strengthening against the Euro. The rate used for budgeting purposes in this edition of the Pocketbook for 2014 and 2015 is 80p.

- Initial entitlements were awarded to the IACS claimant of agricultural land in 2005. They are transferable/tradable and can be sold with or without land, or leased only with an equivalent area of land.

- Most farmland is 'eligible', comprising arable land and permanent pasture but excluding woodland and land in non-agricultural use. 'Permanent crops' (essentially orchards and vineyards) are eligible. The land has to be 'at the farmer's disposal' on 15th May (the application deadline).

- Following the ending of set-aside, English ministers had intended to introduce, as a cross compliance measure under the SPS, a compulsory area of cultivated land in environmental management. This has not been implemented. Instead it was decided to give the voluntary approach, advocated by the CLA and NFU, time to prove it can recapture the environmental benefits of set-aside. The vehicle for this is the 'Campaign for the Farmed Environment' (CFE). Various targets have been set by Defra, for example to increase the amount of land entered into an agri-environment scheme to 70%, to have 170,000 ha of uncropped land and to have at least 204,030 ha of land voluntarily managed outside of agri-environment schemes.

- There are now no supplements for protein crops or energy crops in the UK.

DEDUCTIONS TO THE SINGLE PAYMENT

Initial deductions: A 'National Ceiling', based on past national subsidy receipts led to a 0.17% reduction in England only. Across the UK 4.2% was deducted for the 'National Reserve', to provide payments for special cases, e.g. new entrants since the end of 2002 and purchasers of extra land. These two deductions were made before issuing the initial entitlements in 2005. Up to 10% of direct payments from each sector can be deducted to set up a 'National Envelope' to support specific types of farming or improve product quality/marketing; in the UK this has only been used in Scotland (for beef).

Modulation: There is compulsory 'modulation' (for all EU member states) to fund EU-wide Rural Development projects; this was 3% in 2005, 4% in 2006 and 5% in 2007 and 2008, 7% in 2009 and then increased by 1% for the next three years, taking it to 10% in 2012. Additionally, since 2009 there is an extra 4% on top of the normal EU rate for the element of Single Payment exceeding €300,000. From the amount raised through modulation, member states get at least 80% of its modulated funds back for use in Rural Development programmes and there is an element of compulsory match-funding by member states. The first €5,000 of aid on every farm is exempt from modulation.

Member states may also levy 'voluntary' (national) modulation (to 2013), and the UK levied this at different rates in the devolved administrations. For the UK the agreed modulation rates for payments under €300,000 are shown in the table below for each devolved administration. In 2014 there is no farm level modulation, the new 'Pillar Transfer' rules under the Basic Payment Scheme applies – See Transitional Measures.

Total UK and EU Modulation Rates

%	2005	2006	2007	2008	2009	2010	2011	2012	2013
Scotland	6.5	8.5	10	13	13.5	14	14	14	14
Wales	4.5	4.5	5	7.5	9.2	10.8	11.5	11.5	11.5
N.Ireland	3	8.5	9.5	11	12	13	14	14	14
England	5	10	17	18	19	19	19	19	19

Higher rates of modulation apply in Wales for claims in excess of €300,000; 11% in 2009 rising by 1% per year to 14% in 2012.

Financial Discipline: EU Farm Ministers decide annually what percentage reductions are needed to keep spending within stipulated budget thresholds; as with EU modulation the first €5,000 of aid per farm is exempt. Financial Discipline (FD) had not been necessary from 2005 to 2012. But FD was applied at 2.45% to the 2013 payment to keep within the budget limit. A 'quirk' in the system means the SPS claim year and the EU budget year is one year different and the 2013 payment was made from the new, substantially lower EU Budget (2014-2020).

The new CAP reform's lower exemption rate of the first €2,000 (previously €5,000, see above) was also applied. FD is expected to be 1.3% in 2014 to pay for a new crisis reserve. It may be prudent to put in 0.5% for 2015 and 1% for 2016.

TOTAL PAYMENTS PER FARM

Every farm had a different total payment per hectare each year up to 2011 because their historic payments were unique. In Wales and Scotland these differences will persist until they change from the wholly historic system which starts in 2015 under the new BPS. In England the payment rates in each region (lowland, SDA and moorland) are now the same. Previous editions of the Pocketbook showed examples of how three different English farms' (arable, beef and sheep) payments changed over the period 2005 to 2013. Welsh and Scottish farmers will go through this process, but over a shorter time frame. There will be winners and losers similar to when English farmers undertook the change.

The following are Actual rates of the area payments in 2013 in the three areas (or sub-regions) of England. 'Lowland' covers all non-SDA (Severely Disadvantaged Area) land, which is more than 84% of farmed land.

2013 Flat Rate Area Payments in England

	Lowland	Non-Moorland SDA	Moorland SDA
	£/ha (acre)	£/ha (acre)	£/ha (acre)
Payments before deductions....	270.86 (110)	217.61 (88)	38.01 (15)
Payments after deductions	212.75 (86)	170.93 (69)	29.86 (12)

SDA = Severely Disadvantaged Area   Converted at €1=£0.83605
Deductions at 21.45% (modulation at 19% and FD at 2.45%)

The following are estimates of the flat-rate area payments in 2014 in the three areas (or sub-regions) of England, with €1 = 80p. The estimates are made by The Andersons Centre. From 2014, there is no modulation. However a 12% Pillar Transfer (in England) is introduced under CAP reform, transferring funds from Pillar 1 to Pillar 2 which reduces entitlement values, there are no further cuts unless Financial Discipline is triggered.

Estimated 2014 Flat Rate Area Payments in England

	Lowland	Non-Moorland SDA	Moorland SDA
	£/ha (acre)	£/ha (acre)	£/ha (acre)
Payments	202 (82)	162 (67)	28 (11)

SDA = Severely Disadvantaged Area

Estimated rates for 2015 can be found in the Basic Payment Scheme section below.

3.   MARKET SUPPORT

Market support measures are the other part of Pillar 1 funding, including intervention buying, export subsidies, quotas and tariff barriers. The main measures are tariffs which are unlikely to change much in the short term following the lack of WTO change (see the introduction to this section). Individual UK milk producers have seen their quota increase by 0.5% at the end of each of the 2005/06, 2006/07 and 2007/08 milk years. A further 2% allocation was made at the end of the 2007/08 milk year. As a result of the Health Check individual quotas have increased by 1% for another five years since 31st March 2009. Milk quotas in the EU will end on the 31st March 2015.

Sugar prices are supported within the EU. Following the 2006 reforms, 'institutional' sugar prices have been cut to reach a minimum EU beet price of €26.4 per tonne in 2009 to 2012. Although in Britain, actual prices paid are determined through the Inter-Professional Agreement between British Sugar and the NFU (refer to page 33).

4. THE BASIC PAYMENT SCHEME

A political deal on the main elements of reform to the Common Agricultural Policy (CAP) was concluded on 26th June 2013. This will shape Europe's farm policy from 1 January 2015 to December 2019. But many decisions were left to Member states to decide. In the UK, England, Scotland, Wales and Northern Ireland have all held their own consultations during autumn 2013 and spring 2014. Each of the devolved regions has made its own decisions. At the time of writing most of the broad decisions have been made and where these are different it is shown separately in the text that follows; but some 'farm level' detail was still unavailable.

ENTITLEMENTS AND REDISTRIBUTION

The main change for farmers as a result of reform to the Common Agricultural Policy (CAP) is the introduction of the Basic Payment Scheme (BPS) which replaces the Single Payment Scheme (SPS). In many ways it is similar to the existing scheme, (see earlier for details) with entitlements having to be matched against eligible land which then generates a yearly payment as long as certain land management rules are followed (cross-compliance). But unlike the SPS the BPS forms the 'foundations' of the new support arrangements, with a system of top-up payments that is available from the Pillar 1 budget. The mechanism of the scheme and the additional top-ups are discussed in detail below;

- **_Entitlement Roll-over._** Countries already operating the regional payment system (as in England) can roll-over existing entitlements into the new system. Defra is making use of this. Which means there will be no re-grant of entitlements in England – entitlements farmers hold at the end of 2014 will be converted into BPS ones for 2015. However, if a claimant is holding excess entitlements in 2015 (i.e. more entitlements than they have eligible hectares), the excess entitlements will be confiscated.

- **_Entitlement Grant._** Countries operating on the historic system (including Wales and Scotland) are required to issue new BPS entitlements. However, entitlements will only be granted to those that received a payment (of any size) under the SPS in _2013_. There will be a 'national reserve' set up, comprising up to 3% of funds to deal with hardship claims. Farmers growing certain crops in 2013 (fruit, vegetables, potatoes, ornamentals and vineyards) are eligible to establish entitlements even if they did not claim the SPS in 2013. There are likely to be rules introduced to deal with 'mergers and scissions' of holdings between 2013 and 2015. There are also likely to be rules on transferring the 'right to establish' entitlements (the 'golden ticket'), for those that did not make a claim in 2013, but details were not available at the time of writing.

  In **_Wales,_** the Welsh Government will allocate new entitlements on the basis of land occupied in 2015, with the historic amount for each claimant based on the number of entitlements **_held_** in 2014, not those activated. The claims history will then be divided across all the entitlements established in 2015 to form the historical element of the new entitlement value. This element will decline over the next five years under the Internal Convergence rules – see below.

  In **_Scotland,_** entitlements granted under the BPS are limited to the area claimed in 2013. This means claimants will get entitlements equal to either the area claimed in 2013 or 2015 whichever is the smaller. There will be a 'windfall' profits clause to prevent claimants' history being artificially boosted where land has been given up.

- **_Entitlement Limit._** Member states can limit the number of BPS entitlements granted to either 135% or 145% of the area declared under the SPS in 2009. None of the devolved regions have taken this up.

- *Internal Convergence*. This is the term for the move to a flat rate regional payment in countries currently operating the historic system (e.g. Wales and Scotland). However, there is no requirement for a fully-flat rate to be reached. By 2019 member states are only required to ensure all farmers get at least 60% of the average regional payment. On top of this, losses for individuals can be limited to 30% of their present payment.

  However, *Wales and Scotland* have both decided to phase in the flat rate system fully by 2019. This will be done in equal steps of 20% per year i.e. in 2015 a farmer's entitlement value will be made up of 80% of the historic value and 20% of the flat regional payment (see below). This will mean farmer's entitlement values will change each year until 2019. England went through this process between 2005 and 2012. Wales and Scotland will go through this process over a shorter time frame. There will be winners (extensive producers) and losers (intensive producers). Examples of estimated payment rates are given at the end of this section.

- *Regions.* The flat rate regional payment depends on the region the land falls into. Member states are able to divide their countries into sub-regions so the regional payment rates reflect the amount of farming possible on each hectare. This can make the transition from historic to flat rate less pronounced as the less productive land can be given a lower rate and the better, more productive land, a higher flat rate payment.

  In *England* when the SPS was introduced in 2005, Defra split the country into three regions; Lowland, Severely Disadvantaged Areas (SDA) and Moorland. Defra has decided to keep these regions for the BPS. Entitlements will not be tradable across these regions, but in order to 'move money up the hills', from 2015, the payment rate in the Lowland and the SDA region will be the same. The Lowland rate will be reduced slightly and the SDA rate will increase to match the Lowland value. The Moorland rate will see an increase from current levels.

  Wales has decided to create three regions – Moorland, Severely Disadvantaged Areas (SDA) and a combined Disadvantaged Areas (DA)/ Lowland region. Moorland will be restricted to land above 400m in altitude any 'Moorland' below this line will fall into the SDA flat rate payment region.

  Scotland is also creating three grazing categories. Better land (arable and grassland) will be classed as a single payment region (approx.1.8m ha). Rough grazing will be split to avoid any over compensation for the least productive land. This will be done using the Less Favoured Area Support Scheme (LFASS) classification (see Rural Development Section). Rough grazing in the non-LFA and in LFASS grazing categories B, C and D, will be in one payment region (approx.. 1m Ha). The least productive rough grazing land in LFASS grazing category A will form the third region covering approximately 2m ha. In this region there is a proposal to introduce coupled support of around €25 per ewe.

GREENING

Greening is the biggest change for farmers under the BPS. It is the concept of getting farmers to provide environmental benefits in return for their direct payments. It is seen as a way of making farm support more acceptable to tax payers and voters. Greening payments are set at 30% of the total BPS. Therefore it will change as a result of the 'internal convergence' mechanism set out above.

Under the Rules of 'Equivalence' if a member state can demonstrate to the EU Commission that existing or proposed schemes (national environmental certification schemes) provide equivalent environmental benefit to greening, then this can replace the basic greening requirement. None of the UK administrations have taken up this measure. They have all taken up the three basic EU measures of crop diversification, permanent pasture retention, and Ecological Focus Areas (EFAs) although Scotland in interested in devising an equivalence scheme for 2016.

Under the rules of equivalence, claimants are exempt from greening on organic land although the greening payment will still be made.

- **Land Definitions.** Under greening there are three key types of land, all three categories added together are known as the claimant's eligible area;

  ➤ Permanent Pasture – land that has been in grass for five years or longer. The sixth time it is entered as grass on the claim form it becomes permanent pasture. It doesn't matter if it has been reseeded, it is the length of time the land has been out of the arable rotation. If a catch crop (e.g. stubble turnips have been planted, this could break the sequence but it would have to be demonstrated)

  ➤ Permanent Crops – land in crops that are in place for five years or more without replanting and that yield repeated harvests e.g. vines, orchards, short rotation coppice, Miscanthus, nurseries.

  ➤ Arable Land – any eligible land that is not permanent pasture or permanent crops, including fallow land and temporary grass.

- **Crop Diversification.** Where a claimant's arable land area (as defined above) is between 10-30 hectares a minimum of two crops are required. Three crops will be needed when the arable land area is above 30 hectares. No crop should cover more than 75% of the farm area. Where three crops are required, the two main crops together should be a maximum of 95% of the area. The crop rotation requirement does not apply where;
  ➤ more than 75% of the arable land is used for temporary grass or left fallow (as long as the remaining arable land area is below 30 hectares)
  ➤ more than 75% of the entire holding is permanent or temporary grass (again, subject to a 30 hectare limit on the remaining arable land area).

A crop is defined by its *genus* and *species*. Wheat, barley, oats, oilseed rape, linseed, potatoes, sugar beet etc. are all classed as separate crops. Spring and winter crops are also treated as separate crops. Fallow is a 'crop type', as is temporary grass. There are some oddities though so refer to scheme guidance.

- **Permanent pasture.** Under the existing cross-compliance rules there is already a requirement for permanent pasture to be maintained. This is enforced at member state level. It was originally proposed that this protection of grassland would move down to a farm-level basis. However, it is now optional for member states to retain the implementation at a regional or national level. England, Scotland and Wales have all decided to continue with the national-level enforcement. Under the new rules the overall percentage of permanent grassland in each country compared to the total agricultural area must not fall by more than 5%.

- **Ecological Focus Areas (EFAs).** EFAs will initially be set at 5% of a farm's eligible *arable* land area. This could rise to 7% after 2017 if a study backs the move. Countries are able to choose from a list of possible features to decide what qualifies as an eligible EFA. This includes landscape features (hedges and trees), buffer strips, fallow land, protein-fixing crops, agro-forestry and short-rotation coppice. A matrix system converts linear features (e.g. hedges) into EFA area equivalents and gives some features extra weight. EFAs will not be required on farms where more than 75% of the land is grassland (temporary or permanent) as long as the remaining arable area is less than 30 hectares. Farms with less than 15 Hectares of arable land will also be exempt from the EFA requirement. The table below shows the features each devolved region has chosen. England & Wales have decided to use the standard weighting factors and conversion rates set out in the EU legislation.

Feature	Definition	Conversion Factor m to m²	Weighting	EFA Area
Fallow land	The 'default' EFA option	-	1.0	1m²
Landscape features	Hedges (< 10m wide) Stone Walls [1] Ditches (< 6m wide)	5.0 1.0 3.0	2.0 1 2	10m² 1m² 6m²
Buffer strips [3]	Min. 1m width. Max 10m Must be next to watercourse	6.0	1.5	9m²
Catch crops & green cover [4]	Sown or undersown grass or seed mixtures, not for harvest, must be in place by 1st Oct.	-	0.3	0.3m²
Nitrogen fixing crops	Definitive list of crops still waited. Likely to incl. beans, peas, lupins, soya and Lucerne	-	0.7	0.7m²
Short Rotation Coppice [1]	No inputs	-	0.3	0.3m²
Forested Areas[1]	Areas used to claim the SPS in 2008	-	1.0	1m²

Source: EU Commission

[1] Wales only, [2] Scotland only, [3] England & Scotland only, [4] England & Wales only;

The EFA requirement, apart from woodland (& coppice) options, must be cited adjacent to arable land i.e. hedges between permanent pasture fields are not eligible. In England, Defra has said payments may be delayed for those that use hedges to satisfy their EFA requirement due to the necessary checks that will need to take place.

Scotland has selected fallow, catch crops, nitrogen fixing, field margins (1.5 weighting) and buffer strips for their EFAs. Other weightings as above.

Other Points Regarding Greening

➤ **Double funding and Agri-environment schemes.** This is where farmers are paid twice for the same action. This is not allowed under EU rules. Some Agri-Environment Scheme options are also EFA options and so are seen as double funding so a reduction will have to be made on some Agri-Environment Payments. However, all HLS agreements (and their underpinning ELS agreements) and any ELS agreements that started before 1st January 2012 will not be affected which leaves only about 4,000 ELS schemes. Only Agreements commencing after this date will be affected. Double funding issues relate mainly to in field options as hedges are deemed not to be double funded. Those affected can either take the reduction in ELS (and OELS) payment, add additional options to get their points back to 30 per Ha or withdraw from the Agreement without penalty. If the agreement already has surplus points these can also be used.

➤ **Penalties.** Penalties for not complying with greening will be based on the shortfall in requirement and will range from 0 to 15% for each of the Crop Diversification and EFA rules separately on arable land only i.e. up to a maximum of 30% (100% of the greening payment). From 2017 further administrative penalties for non-compliance will be introduced increasing the penalty to 120% of the greening payment, from 2018 this rises to 125%.

TOP-UP SCHEMES

The Basic Payment Scheme and Greening form the 'foundations' of the new support arrangements, but there will be a system of top-up payments that will be available from the Pillar 1 budget.

- *Young Farmers Scheme*. This is compulsory for member states to implement under Pillar 1. It is funded by a minimum of 2% of the total BPS budget and provides a 25% top-up in the value of entitlements to those under 40 years of age for five years. In Wales and Scotland, the top-up will be equivalent to 25% of the final (2019) payment rate. There will be a limit on how many hectares qualify – the average farm size in the region, but with a minimum and maximum area of 25 and 90 hectares. England and Scotland have gone for the maximum hectares. Wales has gone for the minimum. At 90 hectares the extra payment would be worth around £3,500 per year.

- *Coupled Support*. Countries are able to pay 8% of total BPS funds as coupled payments, plus another 2% for specific aid for protein crops. Countries which have used high levels of coupled support in the past (over 5% of funds) are able to pay 13%, plus the 2% for proteins. Where over 10% of funds have been coupled, a rate higher than 13% may be possible. There will be no coupled payments in England or Wales. The Scottish Government has said around 8% of direct funds will be used for a calf payment similar to the current Scottish Beef Scheme. Animals with 75% beef genetics will receive an annual payment with a higher rate paid on the first 10 animals claimed. Rates are estimated at €170 per head for the first 10 and then €85 for the remainder. In addition (subject to EU approval) there will be a coupled top-up payment for beef producers on the islands in the region of €65 per calf.

- *Redistributive payment*. This is a new concept which provides a top-up in payment on the first few entitlements held by each claimant. It is optional for member states and is limited to the initial 30 hectares, or the average national farm size if larger. The top-up would be capped at 65% of the regional average payment rate, and total funding limited to 30% of the BPS fund. None of the GB regions are taking this up

- *Small Farmers Scheme.* This is optional for member states. Participants would face less stringent cross-compliance regime and not be subject to greening in return for a fixed annual payment. None of the UK administrations have taken this up.

- *Hill Support.* It is possible for member states to pay additional support to hill areas from the Pillar 1 (BPS) budget. This is limited to 5% of total funds and is in the form of a top-up to entitlement values. None of the GB regions are making use of this.

ELIGIBILITY AND RESTRICTIONS ON AID

- *Active Farmer.* To be eligible for the Basic Payment Scheme (BPS) claimants must be an 'active farmer'. The active farmer rule comes in two parts. Firstly, there is a simple 'negative list' of entities not eligible by default for the new Basic Payment , operators of airports, water companies, railways, sports grounds and real estate services. If claimants can prove they have an eligible farming activity they may still be eligible for the BPS. Member states can add to this list with the permission of the EU Commission. Scotland has asked for sporting estates to be added. Secondly, if more than 50% of a claimant's land is in 'areas naturally kept in a state suitable for grazing or cultivation' and they do not comply with the minimum activity rule (see below) the claimant is deemed ineligible.

- *Minimum Agricultural Activity*. Member states are required to set out minimum activity levels on 'areas naturally kept in a state suitable for grazing or cultivation'. Scotland has said it is making every effort to ensure payments are made to active farmers and under the 'Scottish Clause' land with no farming activity will not be eligible. But at the time writing no specific details on how this will be measured had been announced. In Wales there will be stocking rates on saltmarshes and coastal land dunes. In England no specific details had been announced at the time of writing.

- *Minimum Claim size*. The EU's minimum claim size is 1 hectare or €100. Members States can set higher levels if they wish. The minimum BPS claim size in each of the GB regions is

  ➢ England – 5 hectares (up from 1ha)

  ➢ Scotland – 3 hectares (up from 3ha)

  ➢ Wales – 5 hectares (up from 1ha)

- *Degressivity*. The concept of 'degressivity' is new. It is mandatory for all member states. It is a 5% reduction in aid rates above €150,000. The greening element is not affected. Member states can raise levels of degressivity and can be up to 100 per cent and reductions can be banded. Also an optional element within the compromise is the facility for member countries to subtract salaried labour before applying any reduction to direct aid.

  England will levy the minimum EU degressivity requirement of 5% reduction on aid above €150,000.

  Wales has confirmed it is introducing

  o an absolute cap on payments above €300,000;

  o 55% on payments between €250,000 and €300,000,

  o 30% on payments between €200,000 - €250,000 and

  o 15% on payments between €150,000 and €200,000.

  Scotland's Basic Payments will be capped at around £400,000 after labour costs 'part-way' through the transition period. At the time of writing there were no exact dates or details on how labour costs would be calculated.

- *Pillar Transfer*. This replaces modulation. A transfer of funds between the two CAP Pillars is allowed either way, to a maximum of 15% of funds. The rates can be different for each year and can be adjusted in 2018. Any money switched between Pillars has had to be match-funded in the past. This is not required in the BPS. Each of the devolved regions has taken this option at different rates:

  o *England* – 12% with the option to rise to 15% for 2018 and 2019

  o *Scotland* – 9.5%

  o *Wales* – 15%

  o *Northern Ireland* – 0%

- *Financial Discipline*. This is the mechanism by which direct payments are kept within the EU Budget. The threshold for financial discipline will be set at €2,000 (previously it has been €5,000). Payments under this threshold are exempt.

- *External Convergence*. This is the term for all member countries getting a fairer share of Pillar 1 funding. The current plan is that 30% of the gap between a member state's average 'per hectare' payment rate and 90% of the EU average payment should be closed by 2020.

Other Issues

- **Sugar.** Sugar quotas will end on 30th September 2017.

- **Milk Market.** Despite strong pressure from the European Parliament, moves to put some new market management mechanisms in place after the end of milk quotas in March 2015 have been rejected.

- **Conversion Rate.** For countries outside the euro i.e. the UK, the conversion of Pillar 1 aid can be on the average of exchange rates in September. This is instead of simply using the official 30th September exchange rate as currently and should help reduce the effect of currency fluctuations.

TRANSITIONAL MEASURES FOR 2014

As stated in Section 1, the new suite of direct payments including the BPS will commence on the 1st January 2015. But the current CAP legislation is largely written for a period that ran to the end of 2012, meaning the 2013 and 2014 SPS were unaccounted for. However there was no 'sunset' clause in the current CAP legislation so the SPS provisions will carry-on through to 2014. However, the Commission has identified some issues that need addressing to make the SPS work in these years.

Technically, the new BPS legislation started on 1st January 2014, even though the SPS will continue for another year. Which means that parts of the reform applied from 2014 even whilst the old SPS is still operating. The main points are;

- 'external convergence' begins in 2014 - this is the levelling of payment rates between the countries of the EU. It means that the UK funding allocation for the SPS changes – it actually rises from 2014
- the new Degressivity rules apply for 2014 (see previous page)
- all the other main Single Payment rules are rolled-over for another year including entitlements, cross-compliance, IACS, and the Farm Advice Service
- the provisions of the current Rural Development Programmes for 2007-13 are also extended for another year – see Section 4

ESTIMATED PAYMENT RATES

The rates below are estimated by The Andersons Centre for illustrative purposes. This is especially true for Wales and Scotland where every claimant has a different entitlement value based on their history. In these two countries, example farms have been used to try and show how there could be 'winners and losers' as businesses move from the Historic method to a Regional Average Payment.

England
Estimated Flat Rate Area Payments in England

	2013	2014	2015	2016	2017	2018	2019
Lowland £/ha	212.75	202	190	188	187	179	178
(acre)	(86)	(82)	(77)	(76)	(76)	(72)	(72)
Non-Moorland	170.93	162	190	188	187	179	178
SDA £/ha (acre)	(69)	(67)	(77)	(76)	(76)	(72)	(72)
Moorland SDA	29.86	28	54	54	53	51	51
£/ha (acre)	(12)	(11)	(22)	(22)	(217)	(21)	(21)

Converted at €1=£0.83605 in 2013 and €1=80p thereafter. After modulation & financial discipline in 2013. After pillar transfer from 2014 onwards

Wales

In Wales each claimant has a different entitlement value based on their history, over the next five years these will change so that each entitlement in a region has the same value. There will be winners and losers. The first table below estimates how payments will change over the next five years in each of the three regions using a gross entitlement value of €500, €250 and €60 per entitlement in 2013 for the three regions Disadvantaged/Lowland, SDA and Moorland above 400m respectively. By 2019 all entitlements in the same region will have the same value irrespective of their rate prior to 2015.

Estimated Payments for the regions in Wales

	2013	2014	2015	2016	2017	2018	2019
DA/Lowland £/ha	361	306	279	253	228	203	178
(acre)	(146)	(124)	(113)	(102)	(92)	(82)	(72)
SDA £/ha (acre)	181	153	152	151	149	148	147
	(73)	(62)	(62)	(61)	(60)	(60)	(59)
Moorland (above	45	37	32	28	23	19	14
400m) £/ha (acre)	(18)	(15)	(13)	(11)	(9)	(8)	(6)

Converted at €1=£0.83605 in 2013 and €1=80p thereafter. After modulation & financial discipline in 2013. After pillar transfer from 2014 onwards

The table below uses some example farms to show how the payments may change for three different businesses. *Note: They show the average rate per hectare. In practice where a farm's eligible land crosses payment regions, entitlements will have different rates depending on which region they were established in.*

Example A - has 150ha all in the Lowland/Disadvantaged payment region. The business' gross entitlement value in 2013 was €500 per entitlement. This could be an intensive beef finisher or dairy unit.

Example B - a 150ha mixed beef and sheep farm. In 2015 70ha fall within the Lowland/Disadvantaged payment area, 50ha within the Severely Disadvantaged Area (SDA) payment region and 30ha in the Moorland area. In 2013 the gross entitlement value was €250/entitlement.

Example C - is an extensive sheep farm with 300ha of moorland, but 150ha fall below the 400m moorland limit and are therefore in the SDA payment region as from 2015. In 2013 the gross entitlement value was €100/entitlement.

Estimated Payments for example farms in Wales

	2013	2014	2015	2016	2017	2018	2019
Example A	361	320	292	265	238	212	186
£/ha (acre)	(146)	(130)	(118)	(107)	(96)	(86)	(75)
Example B	182	160	156	152	148	145	141
£/ha (acre)	(74)	(65)	(63)	(62)	(60)	(59)	(57)
Example C	73	64	68	72	76	80	84
£/ha (acre)	(30)	(26)	(28)	(29)	(31)	(32)	(34)

Converted at €1=£0.83605 in 2013 and €1=80p thereafter. After modulation & financial discipline in 2013. After pillar transfer from 2014 onwards

Scotland

In Scotland, similar to Wales, each business has its own entitlement value based on their farming history. The first table below estimates how payments will change over the next five years in each of the three regions using a gross entitlement value of €500, €100 and €30 per entitlement in 2013 for the three regions Arable & Grassland, Rough Grazing and Poor Rough Grazing respectively. By 2019 all entitlements in the same region will have the same value irrespective of their rate prior to 2015. Note: there is a proposal to introduce coupled support of around €25 per ewe in the Poor Rough Grazing category.

Estimated Payments for regions in Scotland

	2013	2014	2015	2016	2017	2018	2019
Arable &	350	323	292	262	232	203	174
Grassland	(142)	(131)	(118)	(106)	(94)	(82)	(70)
£/ha (acre)							
Rough	71	63	56	48	41	34	27
Grazing	(29)	(25)	(23)	(19)	(17)	(14)	(11)
£/ha (acre)							
Poor Rough	22	19	17	14	12	10	8
Grazing	(9)	(8)	(8)	(6)	(5)	(4)	(3)
£/ha (acre)							

Converted at €1=£0.83605 in 2013 and €1=80p thereafter. After modulation & financial discipline in 2013. After pillar transfer from 2014 onwards

The example farms below illustrate how claimant's payments may change over the next five years. They are for illustrative purposes only. *Note: They show the average rate per hectare. In practice where a farm's eligible land crosses payment regions, entitlements will have different rates depending on which region they were established in.*

Example A - is a 150ha intensive beef finisher or dairy farm. In 2013 the gross entitlement value was €400/entitlement. In 2015 all the land will be in region 1, arable and grassland

Example B – is a 150ha mixed beef and sheep farm with some arable land. In 2013 the gross entitlement value was €200/entitlement. In 2015 70ha will fall in region 1, arable and grassland; 50ha in region 2, rough grazing; with 30ha falling within region 3, poor rough grazing.

Example C – the final example is an extensive sheep farm, comprising 300ha which will all fall within the poor rough grazing category in 2015. In 2013 the gross entitlement value was €50/entitlement.

Estimated Payments for example farms in Scotland

	2013	2014	2015	2016	2017	2018	2019
Example A	281	253	235	219	202	186	170
£/ha (acre)	(114)	(102)	(95)	(89)	(82)	(75)	(69)
Example B	141	126	119	111	104	97	90
£/ha (acre)	(57)	(51)	(48)	(45)	(42)	(39)	(36)
Example C	36	32	27	22	18	13	8
£/ha (acre)	(15)	(13)	(11)	(9)	(7)	(5)	(3)

Converted at €1=£0.83605 in 2013 and €1=80p thereafter. After modulation & financial discipline in 2013. After pillar transfer from 2014 onwards

5. RURAL DEVELOPMENT

RURAL DEVELOPMENT POST 2014

A new set of national Rural Development programmes is required for the period 2014-2020. Due to the delay in EU budget negotiations and CAP reform, member states have not been able to finalise their Rural Development Programmes in time for the 2014 scheme year. England, Scotland, Wales and Northern Ireland sent theirs for EU Commission approval during summer 2014. At the time of writing these had not received EU approval and therefore specific scheme details were not available, but the sections below give an idea of where funding will be channelled. The previous axes are replaced by 6 'priorities' (LEADER will be retained);

1. fostering knowledge transfer in agriculture and forestry
2. enhancing agricultural competitiveness and enhancing farm viability
3. promoting food chain organisation and risk management in agriculture
4. restoring, preserving and enhancing ecosystems dependent on agriculture
5. promoting resource efficiency and supporting a shift towards a low-carbon and climate-resilient agriculture
6. promoting social inclusion, poverty reduction and economic development in rural areas.

The priorities will contribute to achieving the following objectives:

- The competitiveness of agriculture,
- The sustainable management of natural resources, and climate action,
- A balanced territorial development of rural areas

As many of the current scheme contracts are for more than one year and will carry on for many years until the Agreements are brought to an end (and similar schemes will continue into the next 'period' i.e. Glastir in Wales) brief details of these schemes are also included in the sections below.

ENGLAND 2014 – 2020

In England the new Rural Development Programme will commence on 1st January 2015. Over the next seven years £3.5 billion will be invested in a range of schemes to improve the environment and grow the rural economy. The schemes will centre around three themes:

- The environment (87% of funding)
- Increasing productivity (4%)
- Rural economic growth (9%)

The Environment

The majority of funding will continue to be available for Agri-environmental schemes (£3.1bn). The existing Environmental Stewardship Scheme (ESS) and England Woodland Grant Scheme (EWGS) is being replaced with a single new Environmental Land Management Scheme (NELMS) (this name will change). The aim of the scheme will be to support measures to 'restore, preserve and enhance the natural environment'. The scheme will be open to farmers, foresters and land managers. It will provide three tiers of funding:

- **Site Specific Agreements** – These will be similar to the current HLS agreements, but are expected to be by invitation only. They will offer agreements to only the best environmental sites.

- *Area Specific Agreements* – Priorities for different areas will be identified. Agreements will be scored against these and those offering the best outcomes will be given an agreement. Collaboration is not a pre-requisite.
- *Annual Small Scale Grants* – Funding up to a maximum of £5,000 will be available for capital items such as hedge laying, coppicing and gapping up, or stonewall restoration. This is expected to be open to all, not just those with an Agreement.

Site Specific and Area Specific agreements will normally run for five years, although ten year agreements may be offered if benefits will take longer to achieve. There will be a choice of management options and capital items to choose from depending on the agreement. There will only be one agreement per holding, with no 'underpinning' and there will not be any separate 'strands' for uplands or organics, although there may be specific options for these types of land managers to choose from. The scheme will open in 2015 for applications, the first Agreements will start on 1st January 2016.

At the time of writing specific scheme details were still awaited. These are expected towards the end of 2014.

Increasing Productivity

In the region £140 million will be available to improve the competitiveness of farming and forestry businesses. They will have to bid for funds which innovate, use new technology and the latest research which will improve skills and training in the business. Co-operation and collaboration with other farmers, foresters and others in the land-based sectors together with projects which benefit the environment in a number of ways i.e. tackle environmental problems whilst increasing productivity will be able to bid for a share of the funds. More information will be available on GOV.UK towards the end of 2014.

Rural Economic Growth

Funding may be available through Local Enterprise Partnerships (LEPs) or LEADER Local Action Groups. LEPs will have £177 million to spend. Each LEP will draw up their own priorities around the following themes;

- Knowledge and skills
- Support for small or micro-businesses
- Broadband and renewable energy
- Promotion of rural tourism.
  Information on the different LEPs plans will be made available on GOV.UK

A new LEADER scheme (worth £138 million) will commence on 1st January 2015. This funds programmes run by local community partnerships called Local Action Groups (LAGs) and funds projects which improve the rural economy and create jobs. More information can be found at www.rdpenetwork.defra.gov.uk.

WALES 2014 - 2020

Over the next seven years £953m will be available through the Welsh Rural Development Programme to be invested in a range of schemes to;

- Increase the productivity, diversity and efficiency of farming and forestry businesses. Improving their competitiveness and resilience and helping them move from the 'historic' system of payments to the flat rate system and reducing their reliance on subsidies.
- Improve the environment by encouraging sustainable land management practices and the sustainable management of our natural resources and climate change

- Promote strong, sustainable rural economic growth and encourage community-led local development.

The Welsh Rural Development Plan proposals are expected to get EU approval during autumn/winter 2014 with any new schemes ready to commence at the start of 2015. Funds will be split between five key elements;

- Area-based measures (60% of funds)
- Investment measures (15%)
- Human and Social Capital measures (11%)
- LEADER and local development (10%)
- Technical Assistance (4%)

Area Based Measures

The majority of funding will be available for the Area-based schemes and this will be through a continuation of the current Glastir Programme (see below) with a few new proposals which have been submitted to the European Commission for approval together with the wider Welsh Rural Development plan. Key points from the proposals include;

- Farmers will not be required to participate in Glastir Entry to be eligible to enter other Glastir Schemes
- Online applications will be rolled out in 2015 and will become compulsory in 2016
- The success of the Commons Development Officers will be built upon to encourage collaborative agreements within Glastir Advanced and Glastir Habitat Network
- The Glastir Efficiency Grant will be replaced by a Sustainable Production Grant which will be available to improve economic and environmental performance through capital investment across three themes; nutrient, energy and water efficiency
- The introduction of a small woodland planting scheme, to fund plantings for schemes that are smaller than those eligible under Glastir Woodland Creation
- The introduction of a new Organic Farming Scheme (see below for details) within Glastir.

Glastir

From 2012 Glastir replaced the previous suite of environmental schemes; Tir Gofal, Tir Cynnal, Tir Mynydd, Organic Farming Scheme/Organic Farming Conversion Scheme and Better Woodlands for Wales. Under the Rural Development Programme 2014-2020 Glastir will continue to be the main scheme through which funding for area based measures will be channelled.

Glastir has five elements;

- Glastir Entry (GE)
- Glastir Advanced (GA)
- Glastir Commons (GC)
- Glastir Woodlands (GW)
- Glastir Organic (GO) (New in 2015)

Note the Glastir Efficiency Grants (GEGs) will not be available under the WRDP 2014-2020. Claims for GEGs must be submitted by 31st December 2014

Glastir Entry is open to all farmers in Wales. The first agreements under the new scheme commenced in 2012. Glastir Entry is a whole farm entry level management scheme. Contracts are for five years and applicants must enter all the eligible land they will have full management control of for the full five years. Applicants have to obtain a points threshold for their farm which is either 34 (standard entry level threshold) x total hectarage or 17 (reduced entry level threshold) x total hectarage. To reach the threshold applicants choose from a number of management options. Each option is allocated a set number of points. Occupants can also opt to choose from a list of options in the Regional Package. These are considered to offer the greatest environmental value for their area. If the regional options are chosen the applicant will receive 10% more points per option. Dairy farmers can increase their points by 10% if they choose management options within the 'Dairy Package'. Under Glastir 2014-2020 there are proposals to remove a number of options and change others. Refer to up the most up to date scheme details.

Going forward application windows have been abolished and applications are accepted throughout the year, with a yearly cut-off date. Applications received by 30th September 2014 will have a January 2015 start date. Payment for Glastir Entry is £34 per hectare for all land in the scheme or £17 per hectare for reaching the reduced threshold. There are no different payments for land within the LFA. Claim for payment is made annually on the SAF, the first claim was in 2012.

To be eligible for the scheme, producers also need to comply with the Whole Farm Code; 13 standards of environmental practice. This attracts an additional payment of:

0 – 20 hectares	£15/ha
21 – 50 hectares	£8/ha
51 - 100 hectares	£2.75/ha

Glastir Advanced addresses concerns over soil carbon management, water quality, water quantity management, biodiversity, the historic environment and improving access. Land is assessed against target maps. At this level management is of a prescribed nature, payments consist of both capital and non-capital items. Farmers used to be required to enter GE before they apply to the GA but under proposals put to the European Commission for approval this requirement may be abolished. Those with a reduced entry level threshold are not eligible.

Glastir Commons is available for those who hold rights on Common Land and who have joined together to establish a Grazing Association.

Glasir Woodlands provides funds for woodlands under the Glastir Woodland Creation Grant (WCG) and the Glastir Woodland Management (GWM) scheme. Under the WCG there are three grants; Establishment grants (£500 - £3500/ha, 1st yr), fencing grants (£3.15/m) and Woodland Creation Premium (£300/ha per year for 15 years for farmers). Under the GWM scheme payments are available for managing existing woodlands over 0.5ha. Payments range from £54 to £120/ha. There are proposals for a small woodland planting grant to be made available in the new WRDP 2014 -2020.

Glastir Organic brings support for organic farming in Wales under the Glastir 'umbrella'. Proposals for a new scheme have been sent for approval by the European Commission together with the new Rural Development Plan. Although full details are still unknown at the time of writing the proposed payments rates and key elements are;

- the application window is due to open late summer or early autumn 2014 with agreements commencing on 1st January 2015.
- the new Glastir Organic Scheme will be a stand-alone scheme and farmers joining the organic scheme will remain eligible for other parts of Glastir
- support for ongoing training and skills development will be available
- applicants will need to show they have a business plan in place
- the maximum area supported per holding will be 400 Ha
- conversion and maintenance contracts will be for five years

- Unlike the previous organic scheme there isn't any specific payment for arable crops, but other elements of Glastir have arable cropping options which organic farmers can make use of.
- Land with more than 40% down to horticultural crops in a temporary grassland rotation, as well as top fruit producers will qualify for the highest payments.
- The enclosed land category includes all enclosed lowland. Rough grazing includes enclosed upland, sole grazed commons, grazed woodland, as well as lowland bogs and heaths

The table below summarises the proposed payments;

Glastir Organic Payment Rates

	Conversion £/Ha		Maintenance £/Ha	Certification* £/ha
	Years 1-2	Years 3-5	Years 1-5	
Horticultural	600	400	400	80
Enclosed Land	130	65	65	10
Rough Grazing	15	15	15	3

* Certification costs will be capped at £500 per contract

Note at the time of writing these rates are still subject to EU approval.

Investment Measures

Funding under this element will include:

- ***Investments in physical assets*** - including a scheme to provide grants or loans for the processing and marketing of agricultural products conditional upon the appropriate training and skills being reached

- ***Farm & Business Development*** – funding for the successor to the Young Entrants Support Scheme (see below), grants to support the processing and marketing of non-agricultural products. Support for the farm household to diversify into non-agricultural activities.

- ***Quality Schemes*** – to support entry into Quality schemes

- ***Risk Management*** – subsidising insurance that will extend to losses incurred due to bad weather

- ***Restoration of Forestry Potential*** – support for woodland and habitat restoration to mitigate natural disasters.

Human & Social Capital

The main interventions proposed under this element include:

- ***Knowledge Transfer and Innovation*** – including professional Development and training, demonstration, coaching, workshops, specialist events and short-term farm exchanges study tours aimed at SMEs and micro enterprises. This is likely to build on the current Farming Connect service (see below)

- ***Advisory services*** – expanding on the current Farm Advice Service (see below) beyond just cross-compliance to provide the entry point to the other investment support available under the WRDP

- **Co-operation** – support for co-operation between businesses to aid short supply chains and local markets including those for biomass production. Also there is a proposal to support new and emerging Producer Groups.

LEADER & Local Development

LEADER Local Action Groups (LAGs) will be able to use a community-led local development approach to encourage innovation and achieve rural development. There is also a proposal for a Rural Community Development Fund to tackle rural poverty via community based renewable energy schemes, energy efficiency, etc. including access to broadband.

Technical Assistance

Under this element funds will be available for:

- **Wales Rural Network** – building on the existing scheme to help communicate the opportunities available under the WRDP

- **Glastir Support** – Farmers will be able to get Technical advice and the existing Commons Development Officers' roles will be expanded

WRDP Transitional Measures 2014

Glastir will remain open, applications received by 30th September 2014 will be offered a contract starting on 1st January 2015

The *Young Entrants Support Scheme* (YESS) started in 2010. The scheme has been extended for the 2015/16 period. Applications will be accepted from 1st September 2014 until 30th November 2014. It is available to young farmers (less than 40 years) who are or have just set up as head of a holding for the first time. It provides grant aid of 50% of eligible expenditure up to a maximum of £15,000 whichever is less. It also provides access to a dedicated Young Entrant's Business Enabler Service for advice on training, knowledge transfer and joint venture opportunities together with sign-posted access to funded mentoring services from established farmers and/or processors.

The other main support for farmers in Wales is through *Farming Connect*. This offers one-to-one support, guidance, advice and training. Up to five days subsidised support is available to produce a Whole Farm Plan. A subsidised Skills Development Programme is delivered by Lantra to provide access to practical and regulation linked courses. Through the Farm Advisory Service, help is provided to meet cross compliance measures.

SCOTLAND 2014 - 2020

The proposed Scotland Rural Development Programme (SRDP) 2014-2020 was submitted to the European Commission (EC) in June 2014. The EC is expected to take in the region of six months to consider and approve the program. The aim is for the new SRDP to be open from January 2015. The specific priorities of the new SRDP 2014-2020 are;

- Enhancing the rural economy
- Supporting agricultural businesses
- Protecting and improving the natural environment
- Addressing the impact of climate change
- Supporting rural communities

Over the next seven years there will be about £1.3bn available. The majority of funds will go towards supporting those farming in the hills and agri-environment payments. Below is a summary of the proposed schemes and the budgets available to fund them;

Less Favoured Area Support Scheme (LFASS) (£459m)

This scheme provides essential support to fragile farming businesses in remote and constrained rural areas. The current scheme (see below) will continue, however it will be reviewed and a replacement scheme and designation will be in place by 2018 when the new Areas with Natural Constraints (ANCs) replace the existing LFAs. This scheme will be delivered by the Scottish Government's Rural Payments and Inspections Division (RPID).

Forestry Grant Scheme (£252m)

There will be a range of grants for woodland creation, agroforestry, tree health, woodland improvement, processing and marketing and sustainable management of forests. This scheme will be delivered by RPID and Forestry Commission Scotland.

Agri-environment Climate Scheme (£350m)

The aim of this scheme is to support environmental actions to maintain and enhance Scotland's rich and varied natural environment. It will provide targeted support for land managers to undertake management and capital work for environmental purposes. It will continue with some of the practices currently supported under Rural Priorities (see below). Support for organic conversion and maintenance is expected to be included under this scheme. There will also be £10million of targeted support for slurry stores and £6million for footpaths and other works to support access management. This scheme will be delivered by RPID and Scottish Natural Heritage.

Support for Co-operative Action (£10m)

This will provide funds to help rural businesses work together to deliver larger environmental benefits than could be achieved by businesses on their own. This scheme will be delivered by RPID, Scottish Natural Heritage and Forestry Commission Scotland.

Beef package (£45m)

The aim of this scheme is to see economic and environmental improvements in the beef sector. There will be £32.5 million for support towards genetic resilience, plus targeted support for the beef sector through Knowledge Transfer and the Innovation Fund and the Advisory Service. This scheme will be delivered by RPID, Scottish Natural Heritage and Forestry Commission Scotland.

New Entrants Support (£20m)

This scheme will provide start-up grants for new entrant young farmers of up to 40 years old. Further support will be available for new entrants, regardless of age, to access capital funding to improve their business. This support will be delivered by RPID, Scottish Natural Heritage and Forestry Commission Scotland. Additional support and mentoring will be delivered through the Advisory Service.

Crofting Support Scheme (£14m)

Crofting will continue to be supported under the new SRDP. This scheme will provide grants to crofters to take forward improvements on their crofts which will help to sustain their business. This scheme will be delivered by RPID, Scottish Natural Heritage and Forestry Commission Scotland.

Small Farms Support Scheme (£6m)

This scheme will offer targeted support for small farms that face similar issues as crofters regarding sustainability. The definition of small farms is currently being developed based on discussions with stakeholders. This scheme will be delivered by RPID, Scottish Natural Heritage and Forestry Commission Scotland.

Food and Drink Support (£70m)
In recognition of the fact that the food and drink industry is a key growth sector for Scotland. This scheme will continue to provide support for SMEs in the food and drink sector with start-up grants for new enterprises, and business development grants. This scheme will be delivered through the Scottish Government's Food and Drink Division.

Advisory Service (£20m)
The aim is to have this service available from 2016. It will build on the support already provided under the Whole Farm Review Scheme, providing advice and assistance to farmers, crofters, forest holders and other land managers. This service will be tendered out, with tenders being issued early 2015 ready for a 2016 start.

Knowledge Transfer and Innovation Fund (KTIF) (£10m)
KTIF will assist in the sharing and implementation of innovative ways of improving working practices along with continuing support for Monitor farms. There will be a direct application process for this scheme.

LEADER (£86m)
LEADER enables individuals, communities and businesses to come together to design and implement local development strategies. The LEADER Programme will provide support for the implementation of Local Development Strategies across Scotland. Support will be made available through Local Action Groups who will work with communities and businesses to help them achieve their ambitions. £20million has been allocated for specific support for small business growth, including £10 million for farm and croft diversification, which will also be made available through LEADER.

Technical Assistance (£15m provisional)
Including the Scottish Rural Network for supporting and promoting rural development through the sharing of ideas and best practice. This includes SRDP implementation, evaluation and monitoring.

Broadband (£9m)
Funding will be available to provide support for delivering broadband in rural areas. Delivery options are currently being explored.

Application Process
Under the next Rural Development Regulation there is a proposal to change the application process. A part from applications to the LFASS, there will be two levels of entry;
- Level 1 – applications for grants up to £75,000 with continuous local approval. For forestry the threshold will remain at £750,000
- Level 2 – applications for grants above £75,000 which will be considered nationally by an expert panel. Applications will also be limited to one per holding, per scheme, per year. This is to ensure that funding is spread more fairly in the future.

NORTHERN IRELAND 2014-2020

The Northern Ireland Rural Development Programme (NIRDP) 2014-2020 will have a budget of £623m, this will be allocated across three specific areas:

- **Competitiveness of Agriculture (£287m)** – The Farm Business Improvement Scheme will be the main umbrella scheme. Falling under this will be a portfolio of knowledge transfer and targeted capital investment, central to this will be the Business Investment Scheme (BIS) with £220m of funding available.

- ***Protecting the rural environment (£256)*** – The majority of funding in this area will be allocated to agri-environmental measures through the Environmental Farming Scheme (173.5m). There will also be funding for LFAs and woodland creation and expansion.

- ***Developing rural economies (£80)*** - Funds will be available for a range of measures aimed at encouraging the economic development of rural areas; Rural Basic Services Scheme, Rural Broadband Scheme, Rural Tourism Scheme, Village Renewal Scheme, All Island co-operation scheme, plus running costs for Local Action Groups.

RURAL DEVELOPMENT UNTIL 2014

Rural Development, or Pillar 2, supports environmental protection and improvement of the countryside, and encourages sustainable enterprises and thriving rural communities. The Rural Development regulation sets the legislative framework across the EU, providing a menu of schemes and aid from which member states can choose from. The previous Rural Development Regulation ended on 31st December 2013, under this a range of support measures were allowed under four 'axes', with a minimum percentage of each member state's budget in each:

- Axis 1 Competitiveness (min 10%): training young farmers, advice, food quality, etc.

- Axis 2 Land Management (min 25%): environmental schemes, hill farming (LFA support), forestry and animal welfare.

- Axis 3 Diversification (min 10%): non-farming business, tourism, rural services etc.

- Axis 4 LEADER schemes (min 5%): local partnership programmes for specific problems in certain areas.

Each country had a 7-year Rural Development programme from 2007 to 2013. A brief description is given below as schemes started in that time will mostly continue to completion through the next RDP.

ENGLAND 2007 - 2013

The next section outlines the schemes currently or recently operating in England under the Rural Development Regulation from 2007-2013. The schemes are now closed to new applicants. Many are multi annual Agreements and will continue until their contract ends.

Axis 2 Schemes

Administered by Natural England (NE) and the Forestry Commission and received approximately 80% of funding, the available schemes were:

- Environmental Stewardship Scheme (ESS)

- English Woodland Grant Scheme (EWGS)

- Energy Crops Scheme (ECS)

Environmental Stewardship Scheme (ESS)

The Environmental Stewardship Scheme started in 2005. The scheme is now closed to new applications. It comprises four elements:

- Entry Level Stewardship (ELS)

- Organic Entry Level Stewardship (OELS)

- Higher Level Stewardship (HLS)

- Uplands Entry Level Scheme (UELS)

Changes to the ESS came into force on 1st January 2013 for all new and renewed Agreements. This follows results from the Making Environmental Stewardship More Effective (MESME) project aimed at improving the environmental outcomes from the ESS. The Fourth Edition handbook is the basis for all Agreements from 1st January 2013.

ELS: was designed to encourage a large number of farmers across a wide area to adopt simple environmental management practices such as hedgerow management, stone wall maintenance, low input grassland, buffer strips and arable options. The scheme was non-competitive and open to all as long as scheme requirements were met. Points were awarded for each management option adopted. There was a large range of management options including; hedgerow management, one side 11 points/100m (8 points from 1st Jan 2013), both sides 22 points/100m (16 points from 1st Jan 2013); 2m, 4m, 6m buffer strips attracting 300, 400 and 400 (255, 340, 340 from 1st Jan 2013) points/ha respectively; overwintered stubbles gain 120 points/ha and beetle banks 580 points/ha.

Applicants had to achieve 30 points per hectare to be accepted into ELS. An annual payment of £30 per hectare is made half yearly in arrears. ELS agreements last for five years. Above the moorland line in the LFAs the payment is £8 per hectare for parcels of land over 15ha.

OELS: was open to all farmers with land registered as organic or in conversion and not receiving aid under the Organic Farming Scheme (closed). OELS had similar options to those under ELS and participants receive annual payments of £30 per hectare for carrying out options on the organic land plus an additional £30 per hectare (organic land only) for farming the land organically. There was also an option to apply for organic conversion with a payment of £600 per hectare per year (for 3 years) for top fruit orchards and £175 per hectare per year (for 2 years) for improved land. OELS agreements last for five years.

HLS: was targeted towards achieving significant environmental benefits in high priority areas with the objectives being wildlife conservation, protecting historic environments, maintaining and enhancing landscape quality, encouraging public access and resource protection. It was a competitive application. Payment depends on the management options adopted, and can include a mix of capital items and per hectare payments. HLS agreements were normally for ten years with a break clause for either party after five years.

UELS: Upland ELS replaced the Hill Farm Allowance (HFA) scheme in 2010. The scheme was open to those who farmed within the Severely Disadvantaged Areas (SDAs). Farmers were able to have an ELS agreement over all of their land and enter all their SDA land into the UELS. There are different points targets depending on the classification of the land, see the table below. Producers have to achieve the combined total.

Land Category	ELS Points/ha	UELS Points/ha	Combined Points/ha
SDA Moorland Parcels			
15ha and above	8	15	23
Below 15ha	30	32	62
SDA Land below the Moorland Line	30	32	62

Similar to the ELS, applicants had to achieve the points target by selecting from a menu of 'options'. Once achieved the points equate to the level of payment. SDA Moorland parcels 15ha and above receive £23/ha; all other SDA land receives £62/ha. By meeting the requirements on Moorland parcels above 15ha applicants receive 15 points per ha. By meeting the requirements on Moorland parcels below 15ha and other SDA land the producer receives 11 points per ha. The additional points needed to reach the target must be made up by using the 'options' menu.

The scheme was not available to farmers who had other agri-environmental scheme agreements still running e.g. CSS and ESA schemes. In order that these farmers did not lose out now the HFA has finished, from 2011 there was an Uplands Transitional Payment (UTP). Payments were made to farmers who have an on-going Countryside Stewardship Scheme (CSS) or Environmentally Sensitive Areas (ESA) agreement and who extensively graze eligible land with sheep breeding flocks and suckler cows but not dairy farming or other enterprises such as deer farming.

The 2014 UTP payment (received in March 2014) was £16.62/ha for Moorland and Common Land, Severely Disadvantaged Land (SDA) received £43.88/ha. The full rate is paid on the first 350ha, half rate on the next 350ha. No payment is made on land in excess of 700ha. The 2014 payment was the last year, the UTP is no longer available

English Woodland Grant Scheme (EWGS)

The previous Woodland Grant Scheme (WGS) and the Farm Woodland Premium Scheme (FWPS) were replaced by the English Woodland Grant Scheme (EWGS), administered by Natural England and the Forestry Commission. Under the new Rural Development Regulation for England (RDPE) woodland grant options will be within the New Environmental Land Management Scheme (NELMS).

Energy Crops Scheme (ECS)

The Energy Crops Scheme provided aid for the planting of Short Rotation Coppice (SRC) and Miscanthus (elephant grass). There was a minimum application size of 3 hectares. Agreements were normally for five years. Producers must have been able to demonstrate that there was an end-use for the crop. Grant aid is paid at 50% of the actual expenditure. Applicants submit invoices of their actual costs and are required to provide estimates of likely costs as part of the application process.

Axes 1, 3 and 4 Schemes

The delivery of the socio-economic elements of the RDPE 2007-2013 was managed through the Defra RDPE Delivery Team. More recently key priorities have been improving the competitiveness of farming, skills & knowledge transfer and development of the rural economy. This has been centred on the following schemes:

- Farming and Forestry Improvement Scheme (FFIS)
- Rural Economy Grant (REG)
- Skills and Knowledge Transfer
- Rural Community Broadband Fund
- Paths for Communities
- Dairy Fund

In addition Local Action Groups (LAGs) have been able to support local projects, communities and businesses. These schemes are now closed, under the new Rural Development Plan for England, new schemes are being drawn up using the lessons learnt from FFIS and REG and the other schemes (see earlier section). More details will become available throughout winter 2014.

Farming and Forestry Improvement Scheme (FFIS)

The Farming and Forestry Improvement Scheme aimed to make businesses more profitable and resilient whilst reducing the impact of farming on the environment. The scheme focused on five themes:

- Nutrient management
- Energy efficiency
- Water management
- Animal health and welfare
- Forestry

Grant rates of between 15% and 50% were for projects which met one or more of the above objectives. The application process was in rounds.

Rural Economy Grant (REG)

The Rural Economy Grant provided grants for large scale projects which would result in a significant change in performance – 'game-changing' for farming, forestry, agri-food businesses and micro businesses in rural areas of England. Funding up to 40% of eligible costs was available. The minimum grant was £25,000 up to about £1 million.

SCOTLAND 2007 - 2013

Rural Development Contracts

Previously the SRDP was delivered through a single mechanism known as Rural Development Contracts (RDCs), this was divided into three tiers:

Tier I: The Single Payment Scheme – through the cross-compliance requirements a basic level of environmental protection, food safety and animal welfare is provided.

Tier II: Land Manager's Options - Farmers chose from a menu of options with application at the same time as the Single Application Form (SAF).

Tier III: Rural Priorities – This element was discretionary and competitive and it covered agri-environment, organic, farm business, forestry, young entrants and processing and marketing. Some of these agreements will still be running, but is closed to new applications. Those with an agri-environment or organic scheme which ended in 2013 were given a one year extension.

Less Favoured Area Support Scheme (LFASS)

Under the SRDP 2014-2020 there are proposals to continue the LFASS in a similar format to the current scheme, with a new scheme and land designations being introduced from 2018. It is recognised that there is a problem with destocking in the remotest hill areas. Various policy options have been considered, the latest changes were made to the LFASS in 2011. These included an increase in the payment rates for the Standard Areas and an update of the historic reference on which payments are based. At the same time a new grazing category was introduced for land not currently designated, together with a new variable minimum stocking rate to ensure payments are targeted towards active producers.

The LFASS has been applied for on the annual SAF application. This is expected to continue on the Basic Payment Scheme application form. Eligible hectares are adjusted for non-ring fenced dairy land, variable minimum or maximum stocking density restrictions, grazing category and an enterprise mix multiplier. The adjusted hectares are then paid at the payment rates below depending on the grazing category and location of the land. *There is a minimum payment of £385.*

LFASS Payment Rates

£ per adjusted Hectare	2010		From 2011	
Grazing Category	A & B	C & D	A & B	C & D
Very Fragile	71.35	63.00	71.35	63.00
Fragile	62.10	54.51	62.10	54.51
Standard	37.80	32.50	52.16	34.13

Whole Farm Review

The other main support for farmers in Scotland is the Whole Farm Review, which grants aid for a business review, action plan and implementation, up to £2,400.

ENVIRONMENTAL SCHEME PAYMENTS

There are many agri-environment schemes across the UK which provide annual payments to farmers. Some are now closed to new applicants but were available across all the devolved regions such as the Environmentally Sensitive Areas (ESA) schemes and support for farmers in the LFAs. The main agri-environmental schemes now are Environmental Stewardship in England, In Wales Tir Gofal and Tir Cynnal has been replaced by Glastir, and the Less Favoured Area Support Scheme and Rural Priorities in Scotland. In England the New Environmental Land Management Scheme (NELMS) will be introduced in 2015. The table below summarises the latest payments made for environmental schemes.

Environment Schemes Payments, 2013 (provisional)

		£ Million
England:	Organic Farming Scheme (c)	0
	Environmentally Sensitive Areas (c)	20
	Countryside Stewardship (c)	21
	Uplands Transitional Payment (c)	3
	Environmental Stewardship Scheme	370
Wales:	Organic Farming Scheme (c)	4
	Environmentally Sensitive Areas(c)	0
	Tir Mynydd (c)	0
	Tir Gofal (c)	12
	Tir Cynnal (c)	4
	Glastir	35
Scotland:	Organic Aid Scheme (c)	0
	Environmentally Sensitive Areas (c)	0
	Rural Stewardship (c)	0
	Less Favoured Area Support Scheme	66
	Land Management Contract Scheme (c)	0
	Land Managers Options	6
	Rural Priorities	34
N. Ireland	Organic Farming Scheme (c)	0
	New Environmentally Sensitive Areas	6
	Countryside Management Scheme	20
	Less Favoured Area Compensatory Allowances	25

Source: DEFRA, SGRPID, DARD, WAGDEPC. Agriculture in the UK 2013.
   (c) Schemes that are now closed to new entrants.

IV.   LABOUR

1.   LABOUR COST

There are 8 Bank Holidays in 2015; New Year's Day, Good Friday April 3, Easter Monday April 6, May Bank Holiday May 4, Spring Bank Holiday May 25, Summer Bank Holiday August 31, Christmas Day December 25 and December 28.

STATUTORY MINIMUM WAGE RATES - ENGLAND

The Agricultural Wages Board (England & Wales) ended in 2013 (Scotland, which has its own AWB is not affected). There will be few or no changes to existing agricultural workers contracts, changes to employment contracts should be made with mutual consent.

Workers Employed before 30th September 2013

Terms and Conditions under the Agricultural Wages Order (AWO) remain (unless there is a variation to the employee's terms and conditions of employment). For workers employed prior to 30th September 2013 contracts must not be changed without the consent of both parties. For workers classified as Initial Grade under the 2012 AWO and employed before the 30th September 2013 the minimum wage will increase in line with the National Minimum Wage.

Workers Employed after 30th September 2013

Agricultural workers employed since the 1st October 2013 are subject to the National Minimum Wage (NMW) as follows:

Minimum Wage	21 and over	18-20	Under 18	Apprentice*
1 October 2013 to 30 Sept 2014	£6.31	£5.03	£3.72	£2.68
1 October 2014 to 30 Sept 2015	£6.50	£5.13	£3.79	£2.73

*   *This is for apprentices under 19 or in their first year.*

There are some occasions when the minimum wage is applicable in agriculture. Many farmers are paying a higher wage than legally necessary to attract greater calibre staff. More qualified workers such as machinery operators and livestock handlers command a premium.

Employers can decide on the rate of pay increases and other employment related benefits, with no standard increases dependent on skill level, responsibilities or qualifications. Premium overtime rates and night work are not necessary. From October 2014 accommodation offset is set at £5.08 per day. Dog allowance is also not compulsory but may be covered by expenses. Overtime rates are not statutory for new recruits.

STATUTORY MINIMUM WAGE RATES - SCOTLAND

The Scottish Agricultural Wages Board (SAWB) continues to operate. It has proposed the following rates to apply from the 1st October 2014;

* £6.50/hour for those in the first 26 weeks of employment
* £7.14/hour for those employed for more than 26 weeks by the same employer
* £3.96/hour for workers who undertake a Level 2 Apprenticeship in Agriculture

STATUTORY MINIMUM WAGE RATES - WALES

Whilst the abolition of the Agricultural Wages Board applied to both England and Wales, the Welsh Government has decided to establish its own Wages Board for Wales. Details of the news provisions are not yet available. In the meantime, the rates and rules of the final Agricultural Wages Board continue to apply in Wales. Payment rates are set out in the table below;

STATUTORY MINIMUM WAGE RATES - WALES

Normal Hours (Standard Rates) as if under AWB Rules

Grade		39 Hr Weekly Rate	Hourly Rate*	Overtime per Hour
		£	£	£
1.	Initial Grade Over 16 years	253.50	6.50*	9.75
	Under 16 years	-	3.72*	5.58
2.	***Standard Worker***............	***275.81***	***7.07***	***10.61***
3.	Lead Worker	303.55	7.78	11.68
4.	Craft Grade.....................	325.34	8.34	12.52
5.	Supervisory Grade...........	344.76	8.84	13.26
6.	Farm Management Grade	372.50	9.55	14.32
Apprentice:	Year 1.............................	141.47	3.63	5.45
	Year 2 ~ 16-17 years	145.83	3.74	5.61
	Year 2 ~ 18-20 years	197.34	5.06	7.59
	Year 2 ~ 21 years and over	245.29	6.29	9.54

* No changes have been made to Welsh AWB figures because of legal delays, but the minimum wage increased meaning lowest figures increase accordingly.

TYPICAL ANNUAL LABOUR COST

Estimated for 2014/15 (from 1st October), based on a Standard Worker with a 2% rise.

Average Labour Costs	Weekly	Annual	Hourly
	£		£
Minimum Wage (basic standard worker rate) (1)	281.33	14,629	8.34
National Insurance Contribution and Employers Liability Insurance (2, 3)	41.64	2,165	1.23
Minimum Cost (4)	**322.96**	**16,794**	**9.57**
Overtime, average 10 hrs per working week (45) @ £10.44 (+ NIC, ELI)	107.49	5,590	
Typical cost inc. Overtime (5, 6)	**430.45**	**22,384**	**10.15**

1. *Hours work, excluding overtime*, based on 45 weeks (of 39 hours) per year = 1,755 hours, i.e. statutory holidays (23 days), public holidays (8 days) and illness (3 days), have been deducted.

2. NIC = National Insurance Employer Contribution = 13.8%

3. ELI = Employer's Liability Insurance = 1.0%

4. *Annual cost of cottages* (or net value), value of perquisites, contribution towards payment of the council tax, etc., would have to be added where appropriate.

5. *Hours including overtime;* based on 1755 + 450 (10 hours/week) = 2,205 hours per year

6. *Total average worker's gross earnings* on the above assumptions = £19,498 a year.

2.　LABOUR HOURS AVAILABLE FOR FIELD WORK

This section calculates the theoretical maximum time a single worker could spend on field-work per month in 2015.

Hours available for field-work per worker per month in 2015

	Total Ordinary Hours (1)	Adjusted Ordinary Hours (2)	% workable (3)	Available Hours (4,5)			Total Available Hours (6)		percent o/t at w-ends (7)
				Ordinary	Overtime				
Jan	168	149	50%	75	29	(63)	103	(138)	100%
Feb	160	142	50%	71	30	(60)	101	(131)	76%
Mar	176	160	60%	96	63	(66)	159	(162)	50%
Apr	160	145	65%	94	76	(60)	170	(154)	50%
May	152	139	70%	98	110	(76)	207	(174)	53%
Jun	176	161	75%	121	106	(88)	227	(209)	39%
Jul	184	169	75%	127	109	(92)	235	(219)	38%
Aug	160	147	75%	110	115	(80)	225	(190)	49%
Sep	176	161	70%	113	99	(88)	212	(201)	39%
Oct	176	160	65%	104	76	(66)	179	(170)	45%
Nov	168	149	50%	75	36	(63)	110	(138)	72%
Dec	168	149	50%	75	29	(63)	103	(138)	100%

Ordinary Hours: 8 hours per work day (less 8 bank hols). No deductions have been made for other holidays because they may be taken at various times of the year.

1. *After deducting* for illness (5% Nov. to Feb., 3% March, April and Oct., 2% May to Sept.), and for contingencies and non-delayable maintenance (½ hour/day).

2. *Per cent Workable:* accounts for severe weather, soil conditions e.g. waterlogging etc.

3. *Available Ordinary Hours:* Adjusted Ordinary Hours x Percentage Workable.

4. *Available Overtime Hours: Daylight hours above working day (8 hours)* to a maximum of 4 hours per day and 12 to 14 hours at weekends according to season. Same adjustments for illness and percentage workable. Figures in brackets indicate hours available if headlights used, up to 4 hours/day (summer) and 3 hours/day (winter).

5. *Total Available Hours:* Percentage overtime without headlights available from weekend work as opposed to evenings.

6. *Overtime at weekends:* out of hours fieldwork that is undertaken in daylight.

Additional Notes

7. *Figures relate to medium land.* The percentage workability will be higher with light soils, less with heavy soils. On heavy soils, land may be almost 100% unworkable from late November to early March (or later, according to the season), particularly if un-drained. A rough estimate of variations in workability according to soil type (compared with the figures above) is as follows.

   Heavy land - March, October, November: 30% less; April: 20% less; September: 10% less; May to August: no difference. Light land — October to April: 15% more; May and September: 10% more; June to August: no difference.

8. *It must be remembered that indoor work,* e.g. livestock tending or potato riddling, can be continued over the full working week, i.e. the hours available are the Adjusted Ordinary Hours, plus overtime adjusted back for workability. Also, some handwork in the field has to continue even in rain, e.g. sprout picking.

9. *Percentage workability* varies according to the particular operation, e.g. compare ploughing and harvesting.

3.   SEASONAL LABOUR REQUIREMENTS

CROPS AND GRASS

On the following pages, data on labour requirements for various crops and types of livestock are given. Two levels are shown: average and premium.

The average figures relate to the whole range of conditions and commercial farm sizes, i.e. small and medium-sized farms as well as large; the figures give all farms equal weight.

The premium rates do not denote the maximum rates possible, for instance by the use of especially high-powered tractors under ideal conditions, but relate to rates of work estimated to be obtainable over the whole season, averaging good and bad conditions, with the use of wide implements, relatively large tractors (150hp (111kW) to over 180hp (134kW)) and high capacity equipment in up to 8 hectare fields and over, where no time is wasted. Most farmers with more than 200 hectares (500 acres) of arable land ought to achieve at least the premium levels shown. Those with over 400 hectares (1,000 acres) will have still bigger machines and therefore faster work rates, and thus require 15 to 25% less labour than even the premium levels given.

The rates of work include:

- preparation,
- travelling to fields,
- minor breakdowns and
- other stoppages
- They relate broadly to medium and medium-heavy land

Some jobs, such as ploughing, may be done more quickly on light soils. Operations such as combine harvesting can obviously vary according to many factors to do with the topography and other natural features of the farm.

The usual times of year when each operation takes place are shown; these relate to lowland conditions. They will obviously vary between seasons, soil types, latitude and altitude. In particular, light land can be ploughed over a longer winter period and a high proportion of cultivations for spring crops may be completed in February in many seasons. All such factors must be allowed for in individual farm planning. Conditions in different seasons will also affect, for instance, the number and type of cultivations required in seedbed preparation. Typical monthly breakdowns of requirements are given for various crops.

To illustrate the type of questions that need to be asked for full details of seasonal labour requirements on the individual farm, critical questions affecting timing are listed for cereals.

Note: This data is now old and little new research has been completed to replace it with. However, productivity per labour unit has increased since then.

Winter Cereals

Operations	Labour-hours per hectare Average	Premium	Time of Year
Plough (1)...............................	1.4	1.0	July to October (according to previous crop)
Cultivate (often power harrow).	1.0	0.7	September to October (according to previous crop) (½ Aug if ploughed in July)
Drill (often with power harrows followed by roll)	1.1	0.7	Mid-September to 3rd week October (according to previous crop and soil)
Apply Fertiliser.........................	0.3	0.2	
Spray	0.3	0.2	October-November
Top Dress (three times [2]).......	0.9	0.6	March and April
Spray (three or four [2])............	1.0	0.5	March-June
Combine, Cart Grain, Barn Work	2.5	1.9	Mid-Aug to approx. 10th Sept
Later Barn Work (3)	0.7	0.4	September to June
Total...	**9.2**	**6.2**	
Straw: Bale	1.3	0.8	Mid-August to end
Cart	3.5	2.6	September

Typical Monthly Breakdown

Month	Average	Premium	Notes
October.....................................	2.4	1.7	Approx. 60% of Ploughing,
November.................................	—	—	Cults., Drill, Harrow
December	—	—	
January	—	—	
February	—	—	
March	0.4	0.2	Part Top Dress
April	0.8	0.5	Part Top Dress, Spraying
May	0.3	0.2	Spraying
June	0.3	0.2	Spraying
July..	—	—	
August	1.7 (+2.4 Straw)	1.3 (+1.7 Straw)	⅔ of harvesting (4)
September (harvest).................	0.9 (+2.4 Straw)	0.6 (+1.7 Straw)	⅓ of harvesting (4)
September (prepn. drill)............	1.7	1.1	40% of Ploughing, Cults., Drill, Harrow

1. *Some cereal crops* are direct drilled or drilled after reduced, or minimal, cultivations, i.e. without traditional ploughing. Direct drilling reduces man-hours per hectare by about 2.5 (average) or 1.8 (premium), and minimal cultivations by about 1.2 (average) and 0.9 (premium).

2. *This is for winter wheat;* winter barley will often have one less top dressing and spraying and oats two less. Also see next page for harvest times for winter barley and oats.

3. *Later barn work* is excluded from monthly breakdown.

Spring Cereals

Operations	Labour-Hours per hectare		Time of Year
	Average	Premium	
Plough (1)	1.4	1.0	July to October (according to previous crop and soil type)
Cultivate (often power harrow)	1.0	0.7	March (½ in second half February on light land)
Apply Fertiliser	0.3	0.2	
Drill (often with power harrow), plus roll	1.2	0.8	March (½ at end February on light land)
Top Dress (once, some possibly twice)	0.4	0.2	
Spray (two or three)	0.7	0.3	May
Combine, Cart Grain, Barn Work	2.4	1.8	Last ¾ of August (affected by variety and season)
Later Barn Work (2)	0.6	0.4	September to June
Total	**8.0**	**5.4**	
Straw: Bale (unmanned sledge)	1.3	0.8	Mid-August to end
Cart	3.5	2.6	September

Typical Monthly Breakdown

Month	Average	Premium	Notes
October	0.4	0.3	Ploughing. How much in
November	0.8	0.5	October depends on area
December	0.2	0.2	W. Wheat, Potatoes, etc.
January	—	—	
February	—	—	
March	2.4	1.6	All Cults. Drilling, Rolling, (nearly half in February on light land)
April	—	—	
May	1.1	0.6	Spray and Top dress
June	—	—	
July	—	—	
August (3)	2.4 (+2.6 Straw)	1.8 (+1.8 Straw)	Harvesting
September	— (+2.2 Straw)	— (+1.6 Straw)	

1. *Autumn drilling* preferable if possible to allow frost to crumble soils

2. *Later barn work* excluded.

3. *This is for spring barley*; spring wheat and oats partly September.

Crop Timings in a Normal Season:

Winter Wheat

Drilling mid-September to 3rd week October.

Harvesting mid-August to approx. 10th September.

Winter Barley

As for winter wheat, except that:

- Ploughing unlikely to start before cereal harvest, as usually follows a cereal crop.
- Harvesting some weeks earlier: mid-July to approx. 10th August.

Winter Oats

As for winter wheat, except that:

- Drilling usually first full half of October.
- Harvesting earlier (late July or first half of August).

Spring Barley

Drilling end of February to very early April

Harvesting last half of August to early September

Spring Wheat

As for spring barley, except that:

- Drilling on average 1-2 weeks earlier (should finish in March) - lose more if later than barley.
- Harvesting, on average, 2 weeks later: last week August/first half of September (two-thirds in September).

Spring Oats

As for spring barley, except that:

- Drilling usually a little earlier.
- Harvesting is later than spring barley, earlier than spring wheat: end of August/beginning of September.

Critical Questions affecting Timing for Spring-sown Cereals

1. Previous crops.
2. Will the crop be ploughed traditionally, chisel ploughed, subsoiled, minimally cultivated, or direct drilled?
3. Months when winter ploughing is possible, on average (where relevant).
4. Is spring ploughing satisfactory (where relevant)?
5. Average period of cultivations and drilling.
6. Earliest dates for starting and finishing spring cultivations/drilling and latest dates for starting and finishing cultivations/drilling, ignoring extreme seasons (1 year in 10).
7. Effect on yield if drilling is delayed.
8. Is the crop rolled (a) within a few days of drilling or (b) later?
9. (a) Average period of harvesting.
   (b) Earliest dates for starting and finishing harvest, and latest dates for starting and finishing harvest, ignoring extreme seasons (one year in ten).

Critical Questions affecting Timing for Autumn-sown Cereals

1. Previous crops (affects time available and need for ploughing and cultivations).

2. Will the crop be ploughed traditionally, chisel ploughed, subsoiled, minimally cultivated, or direct drilled?
3. Earliest and latest drilling date, by choice.
4. Effect on yield if drilling is delayed.
5. Autumn weed control?
6. In the spring: (a) whether crop is rolled, and when,
                  (b) whether crop is harrowed, and when,
                  (c) time of top dressings,
                  (d) number of spray applications.
7.   (a) Average period for harvesting.

       (b) Earliest dates for starting and finishing harvest, and latest dates for starting and finishing harvest, ignoring extreme seasons (1 year in 10).

Maincrop Potatoes

Operations	Labour-Hours per hectare		
	Average	Premium	Time of Year
Plough	1.4	1.0	September to December
Cultivating, Ridging, De-stoning/			
Clod Sep. (as required)	6.5	5.0	March, early April
Plant and Apply Fertiliser (1)	4.5	3.5	Last quarter of March, first
Apply Herbicide	0.3	0.2	three-quarters of April
Spray for Blight (av. 6 times)	1.2	0.9	July, first half August
Burn off Haulm	0.3	0.2	End September, early
			October
Harvest, Cart, Clamp (2)	15.0	10.0	End September, October
Work on Indoor Clamp	4.8	3.2	November
Riddle, Bag, Load	40.0	30.0	October to May
Total	**74.0**	**54.0**	

1. *Automatic planter.* Hand-fed planters: approx. 12hrs plus 8 (could be casual labour).
2. *Mechanical harvester,* excluding up to 25 hours for picking off on harvester - usually casual labour. None may be needed on clod and stone-free soils. Hand harvesting: additional approx. 80 hours of casual labour.

Typical Monthly Breakdown

Month	Average	Premium	Notes
October	12.2	8.2	80% of harvest, ½ burn off
November	5.9	4.0	Clamp work and ¾ plough
December	0.3	0.2	¼ plough
January	—	—	
February	—	—	
March	7.8	6.0	All fert', ½ cults', ¼ plant
April	3.5	2.7	½ cult's, ¾ plant
May	—	—	
June	—	—	
July	0.9	0.7	3 blight sprays
August	0.3	0.2	1 blight spray
September	3.1	2.0	20% harvest, ½ burn off

These figures exclude casual labour and riddling.

Early Potatoes

Operations	Labour-Hours per hectare		Time of Year
	Average	Premium	
Plough	1.4	1.0	September to December
Cultivating, etc.	6.5	5.0	Late February, early March
Plant and Apply Fertiliser	4.5	3.5	Late February, early March
Apply Herbicide	0.3	0.2	1st half March (some in February on light land or in early season)
Further Spraying	0.3	0.2	
After-Cultivation/Spray	0.3	0.2	April, early May
Harvest, bag, load	30.0 (1)	25.0 (2)	2nd week June onwards. All June or till mid-July

1. Excluding 80 hours picking—usually casuals.
2. Excluding 60 hours picking—usually casuals.

Second Early Potatoes

Operations	Labour-Hours per hectare		Time of Year
	Average	Premium	
Plough	1.4 (1)	1.0 (1)	September to December
Cultivating, etc	6.5 (1)	5.0 (1)	March
Plant and Apply Fertiliser	4.5 (1)	3.5 (1)	March
Apply Herbicide	0.3 (1)	0.2 (1)	Half 2nd half March, half 1st half April
Further Spraying	0.9 (1)	0.7 (1)	End April, May, early June
Harvest	15.0 (1)	10.0 (2)	Mid-July to end August

1. *Spinner or elevator-digger*, excluding picking and riddling—usually casual labour.
2. *Mechanical harvester*, excluding picking off on harvester/riddling - usually casual.

Sugar Beet

Operations	Labour-Hours per hectare		Time of Year
	Average	Premium	
Plough	1.4	1.0	September to December
Seedbed Cults	3.2	2.2	Mainly March (some early April. Some late February in good seasons)
Load, Cart, Apply Fertiliser	0.7	0.4	
Drill (and Flat Roll)	1.8	1.1	Between mid-March and mid-April
Spray (herbicide: pre- and post-emergence)	0.6	0.3	Late March/April
Spray (x 2)	0.6	0.3	May/June
Spray (aphis)	0.3	0.2	July
Harvest (machine)	14.0	9.0	End September, October, November
Load	3.4	2.5	End September to early January
Total	**26.0**	**17.0**	

Typical Monthly Breakdown

Month	Average	Premium	Notes
October.............................	7.2	4.6	45% harvest; + loading
November	8.2	5.3	45% harvest; ¾ ploughing; + loading
December	1.0	0.8	¼ ploughing; + loading
January	0.5	0.4	Loading
February	—	—	
March	3.8	2.3	Fert., most cults., some drilling
April	2.5	1.7	Some cults., most of drilling
May	0.3	0.2	Spray
June	0.3	0.15	Spray
July...................................	0.2	0.15	Spray
August	—	—	
September........................	2.0	1.4	10% harvesting; + loading

Vining Peas

| Operations | Labour-Hours per hectare | | Time of Year |
	Average	Premium	
Plough	1.4	1.0	September to December
Cults, Fert. and Drill..................	2.3	1.6	Mid-Feb. to April
Post Drilling and Spraying..........	1.5	0.8	
Harvesting	19.0	14.0	July and early August
Total..	**24.2**	**17.4**	

Drilling is staggered in small areas through the season, ranging from early varieties to late varieties.

Dried Peas

| Month | Labour-Hours per hectare | | Notes |
	Average	Premium	
October.......................................	1.2	0.8	
November...................................	0.8	0.5	Stubble cult., Plough
December	—	—	
January	—	—	
February	0.2	0.1	Cult. x 2, harrow; drill & fert.
March	2.8	1.9	(80% March); light harrow
April	0.6	0.4	roll; and spray
May	2.5	1.2	
June	0.2	0.2	Scare pigeons; spray
July..	1.8	1.1	Possible spray desiccant;
August	2.2	1.3	combine and cart, dry
September...................................	0.5	0.3	Stubble cult.

Assumes direct combining.

Field Beans

Winter Beans

Operations	Labour-Hours per hectare		Time of Year
	Average	Premium	
Broadcast Seed	0.6	0.4	
Apply Fertiliser...........................	0.3	0.2	
Plough	1.4	1.0	September/October
Power Harrow.............................	1.0	0.8	
Spray (pre-emergence)	0.3	0.15	
Spraying (two or three times)	0.8	0.35	Spring
Combine and cart and			
Barn-work...................................	3.0	2.4	August

Spring Beans

Operations	Labour-Hours per hectare		Time of Year
	Average	Premium	
Plough	1.4	1.0	September to December
Cultivate (often power harrow)...	1.0	0.7	
Apply Fertiliser...........................	0.3	0.2	
Drill, Roll	1.2	0.8	End Feb, early March
Spray (two or three times)	0.8	0.4	
Combine and cart and			
Barn-work...................................	3.0	2.4	September

Winter Oilseed Rape (*Desiccated*)

Month	Labour-Hours per hectare		Notes
	Average	Premium	
October...........................			
November.........................	0.6	0.3	Spray herbicide and
December			insecticide if necessary
January	—	—	
February	—	—	
March			
April	0.8	0.4	Top dress twice
May	—	—	
June	—	—	Desiccate (1st half July);
July.................................	2.4	1.7	combine (½ 2nd half July
August	2.0	1.4	½ 1st half Aug.); dry
August	1.6	0.9	Cults. (x 2), spray, drill, fert.;
September	1.6	0.9	harrow, roll, barn work (0.5)

Herbage Seed (first production year)

Undersown

Operations	Labour-Hours per hectare		Time of Year
	Average	Premium	
Undersown	0.6	0.4	March, April
Roll..	⎧ (0.6	0.4)	Straight after drilling
	⎨ 0.4	0.3	September
	⎩ 0.4	0.3	Late February, March
Harvest (by Combine): Mow	1.4	0.9	3 to 4 days before combining
Combine and Cart......................	4.5	3.5	Ital. Ryegrasses and Early Perennials: late July. Intermed. Perennials: late July/early August. Late Perennials/White Clover: mid-August
	6.0	4.5	Meadow Fescue: early July
	7.0	5.0	Cocksfoot: early July
	10.0	7.0	Timothy: mid-August Red Clover: late September

Direct Drilled in Autumn

Operations	Labour-Hours per hectare		Time of Year
	Average	Premium	
Plough	1.4	1.0	
Seedbed Cults.............................	2.2	1.6	Depends on previous crop—
Load, Cart, Apply Fertiliser........	0.3	0.2	Usually July or August
Drill (with harrows behind)	0.8	0.6	As early as previous crop allows. This may be up to mid-Sept for ryegrass without detriment to the yield.
Roll (soon after drilling).............	0.6	0.4	Meadow fescue and cocksfoot are best sown no later than July and it is risky to sow Timothy much later than this.

Grass

Production

Operations	Labour-Hours per hectare		Time of Year
	Average	Premium	
Plough	1.4	1.0	Autumn drilling: may not
Seedbed Cults.............................	2.2	1.6	
Load, Cart, Apply Fertiliser........	0.3	0.2	
Drill*	0.7	0.5	Mid-March to mid-April (1) or end July to mid-Sept.
Roll..	0.6	0.4	Soon after drilling
Load, Cart, Apply Fertiliser* (three lots)	0.9	0.6	March to mid-August (2)
Top*	1.3	0.8	Mid-June to mid-July; if grazed only.

1. * These operations apply only where the seeds are undersown in a spring cereal crop soon after drilling. One extra harrowing and rolling is needed if undersown in an autumn-sown cereal crop.
2. *Spring drilling* may continue to mid-May to enable extra cleaning cultivations or the application of farmyard manure.
3. *P. and K.* may be applied in September - especially on undersown ley in year sown.

Conservation

Operations	Labour-Hours per hectare		Time of Year
	Average	Premium	
Plough	1.4	1.0	Autumn drilling: may not
Hay (5.5 tonnes per hectare)			
Mow	1.2	0.9	
Turn, etc	2.6	1.9	Two-thirds June, one-third
Bale......................................	1.3	0.9	July
Cart.......................................	6.0	4.5	
Total per hectare..........................	11.1	8.2	
Total per tonne............................	2.0	1.5	
Silage (17 tonnes per hectare)			
Mow	1.2	0.9	
Turn, etc	0.7	0.5	Two-thirds May, one-third
Load......................................	2.3	1.7	June
Cart.......................................	3.0	2.3	
Clamp...................................	2.3	1.7	
Total per hectare..........................	9.5	7.1	
Total per tonne............................	0.56	0.42	

Specialised Equipment Prices for Grass Conservation: see page 163.

Typical Monthly Breakdown

Production (figures averaged over the life of the ley)

	1-year ley undersown in spring		3-year ley undersown in autumn (1)		1-year ley drilled		3-year ley drilled	
	Ave.	Prem.	Ave.	Prem.	Ave.	Prem.	Ave.	Prem.
March	0.9	0.5	0.7	0.5	0.6	0.3	0.6	0.3
April	0.9	0.5	0.7	0.5	0.6	0.3	0.6	0.3
May	0.6	0.3	0.6	0.3	0.6	0.3	0.6	0.3
June	0.6	0.3	0.6	0.3	0.6	0.3	0.6	0.3
July	0.6	0.3	0.6	0.3	0.6	0.3	0.6	0.3
August	0.3	0.2	0.3	0.2	5.0	3.4	1.9	1.4
September...	0.6	0.3	0.3	0.2	3.2	2.2	1.4	1.0

1. *If ploughed after a cereal crop,* drilled early August to mid-September.

	1-year ley drilled in autumn (1)		3-year ley drilled in spring		Permanent Pasture	
	Ave.	Prem.	Ave.	Prem.	Ave.	Prem.
March	3.0	2.1	1.4	1.0	0.6	0.3
April	1.8	1.2	0.9	0.7	0.6	0.3
May	0.3	0.3	0.6	0.3	0.6	0.3
June	0.6	0.3	0.6	0.3	0.6	0.3
July	0.6	0.3	0.6	0.3	0.6	0.3
August	0.3	0.2	0.2	0.2	0.3	0.2
September..........	—	—	—	0.2	0.2	0.2
October..............	0.9	0.5	0.6	0.3	—	—
November	1.4	1.0	1.0	0.3	—	—
December	0.7	0.5	0.6	0.2	—	—

Conservation

	Hay				Silage			
	per hectare		per tonne		per hectare		per tonne	
	Av.	Prem.	Av.	Prem.	Av.	Prem.	Av.	Prem.
May	—	—	—	—	6.3	4.7	0.37	0.28
June	7.4	5.6	1.3	1.0	3.2	2.4	0.19	0.14
July	3.7	2.6	0.7	0.5	—	—	—	—

Kale

Production

Operations	Labour-Hours per hectare		Time of Year
	Average	Premium	
Plough	1.4	1.0	September onwards
Seedbed Cults.............................	2.2	1.6	March, April, early May
Fertiliser	0.3	0.2	April, early May
Drill	1.3	1.0	May
Roll...	0.6	0.4	Straight after drilling
Spray (weed killer)	0.3	0.2	6 weeks after drilling

Catch Crop

Kale may be drilled up to the first week of July; the crop will be smaller but either an early bite or silage crop may have been taken from a ley earlier in the year, or the ground may have been fallowed and thoroughly cleaned during the spring and early summer. The smaller crop is also easier to graze using an electric fence.

The above operations will still apply although the times of the year will obviously be different, but there may be an additional three or so rotavations and two or three heavy cultivations if fallowed for the first half of the year or ploughed after an early bite. This means approximately an extra 10 (average) or 8 (premium) man-hours per hectare in April, May, June.

FIELD SCALE VEGETABLES

(Labour hours per hectare unless otherwise stated)

Cabbage Transplanting	Hand 150-160. Spring cabbage, Sept.-Oct.; summer, April; autumn, May-June Machine (3.5 gang). Spring cabbage 75, summer 85, autumn 100. Pulling and dipping plants. 20 per hectare transplanted.
Cabbage Harvesting	Early spring cabbage, 210, Feb.-April; hearted spring, 250, April-June; summer, 220, June-July; autumn, 220, Oct.-Dec.
Brussels Sprouts Transplanting	45 (machine) to 55 (hand), May-June.
Brussels Sprouts Picking	320-400: picked over 3-5 times, maximum approx. 3 hectares per picker per season. Early sprouts, Aug.-Dec.; late, Nov.-Mar.
Peas Hand Pulling	475-525 (150 per tonne). Early, June; maincrop, July-Aug.
Runner Beans (Picked)	Harvesting. 625 (175 per tonne), July-Sept.
Runner Beans (Stick)	Harvesting. 675, July-Sept.
Runner Beans (Stick)	Erecting Canes and String. 100-150, May-June.
Carrot Harvesting.	Elevator-digger: 260 (1 man + 12 casuals, 20 hours per hectare). Earlies, July-Aug.; maincrop, Sept.-Feb. Harvester: 30 (3 men, 10 hours per hectare). Riddle and Grade: (1° per tonne), Dec.-Feb.
Beetroot Harvest and Clamp.	25, Oct.-Dec. 12-15 man-hours per tonne to wash and pack.

Source: The Farm as a Business, Aids to Management, Section 6: Labour and Machinery. (N.B. This data is now dated, but it is still the latest known to the author.)

LABOUR FOR LIVESTOCK

This data is updated for 2015

Dairy Cows

Time Required per Cow Depending on Yield.

Yield of Cow	5,500	7,000	8,000	9,000
	hours per cow per month			
January	2.0	2.5	3.1	3.8
February	1.9	2.5	3.1	3.8
March	1.8	2.5	3.1	3.8
April	1.6	2.4	3.0	3.8
May	1.6	2.1	2.7	3.5
June	1.6	2.1	2.6	3.2
July	1.6	2.1	2.6	3.2
August	1.6	2.1	2.6	3.2
September	1.6	2.2	2.8	3.5
October	1.8	2.4	3.1	3.8
November	1.9	2.5	3.1	3.8
December	2.0	2.5	3.1	3.8
Total per Cow per Year	21	27.9	34.9	43.2
Average Seconds per Litre	*13.7*	*14.3*	*15.7*	*17.3*

No time is allocated here for dairy young stock. This schedule is based on a 100-cow herd. Low yielding cows tend to spend more time at grass and less housed. High milk yielders take more management time.
13.7 seconds per litre = 1 man per 725,000L
17.3 seconds per litre = 1 man per 575,000L
The most labour efficient milk producing operations in the UK achieve over 800,000 litres per employed man.

Hours staff Requirement per Cow per Year.

	Cow Annual Milk Yield (L)			
	5,500	7,000	8,000	9,000
Cows per Herd				
60	21.9	29.1	36.4	45.0
100	21.0	27.9	34.9	43.2
150	20.0	26.6	33.2	41.1
300	17.5	23.3	29.1	36.0
500	15.0	19.9	24.9	30.9

Labour Cost per Litre

ppl	Cow Annual Milk Yield (L)			
	5,500	7,000	8,000	9,000
Cows per Herd				
60	3.96	4.14	4.53	4.98
100	3.80	3.97	4.35	4.78
150	3.62	3.78	4.14	4.55
300	3.17	3.31	3.62	3.98
500	2.72	2.84	3.10	3.42

Earnings. The average earnings of 'dairy herdsmen' in 2011/12 is estimated to be £27,594 a year and working 2,770 hours (10 hours for 277 days). This includes relief milking etc. but no cover for young stock or fieldwork, such as hay and silage making.

Dairy Followers and Beef

No recent survey work has been published on labour requirements for beef animals and dairy followers. The following data is therefore only 'best estimates'. They are for average performance and average conditions, excluding fieldwork. Substantial variations occur, e.g. through differing management styles or economies of scale with differing herd sizes.

Calves (per head, early weaning)

Age Group	Labour hours per month	
	Average	Premium
0-3 months	2.3	1.6
3-6 months	0.9	0.6
(av. 0-6 months	1.6	1.1)
6-12 months, yarded	1.1	0.8
6-12 months, summer grazed	0.3	0.2
(av. 0-12 months, during winter (1)	1.3	0.9)
(av. 0-12 months, during summer (1)	0.9	0.6)

1. *Assuming 6 to 12-month olds housed in winter and grazed in summer, and calvings or calf purchases fairly evenly spaced throughout the year.*

Stores (per head)

Yearling, housed	1.0	0.7
2 year olds and over, housed	1.4	0.8
Out-wintered store	0.7	0.5
12 months and over, summer grazed	0.2	0.1

Dairy Followers

(Per 'replacement unit', i.e. calf + yearling + in-calf heifer.) (1)		
During winter	2.9	2.0
During summer	1.2	0.8

1. *Assuming calvings fairly evenly spaced throughout the year and heifers calving at 2 to 2.5 years old.*

Beef Finishing (per head)

Housed	1.8	1.2
Summer Grazed	0.2	0.1
Intensive Beef (0-12 months)	1.3	1.0

Suckler Herds (per cow)

Lowland Single suckling (av. whole year)	0.9	0.6
Lowland Multiple suckling (av. whole year)	2.9	2.1
Upland/Hill Single suckling (av. whole year)	1.1	0.7

Sheep *(per Ewe)*

	Labour hours per month	
	Average	Premium (4)
January..	0.3	0.2
February..	0.3	0.2
March..	1.0 (1)	0.7
April...	0.4	0.25
May..	0.3	0.2
June..	0.4 (2)	0.3
July..	0.2	0.15
August..	0.2	0.15
September..	0.25	0.15
October...	0.25	0.15
November..	0.2	0.15
December..	0.2	0.15
Total..	4.0 (3)	2.75

1. Assuming mainly March lambing.
2. 0.3 if shearing is by contract.
3. A full-time shepherd, i.e. one who did no other work on the farm, would have to have a flock of at least 600 ewes for the average 4 hours per ewe per year to be achieved, assuming full-time assistance during lambing time.
4. In a national survey conducted in 1999 the average annual requirement for flocks exceeding 500 ewes was 2.9 hours.

Pigs

Age Group	Labour hours per month	
	Average	Premium
Breeding and Rearing, per sow..................................	1.5	1.20
(Average 130 sows per worker, Premium 160)		
Feeding only, per 10 pigs.......................................	1.6	1.25
No. at a time, per worker:		
Average 1,200 per man, Premium 1,600		
No. per year, per worker:		
Average: 6,000 porkers, 4,800 cutters, 4,450 baconers		
Premium: 8,000 porkers, 6,400 cutters, 5,750 baconers		
Breeding, Rearing and Feeding, per sow (with progeny)		
Porkers, average 90 sows per worker, premium 110.........	2.4	2.0
Cutters, average 80-85 sows per worker, premium 100-105	2.6	2.1
Baconers, average 75-80 sows per worker, premium 95-100	2.8	2.2

Poultry *(large scale, automated)*

	Labour hours per month
Laying hens: battery cages (18,000 per full-time worker)	1.1 per 100
free range	4 per 100
Broilers: 32,500 at a time per full-time worker*	
(225,000 a year)	1.0 per 100

* additional help needed for catching and cleaning out (included in labour hours/ month)

4.   STANDARD MAN DAYS

Standard Man Days (SMD) is a general estimate of the farm labour requirement per enterprise. A SMD is 2,200 hours per year. This is 45 weeks' work of 39 hours (after holidays, illnesses etc. have been deducted), plus an average of 10 hours overtime per week (45 x 49 = 2,205). These total hours are converted into 275 notional 8-hour Standard Man Days. This figure includes an assessment for overtime but can be increased by further overtime working.

Every farm enterprise requires a number of SMDs per unit of production (per hectare, per cow etc.). The total SMD requirement for each enterprise is therefore calculated by multiplying by the size of the operation. The total labour needed on the holding is the sum of all the individual enterprises. An additional 15% has then traditionally been added to account for general maintenance, repairs and management. The total SMD requirement is then divided by 275 to find the number of full-time employees that will be required. This system can work when the labour requirement is constant during the year – e.g. some livestock enterprises. However, when labour use is seasonal, e.g. most field operations, it does not show the 'peaks and troughs' that are crucial in labour planning. It also fails to reflect that daylight hours, soil conditions, rainfall etc. will alter the amount of time available for fieldwork during the course of the year. SMD also does not recognise the efficiency of larger units, so SMD requirements fall per unit as the enterprise grows.

Crops (per hectare)	S.M.D.s
Winter Feed Wheat	
Winter Milling Wheat	
Spring Wheat	
Winter Feed Barley	1.15 /
Winter Malting Barley	1.75 (1)
Spring Malting Barley	
Winter Oats	
Spring Oats	
Winter Oilseed Rape	1.10
Spring Oilseed Rape	1.00
Linseed	1.00
Winter Field Beans	0.90
Spring Field Beans	0.95
Dried Peas	1.60
Lupins	1.50
Vining Peas	3.00
Maincrop Potatoes	9.25 (2)
Early Potatoes	5.50 (2)
Sugar Beet	3.00
Herbage Seed (Ryegrass)	1.40
Hops	9.50 (2)
Kale (grazed)	1.40
Silage:~ one cut	1.60 (3)
two cuts	2.80 (3)
Grazing only	0.40 (3)
Hay for sale	1.80 (3)
Let Keep	0.40 (3)
Bare fallow / set-aside	0.20
Rough Grazing	0.20

Livestock *(per head)* *(4)*

Dairy Cows..	4.00
Bulls	3.50
Beef Cows (single suckler including calf):	
lowland..	1.35
upland/hill	1.68
Cereal Beef (0-12 months) (5)...	1.90
18-month Beef (5)	1.60
Grass Silage Beef (5)...	1.90
Finishing Suckler bred stores:	
Grass	1.10
Winter	1.10
Calves; to 6 months (5)..	1.20
Ewes: lowland..	0.50
upland...	0.45
hill...	0.40
Rams..	0.50
Winter Finishing Store Lambs..	0.30
Sows (including weaners to 30kg)...	2.25
Boars	2.00
Other Bacon Pigs...	0.25
Laying Birds: battery cages..	0.017
free range	0.06
Pullets reared (5)...	0.005
Broilers (5)	0.002

1. 1.15 if straw ploughed in; 1.75 if straw harvested. Highly mechanised larger farms will require no more than 0.75 S.M.D./ha of direct labour for cereals and other combinable crops (assuming straw ploughed in).

2. Excludes casual labour for harvesting.

3. Excludes any reseeding carried out – this is likely to be around 0.6 S.M.D./ha in the year reseeding is carried out.

4. Note that for grazing livestock, the S.M.D.s per head exclude field work, e.g. grass production and silage making, i.e. the labour for these has to be added to give total labour for these enterprises.

5. For these livestock, S.M.D. per annum should be based on numbers produced (sold) during the year. For all other livestock, average numbers on the farm at any one time during the year should be used (i.e. average of numbers at end of each month).

7. 'Other Cattle' can refer to both beef animals and dairy followers (ref. detail on page 185).

V. MACHINERY

1. AGRICULTURAL MACHINERY PRICES

This schedule is for 2015 purchase of new machinery, net of discounts and ex. V.A.T. Since 2003, machinery price inflation has been significant as a result of dearer raw materials and currency fluctuations. Machinery price inflation in 2011 was 3%. From 2011 to 2012, price changes were relatively static with a small rise in the cost of tractors, whilst other machinery items actually reduced slightly in price. From 2012 to 2013, all machinery costs rose by 1.3%. Over 2014, it is expected that machinery prices will rise slowly by around 1% (included in the schedule). Prices shown are a range as prices vary between makes and models. Machines with a star '*' denote those used in subsequent 'farmer' cost' calculations.

Tractors

		£ Range	
(a) Two-Wheel Drive			
80-90 hp		30,300	35,350
90-100 hp		30,300	36,865
(b) Four- Wheel Drive			
* 100-120 hp		43,430	58,580
* 125-140 hp		48,480	64,640
* 150-180 hp		64,640	80,800
180-220 hp		75,750	95,950
225-270 hp		85,850	126,250
(c) High Road Speed (50 Km /hour)			
155-175 hp		72,720	90,900
190-220 hp		82,820	106,050
(d) Crawlers - rubber tracks			
* 230-300 hp		155,540	171,700
340-400 hp		171,700	196,950
450-550 hp		207,050	252,500

Cultivating Equipment

(a) Ploughs

		Mechanical Adjustment		Variable width Hydraulic Adjustment	
Reversible:					
3-furrow		10,100	12,625	—	
4-furrow		12,120	14,645	14,645	17,170
* 5-furrow		15,655	17,675	18,685	20,705
6-furrow		17,170	22,220	20,200	25,250
7-furrow (mounted)		26,260	29,290	30,300	33,835
8-furrow (mounted)		30,300	35,350	35,350	40,400
(b) Furrow Presses					
1.6-1.8 m double row				3,788	4,293
2.0-2.4 m double row				4,040	5,050
* 2.6-3.0 m double row				5,555	8,080
3.2-3.6 m double row				8,080	11,110
3.8-4.0 m double row				10,100	14,140

(c) *Front Presses (excluding linkage)*

1.5 m single row	2,727	3,232
3.0 m single row	3,788	6,060
* 4.0 m single row — hydraulic folding	6,565	8,585

(d) *Front Press Linkage*

1.0 to 2.0 tonne	5,050	7,070

(e) *Other Cultivating Equipment*

* Sub Soiler 2-3 leg	4,040	5,050
Shakarator (3m)	9,595	13,130
Stubble Cultivator (3m)	7,070	12,120
* (heavy duty) (4m) hydraulic folding	14,140	19,190
(6 m): hydraulic folding	17,170	27,270
* Spring-tine Cultivator (3-4 m):	2,525	4,040
(5-6 m): hydraulic folding	6,565	10,100
Tine / Disc Cultivator Combinations		
(3-4 m) mounted	12,120	22,220
* (5-6 m) trailed	25,250	45,450
* Disc Harrows (3.6 - 4.4 m): trailed	13,130	21,210
(4.4-6.0 m): trailed folding	25,250	40,400
* Harrows (5-6 m): light-medium, hydraulic folding	3,030	5,050
* Rotovator (up to 135 hp tractor)	8,080	10,100
(200 hp tractor)	13,130	16,160
Power Harrow (with packer roller)		
(3 m)	7,575	9,595
* (4m)	12,120	15,150
(4-6m): folding	22,220	30,300
* Rolls: Triple gang, hydraulic folding (6 m)	7,575	12,120
Five gang, hydraulic folding (12m)	17,170	22,220

Fertiliser Distributors, Seed Drills, Sprayers

(a) *Fertiliser Distributors*

Mounted Spinners		
(700-1,200 litre): twin disc, hydraulic control	3,030	7,070
(1,300-1,700 litre): twin disc, hydraulic control	5,050	8,585
* (1,650-2,300 litre): twin disc, electronic control	8,080	12,120
(3,200 litre): twin disc, electronic control	12,120	16,160
Bag lifter (850-1,000kg)	2,020	2,525

(b) *Seed Drills*

Grain: 3 m, gravity fed	7,070	10,100
* 3-4 m, pneumatic	13,130	17,170
6 m, pneumatic	18,180	25,250

(c) *Combined Cultivator and Pneumatic Drill*

3-4 m	18,180	28,280
6 m	35,350	60,600

(d) *Combined Power Harrow and Pneumatic Drill*
*	3-4 m	....	18,180	30,300
	6 m	....	40,400	60,600

(e) *Direct Drill (6m)* — 30,300 | 60,600

(e)	*Direct Drill (6m)*	30,300	60,600
	Precision Maize Drill (6 row)	15,150	25,250

(f) *Sprayers*
	Mounted, 600-800 litre tank, 12 m boom	3,030	6,060
	Mounted, 1,000-1,800 l, 20-24 m hydraulic boom	14,140	21,210
*	Trailed, 2,500-3,000l tank 18-24 m boom	28,280	40,400
	Trailed, 3,000-4,500l tank 24-36 m boom	35,350	55,550
	Self-propelled sprayers,		
	2,500-4,000l, 24-36 m boom	90,900	131,300
	5,000-6,000l tank, 24 - 36m boom	101,000	161,600

Grass Conservation and Handling Equipment

(a) *Silage Equipment*
*	Forage Harvester: trailed, precision chop	30,300	45,450
	Self-propelled (3 m pick-up 400-600 hp)	151,500	222,200
	Maize attachment, 8 row	32,320	38,380
	Silage Trailer, 12 tonne, tandem axle	10,100	13,635
	Silage Trailer, 14 - 16 tonne, tandem axle	13,130	17,170
	Buckrake (push off)	3,535	7,070

(b) *Haymaking Equipment*
	Mowers 1.5-1.8 m, 1-2 drum	2,828	3,838
*	Disc Conditioner, mounted (2.4-3.2 m)	8,585	13,635
	trailed (3.2 - 3.8 m)	15,150	18,180
*	Rake: single/double rotor, 3.2m-4.5m range	4,040	7,575
	multiple rotors 8-10m range	15,150	28,280
	Tedder/swather		
*	5-7 m, 4-6 rotors	5,555	9,595
	8-11m multiple rotors	12,120	24,240
	Balers and Bale Handling: see 5(c) and (d) below		

(c) *Silage Handling Equipment*
	Silage shear bucket	2,020	3,030
	Silage grab	1,768	2,778
	Big Bale Silage Feeder, mounted	10,100	15,150
	Diet-feeder Wagon (6 tonne)	17,170	24,240
	Clamp Silage Mixer (10 tonne)	24,240	30,300

Grain and Straw Harvesting and Handling Equipment

(a) *Combines*

Engine size hp	Cutterbar width metres (feet)			
220-249	4.5-5.5 (14-18)	....	101,000	141,400
250-299	5.4-6.6 (18-22)	....	121,200	171,700
300-399	6.0-7.7 (20-25)	....	131,300	202,000
400+	7.7-10.6 (25-35)	....	202,000	373,700

(b)	Yield monitoring/mapping	8,080	11,110
	Self-levelling options	12,120	18,180
(c)	Balers		
*	Conventional Balers	10,605	13,130
*	Round balers, twine tying and net wrap	20,200	30,300
*	Big Square Balers	80,800	111,100
(d)	Bale Wrappers		
	Big Bale Wrapper: trailed	9,090	14,140
	Big Square Bale Wrapper: trailed	20,200	28,280
	Combined Baler and Wrapper	40,400	55,550
	Bale Trailers, 30 ft - 35 ft long	3,535	5,050
	Accumulator, flat 8, mechanical	2,525	4,040
	Big bale accumulator	10,100	15,150
	Big Bale Shredder, silage or straw	6,060	9,090
(e)	Drying, Handling, Feed Processing Equipment		
	Grain driers and Grain storage:		
	Cleaner/grader, 10-20 tonnes/hour	10,100	16,160
	Grain augers 150 mm, 6-8.5 m, with trolley	2,020	3,030
	Grain conveyors, (25-50t/hour)	1,515	2,525
	Hammer mill, 7.5-15 kW	4,040	5,050
	Roller mill, 4-5.5 kW	3,283	4,040
	Mixer, 750-1000 kg	4,545	5,050
	Mill and mixer, 1,000-1,300kg, 3.7-5.5 kW	7,070	9,090

Potato, Sugar Beet and Vegetable Machinery

(a)	Potato Machinery		
*	De-stoner	45,450	55,550
*	Bedformer, 1 bed	5,050	8,080
	Bed tiller (1 bed)	9,090	13,130
*	Planter: 2 row mounted	12,120	25,250
	6 row	35,350	45,450
	Haulm pulveriser (2 row):	6,565	9,090
*	Harvesters trailed: 2 row elevator manned/unmanned	75,750	101,000
	2 row, self-propelled	151,500	202,000
	4 row, self-propelled	353,500	454,500
	Store loader (heavy duty)	25,250	30,300
	Self-unloading hopper, 3-5 tonnes	11,110	14,140
	Clod separator	11,110	14,140
	Sizer, 5-30 tonnes/hour	11,110	15,150
	Barrel washer, 8-10 tonnes/hour	25,250	35,350
	Roller inspection table, 1.2 x 2.4 m	3,030	6,060
	Weigher, automatic, 8-10 tonnes/hour	7,575	10,100
	Box tipper with cross conveyor	15,150	25,250
	Box filler, automatic	15,150	20,200

Bag stitcher (hand held)	....	505	1,515
Complete out of store grading line: 20 tonnes/hour		60,600	151,500
30 tonnes/hour	....	101,000	202,000

(b) Sugar Beet Machinery

*	Precision Drill: 6 row (pneumatic)	....	11,110	15,150
	12 row-18 row (pneumatic)	....	20,200	40,400
*	Hoe:	6 row-12 row (heavy duty)	....	8,585	14,140
	Harvesters:	Trailed, 2 row, tanker	....	70,700	85,850
		Trailed, 3 row, tanker	....	90,900	101,000
		Trailed, 4 row, tanker	....	95,950	106,050
*	Self-propelled, 6 row, 18 tonne tank	....	343,400	404,000
	Cleaner-loader, with engine, 1-3 tonnes per minute		20,200	35,350
	Fodder beet harvester	....	10,100	90,900

(c) Vegetable Machinery

Onion windrower	....	11,110	13,130
Root crop digger: 1 webb	....	7,575	8,585
2 webbs	....	9,090	11,110
Top lifting vege single row, bunker	....	55,550	70,700
twin row, bunker/elevator	....	95,950	126,250
four row, elevator	....	131,300	156,550
four row, self-propelled	....	343,400	393,900
Leek harvester (mounted)	....	25,250	40,400

Dairy Equipment

Water heater	....	808	1,818
Heat recovery unit	....	2,525	5,050
Plate Cooler	....	1,515	4,040
Variable speed vacuum pumps	....	9,090	11,110
Cow collars for heat-time monitoring (£ per cow)	....	71	91
Electronic auto-shedding systems	....	8,080	14,140
Auto-dipping and flushing system (£ per stall)	....	808	1,010

General

	Trailer, 12 tonne tipping; grain/silage	10,100	13,130
*	Trailer, 14t tipping, tandem axle; grain/silage	11,110	16,160
*	F.Y.M. Spreader, (10 - 12 tonne)	11,110	16,160
	(12 - 14 tonne)	15,150	20,200
*	Loaders, front mounted	5,555	9,090
*	Materials Handler, telescopic boom (2.5-3.0 tonne)	40,400	60,600
	Skid steer loader (500-600 kg)	15,150	22,220
	Quad Bikes	3,535	6,565
	Vacuum Tankers (5,000-6,000 litre)	5,050	7,070
*	Low Ground Pressure Tankers (9,000-11,000 litre)	12,120	16,160
	Slurry pump	4,040	5,050
	Slurry separator	28,280	35,350
	Cattle crush	1,010	2,020
	Cattle crush with weigher	2,020	3,030
	Cattle trailer (twin-axle)	3,535	5,050
	Yard scrapers	505	1,010
	Rotary brush (2-2.5 m)	2,020	2,525
*	Flat roll, ballastable (2.5-3 m)	1,263	2,020
*	Pasture topper (2.0-3.0 m)	1,212	2,525
	Hedge cutter:		
*	hydraulic angling; flail head	12,120	18,180
	7.6m reach, 1.3m flail head, double sided	28,280	35,350
	Ditcher: fully slewing	9,595	12,120
	Post hole digger	1,212	2,020
	Post hole driver	1,515	3,535
	Saw bench	1,515	2,525
	Log splitter	808	1,212
	Welder	253	1,515
	Angle Grinder	25	202
	Compressor	253	808
	Farm Security Camera (single basic camera)	101	202
	Farm Security Camera System (automatic and wireless)	1,111	1,414
	Tractor Guidance System (basic)	808	1,515
	Auto-Steer Guidance System	7,070	12,120

2. CONTRACTORS' CHARGES, AVERAGE FARMERS' COSTS, AND RATES OF WORK

Contractors' charges vary widely according to many factors: these are estimates for 2015. Farmer-contractors sometimes charge less than dedicated contractors, since some of their overheads and fixed costs are largely *considered* covered by their own farming operations, but the service may not always be so complete, including specialist advice or access to new technology.

Farmers' own costs (including the value of the farmers' own manual labour) vary even more widely; those given (for 2015) are averages in every respect as costs will vary according to soil types, size of farm, and so on; they are based on accounting cost procedures in that labour, tractor and machinery fuel, repairs and depreciation are included - no allowance has been added for general farm overheads, interest on capital, supervision/management or under-occupied labour during slack times. They assume four-wheel drive 130 hp tractors for heavy work such as ploughing, cultivations and drilling and 165 hp tractors are assumed for work with a very high power requirement such as heavy discing, sub-soiling and deep ploughing. An additional fuel allowance for very heavy work has been added (i.e. higher than the average consumption assumed in the tractor costs schedule). Four-wheel drive 110 hp tractors are assumed to be used for most other operations (these individual tractor costs are shown in the tractor costs schedule on page 203). The figures should not be used for partial budgeting. The machinery used in the calculations for farmers' costs is identified by a 'star' * adjacent to specific items of equipment in the machinery list in the previous section (an average has been used for the purchase price).

The contract charges and average farmers' costs are put side-by-side for tabular convenience, not to facilitate comparisons. Apart from the fact that contractors' charges must cover expenses omitted from the farmers' cost, the advisability or otherwise of hiring a contractor for a particular job depends on many factors (e.g. timeliness), varying widely according to farm circumstances; therefore, there are advantages and disadvantages not reflected in a cost comparison alone.

Assumptions: Contractors' costs are particularly sensitive to many factors including fuel costs, capital machinery prices, and local demand versus competition. Contractors' charges are based on red diesel at 70ppl whilst the farmers' cost calculations are based on fuel at 62ppl. The reason for the difference is due to timings and because it is unlikely that contractors' charges would reduce due to a small fall in fuel prices. However, many contractors are now making individual arrangements with customers regarding fuel (i.e. prices quoted before fuel – therefore using the farmer's fuel when on site). The contractor charges shown below are inclusive of fuel and do not reflect this trend. Tractor costs are taken from those on page 203. The rates of work include preparation, travelling to and from the fields and allow for minor breakdowns and other stoppages.

Machinery rings. Prices charged by farmers offering services through machinery rings are extremely variable but are generally between average farmers' costs and contractors' charges. There are exceptions, which mainly relate to relatively expensive items of machinery (e.g. precision drills, de-stoners and combine harvesters), where the charges for services offered through machinery rings are close to and often less than average farmers' costs. Machinery and Labour rings are great examples of Joint Ventures that can deliver significant cost savings for all of the farming businesses involved. Structures and circumstances often vary considerably between organisations / groups involved.

Acknowledgement. The estimates for contractors' charges are kindly supplied by the National Association of Agricultural Contractors (as collected through their survey).

* *All costs below are per hectare unless otherwise stated. The figures represent a national average.*

Average Contractors Charges & Farmers Costs of Performing Mechanical Operations

Operation	Contract Charge £/ha *	Farmer's Average Cost £/ha *	Days Use Per Year	Average Rate of Work (Ha per 8 hr day)
Cultivations				
Ploughing – light land	57.48	56	30	7
– heavy land	62.20	60	30	6.5
-- with furrow press	6.67	9	30	6
Deep ploughing (over 30cm)	70.13	85	25	5.5
Rotovating - ploughed land	64.67	84	18	5
- grass		106	18	4
Sub-soiling/Flat Lifting	57.43	63	10	6
Mole-ploughing – single leg	95.63			
Stubble cultivating	38.30	35	20	12
Discing: Shallow	40.10			
Deep	42.80	46	20	10
Power harrowing – Deep/on ploughing	53.10	42	20	9
Shallow/seedbed prep	49.57			
Spring-tine Harrowing	30.89	21	20	12
Pressing	33.66	24	10	
One-pass tillage train (solo/discordon etc)	66.72	56	20	15
Rolling – flat (grassland)	24.09	19	10	12
– ring (seedbeds)	17.30	14	10	20
Drilling				
Rape drilling with flatlift/subsoiler	66.10	63	10	6
Cereal drilling – conventional	40.77	29	12	14
Combi-Drilling	59.40	55	12	9
Tyre Drill (Vaderstad)	46.95	44	12	18
Direct Drilling	52.63	51	12	15
Sugar beet drilling	50.24	49	5	10
Grass seed (broadcast)	21.62	24	2	11
Grass seeding with harrow (e.g. Opico)	29.23			
Cross drilling grass	79.07			
Chain Harrowing	22.61			
Maize Precision Drilling	44.48			
Maize Drilling Under Plastic	117.37			
Fertilising & Spraying				
Fertiliser distribution	12.03	8	15	45
Extra for variable rate application	3.71			
Lime spreading (per tonne)	4.50/tonne			
Spraying (based on 200 l/ha & 24m boom)	13.59	11	20	45
Extra if less than 50 acres (20 ha)	5.07			
Liquid Fertiliser	15.20			
ATV spraying (£/hr)	38.73/hr			
Slug-pelleting	8.28			
Avadex Spreading	16.56			

Operation	Contract Charge £/ha *	Farmer's Average Cost £/ha *	Days Use Per Year	Average Rate of Work (Ha per 8 hour day)
Combining				
Combining cereals	85.87	77	14	20.4
Extra for straw chopper on combine	6.60	*Farmer's cost assumes*		
Extra for seeding (Autocast)	8.03	*average of all machine sizes*		
Extra for yield mapping	2.47	*and harvested areas*		
OSR harvesting – out of windrow	82.78			
– direct combining	89.57	77	14	20.4
Combining peas/beans	94.52	77	14	20.4
Combining grain maize	103.16			
Swathing OSR	40.77			
Grain carting to barn (per hour)	37.54/hr	30.94 /hr		
Grass & Forage				
Topping margins per hour	46.15/hr			
Grass topping	33.11	24	3	12
Grass mowing	28.29	30	10	12
Tedding	15.72	14	10	20
Raking	15.79	21	3	20
Forage harvesting only – first cut	63.26	57	6	16
- other cuts	53.62	45	6	20
Forage harvesting, cart (3 trailers) and clamping	117.15			
Whole Crop forage harvesting, cart (3 trailers) and clamping	159.87			
Complete service – mow, rake, forage harvest, cart (3 trailers) and clamp	161.70			
Maize harvesting incl carting (3 trailers) and clamping	160.94			
Extra forage trailer (per hour)	38.50/hr			
Forage box	99.50/hr			
Baling				
Baling (per bale) - 'small'	0.52/bale	0.35 / bale	10	5.6
- 80cm × 70cm	3.58/bale			
- 120cm × 70cm	4.45/bale	4.34 / bale	25	20
- 120cm × 130cm	6.75/bale			
- Round 120cm	2.75/bale			
- Round 150cm	3.30/bale	2.32 / bale	20	13.6
Bale-wrapping – Round 120cm (6 layers)	5.73/bale			
- Round 120cm (with 4 layers)	5.03/bale			
- Round 120cm (without plastic)	2.15/bale			
- Square 120cm × 70cm (6 layers)	6.20/bale			
- Square 120cm × 70cm (4 layers)	5.25/bale			
- Square120cm × 70cm (without plastic)	2.23/bale			

Operation	Contract Charge £/ha *	Farmer's Average Cost £/ha *	Days Use Per Year	Average Rate of Work (Ha per 8 hour day)
Root Crop Operations				
Potato harvesting – harvesting only	778.37	432	20	2
- Harvesting and carting	976.05	679		
De-stoning potato land	259.46	214	18	2.5
Potato ridging	69.19	39	5	9
Potato Planting	200.08	122	16	3
Sugar beet harvesting - harvesting only	240.92	306	20	8
- Harvesting and carting	291.58			
Irrigation (25 mm application / ha)	98.00			
Manure Handling - *see below for telehandler costs for loading*				
FYM spreading – tractor and rear discharge :	43.00/hr	47	per hour	
- tractor and side discharge spreader	38.88/hr			
Slurry spreading – tanker	43.42/hr	47	per hour	
- umbilical	77.00/hr			
- extra pump	37.56/hr			
Slurry injection	52.00/hr			
General / Rural Maintenance				
Hedge cutting - flail	34.59/hr	36	per hour	
- saw-blade	40.67/hr	44	per hour	
Hedge laying	15.00/metre			
Fence erection (with materials)				
– post and 4 Barb	4.92/metre			
– post, stock net & 2 Barb	5.92/metre			
– post and 3 rails	16.00/metre			
Quad Bike (including man)		15	per hour	
Tractor + Post Knocker + Man	38.29/hr			
Ditching using 360 deg digger	35.13/hr			
Tractor + trailer + man	37.92/hr	31	per hour	
100 – 150 hp Tractor + man	34.14/hr			
150 – 220 hp Tractor + man	37.44/hr	*See tractor costs schedule*		
220 – 300 hp Tractor + man	51.50/hr	*for farmer's average cost*		
300 hp + Tractor + man	64.00/hr			
Forklift/Telehandler + Man	36.65/hr	30	per hour	
Livestock Husbandry				
Sheep dipping	1.25/head			
Sheep jetting / showering	0.88/head			
Sheep – shearing	1.65/head			
-- rams	3.30/head			
-- crutching	0.70/head			
Sheep ultrasound scanning	1.00/head			
Cattle ultrasound scanning	2.00/head			
Foot trimming – sheep	1.00/head			
- cattle	10.00/head			
- bulls	20.00/head			
Tractor + Man + Feeder Wagon		36	per hour	
Mobile Feed Mixing and Processing (£/t)	19.00/tonne			

Purchase, Hire Purchase and Contract Hire of Machinery

The farmer's cost for the various operations shown in the table above assume the machinery and equipment is purchased outright. There is no interest charge included in the calculations for the capital required to purchase the machinery. However, a farming business may choose to purchase the machinery through a hire purchase (HP) agreement. This is where a deposit is paid up-front followed by a number of monthly or annual payments. The benefits of HP agreements are purely cash flow, allowing a business to spread the cost over say 3 years. For new equipment, the interest charge may be very low or even 0%, whereas using HP agreements to finance used machines will usually incur an interest rate currently of 3-7%. Once the HP agreement ends (i.e. all payments are complete), the farmer owns the item of machinery outright.

Alternatively, some businesses choose to use contract hire (CH) agreements. This involves paying a rental charge for the use of an item of equipment for a set period of time. At the end of the period, the machine is returned to the company (although sometimes opportunities exist to negotiate a price to buy the machine). Contract hire agreements usually include a full service, maintenance and repair plan. The main advantage of these agreements is the ability to plan and budget costs, as the farmer/contractor is 100% confident of the exact cost of operating that machine, with no un-expected repair bills or no need to budget what it will be worth when you come to trade-in the machine. These are becoming popular with large arable and contracting businesses.

Another option which is increasingly popular is to use short-term hire agreements to hire key items of machinery as and when required. For example, many arable businesses contract hire combines and/or additional tractors at harvest time when extra machinery is required. This allows them to access new technology without having large sums of capital tied up in machinery that sits idle for much of the year. The most cost-effective option depends very much on the specific circumstances of the farm business and will be determined by factors such as ability to access capital, annual usage and life expectancy.

Contract Charge for All Operations

For cereals and combinable break crops, 'stubble to stubble' charges (i.e. up to and including combine harvesting and carting the grain to store) are typically £333 to £420/ha (£135-170/acre). Variations depend upon such factors as distance away, area contracted, size of fields, type of terrain, quality of soil, level of inputs and which party provides the storage. Local competition also has a significant bearing on prices, as with all contract charges. Some regions of the UK are very competitive when it comes to certain contract operations, for example hedge cutting or 'tractor and man' provision.

One sometimes views farmers' total power, machinery and labour costs compared with stubble to stubble contractors' charges. It has of course to be remembered that the former include many cost items not included in the latter, e.g. the cost of farm vehicles, fixed plant such as grain stores and general farm maintenance.

Contract Farming Agreements

Generally these are formalised with a written agreement which sets out the terms for the "Farmer" (who can be a landowner or tenant) and a "Contractor". The "Contractor" can be a neighbouring farmer or traditional contractor. "Contractor" remuneration includes a guaranteed basic payment (fee). The basic payment is usually between £210 and £275/ha (£85-£110/acre) for combinable crops and should cover the majority of the fixed costs of the operation. However, it should not offer any margin for the contractor to incentivise him to farm the farm to the best of his ability and therefore generate the maximum return to the farmer and contractor through the share of the divisible surplus

Following deduction of agreement running costs (crop variable costs, drying, insurance, interest charges etc.) and the Farmers Basic Payment, the surplus is split between the 2 parties. The split may typically be 70%-80% to the Contractor and 20%-30% to the Farmer. This incentivises good performance and management from the contractor. A second band of payment rate is sometimes introduced e.g. 50%:50% split above a set level of surplus to enable the farmer to benefit from any significant rises in market prices. This is increasingly the case given the large volatility in cereal prices in recent years.

LIVESTOCK HAULAGE COSTS

The cost of hauling livestock to market, to field, back to winter housing or other movements between grazing is a cost that is often over-looked. The table below demonstrates the farmers cost of hauling livestock per head per journey, for a number of different journey lengths.

Journey Length	£ Per Head Per Journey		
	Ewe	Finished Lamb	Finished Cattle
1 Mile	0.50	0.33	4.97
5 Miles	0.62	0.41	6.17
10 Miles	0.77	0.51	7.68
15 Miles	0.92	0.61	9.19
20 Miles	1.07	0.71	10.70
30 Miles	1.37	0.91	13.71

The costs calculated above include the cost of running a vehicle (pick-up/Landrover), based upon 12,000 miles annual mileage, attributing this cost on a per mile basis to the livestock transport cost (to reflect the fact that the vehicle is also used for many other purposes). The cost of running a livestock trailer (capital cost and repairs/maintenance) is based upon an average sized farm stock trailer with decks, capable of holding 30 ewes, 45 finished lambs, or 3 finished cattle, assuming it is kept for 10 years and used for 40 journeys per year. In arriving at a cost per head, the calculations assume that the trailer is always fully occupied with one of the above livestock numbers. The costs per head by journey length assume one journey; therefore if the journey to market was 30 miles one-way and no return load was bought back (i.e. an empty trailer), the total cost of transporting those livestock to market would in fact be almost double that shown above (although recognising the fact that towing an empty trailer will be much more fuel efficient than when fully loaded). The labour costs calculated above exclude time for loading/un-loading but account for time spent driving between destinations averaging 30mph.

Specialist livestock hauliers charge either on a per day basis or a cost per head for specific journey lengths. As a result, charges vary widely depending upon the specific circumstances, such as distances and the size of groups etc. As a guide, to move breeding sheep from Yorkshire to the Midlands would cost approximately £3/ewe assuming the haulier is able to backload. Costs for hauling lambs to market over a distance of more than 40 miles would cost circa £2.00 - £2.50/lamb and £15-20/head for finished cattle. An articulated lorry and driver, fully equipped for livestock haulage, would typically cost £550-£600/day.

GRAIN HAULAGE COSTS

The average costs per tonne of grain (and oilseed) haulage in Great Britain over the past six seasons are summarised by the HGCA's haulage survey carried out each December. The summarised results for the years 2009 to 2014 are tabulated below:

Summary table of the HGCA Haulage Survey Results

	2009	2010	2011	2012	2013	2014
10 miles	£4.24	£4.54	£4.30	£4.28	£4.92	£4.33
20 miles	£4.81	£5.03	£4.92	£4.90	£5.54	£5.03
40 miles	£5.95	£6.01	£6.15	£6.13	£6.76	£6.42
60 miles	£7.09	£6.98	£7.37	£7.36	£7.99	£7.82
100 miles	£9.38	£8.94	£9.83	£9.83	£10.44	£10.61
150 miles	£12.23	£11.39	£12.90	£12.91	£13.51	£14.10

TRACTOR POWER REQUIREMENTS

		hp/acre		hp/ha		kW/Ha	
		av.	prem.	av.	prem.	Av.	Prem.
Combinable crops:	heavy land	1.20	0.85	3.00	2.10	2.24	1.57
	light land	0.90	0.65	2.20	1.60	1.64	1.20
Mixed cropping:	heavy land	1.35	0.95	3.35	2.35	2.50	1.75
	light land	1.00	0.70	2.50	1.75	1.86	1.30

UK Agricultural Tractor Sales per Year (over 50 HP)

Year	Average Tractor Size HP	Number of Units Sold	Per Cent change y/y
2005	127.6	13,068	-11.4%
2006	128.3	13,566	+ 3.8%
2007	134.0	15,540	+14.6%
2008	138.1	17,104	+10.1%
2009	143.4	15,013	-12.2%
2010	141.7	13,347	-11.1%
2011	144.3	14,094	+5.6%
2012	148.0	13,951	-1.0%
2013	150.4	12,498	-10.4%
2014 (Jan-June)		6,942	

(data from the Agricultural Engineers Association).

3.   TRACTOR HOURS

Crops	Per Hectare Per Annum	
	Average	Premium
Cereals	8.4	6.3
Plus, Straw	1.6	1.2
Potatoes	18.6	13.9
Sugar Beet	11.6	8.7
Vining Peas	9.4	7.0
Dried Peas	6.9	5.2
Field Beans	6.9	5.2
Oilseed Rape	8.4	6.3
Herbage Seeds:- 3 year crop	5.0	3.7
Hops (machine picked)	120.0	90.0
Kale (grazed)	5.2	3.9
Turnips/Swedes (Folded/Lifted)	10/28	8/22
Fallow	0.8	0.6
Grass Ley Establishment	4.2	3.2
Making Hay	4.8	3.6
Making Silage:-		
1st Cut	4.1	3.1
2nd Cut	3.3	2.4
Grazing:-		
Temporary Grass	2.2	1.7
Permanent Grass	1.3	1.0

Livestock	Average Per Head
Dairy Cows	6
Other Cattle over 2 years	5
Other Cattle 1-2 years	4
Other cattle 0.5-1 year	2.25
Calves 0-0.5 year	2.25
Housed Bullocks	3
Sheep (per ewe)	1.25
Store Lambs	0.8
Sows	1.75
Other Pigs over 2 months	1
Laying Birds	0.04

1. *For livestock*, annual requirements are per head requirements above multiplied by average numbers during the year (i.e. average numbers at end of each month).

2. *As with labour*, the number of tractors required by a farm depends more on the seasonal requirements and number required at any one time than on total annual tractor hours. These can be calculated from the seasonal labour data provided earlier in this book. The soil type and size/power of tractors purchased are obviously other relevant factors. The table below gives a guide to the typical horse power requirements on arable farms. All figures are for 2015

4.   TRACTOR COSTS

	Four-Wheel Drive Tractors			
	110 h.p.		130 h.p.	
Initial Cost................................	£51,005		£56,560	
	per year	per hour	per year	per hour
	£	£	£	£
Depreciation................................	4,080	8.16	4,525	9.05
Insurance................................	383	0.77	424	0.85
Repairs and Maintenance................	1,275	2.55	1,414	2.83
Fuel and Oil................................	3,194	6.39	3,920	7.84
Total	8,932	17.86	10,283	20.57

			Crawler	
	165 h.p.		265 h.p.	
Initial Cost................................	£72,720		£163,620	
	per year	per hour	per year	per hour
	£	£	£	£
Depreciation................................	5,818	11.64	13,090	26.18
Insurance................................	545	1.09	1,227	2.45
Repairs and Maintenance................	1,818	3.64	4,091	8.18
Fuel and Oil................................	5,527	11.05	10,356	20.71
Total	13,708	27.42	28,763	57.53

Figures are estimates calculated for 2015. Depreciation assumes all tractors are sold for 20% of their original value after 10 years of life. The depreciation schedule shown on page 205 demonstrates the average annual fall in value of machinery over its life (column 2 is applicable to tractors). Annual repair costs have been calculated at 2.5% of initial cost for all tractors. This assumes the majority of basic servicing work carried out by the farm's own labour. No interest on capital has been included. Fuel is charged at 62p/litre plus a 5% allowance for oil. Fuel usage data has been reviewed and refined over the past year.

The hourly figures are based on a use of 500 hours per year. A greater annual use than this will mean higher annual costs but possibly lower hourly costs. On some larger farms and within many contracting businesses, many tractors do up to, and even over, 1,000 hours per year. Earlier replacement at a given annual use will increase depreciation costs per hour but should reduce repair costs. The hourly figures are averages for all types of work: heavy operations such as ploughing obviously have a higher cost than light work. The variability of fuel usage is significant depending upon the type of work (light work vs. heavy cultivations) and can vary by up to 80%. The figures shown attempt to depict the average consumption from all types of work.

Typical Contract Hire Charges (see page 199) for tractors are shown below (prices exclude insurance but include repairs/maintenance):

	Short-Term (8-10 weeks)	52 weeks Contract
110 hp tractor:	£430 - £490 / week	£160 - £190 / week
130 hp tractor:	£460 - £520 / week	£190 – £210 / week
165 hp tractor:	£675 - £775 / week	£260 - £285 / week
290 hp tractor (wheeled):	£1,100-£1,375 / week	£350 - £450 / week
130 hp telehandler	£500 - £550 / week	£250 - £300 / week
16 tonne Grain Trailer	£250 – £270 / week or £60-£70/day	

5.   ESTIMATING ANNUAL MACHINERY COSTS

Annual machinery costs consist of depreciation, repairs, fuel and oil, contract charges, and vehicle tax and insurance. These can be budgeted in three ways;

1)   using information on past machinery costs on the farm (e.g. management accounts),

2)   per hectare, by looking up an average figure for the district, according to the size and type of farm. Approximate levels are shown in the tables of whole farm fixed costs (page 216). This is obviously a guide only and masks huge variations between farms.

3)   Fully detailed calculations, costing and depreciating each machine in turn, including tractors, estimating repairs and fuel costs for each, and adding the charges for any contract work. The following tables give, for different types of machinery, estimated life, annual depreciation, and estimated repairs according to annual use.

ESTIMATED USEFUL LIFE OF POWERED MACHINERY IN NORMAL USE

Estimated Useful Life (years)	Annual Use (hours)				
Equipment	25	50	100	200	300
Group 1:					
Ploughs, cultivators, toothed harrows, hoes, rolls, ridgers, potato planting attachments, grain	12+	12+	12+	12	10
Group 2:					
Disc harrows, corn drills, grain drying machines, food grinders and mixers	12+	12+	12	10	8
Group 3:					
Combine harvesters, pick-up balers, rotary cultivators, hydraulic loaders	12+	12+	12	9	7
Group 4:					
Mowers, forage harvesters, swath turners, rakes, tedders, hedge cutting machines, semi-automatic potato planters and transplanters, unit root drills, mechanical root thinners	12+	12	11	8	6
Group 5:					
Fertilisers, combine drills, FYM spreaders, elevator potato diggers, spraying machines, pea cutter windrowers	10	10	9	8	7
Miscellaneous:					
Beet harvesters	11	10	9	6	5
Potato harvesters	—	8	7	5	—
Milking machinery	—	—	—	—	20+

	Annual Use (hours)					
	500	750	1,000	1,500	2,000	2,500
Tractors	12+	12	10	7	6	5
Electric motors	12+	12+	12+	12+	12	12

DEPRECIATION: AVERAGE ANNUAL FALL IN VALUE

Age of Machine	Complex. High depreciation rate		Traditional machines		Simple equipment: Low depreciation rate	
	Annual % Dep'n	Total % Dep'n	Annual % Dep'n	Total % Dep'n	Annual % Dep'n	Total % Dep'n
1	37.5	37.5	28	28	22	22
2	25	50	19	38	16	32
3	20*	60	15.3	46	13.7	41
4	16.5†	66	13.3*	53	12	48
5	14.2‡	71	11.8	59	10.8	54
6	12.5	75	10.7†	64	9.8	59
7	11.3	79	9.8	68.5	9.1*	64
8	10.3	82	9.0‡	72	8.4	67
9	9.3	84	8.2	74	7.7	69
10	8.5	85	7.5	75	7†	70

Complex: Machines such as potato harvesters, mobile pea viners, etc.
Traditional Machines: with many moving parts, e.g. tractors, combines, balers, forage harvesters
Simple Equipment: with few moving parts, e.g. ploughs, trailers

* Typical frequency of renewal with heavy use.

† Typical frequency of renewal with average use.

‡Typical frequency of renewal with light use.

These figures have been updated from a survey of machinery sale prices undertaken in 2014. Depreciation is calculated from the new price, asking price of the second hand machine, and its age. The asking price has been discounted by 5% to account for price negotiations. Prices for a variety of machinery and equipment types have been collated and categorised according to complexity.

Example: If a tractor (Traditional Machine) costing £80,000 is 5 years old, the value of the machine has depreciated on average by 11.8% per year, totalling a 59% fall in value. This means the tractor is now worth £32,800. The chart shows the rise of depreciation over the ten year period.

Depreciation of Machinery Categories over 10 years

DEPRECIATION: PERCENTAGE RATES

Straight-Line

Trade-in, Second-hand or Scrap Value as % of New Price

Years Retained	5%	10%	20%	25%	33%	40%	50%	60%
3	—	—	—	—	—	20	16	13
4	—	—	—	—	17	15	12	—
5	—	—	—	15	13	12	—	—
6	—	—	13	12	11	10	—	—
8	—	11	10	9	—	—	—	—
10	9	9	8	—	—	—	—	—
12	8	7	—	—	—	—	—	—
15	6	—	—	—	—	—	—	—

Example: If a machine costing £10,000 is retained for 8 years, at the end of which the trade-in value is 20% of the new price (i.e. £2,000), the average depreciation per annum has been £8,000 over 8 years = £1,000 (i.e. 10% per year of the new price).

Formula to calculate percentage = ((NP – TiV) / AoM) / NP x 100

NP   New Price

TiV   Trade in Value

AoM   Age of Machine

Diminishing Balances

Trade-in, Second-hand or Scrap Value as % of New Price

Years Retained	5%	10%	20%	25%	33%	40%	50%	60%
3	—	—	—	—	—	26	21	16
4	—	—	—	—	24	20	16	—
5	—	—	—	24	20	17	—	—
6	—	—	23	20	17	14	—	—
8	—	25	18	16	—	—	—	—
10	25	20	15	—	—	—	—	—
12	22	17	—	—	—	—	—	—
15	18	—	—	—	—	—	—	—

Example: If a machine costing £10,000 is retained for 4 years, at the end of which the trade-in value is 40% of the new replacement price, the annual depreciation on the diminishing balances method is:

Year 1, £2,000 (i.e. 20% of £10,000);

Year 2, £1,600 (i.e. 20% of £8,000 [the written-down value]);

Year 3, £1,280 (i.e. 20% of £6,400); Year 4, £1,024 (20% of £5,120).

The total written-down value at the end of Year 4 is therefore £4,096 (i.e. £10,000 less the total depreciation of £5,904). This is approximately 41% of the new price. (Taking the percentages in the above table to decimal places would give the trade-in prices stated more precisely).

ESTIMATED ANNUAL COST OF SPARES AND REPAIRS

These figures are based on a percentage of purchase price* at various levels of use

	Annual Use *(hours)*				Additional 100 hours
	500	750	1,000	1,500	use add
	%	%	%	%	%
Tractors	3	3-4	5	7	0.5

	Annual Use *(hours)*				Additional 100 hours
	50	100	150	200	use add
Harvesting Machinery:	%	%	%	%	%
Combine harvesters, self-propelled forage harvesters, self-propelled potato harvesters	1.5	2.5	3.5	4.5	2
Trailed forage harvesters, pick-up balers, potato & sugar beet harvesters	3	5	6	7	2
Other Implements and Machines:					
Ploughs, Cultivators, Toothed harrows, Hoes, Elevator potato diggers	4.5	8	11	14	6
Rotary cultivators, Mowers, Pea cutter-windrowers	4	7	9.5	12	5
Disc harrows, Fertiliser distributors, Farmyard manure spreaders, Combine drills, Potato planters with fertiliser attachment, sprayers, Hedge-cutting machines.	3	5.5	·7.5	9.5	4
Swath turners, Tedders, Side-delivery rakes, Unit drills, Flail forage harvesters, Semi-automatic potato planters and transplanters, Down-the-row thinners	2.5	4.5	6.5	8.5	4
Corn drills, Milking machines, Hydraulic loaders, Potato planting Attachments	2	4	5.5	7	3
Grain driers, Grain cleaners, Rolls, Hammer mills, Feed mixers Threshers	1.5	2	2.5	3	0.5

* When it is known that a high purchase price is due to high quality and durability or a low price corresponds to a high rate of wear and tear, adjustments to the figures should be made.

Service Plans

Most tractor manufacturers now offer extended warranties or comprehensive service plans to cover the cost of all servicing, maintenance and repairs beyond the regular manufacturer warranty. This is usually for a pre-agreed period of time or maximum number of hours (usually this expiry date is determined by which comes first). Costs and offerings vary hugely between manufacturers and tractor models but the following gives an approximate guide. A 'standard' maintenance and repair plan for a 130hp tractor doing 500 hours per year for 5 years would cost an average of £1,300-£1,500/year. This is for a 'standard' maintenance and repair plan to include all servicing, most replacement parts, filters, maintenance fluids and routine labour. There are also 'premium' plans available to go a stage further and protect further parts of the machine. There are, however, always exclusions from these agreements such as tyres, glass and provisions for negligence. Given the rising cost of repairs (and machinery dealer labour costs), such plans can be beneficial for farming businesses, particularly contractors who can fix their repair costs. This therefore helps with budgeting and setting prices to charge customers. This also gives peace of mind in the knowledge that the services were carried out by a qualified technician at the correct service intervals, rather than by farm staff who may lack knowledge and also can be undertaken on a rather ad-hoc basis, particularly during busy times of the year.

Tyres

The length of time a set of tractor tyres last before they need to be replaced will vary significantly depending upon a number of factors. These include soil type (stone content is the main determinant of tyre wear), the amount of yard work undertaken (feeding, loading grain etc), and the amount of road travelling undertaken. Many tractors will do in excess of 5,000 hours on a set of tyres assuming the machine does not do excessive road work. Front tyres on loader tractors are likely to require replacement earlier than rear tyres due to the weight of the loader (and items lifted) and the associated increase in wear that this creates. Costs vary significantly between makes and sizes. It is not our intention to list prices for all types of tyres but as a guide new standard rear tyres for a 130 hp tractor would cost between £500-£800 + VAT each and for standard front tyres they would cost in the region of £325-£475 + VAT each. Therefore, the cost to replace the full set of tyres would be approximately £2,100, plus the cost of fitting. This could be done on-farm where the correct equipment is held, otherwise most tyre fitters / tractor dealers would fit these. Typical labour charges for technicians vary between £30/hour to £60/hour. The cost of larger tyres for tractors in the 160-180 hp range, say for 650mm width on the rear, could cost £1,500-£2,200 each including the cost of fitting. Larger and even flotation tyres are becoming increasingly popular for field-work in an attempt to reduce soil compaction. These will cost significantly more to purchase.

6.   PRECISION AGRICULTURE

Precision farming is a method of farm management fundamentally centred on responding to very detailed variation in resource capability. The term has been adopted in recent years as a technology to map resource capacity such as land fertility or machinery passes so that each resource unit can be treated individually and precisely to maximise its productive capacity. It is estimated that about two thirds of UK arable land is farmed using precision farming technology, dominated by the larger farms.

Two main technologies exist. The first is nutrient mapping to determine the nutrient balance at a very precise level of field area so that applications can be tailored according to the requirement or yield potential of that precise piece of land. The second is automatic or assisted steering to ensure the machinery covers precisely the right ground without overlaps or leaving gaps. This is also used for controlled traffic; keeping all vehicle types solely on a precise layout of tramlines each year so reducing compaction and soil structure damage.

The cheapest and most cost effective piece of precision farming equipment is a tape measure. For example, measuring the 'operating' width of machinery compared with size of tramlines to identify overlap is a critical starting point. Precision farming is of most benefit to farmers who are least precise in their resource allocation. This might be through poor machinery use or considerable variation of in-field nutrient variation. Larger, more extensive operations that have less management and labour per hectare to examine and treat each small parcel of land (or other resource) individually, will be able to benefit more greatly through automated measurements of resource capacity such as soil fertility or pH in different areas. They can also benefit more by spreading the capital cost over more hectares.

Economic benefits result from better allocated inputs leading to savings of inputs, or higher yields. Inputs saved could include seed, fertilisers, sprays, machinery use, fuel and labour. Faster work-rates achieved can mean achieving more in periods of optimal weather conditions. Environmental benefits can also be achieved through correct input allocations.

Table of benefits for Assisted Steer Technology (HGCA Review 71)

Level	Arable area	Accuracy	Machines Adapted	cost £/ha	benefit £/ha	net £/ha
Assisted Manual Steer	300 Ha	+/- 40cm	2	1.25	2.50	1.25
Mid-Level DGPS*	500ha	+/- 10cm	2	12	14	2.00
RTK**	500ha high value crops	+/- 2cm	3	20	22	2.00

* DGPS = Differential Global Positioning System   ** RTK = Real Time Kinetic

A HGCA publication 71 (2009) suggests that costs of automated steering might be in the region of the table above, although this will vary considerably according to crops, yields and values between farms and years. The report continues that the cost of mapping crop canopy maps on a 500 hectare farm is likely to cost about £3 per hectare and, £6.50 for nitrogen sensing. Other analyses have variable costs like compaction sensing at about £12 per hectare and seed rate maps at £1 per hectare.

The cost of individual soil tests for N, P, K and Mg is about £8 per sample.

Godwin R. J. An Economic analysis of the potential for precision farming in UK cereal production Biosystems Engineering, Volume 84, Issue 4 2003

Knight S., Miller P. and Orson J. An up to date cost/benefit analysis of precision farming techniques to guide growers of cereals and oilseeds. HGCA Review 71. 2009

Acknowledgement: thanks to Ian Beecher-Jones 07967 637 985

7. FIELD DRAINAGE

Estimated for 2015

1. Field drainage is one of those farm investments which has in many cases been over-looked in recent years. Most agricultural land has been drained at some point historically, although some will have been done over 100 years ago (clay pipes). Much was re-drained in the 1960's and 1970's when significant grants were available to assist with the capital cost. Despite the age of some of these systems, many still function, although do require regular maintenance. This may include clearing out-falls, cleaning out ditches, or even using high pressure systems to clean field drains (jetting).

2. The costs of installing drains per metre are shown below. These costs include the cost of operating a trenching machine, supplying and laying the perforated plastic pipe to an average depth of 800 mm by trencher with 40/20mm cleaned washed porous fill (drainage stone) laid over the pipe to within 375mm of the surface. Costs as follows:-

60 – 80mm diameter	£5.00 - £5.75/metre
80 – 100mm diameter	£5.25 - £6.00/metre
100 – 120 mm diameter	£6.00 - £7.00/metre
120 – 160 mm diameter	£7.00 - £10.00/metre

The costs above include the cost of and laying porous backfill (drainage stone). However, this is not essential, and soil can be used as backfill. This could save £2.75-£4.00 per metre in cost depending upon the depth of the trench required to get the falls correct and the type of drainage stone selected. However, porous backfill greatly enhances the effectiveness of drains by keeping the openings in the pipe clear and enabling fast penetration of water into the drain. The above rates apply to comprehensive schemes of 4 hectares or more. Smaller areas and patching up work can cost up to 50% more. This is because of the cost of transporting and tracking trenching equipment across fields for small areas of work. Patching up / repairing old drainage systems is common practise as a cheaper alternative to new comprehensive systems.

Digging new open ditches (1.8m top width, 1.25m depth) costs £2.20-£3.00 per metre compared with improving existing ditches at £1.20 to £1.80 per metre depending upon the amount of material that needs to be removed. However, most contractors would charge on an hourly basis for this work with a 360 digger at approximately £35/hour.

Mole draining will cost in the region of £74-£94 per hectare (see contractor charges). Mole draining is effectively a secondary drainage method which is used where a drainage system already exists. The mole plough creates a cavity for the water to travel through. This practise is best suited to heavy land / clay based soils, where mole cavities will remain in place for some time.

3. *Total Costs* per hectare for complete schemes will vary depending on the distance between laterals, soil type, size of area to be drained, region of the country and the time of year when the work is to be undertaken. The cost of a scheme with 20m spacing between laterals and using permeable backfill will typically be in the range of £2,400 to £3,500 per hectare (£980-£1,400 per acre). Comprehensive schemes using little / no permeable backfill will cost circa £1,550 - £2,250 per hectare. Backfilling with soil, rather than with permeable material (washed gravel), may reduce the cost by almost half but is only possible on certain soil types. Certain soil types which are particularly suitable for mole drainage may permit spacing between laterals to be increased to 40m or even 60-80m in some instances. Where this is possible costs will be reduced proportionately.

8.   IRRIGATION COSTS

Estimated for 2015

Capital Costs

1. Pumps (delivering from 20 to 200 cubic metres per hour from a surface water source), complete with monitoring equipment:-

Tractor PTO driven (pump only)	£800 - £4,000
Diesel engine driven pump unit	£12,500 - £25,000
Electric motor driven pump unit	£22,000 - £32,000
Optional remote/wireless monitoring controls	£500 - £1,500
Variable speed drive option – fitted to electric motor	£800 - £5,000

    Individual pumps for mounting on diesel engines range in price from £2,000 to £11,000 for capacities of between 50 and 250 cubic metres per hour. A sophisticated system, including pump house, pumps and control equipment to feed an irrigation system from a reservoir to cover a total area of approx. 400 ha (as and when required) would cost approximately £30,000 - £40,000 to construct and install.

2. Pipelines (averages £ per metre):-

    Portable: (excl. valve take offs) 50mm: £4.00; 75 mm: £5.25; 100 mm: £7.50; 125 mm: £8.75; 150 mm: £11.00.

    Permanent underground galvanised pipe 12 bar rating (supply and laying) per metre: 80 mm: £10.00 - £13.50; 100 mm: £15.00 - £19.50; 150 mm: £25.00 - £32.00; 200 mm: £54.00 - £62.00.

    Hydrants: 100 mm x 100 mm: £200-£275; 150 mm x 125 mm: £310-£430.

3. Application Systems:-

    (a)   Hose reel systems (average cost per machine) complete with rain gun:

	Hose Length	Output	Acre Inches Per Day	Manual Controls	Electric Controls
Small	180-250m	5-25m³/hr	4.5-5.5	£8,500 - £9,500	
Medium	300-400m	40-80m³/hr	17-20	£19,000 - £21,000	+ £3,000
Large	450-650m	70-120m³/hr	28-33	£40,000 - £45,000	

    (b)   Irrigation booms (average cost per unit):

Small	14m boom (20m wetted width)	£1,800 - £2,300
Medium	30m boom (40m wetted width)	£4,500 - £6,000
Large	50m boom (60m wetted width)	£8,000 - £12,000

    (c)   Pivot and linear systems:

Small Linear	200m width	£45,000 - £55,000
Large pivot	600m radius (113ha)	£60,000 - £85,000

    (d)   Traditional portable hand move sprinkler systems (very specialist and not widely found):

    75mm diameter, sprinkler line assemblies:

1 move/day/six day cycle	£800 - £1,100/ha
2 moves/day/six day cycle	£400 - £550/ha
3 moves/day/six day cycle	£300 - £375/ha

(e)   Solid set sprinkler lines – semi-permanent systems (very specialist and not widely found):

63mm dia. pipework assemblies at 18m x 18m triangulated spacing	£1,500 - £1,800/ha
As above but with infra-red automated hand-held controls	£1,700 - £2,100/ha

(f)   Specialist Drip Irrigation systems typically use a tape. 25mm tape (excluding the header mains, control valves and filtration equipment) will cost approximately £0.50-£0.55 per metre.

4.   Total:

If no source works are needed, as with water from a river, or pond, total capital costs are likely to vary between £1,200 and £2,300 per hectare requiring irrigation at regular intervals, depending on the site layout, levels of sophistication and automation of the system installed. The capital cost of constructing a reservoir to store irrigation water, usually filled during the winter, is typically in excess of £1.25/m^3 for clay-lined reservoirs (although considerable variations will exist depending on precise circumstances). Lining and fencing could double this cost. This cost could be off-set partly by the sale of sand / gravel depending upon the location. In addition, there may be a need for pump houses and other infrastructure depending upon the circumstances. New time limited abstraction licences are difficult to obtain, especially for summer abstraction. Hence there is an increasing trend towards constructing reservoirs that can be used to store water abstracted during the winter months.

Water Sources

An abstraction licence is required if more than 20m^3 (4,000 gallons) of water per day are taken from surface or underground sources. A temporary abstraction licence is sufficient if more than 20m^3 of water per day is to be taken for less than 28 days, whereas a full abstraction licence is required if more than 20m^3 of water per day is to be taken for more than 28 days. If abstracting more than 10m^3 per day in Scotland, you must obtain authorisation from SEPA. If abstracting less than 10m^3 per day in Scotland, and comply with certain General Binding Rules (GBR), you do not require authorisation. Abstraction charges vary widely calculated by a formula combining the following factors together:

- Volume – annual licensed
- the Source Factor; whether the source is Environment Agency unsupported, supported or tidal
- The Season Factor; summer, winter or all year round
- The loss factor – high, medium, low or very low, depending upon what the water is authorised to be used for under the licence
- A minimum annual charge of £25

There are 22 regions 'supported' by the Environment Agency in 2014/15. Abstraction from these rivers is 3 times dearer than 'unsupported' sources. Abstraction from tidal sources costs 20% of 'unsupported' sources.

Winter abstraction charges (authorised for abstraction between 1st November to 31st March) cost 16% of all-year abstraction charges. Summer charges (1st April to 31st October) are 160% of the all-year charge.

An application charge of £135 and advertising administration charge of £100 is due, alongside an annual subsistence charge which comprises the Standard Unit Charge (SUC) and the Environmental Improvement Unit Charge (EIUC). Annual subsistence charges are not payable for temporary licences. The charges for 2014/15 are as follows:-

Region (£/1000m³)	Standard Unit Charges	Environmental Improvement Unit Charge (EIUC)
Anglian	27.51	9.96
Midlands	14.95	6.19
Northumbria	29.64	0.00
Yorkshire	11.63	0.00
North West	12.57	8.91
Southern	19.23	8.26
South West inc. Wessex	19.71	0.00
Thames	13.84	8.24
Natural Resources Wales	15.16	0.00

Most abstractors must provide the Environment Agency with accurate records (known as 'returns') of how much water is taken in order to enable them to balance water resources between different users and check compliance with licence conditions. If a licence is in place and you have not extracted any water, a 'nil' return must be submitted.

Water Costs

A typical extraction cost for a non-tidal, non-supported farm in East Anglia for 25mm per hectare (250m³ per hectare) would be £1.65/ha for winter abstraction only (0.66p/m³), £10.31/ha for all year abstraction (4.12p/m³) and £16.49/ha (summer only abstraction) (6.60p/m³). The same for an acre-inch would equate to £0.68, £4.24 and £6.78 respectively. This is clearly just the cost for the water. The capital invested plus the labour and any power requirement should also be accounted for which will vary according to individual circumstances. Mains water at 155p per m³ would cost £388 per application of 25mm per hectare (£159/acre inch).

Overall Operating Costs

Because of variations in individual farm circumstances in terms of source works and the irrigation system used, the overall cost of applying 25mm per hectare can range widely, from £85 to £155/ha. Very sophisticated systems distributing mains water over intensive specialist crops could be much more expensive.

Conversions and Calculations

The (approximate) imperial equivalents for metric values commonly used in irrigation are as follows:

- 1 cubic metre = 1,000 litres = 220 gallons (1 million gallons = 4,546 cubic metres).
- A pump capacity of 100 cubic metres per hour is equivalent to 22,000 gallons per hour (367 gallons per minute).
- 1,000 cubic metres is sufficient to apply 25 millimetres of water over 4 hectares, which is approximately equivalent to applying 1 inch over 10 acres. An acre inch is therefore 100 cubic meters (22,000 gallons), or a hectare centimetre is 100 cubic meters.
- The cost/volume conversion from a hectare of 25mm depth to an acre-inch is 0.411 or 2.433 from an acre-inch to a hectare 25mm.

9.   GRAIN DRYING AND STORAGE COSTS

Drying (estimate for 2015)

Capital Costs: vary widely according to type and capacity of drier. A standard 20 tonne per hour continuous flow drier, suitable for a 350 hectare arable unit would cost in the region of £110,000 – £150,000 including the wet bin and associated handling requirements (to feed the drier and empty it). Over 15 years, this capital cost represents £3.87 for every tonne of grain regardless of drying requirements (assuming no residual value). Amortised (i.e. cost to repay capital and interest) at 6% and assuming only 75% of the grain requires drying, over the 15 year period, this figure rises to £7.97/tonne dried. This figure changes dramatically by changes to throughput and longevity.

Annual fixed costs: being fitted and immobile, grain dryers have a low resale value (mobile dryers do have good second hand value). *Depreciation* is calculated as the capital value divided by the longevity and tonnes per year. This ranges from £5.99 to £1.95 per tonne depending on capacity and annual throughput. *Maintenance* tends to be low at around 2% of purchase value, rising as the dryer ages. *Insurance*; 1.25% of current value.

Running costs: *Fuel*: A useful 'rule of thumb' is 1 litre of fuel per 1% moisture per tonne. However, this will vary considerably between different machines and drying systems. Thus drying each tonne by an average of 5% points at 62ppl will cost £3.10 per tonne in fuel. *Electricity* use is 17.5Kw/hr for the burner and dischargers, as much again for the handling apparatus, totalling 35Kw/hr. Over a season, (approximately 85 hours use) at 10p/kWh is £298. This represents 18p per tonne of grain dried. Little labour is required for modern automatic driers. There could be a further cost requirement to cool the grain in store after being dried. This cost varies depending upon the system used – pedestals or on-floor blowing are common. The cost of suitable fans vary but can be obtained for £1,500 - £4,000 depending on requirements. With the introduction of the Renewable Heat Incentive, there are now opportunities to use renewable fuels (woodchip, straw) to reduce drying costs. There are a number of burners on the market which are fired by renewable fuels that produce hot air to then dry grain on-floor.

Overall operating costs for a fixed machine of 20t/hr output (on a 350 ha arable farm) therefore equate to £10.47 per tonne of grain dried (assuming 75% dried). Per tonne of total grain produced by the farm the cost is £7.85. *Mobile batch driers are much cheaper to buy, in the region of £35-45,000 for a 16t – 20t machine, but these can require more handling of grain (forklift and trailers) unless they are automatic and sited suitably. Therefore the capital costs per tonne are often much lower but the running costs can be much higher. These machines are popular on many farms, however, offering flexibility and are a viable alternative where a suitable electrical connection is not available.* There has been considerable investment in grain storage and drying facilities in recent years, which has been much needed, with many businesses having old and often inefficient facilities.

Central grain stores offer grain drying services for about £7.00 to £12.00 per tonne for 5% moisture drying for members and non-members respectively. Contractors' charges are typically around £12.00 – 16.00 per tonne for drying grain by 5% moisture.

Storage (estimate for 2015)

Capital Costs: from approximately £85 per tonne (on-floor concrete floor and concrete walling) to £150 per tonne (on-floor storage in a purpose-built building with drying floor and stirrers). This cost can rise to over £300 per tonne for an elaborate plant, including pit, elevator, conveyors, ventilated storage bins, catwalk etc. in a new building. *See page 226.*

Depreciation and Interest: £250/t depreciated over 25 years is £10.00/t per year. Interest/opportunity cost of £250/t at 6% is £7.50/t/year (i.e. on the average capital employed). *Fuel and Repairs:* £2.50 per tonne (1%). *Interest on Grain Stored*: 68p/month with grain at £135/t at 6% interest.

Contract Storage: typically £1.50 - 2.50/t per month with a handling charge of around £2.00 - £2.50 per tonne for loading into store and out of store. Large grain merchants offer storage including haulage for around £10/t for the four month period September to December (giving flexibility on marketing where no on-farm storage is available) with a further charge of £1.50/t per month for every additional month stored prior to sale post-Christmas.

VI.   OTHER FIXED COSTS DATA

1.   WHOLE FARM FIXED COSTS

The following are a broad indication of the levels of fixed costs per hectare (acre) for various types and sizes of farm, estimated for 2015, including the value of unpaid family manual labour, including that of the farmer and his wife. The figures are based on the actual results from the Farm Business Survey (FBS) for the 2013-12 year (February to February), adjusted for subsequent changes in costs. The FBS is based on a sample of farms which does change over time, so there is not a consistent sample. This just emphasises that the costs given below should be used only as an indication and must be adjusted according to individual situations; see also further notes on the use of this data below.

The FBS is conducted by a consortium of Universities and Colleges across England on behalf of Defra. Although the survey is limited to England, the figures within this section are likely to be broadly applicable to most parts of the UK. The FBS has undergone an overhaul in recent years. Specific regional reports are no longer published - although they can be accessed via the FBS website (see www.farmbusinesssurvey.co.uk). In addition, the farm types have been standardised across the country. They are now based on Defra's standard farm classifications. This has meant that some categories of farm have disappeared (mainly the 'mixed' ones such as dairy & arable, and arable & lowland livestock). All of these costs can of course vary widely according to many factors, especially the intensity of farming, e.g. the number of cows per 100 hectares on dairy farms, or the hectares of intensive crops on general cropping farms.

The figures provided are averages. 'Premium' farms of the same level of intensity can have labour, machinery and general overhead costs at least 20% lower. However, the most profitable farms are often more intensive. They therefore have higher fixed costs associated with the great intensity - but with substantially higher total farm gross margins. Thus it is the net amount (Gross Margin – Fixed Costs) that matters.

The 'small' farm categories relate only to full-time holdings and do not include very intensive holdings occupying very small areas.

The term 'fixed costs' is used here as it is in gross margin analysis and planning; a full explanation of the differences between fixed and variable costs in this context is given on pages 1 and 2. Note that all casual labour and contract work has been included under fixed costs. In calculating enterprise gross margins on the individual farm these costs are normally allocated as variable costs if they are specific to a particular enterprise and vary approximately in proportion to its size, i.e. are approximately constant per hectare of a particular crop or per head of livestock. Otherwise they are included as fixed costs. In both cases, however, they could be regarded as substitutes for regular labour and/or the farmer's own machinery - which are both items of fixed cost. It is therefore simpler if both are included, fully, as fixed costs. If one is comparing results from accounts set out on a gross margin basis, and some or all of the casual labour and contract work have been included as variable costs (especially on cropping farms, e.g. for potato harvesting using casual labour or a contractor's machine), the necessary adjustments need to be made in making the comparisons.

Notes on the Schedules

1. *Unpaid Labour:* Refers to the value of unpaid family manual labour, including that of the farmer and his wife.

2. *Machinery Depreciation:* This is based on current (i.e. replacement) cost. This gives a truer reflection of the real loss of value of machinery (as is apparent when replacement becomes necessary). It also allows easier comparison between different businesses.

However, many farm accounts calculate depreciation on the 'historic' (i.e. original) cost of the machinery. This will tend to produce a lower figure. Depending on the age of the machine, and bearing in mind recent strong increases in machinery prices, the historic method may underestimate depreciation by 10-20%. Note that both the Depreciation item and Repairs include vehicles.

3. *Leasing Charges:* The capital element, but not the interest, is included in depreciation; the proportion paid as interest varies according to the rate of interest paid and the length of the leasing period, but is typically 7%-10%.

4. *Machinery Running Costs:* This includes fuel, oil, repairs, servicing and vehicle tax and insurance. Separate figures for these elements are no longer available. As a general rule, fuel might make up a little over half of all such costs.

5. *General Overheads:* include general farm maintenance and repairs, office expenses, water, insurance, fees, subscriptions, etc.

6. *Rent & Interest:* Rent now only relates to the actual rent paid by the average farm in that particular category. It is no longer an imputed rent for all land farmed by the business; thus, a fully owned-occupied farm will have no rental costs. Interest used to be excluded but now actual interest paid by the average farm in that particular category is shown.

In making comparisons with fixed costs taken from farm accounts it is important to note that in the figures below unpaid manual labour is included; farm accounts will rarely include this. Also the figures below include average rent and interest; in farm accounts these will vary widely depending on the farm tenure and borrowing. Very low 'target' figures given in press articles often omit these items and can therefore be misleading; usually, too, they relate only to large, very well appointed farms. If an 'opportunity cost' for owner-occupied land (often fully paid for many years ago) is included, then the cost level rises further. Note too that the figures given below do not include management, whether paid or unpaid. The margin after deducting the fixed costs below from the total gross margin plus any other farm receipts represents the total return to management and own capital in the business.

Labour, machinery and buildings are the main items of 'fixed' costs subject to change with major alterations in farm policy. Each has a separate section in this book.

Mainly Dairying

	Under 75 ha (Under 185 acres)		75 - 125 ha (185 - 310 acres)		Over 125 ha (Over 310 acres)	
Regular Labour (paid)	90	(36)	150	(61)	290	(117)
Regular Labour (unpaid)	730	(295)	525	(212)	250	(101)
Casual Labour	30	(12)	35	(14)	50	(20)
Total Labour	**850**	**(344)**	**710**	**(287)**	**590**	**(239)**
Machinery Depreciation	165	(67)	190	(77)	185	(75)
Machinery Running Costs	155	(63)	180	(73)	200	(81)
Contract	115	(47)	135	(55)	150	(61)
Total Power & Machinery...	**435**	**(176)**	**505**	**(204)**	**535**	**(217)**
Farm Maintenance	45	(18)	60	(24)	70	(28)
Water & Electricity	160	(65)	170	(69)	145	(59)
General Overhead Expenses ..	95	(38)	90	(36)	80	(32)
Total Overheads	**300**	**(121)**	**320**	**(130)**	**295**	**(119)**
Rent & Interest	125	(51)	170	(69)	200	(81)
Total Fixed Costs	**1710**	**(692)**	**1705**	**(690)**	**1620**	**(656)**

Mainly Cereals

	Under 175 ha (Under 430 acres)		175 - 300 ha (430 - 740 acres)		Over 300 ha (Over 740 acres)	
Regular Labour (paid)	40	(16)	70	(28)	90	(36)
Regular Labour (unpaid)	230	(93)	155	(63)	100	(40)
Casual Labour	10	(4)	10	(4)	10	(4)
Total Labour	**280**	**(113)**	**235**	**(95)**	**200**	**(81)**
Machinery Depreciation	130	(53)	140	(57)	135	(55)
Machinery Running Costs	100	(40)	130	(53)	110	(45)
Contract	95	(38)	65	(26)	65	(26)
Total Power & Machinery...	**325**	**(132)**	**335**	**(136)**	**310**	**(125)**
Farm Maintenance	30	(12)	20	(8)	25	(10)
Water & Electricity	65	(26)	60	(24)	55	(22)
General Overhead Expenses ..	80	(32)	65	(26)	75	(30)
Total Overheads	**175**	**(71)**	**145**	**(59)**	**155**	**(63)**
Rent & Interest	105	(42)	125	(51)	120	(49)
Total Fixed Costs	**885**	**(358)**	**840**	**(340)**	**785**	**(318)**

Large-Scale Cereal Farms (over 500 ha (1,250 acres))

Data from the Farm Business Survey indicates there are further economies of scale for cereals farms at even larger farm sizes. There are likely to be wide variations depending on the precise scale of these businesses (some of which are very large). The following figures may be used as a guide; Labour - £155 per ha (of which paid labour £95); Power & Machinery - £275 per ha; Other Overheads - £195 per ha; Rent & Interest - £135 per ha. This totals £760 per ha (£308 per acre).

Data for larger-scale General Cropping farms (see below) is not so conclusive. Costs on a 'per ha' basis do not necessarily seem to fall as farm size increases. This may be due to the larger proportion of (higher cost) root crops and vegetables seen on larger farm sizes.

General Cropping

	Under 150 ha (Under 370 acres)		150 - 225 ha (370 - 560 acres)		Over 225 ha (Over 560 acres)	
Regular Labour (paid)	55	(22)	85	(34)	145	(59)
Regular Labour (unpaid)	320	(130)	220	(89)	165	(67)
Casual Labour	20	(8)	35	(14)	70	(28)
Total Labour	**395**	**(160)**	**340**	**(138)**	**380**	**(154)**
Machinery Depreciation	140	(57)	150	(61)	160	(65)
Machinery Running Costs	140	(57)	160	(65)	165	(67)
Contract	100	(40)	100	(40)	100	(40)
Total Power & Machinery...	**380**	**(154)**	**410**	**(166)**	**425**	**(172)**
Farm Maintenance	25	(10)	25	(10)	35	(14)
Water & Electricity	85	(34)	85	(34)	90	(36)
General Overhead Expenses ..	65	(26)	90	(36)	70	(28)
Total Overheads	**175**	**(71)**	**200**	**(81)**	**195**	**(79)**
Rent & Interest	100	(40)	160	(65)	135	(55)
Total Fixed Costs	**1050**	**(425)**	**1110**	**(449)**	**1135**	**(459)**

* With potatoes and/or sugar beet and/or field vegetables; grade 1 or 2 land.

Mainly Sheep/Cattle (lowland)

	Under 90 ha (Under 220 acres)		90 - 125 ha (220 - 310 acres)		Over 125 ha (Over 310 acres)	
Regular Labour (paid)	25	(10)	45	(18)	45	(18)
Regular Labour (unpaid)	480	(194)	350	(142)	265	(107)
Casual Labour	10	(4)	15	(6)	15	(6)
Total Labour	**515**	**(208)**	**410**	**(166)**	**325**	**(132)**
Machinery Depreciation	90	(36)	95	(38)	105	(42)
Machinery Running Costs	85	(34)	90	(36)	100	(40)
Contract	55	(22)	55	(22)	60	(24)
Total Power & Machinery...	**230**	**(93)**	**240**	**(97)**	**265**	**(107)**
Farm Maintenance	25	(10)	30	(12)	25	(10)
Water & Electricity	65	(26)	70	(28)	65	(26)
General Overhead Expenses ..	65	(26)	55	(22)	40	(16)
Total Overheads	**155**	**(63)**	**155**	**(63)**	**130**	**(53)**
Rent & Interest	70	(28)	75	(30)	100	(40)
Total Fixed Costs	**970**	**(393)**	**880**	**(356)**	**820**	**(332)**

Mainly Sheep/Cattle (upland)

	Under 130 ha (Under 320 acres)		130 - 230 ha (320 - 570 acres)		Over 230 ha (Over 570 acres)	
Regular Labour (paid)	20	(8)	15	(6)	35	(14)
Regular Labour (unpaid)	330	(134)	260	(105)	150	(61)
Casual Labour	10	(4)	10	(4)	15	(6)
Total Labour	**360**	**(146)**	**285**	**(115)**	**200**	**(81)**
Machinery Depreciation	60	(24)	65	(26)	65	(26)
Machinery Running Costs	50	(20)	65	(26)	60	(24)
Contract	20	(8)	25	(10)	25	(10)
Total Power & Machinery...	**130**	**(53)**	**155**	**(63)**	**150**	**(61)**
Farm Maintenance	10	(4)	10	(4)	15	(6)
Water & Electricity	40	(16)	40	(16)	35	(14)
General Overhead Expenses ..	25	(10)	20	(8)	25	(10)
Total Overheads	**75**	**(30)**	**70**	**(28)**	**75**	**(30)**
Rent & Interest	45	(18)	55	(22)	70	(28)
Total Fixed Costs	**610**	**(247)**	**565**	**(229)**	**495**	**(200)**

Other Farm Types

The other main DEFRA farm types are '*Mixed*', *Pigs*, *Poultry and Horticulture*. As the name suggests, the mixed category includes all farms where one enterprise is not sufficiently dominant for it to be allocated to one of the categories above. As it includes many different mixes of enterprises, the figures are unlikely to be useful for budgeting purposes.

Due to the intensity and variability of the Pig, Poultry and Horticultural farm types, the presentation of average 'per ha' figures would not be useful. Detailed historic FBS data for the different pig, poultry, and horticulture systems found in England are published on line at the addresses given on page 4. For pigs, Askham Bryan: for poultry and horticulture, Reading, or go to www.farmbusinesssurvey.co.uk.

2.   RENTS

One of the main factors affecting the rental level of agricultural land is the type of tenancy it is let on. There are three main types of agricultural agreements for letting land in England and Wales: Full or Agricultural Holdings Act (AHA) 1986, Farm Business Tenancies (FBTs, under the 1995 Act) and Seasonal Lets of less than 1 year. Since the introduction of the 1995 Act no new AHA tenancies can be created.

The Single Payment Scheme (or Basic Payment Scheme) provisions also need to be taken into account when comparing rents. The situation will vary from farm to farm and differ between the different regions of the countries of the UK. The tenant is the only person who can claim the Single Payment (SP). In seasonal lets (grazing agreements) the Licensor should be the claimant. In an AHA tenancy agreement the rental is struck independently of the Single Payment in that the tenant will have been awarded the Single Payment entitlements in 2005 and at the end of the tenancy the ownership remains with the tenant or his/her successors. With FBTs the assumption is that the tenant is claiming a 'full' SP, and if land becomes available without SP entitlements then rental levels will be lower than those shown below.

Unless otherwise stated the figures in this section relate to farms let with a combination of crops, grass and rough grazing in England; they include housing and buildings, as available.

Agricultural Holdings Act Tenancies:

Rents for land had been tending to fall up to 2007 but this was offset by higher rents for housing and buildings so that overall per hectare rents were stable. Since then improving commodity prices on cereals and general cropping farms have seen rents increasing year on year. The upturn in livestock prices, particularly in the beef sector has seen rents on grazing livestock farms improve quite considerably since 2009. But a difficult year in 2012 which had a knock on effect into 2013 has seen a small impact on rents. The dramatic fall in the beef price during the first half of 2014 could lead to a weakening of grassland rental prices.

The average rent for lowland, excluding woodland and rough grazing for farms under full Agricultural Tenancies is likely to be approximately £190 per ha, *£77 per acre*, in 2014/15. The levels on large mixed arable farms (i.e. including potatoes, sugar beet and/or vegetables) on very good soil, or well-equipped dairy farms, will tend to average £190 to £250 per hectare, *£77 to £101 per acre*. Rents on moderate, below average, quality farms, particularly with full repairing and insuring leases are likely to average £125 to £150 per hectare, *£50 to £60 per acre*.

Farm Business Tenancies:

On average FBT rents will remain higher than those above for AHA tenancies, although this is not always the case especially for lowland cattle and sheep land and dairy land. When reviewing AHA rents the scarcity value is ignored, but FBT rents reflect an open market and therefore the gap is wider. For cereals land of reasonable quality offers have tended to follow the price of a tonne of wheat per acre, but there is currently very little on offer for under £495 per hectare (*£200 per acre*). But this may prove to be a high point, as the experiences of 2012 where agreements made in the autumn left many arable farmers in a loss situation and again low cereal prices budgeted for 2014 may lead to prices stabilising. Local markets for maize and potato land can command high values and even cause agents to try and increase 3-5 year agreements on the back of this but it must be remembered there has to be a rotation. Rents throughout 2014/2015 for arable land are expected to be in the region of £445 to £495 per hectare, *£180 - £200 per acre* with good dairy land in excess of £495 per hectare, *£200* per acre.

Farm Business Survey 2012-13:

The following figures are the latest National Statistics produced by Defra showing the estimates of farm rents in England from the 2012/13 Farm Business Survey (FBS). Results from the 2012/13 Survey are referred to as the 2012 results. It should be borne in mind that rough grazing may be included in the figures given in the table below and the figures relate to the 2012/13 (Feb-Feb) year mainly covering 2012. Some farms are likely to be let at below competitive rates, for various reasons.

Average Rent by Type of Agreement:	£/ha	(acre)
Full Agricultural Tenancies	163	(66)
Farm Business Tenancies for 1 year and over......................	177	(72)
Seasonal Lets of less than one year.....................................	117	(47)

Full Agricultural Tenancies in England:

Average Rent by Farm Type:

(£ per ha [acre])	2008	2009	2010	2011	2012
Cereals	138(56)	148(60)	166(67)	172(70)	184(74)
General Cropping	164(66)	170(69)	192(78)	192(78)	198(80)
Dairy	167(68)	155(63)	180(73)	186(75)	192(78)
Cattle & Sheep (LFA)	54(22)	52(21)	62(25)	66(27)	58(23)
Cattle and Sheep (Lowland)	123(50)	131(53)	139(56)	148(60)	154(62)
All	136(55)	139(56)	152(62)	159(64)	163(66)

Farm Business Tenancies – One year and over:

Average Rent by Farm Type:

(£ per ha [acre])	2008	2009	2010	2011	2012
Cereals	158(64)	167(68)	176(71)	192(78)	211(85)
General Cropping	222(90)	225(91)	249(101)	307(124)	257(104)
Dairy	152(62)	166(67)	169(68)	184(74)	197(80)
Cattle & Sheep (LFA)	65(26)	70(28)	68(28)	78(32)	77(31)
Cattle and Sheep (Lowland)	96(39)	117(47)	119(48)	121(49)	119(48)
All	160(65)	162(66)	162(66)	179(72)	177(72)

Source of Data

DEFRA (Farming Statistics): Farm rents 2012/13 – England. In the past DEFRA rental statistics were collected via the Tenanted Land Survey (TLS) and these were reported on in previous editions of the Farm Management Pocketbook. Following a review in early 2009 DEFRA decided that the Farm Business Survey (FBS) data should be the main source and the Tenanted Land Survey (TLS) should be discontinued. The FBS is an annual survey conducted by trained Interviewers. The FBS collects data at business level and collects data for up to 15 agreements per business, with a sample of around 1,900 farm businesses. The 2013-14 Survey is due to be published in March 2015.

RICS Rural Land Market Survey:

Previous editions of the Pocketbook have included average rental levels these are now available on the Pocketbook website at www.thepocketbook.co.uk

3.   LAND PRICES

SALE VALUE OF FARMLAND, ENGLAND AND WALES

Current Agricultural Land Prices

A CALP/RICS Farmland Price Index (England and Wales) began in 1995. It covers sales of vacant possession land in England and Wales, excluding residential value where more than 50% of total sale price; value of milk quota excluded. It is calculated by dividing total value of sales by total area sold. Figures for the most recent half-yearly periods are subject to revision as further information becomes available.

As can be seen from the table below, the volume of land traded in any year, and included in the Index, is low – probably only between 0.1%-0.2% of the total agricultural area of England and Wales. The relative scarcity of land for sale has helped contribute to the increases in prices seen since the early 2000's. Such a 'thin' market can also make the prices sensitive to a small number of large transactions. For this reason, in recent years, the RICS has moved away from the transaction-based figures presented below, to using opinion-based data as its headline land price figures.

Farmland prices have weathered the economic downturn of recent times far better than other asset classes. 'Lifestyle' purchasers were replaced by farmers keeping the demand and the price of land high as the economy faltered. Since 2009, very low rates of borrowing money and negligible returns for cash investments have fuelled farmland values. This is coupled with tight supply of land and improved farm commodity prices. Once again demand is being driven by commercial farmers; but for the first time in three years demand for 'residential' farmland has grown mirroring that of the wider housing market. Land prices could drop back (along with other asset classes) when base rates rise, leading to higher costs of borrowing money and fixed interest investments start to generate a return. As always there is a wide variation in prices. Farmland prices for the period 1995 to 2000 can be found in previous editions of the Pocketbook or on the Pocketbook website at www.thepocketbook.co.uk

CALP/RICS Farmland Price Index 2005-2013 – Transaction based. (* Provisional)

		Number of Sales	Area sold '000		Weighted Average Price £		Index 1995 =100
			Ha	(acres)	Ha	(acres)	
2005	H1	141	6.0	(14.8)	8,967	(3,629)	173
	H2	164	8.7	(21.5)	9,647	(3,904)	186
2006	H1	173	9.4	(23.2)	9,408	(3,807)	181
	H2	234	15.0	(37.1)	10,376	(4,199)	200
2007	H1	141	7.0	(17.3)	11,153	(4,513)	215
	H2	230	10.8	(26.7)	14,138	(5,721)	273
2008	H1	233	8.9	(21.9)	15,824	(6,404)	305
	H2	278	11.7	(28.9)	16,342	(6,713)	315
2009	H1	181	6.3	(13.8)	15,199	(6,151)	293
	H2	256	11.4	(28.2)	16,126	(6,526)	311
2010	H1	293	5.5	(14.0)	15,177	(6,142)	293
	H2	262	12.0	(29.6)	17,458	(7,065)	336
2011	H1	154	4.2	(10.6)	18,631	(7,540)	359
	H2	273	11.7	(28.9)	20,721	(8,386)	399
2012	H1	166	4.69	(11.6)	20,586	(8,331)	397
	H2	240	7.69	(19.0)	21,053	(8,520)	406
2013	H1				21,601	(8,742)	416
2013	H2*				22,876	(9,258)	441
2014	*Estimate*				*23,475*	*(9,500)*	*452*

Other Land Price Series

In past editions of the Pocketbook, Inland Revenue and Valuation Office (VO) land price returns have been published, covering 30 years up to 1996/97 and 1993-2004 respectively. These series contained detailed splits between vacant possession and tenanted land, farms (including houses and buildings) and bare land, and also by size, land class and region. This information is still available from past editions of the Pocketbook. Data in the VO series does not continue beyond 2004, although limited information is available on the website, www.voa.gov.uk. Previous editions also include the Oxford Institute/Savills (1) Series, 1937-2000. Much of the data included in this section is available from the RICS website – www.rics.org

SALE VALUE OF FORESTS AND WOODLANDS

Forests

The figures in this section relate to planted land sold (over 25 hectares) so that values include the value of the property (land) and the timber. They focus on properties that are predominantly conifer. The decline in timber prices was reversed back in 2010 due to the high price of imported timber; a consequence of a weak Pound. Timber prices have continued to rise since then and have reached their highest levels for more than a decade. The forestry market remained extremely active throughout the year, with the highest level of total area sold since 2009. Strong domestic demand from a number of forestry investment funds and high net worth individuals being the main reasons.

Forestry continues to be attractive to investors especially due to the tax benefits available to owning woodland. Income tax is not payable on timber sales. There is potentially 100% relief on Inheritance Tax (IHT) and any gains attributable to standing or felled timber are exempt from Capital Gains Tax (CGT). 2013 was again a good year for forestry delivering excellent returns and demand going forward is expected to remain high with more opportunities for woodland owners becoming available. As economies start to recover and movement in the development and construction sectors increase, demand for timber both as a material and for fuel should grow further. Woodlands often present opportunities for wind turbines and hydro-electric schemes, whilst biomass projects supported under the Renewable Heat Incentive are likely to boost demand for timber products. But as economies grow, those who invested for the first time during the financial crisis may exit the sector seeking better returns in the short term from other investments, which may see capital values reaching their peak.

Last year there was a move in the market towards larger, more commercial forests helped by more favourable grants being offered for these kinds of properties. This trend continued in 2013. The number of properties sold rose by 16% to 79 in the year to September 2013 compared to 2012 (68) with the area sold significantly up on year earlier levels, by 47% to 13,780ha. The total market value of commercial forestry properties traded throughout GB in 2013 increased by 50% compared to 2012 to £97.25m, the highest value since 1998.

Average forest prices were up by only 2% in the year to September 2013 compared to 2012 to just under £7,100 per stocked Ha, this is the lowest jump since the survey commenced. Although looking back to 2002 the annualised average increase in property values per hectare has been 15.4% considerably better than many other investments. The figures below are for the UK and are predominantly upland with at least 50% coniferous content. Values vary with many factors and only size of block and age are recorded here, but yield class is also important.

Value of Forestland:

By Size Range (approx.)	2012	2013
	£/ha *(£/acre)*	£/ha *(£/acre)*
25 to 50 hectares.............................	6,200 *(2,509)*	6,300 *(2,550)*
51 to 100 hectares...........................	4,500 *(1,821)*	6,200 *(2,509)*
101 to 200 hectares.........................	5,000 *(2,023)*	8,500 *(3,440)*
Above 200 hectares	8,000 *(3,237)*	7,700 *(3,116)*

By Age Band	2012	2012
	£/ha *(£/acre)*	£/ha *(£/acre)*
Young (1 to 10 years)	5,000 *(2,023)*	4,800 *(1,943)*
Mid-rotation (11 to 20 years).........	5,100 *(2,064)*	4,700 *(1,902))*
Semi-mature (21 to 30 years).........	7,000 *(2,833)*	5,100 *(2,064)*
Mature (over 30 years)...................	7,200 *(2,914)*	8,000 *(3,238)*
Mature (over 40 years)...................	5,700 *(2,307)*	8,100 *(3,278)*

Woodlands

The value for small woodland decreased in 2010 as demand from lifestyle buyers for less commercial, more amenity and sporting woodland was hit by the economic climate. As the economic climate picks up this is expected to reverse. Values remain at their highest adjacent to centres of population and for properties of high amenity value. Sales in the South of England are in the £8-12,000/ha range, whereas £2-5,000/ha is more typical for other locations or where amenity values are lower.

Source: UPM Tilhill and Savills, Forest Market Report (2013)

4.   PUBLIC LIABILITY INSURANCE

Public liability insurance is not a legal obligation. However, it is essential if the general public is interacting with your business in any way, whether deliveries, visitors, etc. With a rising emphasis on encouraging the public to understand farming including visiting farms, this should be a necessity for all farms.

These figures don't take into account any additional diversification that may result in further premium. The figures below are per year, per farm. Prices of some providers are the same for each band, as they calculate their quotes differently. Often public liability comes with product and environmental liability. These figures are solely for farming, and not other activities that might take place on a farm such a contract farming, other diversifications such as a shoot, livery or a farm shop.

	Mixed Farm (130 ha)	Dairy (130 ha)	Arable (250 ha)
£5m	£250	£250	£320
£10m	£450	£450	£500

5. BUILDINGS

BUILDING COSTS

Building costs are notoriously variable. Many factors influence a contractor's price, including distance from his yard, size of contract, site access, site conditions, complexity of work, familiarity with the type of work and his current work load. There will also be differences in efficiency and standard of work between contractors and, as is often the case with farm buildings, the absence of detailed specification by the client may mean different contractors will not have quoted for identical buildings. The number of extras that are found to be required after a contract has been agreed will also vary.

The costs given below are an approximate guide. They refer to new buildings, erected by contractor on a clear level site and exclude VAT and grants that may be available. More detailed information is available in the following publications. The books and journals giving general building cost information generally assume knowledge of how to take off quantities for building work.

Specialised Information on Farm Buildings

- Farm Building Cost Guide. Published by SAC Building Design Services, Aberdeen.

- Standard Costs. Published by the Scottish Government. Used when claiming government grants on a standard-cost basis. It can be found at www.scotland.gov.uk/Resource/Doc/158202/0042819.pdf

- The Farm Buildings Handbook. Published by the Rural and Industrial Design and Building Association, Stowmarket.

General Building Cost Information

Books are produced by a number of publishers with annual or more frequent new editions and updates. Examples are Laxton's Building Price Book, Spon's Architects' and Builders' Price Book, and Wessex Comprehensive Building Price Book. Regularly updated cost information is also given in several professional and trade journals.

Constituent Parts

Frame, Roof and Foundations		*per m² floor area*
1.	Open-sided timber framed pole barn with round pole uprights on concrete bases, sawn timber rafters and purlins, high-tensile galvanised steel cladding to roof and gable ends above eaves, hardcore floor, eaves height 4.8 m, 9 m span, no side cladding, rainwater drainage to soakaways.	£80
2.	Open-sided steel portal-framed building with fibre-cement or plastic coated steel cladding to roof and gables above eaves, hardcore floor, eaves height 4.8 m, no side cladding, rainwater drainage to soakaways.	
	9 m span	£135
	13.2 m span	£125
	18 m span	£115
3.	Cost breakdown of 2 above;	
	Materials: portal frame and purlins	26%
	foundations	3%
	roofing	16%
	rainwater and drainage	3%

	hardcore and blinding	2%
	Total Materials	50%
Erection:	portal frame and purlins	19%
	foundations	2%
	roofing	19%
	rainwater and drainage	5%
	hardcore and blinding	5%
	Total Erection	50%

Roof cladding   *per m²*

1. Natural grey fibre-cement, 146 mm corrugations fixed with drive
    screws

Materials	£15.00	
Fixing	£12.50	
Total		£27.50

2. Extra for coloured sheet   £2.50

3. Deduct for translucent sheets   £0.55

4. Deduct for PVC-coated steel   £3.00

5. Deduct for high-tensile corrugated galvanised steel sheeting   £4.00

                                                                                                 per m run

6. PVC 150 mm half-round gutter on fascia brackets, including stop-ends
    and outlets   £27.50

7. PVC 100 mm rainwater pipe with fixings, swan-neck and shoe   £45.00

8. Fibre-cement close-fitting ridge   £40.00

9. Fibre-cement ventilating ridge   £45.00

Walls and Cladding   *per m²*

1. Concrete blockwork, fair faced and pointed both sides

150 mm thick	£50.00
215 mm thick	£70.00
215 mm thick hollow blocks	£70.00
215 mm thick hollow blocks, filled and reinforced	£90.00

2. Extra for rendering or roughcast to blockwork on one side   £25.00

3. Vertical spaced boarding 21x 145 mm with 19 mm gaps including
    horizontal rails, all pressure treated   £28.00

4. Fibre-cement vertical cladding, including rails   £43.00

5. Corrugated high-tensile steel side cladding, including rails   £37.50

6. Wall element: 215 mm thick blockwork, including strip
    foundation (base 750 mm below ground level),
    2.5 m height above ground level   £180 per m run

Floors   *per m²*

1. Concrete floor 100 mm thick, Gen 3 mix, on 150 mm hardcore,
    including excavation: £36.50

Breakdown:

(a)	excavate, level and compact	£3.50
(b)	hardcore	£5.00
(c)	blinding	£2.40
(d)	damp-proof membrane	£2.10
(e)	premixed concrete spread and compacted	£19.00
(f)	float finish	£4.50

2. Extra to above for

(a)	150 mm instead of 100 mm	£6.00
(b)	laying concrete to falls	£2.00
(c)	broom or textured finish	£2.00
(d)	Carborundum dust non-slip finish	£3.50
(e)	insulating concrete	£12.50

3. Reinforced concrete slatted floors for cattle

(a)	cattle loading	£77.50
(b)	tractor loading	£90.00

4. Reinforced concrete slats for pigs — £60.00

5. Insulating floor, including excavation and base

(a)	27 mm expanded polystyrene, 38 mm screed	£52.50
(b)	insulating concrete with lightweight aggregate	£45.00
(c)	as (b) with 20 mm screed	£52.50

6. Form channel in concrete — £5.00 per m run

7. Excavate for cast 1 m3 in-situ concrete bases for stanchions — £140.00 each

Services and Fittings   *per m²*

1. Drainage: 100 mm PVC pipe laid in trench, including 750 mm deep excavation and backfil — £29.00 per m run

Breakdown:

(a)	excavate and backfill	£18.00
(b)	100 mm PVC pipe laid	£10.00

Extras:

(c)	add to (a) for 1 m deep	£4.00
(d)	add to (b) for 150 mm pipe	£7.00

2. Excavate soakaway and fill with stones — £120 each

3. Trap and grid top, 100 mm PVC — £29.00 each

4. Yard gully with heavy duty road grating 400 x 300 mm — £200 each

5. Inspection chamber 900 mm deep, 450 x 600 mm opening and medium duty cast iron cover — £400 each

6. Above-ground vitreous enamel slurry tank on concrete base, 1000 m³ — £55,000 each

7. Reception pit, 20 m³ — £6,000 each

8. Slurry channel beneath (not including) slats, 1.8 m deep, 3m wide — £500 per m run

9. Lighting: 1.5 m 60W single fluorescent unit, including wiring and switch — £135 each

Extras:

(a)	PVC conduit	£6.50
(b)	screwed steel conduit	£12.00

10.	Power: 13A switched outlet	£24.00 each
11.	Diagonal feed fence, fixed, including posts (painted)	£135 per m run
12.	Tombstone feed fence, fixed, including posts (painted)	£145 per m run
13.	Feed bunker	£80 per m run
14.	Hay rack, wall fixing	£85 per m run
15.	Cubicle division, galvanised, fixed in place	£110 each
16.	Fencing: three-rail timber with posts, all pressure treated	£30.00 per m run

17. Gate, 3 m wide, galvanised steel, including posts set in concrete
    (a)   medium duty   £250 each
    (b)   heavy duty   £325 each
    Deduct for painted instead of galvanised finish   £30

Complete Buildings

Fully Covered and Enclosed Barn

Portal frame, 18 m span, 6 m bays, 6 m to eaves, 3 m high blockwork walls with sheet cladding above, 6 m sliding doors at either end, 150mm thick concrete floor   £210 per m² floor area

Cows and Cattle Housing

1.	Covered strawed yard, enclosed with ventilated cladding, concrete floor, pens only, with 4.0 m² per head floor area	£750 per head
2.	Extra to 1 for 4.0 m wide double-sided feeding passage, barrier and troughs	£300 per head
3.	Kennel building	£450 per head
4.	Portal framed building with cubicles	£1,500 per head
5.	Extra to 4 for feed stance, feeding passage, barriers and troughs	£625 per head
6.	Extra to 4 for slatting of cubicle passages	£640 per head
7.	Covered collecting yard, 1.1 m² per cow	£225 per head
8.	Milking parlour building, example: 5.5 x 11.5 m for 8/16 parlour	£20,000
9.	Parlour equipment, herringbone parlours:	
	(a) low level, 1 stall per point	£3,850 per point
	(b) pipeline	£3,150 per point
	(c) extra for meter and auto cluster removal	£2,150 per point
	(d) auto feed dispenser	£900 per point
10.	Dairy building	£335 per m² floor area
11.	Bulk tank and washer	£8.50 per litre
12.	Loose box, 16 m² floor area laid to falls, rendered walls	£350 per m² floor area
13.	Bull pen and open run	£13,500
14.	Cattle crush and 20 m race	£6,500
15.	Slatted floor cattle building for 120 growing cattle (1.7 m² pen space per head) with drive-through feed passage/troughs	£1,500 per head

Silage	*per tonne stored*
1. Timber panel clamp on concrete base with effluent tank	£80
2. Precast concrete panel clamp with effluent tank	£110
3. Glass-lined forage tower and unloader	£250

Waste Storage	*per m³ stored*
1. Lined lagoon with safety fence	£45.00
2. Glass-lined steel slurry silo	
small (400 m³)	£60.00
medium (1,200 m³)	£55.00
large (3,600 m³)	£50.00
3. GRP below-ground effluent tank, encased in concrete	
small (12 m³)	£500
large (36 m³)	£450

Sheep Housing

1. Penning, troughs, feed barriers and drinkers installed in suitable existing building — £38 per ewe
2. Purpose-built sheep shed with 1.35 m² pen space per ewe concentrate troughs, feed passage and barrier for forage feeding — £225 per ewe
   Extras:
   (a) softwood slatted floor panels, materials only — £10.00 per m²
   (b) slatted panels as (a), made up, plus supports — £31.50 per m²

Pig Housing — *per sow and litter*

1. Farrowing and rearing
   (a) Prefabricated farrowing pens with crates, side creep areas, part-slatted floors, including foundations, electrical and plumbing work — £3,500
   (b) Steel-framed farrowing house with insulated blockwork walls, part-slatted pens with side creeps in rooms of eight with off main passage — £3,950
   (c) Flat-deck rearing house 3-6 weeks with fully perforated floors to pens, 0.25 m² per pig pen area — £150 per weaner
   (d) Prefabricated veranda house including foundations, electrical and plumbing work, 0.3m² per pig internal lying area — £120 per weaner

2. Finishing   *per baconer*

    (a) Prefabricated fattening house with part-slatted floors,
        trough feeding   £265

    (b) Prefabricated fattening house with part-slatted floors,
        floor fed   £255

    (c) Steel framed building with insulated blockwork walls,
        part-slatted floors, trough fed   £110

    (d) Automatic feeding systems for items (a), (b) and (c)
        above:
        dry-feed system with ad-lib hoppers   £675
        dry on-floor feeding   £16.00
        wet feeding   £23

3. Dry sows and boars   *per sow*
    (a) Yards with floor feeding   £375
    (b) Sow cubicle system   £600
    (c) Yards with electronic feeders   £1,050
    (d) Yards with individual feeders   £1,250
    (e) Two-yard system with flat-rate feeding   £1,350
    (f) Boar pens as part of sow house   £2,750 each

4. Complete pig unit

    Building costs calculated on basis of three-week weaning,
    23 pigs per sow per year to bacon, excl. external slurry or
    dung storage, feed storage and handling/weighing facilities:
    (a) Breeding and rearing only   £2,100 per sow
    (b) Breeding with progeny to bacon   £3,750 per sow

Poultry Housing and Equipment   *per bird*

1. Intensive enriched cages with automatic feeding and egg
    collection; (new traditional cages were banned from 1st
    January 2003;only enriched cages complete with nest box,
    perches and scratching area are now allowed)   £24.00-£28.00

2. Perchery/barn   £22.00-£27.00

3. Free Range: new sites stocked at 9 birds per m²,   £27.50-£35.00
    existing sites stocked at 11.7 birds per m²   £22.50-£29.00
    smaller mobile units will cost   £32.00 plus

4. Broiler Breeders, deep litter, 0.167 m² per bird   £29.00

5. Pullets (cage and floor reared)   £16.50

6. Broilers, deep litter, 0.05 m² per bird   £9.50-£10.50

7. Turkeys, 20,000 pole barn fattening unit
    (cost varies with size of unit and degree of automation)   £21.00-£28.00

Grain Storage and Drying   *per tonne stored*

1. Intake pit, conveyor, elevator, overhead conveyor and catwalk,
    storage bins within existing building   £240
    extra for low volume ventilation of bins   £95

2.	As 1 in new building	£340
3.	Portable grain walling for on-floor storage in existing building	£55
4.	On floor grain storage in purpose-built building	£125
	Extras:	
	(a) low volume ventilation	£9.00-£10.00
	(b) on-floor drying with above-ground main duct and laterals	£135
	(c) add to (b) for below-ground laterals	£17.00
5.	Sealed towers for moist grain, including loading and unloading equipment	£165-£210

Potato Storage	*per tonne stored*
1. Pallet-box store with recirculation fans	£240
Pallet boxes, 1 tonne	£85
2. Bulk store, building only	£225
Ventilation system: fans, main duct, below-floor lateral ducts	£55

Roads and Fences	*per m length*
3.2 m wide hardcore road with drainage ditches using locally excavated material	£35.00
using imported hardcore (£6.15/m³)	£50.00
extra for bitumen macadam surfacing, two coats	£57.00
Traditional 7-wire stock fence	£8.50
High tensile 7-wire stock fence	£6.50

Construction Equipment Hire	*hourly rate, with driver*
Excavator	£30.00-£40.00
Tipping lorry	£40.00-£55.00
10-tonne crane	£50.00-£70.00
	weekly rate
Concrete mixer, 100 litre (5/3)	£50
Compressor and heavy breaker	£140

STANDARD BUILDING COSTS

Standard costs were published by the Scottish Government on the basis of the cost of farm or casual labour and new materials. The last set of data issued was for 2002 and so the figures are no longer included in The Pocketbook.

STORAGE REQUIREMENTS

Bulk (cubic metres (feet) per tonne):

		M³/tonne	Ft³/tonne
Beans		1.2	(43)
Wheat, peas		1.3	(46)
Barley, rye, oilseed rape, linseed, fodder beet		1.4	(50)
Oats		1.9	(68)
Potatoes		1.6	(57)
Dry bulb onions		2.0	(71)
Concentrates:	meal	2.0	(71)
	cubes	1.6	(57)
Grass silage:	18% DM	1.3	(46)
	30% DM	1.6	(57)
Maize silage		1.3	(46)
Silage: large round bales		2.5	(88)
Wheat straw ⎫		13.0	(464)
Barley straw ⎬ small bales		11.5	(411)
Hay ⎭		6.0	(214)
Wheat straw ⎫		20.0	(714)
Barley straw ⎬ large round bales		18.0	(643)
Hay ⎭		8.0	(286)
Brewers' grains		0.9	(32)

(With straw and hay the storage requirement clearly depends on the packing density; the above are simply typical averages).

Boxes (floor area in square metres (feet) per tonne):

Potatoes:	0.5 tonne boxes, 5 boxes high	0.52	(5.6)
	1.0 tonne boxes, 4 boxes high	0.52	(5.6)
	1.0 tonne boxes, 5 boxes high	0.45	(4.8)

Bags (floor area in square metres (feet) per tonne):

Feedstuffs:	2 bags high	1.6	(17)
Fertiliser:	6 bags high	1.1	(12)
	10 bags high	0.7	(8)

VII.   TAXATION

Note: no responsibility can be taken for any errors or omissions in the information presented in this section or for any action taken on the basis of the information provided. Professional advice should always be sought before taking any decision that may affect your tax position.

1.   INCOME TAX

RATES OF INCOME TAX (2014-15)

	Income Band	Dividends	Interest	Other Income
Basic rate	£0 to £31,865	10	20	20
Higher rate	£31,866-150,000	32.5	40	40
Additional rate	over £150,000	37.5	45	45

For 2014-15 a lower rate of 10% still applies to other savings income (primarily bank and building society interest) up to a limit of £2,880. This 10% rate is not available if taxable non-savings income exceeds £2,880.

ALLOWANCES AND RELIEFS (2014-15)

Personal Allowance

This is £10,000 for 2014-15. The basic personal allowance for income tax is gradually reduced to nil for individuals with adjusted net incomes in excess of £100,000. The reduction is £1 for every £2 over the limit. For 2015-16 the basic personal allowance will rise to £10,500.

The age related allowance if aged 65 to 74 is £10,500, and £10,660 if aged over 75 on 5th April 2013, subject to total income not exceeding the statutory income limit (£27,000 for 2014-15).

Married Couples Allowance

This was abolished from the tax year ended 6th April 2001 except for couples where at least one spouse was born before 6th April 1935. From 2005-06 the allowance has been available to couples in a civil partnership where at least one partner was born before 6th April 1935. The relief is given as a reduction in income tax restricted to the lower of 10% of the allowance (£816.50 for 2014-15) or the total tax liability.

Personal Pension Schemes

Tax relief is obtainable for contributions to a pension. There are limits on how much of the contribution is eligible for relief – both yearly and lifetime. The annual allowance is £40,000 for 2014-15. The lifetime allowance is £1.25m for 2014-15.

2.   PRIVATE COMPANY TAXATION

RATES OF CORPORATION TAX (2013-14)

The rates set out in the table below apply to profits made in any financial year (FY) from 1st April to 31st March. FY14 therefore covers 1st April 2014 to 31st March 20154. Profits are chargeable at the following rates;

Corporation Tax Bandings

	Profits band	per cent tax	
		FY14	*FY13*
Small companies' rate	Up to £300,000	20	*20*
Upper marginal rate	£300,000 to £1.5m	21.25	*23.75*
Main companies' rate	Over £1.5m	21	*23*

Note: The marginal rates shown above are divided by the number of associated companies.

COMPANY TAXATION – OTHER ISSUES

Capital Gains

Capital gains of companies are charged at the appropriate rate of Corporation Tax. The indexation allowance is still available to reduce capital gains made by Companies.

Quotas

Milk quota purchased by a company after 1st April 2002 will attract Corporation Tax relief at the rate of depreciation selected in the accounting policies of the company or 4% per year if not depreciated in the accounts of the company.

Distributions

Dividends are not deductible in arriving at the amount of Corporation Tax profit. However, the recipient of distributions will be credited with a tax payment of 10% of distributions received, which will be deemed to discharge the liability of basic rate (20%) taxpayers. Higher rate taxpayers are liable to pay tax at 32.5% on that part of their dividend income falling above the higher rate limit. Taxpayers with income in excess of £150,000 will be liable to tax on dividends at 37.5%.

Losses

Carry back of losses not set against other income is restricted to one year. Losses can be carried forward and offset against profits of the same trade.

3. AGRICULTURAL BUSINESSES: OTHER ITEMS

ASSESSING SELF-EMPLOYED PROFITS

Self-employed people are assessed for tax in any tax year on the basis of the profits recorded in the annual accounts which end in that tax year, i.e. on a 'current year basis'.

LIVESTOCK

Dairy cows or breeding livestock may be treated on the herd basis or on a trading stock basis;

Herd Basis

Under the herd basis valuation changes are not included in the trading account, nor are additions to the herd, but sales from the herd and replacements are. On the sale of all or a substantial proportion (normally taken as 20% or more) of the herd, no tax is paid on any profit over the original cost price, nor is there any relief for loss.

Trading Stock Basis

Purchases, sales and valuation changes are all included in the trading account. Under this method stock should be valued at the lower of cost (or cost of production) and net realisable value. Where animals are home-produced and it is not possible to ascertain actual costs from farm records the 'deemed' cost may be used. This is 60% of market value for cattle and 75% for sheep and pigs.

STOCK VALUATION: CROPS

Crops should generally be valued at the cost of production (or net realisable value, if lower). Costs which are directly attributable to buying, producing and growing the crops should be included. The deemed cost method allows 75% of market value to be used although this method should only be used where it is not possible to ascertain actual costs.

ALLOWANCES FOR CAPITAL EXPENDITURE

Machinery and Plant

1. The same rules apply whether the machinery and plant is new or second hand. An annual writing down allowance of 18% p.a. is available on a reducing balance basis on capital expenditure incurred on the provision of plant and machinery. Qualifying expenditure is added to the asset 'pool' and the writing down allowances are given on the residue of expenditure in that pool.

2. The Annual Investment Allowance ('AIA') gives 100% relief for the first £250,000. The allowance has been raised to £500,000 from April 2014 to 31st December 2015 of qualifying expenditure per accounting period. The limit is proportionally increased or decreased where the chargeable period is longer or shorter than a year. A group of companies can only receive a single allowance. Expenditure on cars does not qualify, although expenditure on long life assets, or on 'integral features' can be claimed.

3. An 8% rate applies to expenditure incurred on certain listed 'integral features' in a building and on long life assets. Expenditure brought forward will obtain the 8% rate.

4. 100% first year allowances can be claimed for expenditure incurred by any business on designated energy-saving plant and machinery and environmentally beneficial technologies and products. The lists of items which qualify can be found on the Government's Energy Technology Product lists, which is at www.eca.gov.uk.

Cars

Motor cars purchased before April 2009, costing more than £12,000 are included in a separate 'pool' in the year of purchase, on which a 20% writing down allowance is available.

For expenditure on motor cars purchased in or after April 2009, the regime is based on CO_2 emissions. Cars with CO_2 emissions exceeding 160gm/km are allocated to the 8% special rate pool. All other cars go into the general 18% rate pool. For unincorporated businesses, cars have their own separate pools where there is an element of private use.

Machinery Leasing

Tax allowances for rental payments on financial leases are spread to reflect the commercial depreciation of the asset. This may mean that full tax relief for rental payments may not be gained in the years in which the payments are made.

Buildings

Farm buildings, fencing, drainage and other improvements (including up to one-third of farmhouses) used to qualify for a writing-down allowance of 4% annually, given equally over 25 years. These allowances have now been completely phased out.

LOSSES

Losses can normally be set against other income in the year they are incurred and in the prior year. If other income is insufficient in the year when the loss occurs and in the prior year, unrelieved losses can be carried forward and set off against future profits from the same trade. Special rules apply to prevent abuse of loss relief provisions by 'hobby' farmers who are not running their farms on a commercial basis with a view to producing a profit: normally losses are disallowed against other income after 5 consecutive years of loss. Trading losses may be set against capital gains in the same year as the loss.

PROFIT AVERAGING

This relief is to enable farmers, other than companies, to average their taxable profits over two consecutive years. Where the difference between the profits of two consecutive years is 30% or more of the higher profits, the total profits for the two years are equally divided between the two years. Marginal relief is available where the difference is less than 30% but more than 25% of the higher profits. Profit for the purposes of tax averaging calculations is after the deduction of capital allowances. There is a two year limit in which to make the claim:

- 95 gm/km or less are eligible for 100% first year allowances;

- 95 – 130 gm/km go onto the general 18% pool;

- Over 130 gm/km have an 8% annual allowance.

4.   CAPITAL GAINS TAX

APPLICATION AND RATES

Applies to capital gains made by an individual. Capital gains accruing to companies are chargeable to Corporation Tax. A capital gain is the difference between the acquisition value and the sale price. The first £11,000 of capital gains realised by an individual in a tax year are covered by their annual exemption.

Disposals of non-business assets attract capital gains tax of 18% for basic rate taxpayers or 28% for higher and additional rate taxpayers. The rate of CGT is 18% where total taxable gains and income, after taking into account all allowable deductions including losses, personal allowances and the CGT annual exemption, are less than the upper limit of the income tax basic rate band. The 28% rate will apply to gains or any parts of gains above this limit.

Exempt assets include a principal private residence (e.g. farm house, if non-exclusive business occupation applies) if occupied as such, normal life assurance policies, animals and tangible movable properly (i.e. chattels) disposed of for £6,000 or less.

Capital Gains Tax is chargeable only on the disposal (including gifts) of assets. Capital Gains Tax is not payable on death. Payment of Capital Gains Tax is due on 31st January following the tax year of disposal.

RELIEFS

Losses

Should a transaction produce a loss, this may be set against any long term chargeable gains arising in the same year or, if these are insufficient, those accruing in subsequent years. Losses brought forward will be used only to the extent necessary to reduce untaxed gains for the year to £11,000.

Where a trading loss can be set against other income in the same or prior year for income tax purposes, any unused loss can be set against capital gains for those years.

Improvements

Spending that has increased the value of the asset can be offset against any gain. In the case of agricultural property, allowance would be made for any capital expenditure undertaken to improve the property.

Indexation and Taper Relief

Indexation and Taper relief for individuals has now been abolished for any disposals taking place on or after 6th April 2008. Indexation allowance is still available for capital gains arising in companies.

Entrepreneurs Relief

Entrepreneur's relief applies to certain disposals of business assets by an individual. The relief, which must be claimed, gives a reduced effective rate of Capital Gains Tax of 10% for eligible gains of up to £10m for disposals after 6th April 2011 (lower limits applied before this date). The limit is a lifetime limit per individual. The assets which qualify for entrepreneurs' relief are in line with those which qualified for business asset taper relief. This covers:

- a trading business carried on by an individual alone or in partnership;

- assets of such a trade following cessation;

- shares or securities in a trading company where the individual owns 5% or more and is an officer or employee

The conditions for the relief must have been satisfied throughout a qualifying period of a year before the disposal.

Editorial Note: *The rules for Entrepreneurs' relief are complex, particularly in cases of disposals of part of the business. The rules are similar to the previous Retirement Relief and are particularly tricky in cases of disposals of farmland and related assets and trade. It is recommended that professional advice is sought where it is anticipated claiming this relief, particularly as given the increase in the lifetime allowance combined with the increase in tax rate for non-business assets, the tax savings can be greatly increased.*

Rollover

Payment of tax may be deferred on gains accruing from the sale of business assets (including land and buildings occupied and used for trade purposes, fixed plant and machinery, milk quotas, and from the sale of shares in a family business) if part or all of the proceeds are spent on acquiring new qualifying assets. The tax is deferred by deducting the gain from the acquisition price of the new asset. It can only be claimed if the new asset is acquired within 12 months before and 3 years after the disposal of the old assets. Disposal and acquisition dates for Capital Gains purposes are generally contract, not completion, dates.

Holdover

Payments of tax may be deferred where disposal is by gift. This relief only applies to gifts of business assets, land which qualifies for agricultural property relief at either the 100% or 50% rate under Inheritance Tax (see next section) and gifts which lead to an immediate charge to Inheritance Tax (e.g. gifts into a discretionary trust). The amount of the chargeable gain which would normally have accrued to the donor will be held over; the value at which the donee is deemed to acquire the asset will be its market value reduced by the amount of the donor's chargeable gain held over. Where deferral is not available, payment of tax by interest bearing annual instalments over 10 years will be allowed for gifts of land, controlling share holdings and minority share holdings in unquoted companies.

5.   INHERITANCE TAX

APPLICATION AND RATES

This tax is charged on lifetime gifts and transfers on death. The rate for 2014-15 is 40%, on amounts chargeable to Inheritance Tax above the nil rate band of £325,000.

The nil rate band is potentially increased for surviving spouses or civil partners who died on or after 9th October 2007. From this date the nil rate band may be increased by the unused proportion of the deceased spouse or civil partners nil rate band.

Outright gifts to individuals are exempt from tax at the time of the gift. If the donor lives for a further seven years then the transfer is fully exempt. Gifts into accumulation and maintenance trusts and interest in possession trusts no longer receive special treatment - all other gifts will be taxed at half the above rates at the time of the transfer.

Tax is charged on the value of an individual's estate at death plus the value of all gifts made within seven years of death. Allowance is made for any tax paid on lifetime gifts included in the value of the estate on death. Relief is given for outright gifts made more than three years before death according to the following scale:

Years between gift and death	0-3	3-4	4-5	5-6	6-7
Percentage of the full tax charge	100%	80%	60%	40%	20%

Exemptions include: transfers between husband and wife; the first £3,000 of gift made by a donor in the income tax year and separately up to £250 per year to any number of persons; gifts made out of income which form part of normal expenditure; marriage gifts within limits of £5,000 for a parent, £2,500 for a lineal ancestor and £1,000 for other donors.

RELIEFS

Agricultural Property Relief

Relief may be available for agricultural land. Subject to a general rule that the agricultural land must have been occupied by the transferor (or by his controlled company) for two years, or owned by the transferor for 7 years and occupied for agricultural purposes by someone else before any relief is granted. The relief is at two different rates. If the basis of valuation is vacant possession (or there is the right to obtain it within 12 months), the taxable value of the land is reduced by 100%. If the basis of valuation is tenanted value, the taxable value of the land is reduced by 50% of that tenanted value. Ownership and occupation periods normally include prior periods of ownership or occupation by husbands and wives. From 1st September 1995, 100% relief applies to new lettings of agricultural land as Farm Business Tenancies. Agricultural Relief includes agricultural land in the European Economic Area (EEA).

Editorial Note: There has been much publicised activity and tax cases concerning APR claims, particularly attempts by the Inland Revenue to reduce or deny the relief on claims for farmhouses. Care must be taken to protect the relief particularly where the attached land is either let out on a Farm Business Tenancy or under a contract farming arrangement.

Business Property Relief

Relief is also available in respect to 'business property' transferred during lifetime or on death. The relief extends to the business assets of a proprietor and the interest of a partner or controlling shareholder in the business capital of a company. The value of such property, providing certain tests are satisfied (e.g. it has been owned by the transferor for two years preceding transfer), is reduced by 100%. Where a partner or controlling shareholder owns assets (e.g. land) that the business uses, the value will be reduced by 50%. Shareholdings in unquoted companies receive a 100% reduction in market value.

Lifetime gifts of property eligible for Agricultural and Business Property Relief have to be retained (or replaced by similar property) until the death of the donor (or earlier death of the donee) if those reliefs are to be available when the tax (or additional tax) becomes payable subsequent to the donor's death

In the case of the transfer of property eligible for APR and BPR, the tax can be paid by annual instalments over ten years free of interest.

6.   STAMP TAXES

Stamp Duty is charged at 0.5 per cent of consideration paid (purchase by cash, other stocks or shares) on the transfer of shares and securities.

Stamp Duty Land Tax is charged on the transfer of an interest in land; both sales and leases. With sales of property the tax is levied on a percentage of the sale value of the property. The rates applicable to transactions since March 2014 are:

Residential property	Rate	Non-residential and mixed use	Rate
Value up to £125,000...........	nil	Value up to £150,000..............	nil
£125,001 to £250,000	1%	£150,001 to £250,000..............	1%
£250,001 to £500,000	3%	£250,001 to £500,000..............	3%
£500,001 to £1,000,000	4%	£500,001 or more....................	4%
£1,000,001 to £2,000,000	5%		
£2,000,001 or more..............	7%		

Purchased of property other than individuals with a value of over £500,000 are subject to a 15% rate as from March 2014.

Stamp Duty Land Tax is payable on leases calculated according to the net present value of the rent payable over the term of the lease.

7.   VALUE ADDED TAX

Agricultural businesses with a turnover of taxable goods and services in excess of £81,000 per annum must register for VAT. Businesses with a turnover below this limit may apply for voluntary registration. The standard VAT rate has been 20% since January 2011. Most agricultural products are zero rated for VAT purposes. VAT has to be paid on certain inputs. Registered businesses are eligible to reclaim the tax paid where the goods or services purchased have been used in the production of zero-rated supplies.

A flat rate scheme is available to farmers as an alternative to registering for VAT. Farmers under the flat rate scheme do not have to submit tax returns or account for VAT and consequently cannot reclaim tax. They can, however, charge (and keep) a flat rate addition of 4% when they sell to VAT registered customers goods and services which qualify. This addition is not VAT but acts as compensation for losing input tax on purchases. The registered person paying the flat rate amount to the farmer can recover it as if it were VAT, subject to the normal rules for reclaiming. The local VAT office may refuse to issue a certificate to participate in the flat rate scheme if this would mean the farmer would recover substantially (£3,000) more than through the normal system.

A flat rate scheme operates for small businesses generally and is an alternative that farmers can use if they have taxable supplies of no more than £150,000 and a total business income of no more than £187,500. This scheme operates in a different way to the flat rate scheme for farmers in that a business charges the normal rate of VAT on sales. However, the VAT which the business has to remit to Customs and Excise is calculated by multiplying the value of gross sales by a rate specified for each particular trade sector. The rate for agriculture is 6.5% since January 2011 except for businesses supplying agricultural services, when the rate is 11%.

Editorial Note*: Farmers and landowners must always consider the VAT implications when considering any new or more farming activities on the land or within the buildings, particularly where supplies are made the public who cannot recover any VAT which may be charged on the service or goods provided from the farm.*

8.   NATIONAL INSURANCE

The tables below set out the National Insurance contributions for the 2014-15 year;

Class 1 (not contracted out)

Employee's weekly earnings	Employee
£153 or less...	Nil
£153.01 to £805	12%
Over £805	2%

Employer contributions are 13.8% on weekly earnings over £153

Class 2

Self-employed flat rate .... £2.75 a week

Class 3

Non-employed (voluntary) flat rate .... £13.90 a week

Class 4

Self-employed. On profits or gains
between £7,956 and £41,865 .... 9%
over £41,865 .... 2%

VIII.   FARM BUSINESS MANAGEMENT

1.   DEFINITIONS OF FARM MANAGEMENT TERMS

VALUATIONS AND CAPITAL

Valuations

Valuation is essentially a process of estimation. Alternative methods are possible, according to the purpose intended. The basis should be consistent throughout the period or any series of figures.

1. *Saleable crops in store.* At estimated market value less costs still to be incurred, e.g. for storage and marketing. Both may be estimated either at the expected date of sale or at the date of valuation.

2. *Growing crops.* Preferably at variable costs to the date of valuation, although estimated total cost can alternatively be used.

3. *Saleable crops ready for harvesting* but still in the ground. Preferably as valued in point 1 above, less estimated harvesting costs, although they can alternatively be treated as described in point 2 above.

4. *Fodder stocks (home-grown).* Normally at variable costs when calculating gross margins although this can be misleading for management purposes. Alternatively at estimated market value (based on hay-equivalent value according to quality). Fodder crops still in the ground, e.g. kale, treated as point 2 above.

5. *Stocks of purchased materials (including fodder).* At cost (net of discounts).

6. *Machinery and equipment.* Original cost (net of grants and discounts), less accumulated depreciation to date of valuation – this gives a valuation on the 'historic' cost basis. Alternatively at estimated market value.

7. *Livestock.* At current market value, less cost of marketing. Fluctuations in market value expected to be temporary should be ignored.

Capital

Tenant's Capital. The estimated total value of capital on the farm, other than land and fixed equipment. There is no easy way of determining this sum precisely and estimates are made in several ways depending on the information available and the purpose for which the estimate is required. One method is to take the average of the opening and closing valuations (at either market value or cost) of livestock, crops, machinery and stores (feed, seed, fertilisers). See also pages 246 (following section).

Landlord's Capital. Value of the land and fixed equipment (including buildings).

OUTPUT TERMS

Revenue (or Income). Receipts adjusted for debtors at the beginning and end of the accounting period. Items such as CAP support, revenue grants, contract receipts and wayleaves are included.

Returns. Revenue adjusted for valuation changes (add closing, deduct opening, valuation).

Gross Output. Returns plus the value of produce consumed in the farmhouse or supplied to workers for which no payment is made, less purchases of livestock, livestock products and other produce bought for resale.

Enterprise Output. The total value of an enterprise, whether sold or retained on the farm. It therefore equals Gross Output of the enterprise plus the market value of any of the products kept on the farm (transfers out). Following 'decoupling' the Single Payment should not be apportioned to individual enterprises. Products transferred from another enterprise to be used in the production of the enterprise whose output is being calculated are deducted at market value (transfers in). Instead of the accounting year the "harvest year" can be used for crops which means valuations may not be relevant.

(Enterprise) Output from Forage. Primarily the sum of the enterprise outputs of grazing livestock, but includes keep let and occasional sales, e.g. of surplus hay, together with an adjustment for changes in the valuation of stocks of home-grown fodder. However, fortuitous changes in stocks caused by yield variations due to the weather, the severity or length of the winter, or minor changes in livestock numbers or forage area can be either ignored (if small in relation to total annual usage) or included in miscellaneous output.

Adjusted Forage (Enterprise) Output. Output from Forage less rented keep and purchases of bulk fodder.

Standard Output. The average enterprise output per hectare of a crop or per head of livestock calculated from average yield data and either national or local average price.

INPUT TERMS

Expenditure. Payments adjusted for creditors at the beginning and end of the accounting period. Capital expenditure is not included.

Costs. Expenditure adjusted for valuation changes (add opening, deduct closing, valuation), with the following adjustments: Add; depreciation on capital expenditure including machinery, any loss made on machinery sales (add to depreciation) and the value of payments in kind to workers if not already included in their earnings. Deduct; purchases of livestock, livestock products and other produce bought for resale, any profit made on machinery (deduct from depreciation), allowance for private use of farm vehicles (deduct from machinery costs), the value of purchased stores used in the farmhouse (e.g. electricity) or sold off the farm (deduct from the relevant item).

Inputs. Costs with the following adjustments, made in order to put all farms on a similar basis for comparative purposes. Add: the value of unpaid family labour, including the manual labour of the farmer and his wife, and, in the case of owner-occupiers, an estimated rental value (based on average rents of similar farms in the area), less any cottage rents received. Deduct: any mortgage payments and other expenses of owner-occupation, interest payments and the cost of paid management. A proportion of the rental value of the farmhouse may also be deducted.

Fixed Costs. See pages from 216 whole Farm Fixed Costs.

Variable Costs. See page 1.

MARGIN TERMS

Management and Investment Income. Gross Output less Inputs. It represents the reward to management and the return on tenant's capital invested in the farm, whether borrowed or not. It is mainly used for comparative purposes, all farms having been put on a similar financial basis by the adjustments made to costs in calculating Inputs.

Net Farm Income. Management and Investment Income, less paid management, plus the value of the manual labour of the farmer and his wife. It represents the return to all tenant's type capital and the reward to the farmer for his manual labour and management.

Profit (or Loss). Gross Output less Costs. This represents the surplus or deficit before imputing any notional charges such as rental value or unpaid labour. In the accounts of owner-occupiers it includes any profit accruing from the ownership of land.

Farm Business Income. This term is increasingly being used in FBS costings, and is similar to 'Profit' above. It represents the return to all unpaid labour and to all their own capital in the farm business including land and farm buildings.

Gross Margin. See page 1.

Net Margin. A term sometimes used to denote Gross Margin less direct labour and machinery costs charged to an individual enterprise. This is not, however, nationally accepted terminology. Increasingly Net Margin in the enterprise context is being used to denote the profit of an enterprise by taking its gross output less its 'complete enterprise costs', but see page 2.

AREA TERMS

Total Hectares. All hectares comprising the farm.

Hectares. Total hectares less areas of woods, waste land, roads, yards, buildings, etc.

Adjusted Hectares. Hectares reduced by the conversion of rough grazing into the equivalent hectares of average quality grassland. This is the figure often used for lowland farms when calculating "per hectare" results.

Forage Hectares. Total hectares of forage crops grown, less any hectares exclusively used by pigs or poultry and the area equivalent of any home-grown fodder fed to livestock reared in cereal systems. Also, the area of rough grazing is converted to its grassland equivalent (see Adjusted Hectares). Forage crops are all crops including grass, rough grazing, maize and whole crops grown specifically for grazing livestock, but excluding catch crops and crops harvested as grain and pulses.

Adjusted Forage Hectares. Forage hectares adjusted as follows. Add area equivalent of keep rented, deduct area equivalent of keep let; deduct the area equivalent of occasional sales of fodder, e.g. surplus hay, and seed cuts (note: hay and seed grown regularly for sale should be regarded as cash crops, not forage crops); add or deduct the area equivalent of planned changes in the valuation of stocks of home-grown fodder (fortuitous changes in stocks resulting from weather conditions may be ignored); convert rough grazing into their grassland equivalent if not already done. The following adjustments also may be made: add the area equivalent of catch crops and of grazing from cash crops of hay or seed: add the area equivalent of purchased fodder.

In calculations such as Gross Margins per Forage Hectare, Adjusted Forage Hectares are usually used. If the area equivalent of purchased fodder has been added, the cost of purchased fodder must not be charged as a variable cost: this is probably the best calculation for comparative purposes. Alternatively, when considering all the grazing enterprises taken together, purchased fodder can be deducted as a variable cost and no addition made for its area equivalent.

2. CAPITAL REQUIREMENT AND RETURN

TENANT'S CAPITAL

1. *Machinery.* Costs of new machinery are given on pages 189. Written-down values in 2015 are likely to average £545-£750 per hectare (£221-£304/acre) of actively farmed land (excluding fallow and rough grazing) taking all farm types together. Average values for different farm types are given on the next page.

2. *Breeding Livestock.* The 2015 average of breeding livestock value per hectare can be anything up to £1,600 (£650/acre) for an intensive (outdoor) dairy/livestock farm. Intensive (housed) pig and poultry units will be substantially more but a relatively meaningless figure. Approximate average market values of various categories of breeding livestock (of mixed ages in the case of adult stock) are as follows (actual value will vary according to average age and weight, quality and breed):

Average market values of various breeding livestock

| | **Breeding Herd** | | |
	Newly calved	Average	Cull**
Holstein/Friesian Dairy Cows	£1,600	£1,100	£500
Channel Island Dairy Cows	£1,250	£760	£270
Suckler Beef Cows:	£1,200*	£775	£550
Pure-bred Beef Cows	£1,900*	£1,125	£550

* *Calf at Foot < 3 months*
** *based on £1.10/kg DW*

| | **Replacements** | | |
	Holstein Friesians	Ayrshires and C.I. Breeds	Beef Cattle
In Calf Heifers	£1,350	£1,125	£1,100
1-2 years	£1,000	£800	£780
6-12 months	£630	£500	£600
Under 6 months	£325	£250	£200

	Other Livestock
Ewes (2 ½ years old / one lamb crop)	£130
Rams (2 ½ years old / one mating season)	£350
Sows and In-Pig Gilts	£210
Boars	£750

3. Working Capital. This is defined as the current assets of a business less its current liabilities. It is the liquid capital needed to finance the cash flow through the production cycle, the length of which varies considerably between different crop and livestock enterprises and different combinations of these enterprises. It can include the cost of purchased fattening stock, feed, seed, fertilisers, regular labour, machinery running costs, general overhead costs, rent and living expenses. This capital will vary between farm business types. Specialist root crop and vegetable farm businesses will have significantly higher working capital requirements than livestock and combinable cropping businesses. The only accurate way to estimate working capital requirement is to complete a full cash flow estimate for the production cycle of the business.

Average Tenants Capital per Hectare

Average Tenant's Capital for different English farm types for 2015:

Farm Type Group	Average No. Hectares	Breeding Livestock ***	Crops, Cultivns., Stores	Machinery and Equipment*	Total Tenant's Capital	
**		£/ha	£/ha	£/ha	£/ha	£/acre
Mainly Dairying:						
under 75 ha	60	1,100	210	975	2,285	925
75 to 125 ha	85	1,240	270	1,020	2,530	1,025
Over 125 ha	170	1,510	315	1,100	2,925	1,185
Average	140	1,470	310	1,090	3,010	1,220
Mainly Cereals:						
under 185 ha	170	30	660	780	1,470	595
185 to 320 ha	270	50	730	790	1,570	635
over 320 ha	550	40	660	775	1,475	600
Average	290	40	660	780	1,480	600
General Cropping:						
under 150 ha	125	30	570	805	1,405	570
150 to 225 ha	185	-	760	915	1,675	680
over 225 ha	450	50	640	815	1,5050	610
Average	280	35	530	875	1,440	585
Mainly Sheep/Cattle (Lowland):						
Under 100 ha	80	445	125	600	1,170	475
100 to 150 ha	125	465	105	520	1,090	440
Over 150 ha	240	510	120	455	1,085	440
Average	130	480	120	530	1,130	460
Mainly Sheep/Cattle (Upland SDA):						
under 130 ha	100	530	60	525	1,115	450
130 to 230 ha	140	560	60	460	1,080	440
over 230 ha	300	540	55	360	955	385
Average	175	545	60	450	1,055	430

*   Based on current (i.e. replacement) costs.

**   Size range estimated from survey data

***   Trading Livestock or crops in store are not included as they are not assets of production and will vary according to marketing styles and time of year

The above (deliberately rounded) data is based on Farm Business Survey results for England compiled annually by University/Colleges centres (as listed on page 4). The values of milk quota and Basic Payment entitlements are excluded as are other assets not named above, such as debtors.

RETURN ON CAPITAL

Tenant's Capital

Return on tenant's capital is calculated by taking the management and investment income (MII) of a business as a percentage of the tenant's capital (see definitions in section VIII.1). Because MII is before deduction of any interest, this return is 'gross', i.e. before allowing for cost of finance. However, it should be borne in mind that MII includes no charge for management but that a rental value for owner-occupied land and the value of the unpaid labour of the farmer and wife have been deducted.

Landlord's Capital

The return on landlord's capital is calculated by taking the rental income, less any ownership expenses (mortgage, insurance, repairs etc.), expressed as a percentage of the land value. With farmland in 2015 averaging, possibly £22,000 per hectare (£8,900 per acre) (see page 223) with vacant possession (assuming no special amenity or house value), an average lowland existing rent of, say, £300 per hectare (£120 per acre) (see page 221), and assuming ownership expenses at £87 per hectare (£35 per acre), the (net) return of £213 per hectare (£86 per acre) averages 1%. This takes no account of land valuation change.

If land is taken at its tenanted value, with an assumed vacant possession premium of say one-third foregone, the return increases to 1.53%. Full repairing and insurance leases clearly raise the returns above these levels. Above average quality farms command higher rents but also obviously command higher prices than the average levels quoted above.

Return on Capital to Individual Enterprises

On a mixed farm it is difficult to ascertain the return on enterprise capital, except perhaps for a full-time pig or poultry enterprise. It would also be of limited use. It would require the arbitrary allocation both of costs and capital inputs that are common to several, or all, of the enterprises on the farm.

What is relevant and important is the extra (net) return from an enterprise either to be introduced or expanded, as calculated by a partial budget, related to the extra (net) capital needed. The 'net' in brackets relates to the additional returns to gross margins less any additional (or plus any reduction in) 'fixed' costs, bearing in mind that another enterprise may have to be deleted or reduced in size; and, regarding capital, to the fact that deletion or reduction of another enterprise may release capital.

In most cases of 'marginal' substitution, it is differences in the value of breeding livestock and differences in variable costs that are particularly relevant, but the timing of both inputs and sales are also obviously very important.

'Marginal' Capital Requirements

These are for small changes in crop areas or livestock numbers and can be estimated as follows:

- Crops: variable costs until payment of sale.
- Dairy Cows and Egg Production: value of the cow* or hens, plus food until payment of product.
- Other Breeding Livestock: average value of stock*, plus variable costs to sale (payment) of the progeny (e.g. lambs) – or their transfer to another enterprise (e.g. weaners to the pig fattening enterprise).
- Rearing Breeding Livestock (e.g. heifers, shearlings, gilts, pullets): cost of the calf, lamb, weaner or chick, plus variable costs until they produce their first progeny/milk/eggs.
- Fattening Livestock and Production of Stores: cost of stock, plus variable costs till sale.

* Value of breeding stock, including dairy cows: either the average value over their entire breeding or milk producing life (see table on page 246) or their value when they first produce progeny can be taken. The latter will give the lower return on (marginal) capital and is thus the severer test.

Home-reared stock: where stock to be used for milk or egg production, breeding or fattening are home-reared, there are two possibilities:

(a) either they can be valued at variable costs of production when they are transferred from the rearing to the 'productive' enterprise; in this case the return on (marginal) capital will be estimated over the combined rearing and 'productive' enterprise.

(b) or they can be valued at market value at point of transfer. This is the procedure if one wishes to work out a return on (marginal) capital for the rearing and the 'productive' enterprises separately.

Return on 'Marginal' Capital

This is sometimes expressed as the gross margin less fuel and repair costs of the enterprise expanded as a percentage of the 'marginal', or extra capital. However, two points have to be remembered:

(a) If another enterprise has had to be reduced in size to enable the enterprise under consideration to be expanded, the capital released and the gross margin forfeited by reducing the size of the first enterprise must be brought into the calculation in estimating the net result of the change.

(b) All the above statements on 'marginal' capital refer to small changes. If the change is large enough to cause changes in labour, machinery or building requirements, the capital changes brought about may be considerably greater.

Return on Investments in Medium-Term and Long-Term Capital

This calculates the Rate of Return and the Discounted Yield.

Example: If a £5,000 investment results in an annual net return of £500 (after deducting depreciation, but ignoring interest payments) and with no capital salvage value:

$$\textit{Rate of Return on Initial } \text{Capital} = \frac{500}{5,000} \times 100 = 10\%$$

$$\textit{Rate of Return on Average } \text{Capital} = \frac{500}{2,500} \times 100 = 20\%$$

It is more accurate to calculate the '*Discounted Yield*', which is the discount rate that brings the present value of the net cash flows (which means ignoring depreciation) to the value of the investment. The tables on pages 255 may be used.

'Short-Cut' Estimates of the Discounted Yield on Depreciating Assets

The Discounted Yield falls between the simple Rates of Return on Initial and Average Capital. In fact, for investments lasting 5 to 15 years, when the Rate of Return on Initial Capital is 10 per cent and on Average Capital 20 per cent, the Discounted Yield will be almost exactly halfway between, i.e. about 15 per cent. However, this is only so providing the anticipated annual net cash earnings are fairly constant — or fluctuate unpredictably around a fairly constant level.

There are three circumstances when the Discounted Yield will get closer to the Rate of Return on Initial Capital (i.e. the lower per cent return) and further from the Rate of Return on Average Capital:

(a) The longer the life of the investment.

(b) The higher the Rate of Return.

(c) The higher the net cash flow is in the later years of the investment compared with the earlier years.

When the opposite circumstances occur, the Discounted Yield will be closer to the Rate of Return on Average Capital (i.e. the higher per cent return).

Granted that there are inevitably varying degrees of estimation and uncertainty in calculating future net annual earnings of investments, the following short-cuts might reasonably be used where the annual net cash earnings are expected to be fairly constant — or fluctuate unpredictably (e.g. through weather effects on yields) around a fairly constant level. (W.O. period = write-off period; R.R.I.C. = rate of return on initial capital).

1. Where

   (i)   the W.O. period is 5 years or less,

   (ii)   the W.O. period is 6 - 10 years and the R.R.I.C. is 15 per cent or less,

   (iii) the W.O. period is 11 - 20 years and the R.R.I.C. is 10 per cent or less,

calculate the Return on Capital as being approximately midway between the Rates of Return on Initial and Average Capital, i.e. by calculating the Rate of Return on 2/3 of the original investment.

For example, following the earlier example above:

$$\frac{500}{3,333} \times 100 = 15\%.$$

2. Where

   (i)   the W.O. period is 6 to 10 years and the R.R.I.C. exceeds 15 per cent,

   (ii)   the W.O. period is 11 to 20 years and the R.R.I.C. is between 10 per cent and 25 per cent,

   (iii) the W.O. period exceeds 20 years and the R.R.I.C. is 10 per cent or less,

calculate the Return on Capital on 80 per cent of the original investment.

For example, again following the earlier example:

$$\frac{500}{4,000} \times 100 = 12.5°\%.$$

3. Where

   (i)   the W.O. period is 11 to 20 years and the R.R.I.C. exceeds 25 per cent,

   (ii)   the W.O. period exceeds 20 years and the R.R.I.C. exceeds 10 per cent, take the Return on Capital to be the R.R.I.C.

In borderline cases, use method 1 rather than 2, or 2 rather than 3 if there is a tendency for the cash flow to be higher in the earlier years, e.g. because of tax allowances on machinery. Take 2 rather than 1, and 3 rather than 2, if the likelihood is that the cash flow will be lower in earlier years and increase in later years.

However, where the annual cash flow is expected to vary (apart from unpredictable fluctuations) it is safer to make the full D.C.F. calculation. This is particularly so where the variation is both up and down and where further periodic investments are to be made during the life of the project.

3.   INTEREST RATES

Rate of interest on Bank Loans

Typically 3.0% to 3.5% above Base Rate. Main range is 1.5% above to 4.0% above. Extremes are likely to be 0.8% above and 7% above. Particularly low margins over base have become rare, especially for new lending agreements. Annual arrangement fees based on the total facility can add substantially to the cost of borrowing. At the time of writing, base rate was at an all-time low since 2009 at 0.5%, but the Bank of England had started preparing borrowers for a rate rise at some point, possibly by or during 2015. It would be prudent for budgeting purposes to allow an additional 0.5% by the end of 2015.

Fixed Rates

New fixed rates on long term borrowing such as mortgages have been increasing in the light of the above paragraph. The table gives typical mortgage rates on domestic dwellings.

Typical Fixed Rates on Residential Mortgages

Fixed Rate	95% LTV*	75%	60% LTV*
2-year	4.9%	4.2%	1.8%
5-year	5%	4.4%	3.2%
10-year	n/a	4.6%	4%

* *LTV = Loan to Value (the percent the financier loans against the capital value)*

Annual Percentage Rate (APR)

This is the effective rate of interest calculated on an annual basis and should be used when seeking to make a true comparison between interest charges on money borrowed from different sources. The APR allows for the fact that when interest is applied to accounts at half yearly, quarterly or monthly intervals an element of compounding will arise.

For example, £100 borrowed for one year at a quoted annual nominal interest rate of 6% (e.g. 5.5% over base rate of 0.5%) with interest charged quarterly, will lead to an accumulated interest charge of £6.136 (i.e., giving an APR of just under 6.14%). The higher the annual nominal interest rate and the more frequently the interest charges are applied to the account, the more pronounced the compounding element becomes. For example, an annual nominal interest rate of 10% produces an APR of 10.25% with half yearly charging, 10.38% with quarterly charging and 10.47% with monthly charging.

In the case of some loans and hire purchase agreements, interest charges may be quoted as a flat rate on the original amount borrowed. The APR will be considerably greater than the flat rate if the loan is repaid by equal periodic instalments, comprising part capital and part interest, so that the borrowing is completely repaid by the end of the agreed term. For example, the APR for a loan at a flat rate of interest of 8% repaid by monthly instalments over 5 years will be 15%. The shorter the repayment period, and the more frequent the payments, the higher is the APR compared with the flat rate.

The Real Rate of Interest.

When preparing simple profit and loss budgets to estimate how worthwhile an investment in a fixed asset (machinery, buildings, land) is, it is usual to price inputs and outputs at present-day values even when most costs and returns are expected to rise due to inflation over the life of the investment. Where this real terms approach is adopted a more realistic estimate of the effect on profitability can be gained by basing charges for capital on the real rate of interest rather than the APR.

The real rate of interest is the APR adjusted for the annual rate at which prices relevant to the investment are expected to increase. A crude estimate of the real rate of interest can be obtained by simply subtracting the expected rate of price increase from the APR; for example, if the APR were 8% and the expected rate of inflation 3%, the real rate of interest would be $8 - 3 = 5\%$.

4.   FINANCIAL RATIOS

Common Ratios

The following ratios are standard guidelines:

% of Gross Output	Arable	Dairy	Mixed	Upland
Variable Costs	32	39	37	47
Labour+	12	15	21	17
Machinery	18	17	19	14
Sundry Fixed Costs	9	9	10	12
Rent & Interest	12	13	9	8
Profit *	17	17	4	2
Basic Payment Support	14	5	14	19

+ *including drawings*
* *to cover, tax, capital repayments, reinvestments*

It has to be borne in mind that these are indeed only rough guidelines and need to be considered with great care. Values vary with type of farming and size of farm. It is often unclear how some items are being measured, especially whether unpaid manual labour of the farmer and family has been included or whether a rental value has been allowed for owner-occupied land. In the table above, variable costs of about 30% would be found on cereals type farms, leaving 40% for labour, machinery and sundry fixed costs. On intensive livestock farms variable costs of 40% would be expected, leaving only 30% for fixed costs. Higher rent and finance can be justified on more profitable farm systems.

The Basic Payment as a percentage of output is also included to compare against profit. It identifies the dependence of several farm businesses to direct subsidy.

Farm Survey Ratios

The following are rounded averages based on farm surveys in recent years on a large sample of all types of farm, assuming a Management and Investment Income (see page 244) of 10% of Total Output is made. It is to be noted that Total Output includes the market value of any production retained for use/consumption on the farm (e.g. cereals for feed or seed). Unpaid labour (value of manual labour by the farmer and spouse) is included. Rent includes the rental value of owner-occupied land and interest charges are not included in the costs. Casual labour and all contract work are included in fixed costs. Costs are a lower proportion and the margin a higher proportion in profitable years (and on more profitable farms), and *vice-versa* in low profit years.

Average Financial Ratios from Farm Business Survey (England)

	% Total Output	% Total Gross Margin	% Total Fixed Costs
Variable Costs:			
(excl. casual labour and contract work)	32.5		
Fixed Costs:			
Labour: Paid (inc. casuals) ⎫	20	30	33
Labour: Unpaid ⎭			
Power & Machinery			
(inc. contract work)	20	30	33
Labour & Machinery	40	60	66
Rent/Rental Value	12.5	19	21
General Overheads	7.5	11	13
Total Fixed Costs	60	90	100
Margin	**7.5**	**10**	-

Total Gross Margin = 67.5% of Total Output

Lending Criteria

Another set of standards widely used by lending and leasing institutions looks at total Finance Charges (rent, interest, leasing charges, etc.), as a percentage of Gross Output and Gross Margin;

Finance as a % of Gross Output	Finance as a % of Gross Margin	Lending Criteria
0-10%	0-15%	Normally very safe
11-15%	16-22.5%	Common range, should be safe
16-20%	23-29%	Care required
20% plus	30% plus	Potentially dangerous

As lenders will be well aware, however, these ratios too must be regarded with caution and in conjunction with the farm's level of net worth (% equity) and its trend in recent years, recent trends in its profitability and the potential borrower's record of expenditure both on and off the farm, together with his or her character and potential. Also, of course, some enterprises / types of farming are more risky than others.

DISCOUNTING TABLE

Discount Factors for Calculating the Present Value of Future (irregular) Cash Flows

Year	Percentage																	
	2%	3%	4%	5%	6%	7%	8%	9%	10%	11%	12%	13%	14%	15%	16%	18%	20%	25%
1	0.980	0.971	0.962	0.952	0.943	0.935	0.926	0.917	0.909	0.901	0.893	0.885	0.877	0.870	0.862	0.847	0.833	0.80
2	0.961	0.943	0.925	0.907	0.890	0.873	0.857	0.842	0.826	0.812	0.797	0.783	0.769	0.756	0.743	0.718	0.694	0.64
3	0.942	0.915	0.889	0.864	0.840	0.816	0.794	0.772	0.751	0.731	0.712	0.693	0.675	0.658	0.641	0.609	0.579	0.51
4	0.924	0.888	0.855	0.823	0.792	0.763	0.735	0.708	0.683	0.659	0.636	0.613	0.592	0.572	0.552	0.516	0.482	0.41
5	0.906	0.863	0.822	0.784	0.747	0.713	0.681	0.650	0.621	0.593	0.567	0.543	0.519	0.497	0.476	0.437	0.402	0.33
6	0.888	0.837	0.790	0.746	0.705	0.666	0.630	0.596	0.564	0.535	0.507	0.480	0.456	0.432	0.410	0.370	0.335	0.26
7	0.871	0.813	0.760	0.711	0.665	0.623	0.583	0.547	0.513	0.482	0.452	0.425	0.400	0.376	0.354	0.314	0.279	0.21
8	0.853	0.789	0.731	0.677	0.627	0.582	0.540	0.502	0.467	0.434	0.404	0.376	0.351	0.327	0.305	0.266	0.233	0.17
9	0.837	0.766	0.703	0.645	0.592	0.544	0.500	0.460	0.424	0.391	0.361	0.333	0.308	0.284	0.263	0.225	0.194	0.13
10	0.820	0.744	0.676	0.614	0.558	0.508	0.463	0.422	0.386	0.352	0.322	0.295	0.270	0.247	0.227	0.191	0.162	0.11
11	0.804	0.722	0.650	0.585	0.527	0.475	0.429	0.388	0.350	0.317	0.287	0.261	0.237	0.215	0.195	0.162	0.135	0.09
12	0.788	0.701	0.625	0.557	0.497	0.444	0.397	0.356	0.319	0.286	0.257	0.231	0.208	0.187	0.168	0.137	0.112	0.07
13	0.773	0.681	0.601	0.530	0.469	0.415	0.368	0.326	0.290	0.258	0.229	0.204	0.182	0.163	0.145	0.116	0.093	0.06
14	0.758	0.661	0.577	0.505	0.442	0.388	0.340	0.299	0.263	0.232	0.205	0.181	0.160	0.141	0.125	0.098	0.078	0.04
15	0.743	0.642	0.555	0.481	0.417	0.362	0.315	0.275	0.239	0.209	0.183	0.160	0.140	0.123	0.108	0.084	0.065	0.04
20	0.673	0.554	0.456	0.377	0.312	0.258	0.215	0.178	0.149	0.124	0.104	0.087	0.073	0.061	0.051	0.037	0.026	0.01
25	0.610	0.478	0.375	0.295	0.233	0.184	0.146	0.116	0.092	0.074	0.059	0.047	0.038	0.030	0.024	0.016	0.010	.004
30	0.552	0.412	0.308	0.231	0.174	0.131	0.099	0.075	0.057	0.044	0.033	0.026	0.020	0.015	0.012	0.007	0.004	.001

Example: The Present Value of £2,000 received 10 years from now, at 8 per cent discount rate of interest = 2,000 x 0.463 = £926.

Conversely, £926 invested now, at 8 per cent compound interest, will be worth £2,000 in 10 years' time.

ANNUITY / DISCOUNTING TABLE B

Discount Factors for Calculating the Present Value of Future Annuity (i.e. Constant Annual Cash Flow) Receivable in Year 1 to n inclusive.

Year	2%	3%	4%	5%	6%	7%	8%	9%	10%	11%	12%	13%	14%	15%	16%	18%	20%	25%
1	0.980	0.971	0.962	0.952	0.943	0.935	0.926	0.917	0.909	0.901	0.893	0.885	0.877	0.870	0.862	0.847	0.833	0.80
2	1.942	1.913	1.886	1.859	1.833	1.808	1.783	1.759	1.736	1.713	1.690	1.668	1.647	1.626	1.605	1.566	1.528	1.44
3	2.884	2.829	2.775	2.723	2.673	2.624	2.577	2.531	2.487	2.444	2.402	2.361	2.322	2.283	2.246	2.174	2.106	1.95
4	3.808	3.717	3.630	3.546	3.465	3.387	3.312	3.240	3.170	3.102	3.037	2.974	2.914	2.855	2.798	2.690	2.589	2.36
5	4.713	4.580	4.452	4.329	4.212	4.100	3.993	3.890	3.791	3.696	3.605	3.517	3.433	3.352	3.274	3.127	2.991	2.69
6	5.601	5.417	5.242	5.076	4.917	4.767	4.623	4.486	4.355	4.231	4.111	3.998	3.889	3.784	3.685	3.498	3.326	2.95
7	6.472	6.230	6.002	5.786	5.582	5.389	5.206	5.033	4.868	4.712	4.564	4.423	4.288	4.160	4.039	3.812	3.605	3.16
8	7.325	7.020	6.733	6.463	6.210	5.971	5.747	5.535	5.335	5.146	4.968	4.799	4.639	4.487	4.344	4.078	3.837	3.33
9	8.162	7.786	7.435	7.108	6.802	6.515	6.247	5.995	5.759	5.537	5.328	5.132	4.946	4.772	4.607	4.303	4.031	3.46
10	8.983	8.530	8.111	7.722	7.360	7.024	6.710	6.418	6.145	5.889	5.650	5.426	5.216	5.019	4.833	4.494	4.192	3.57
11	9.787	9.253	8.760	8.306	7.887	7.499	7.139	6.805	6.495	6.207	5.938	5.687	5.453	5.234	5.029	4.656	4.327	3.66
12	10.58	9.954	9.385	8.863	8.384	7.943	7.536	7.161	6.814	6.492	6.194	5.918	5.660	5.421	5.197	4.793	4.439	3.73
13	11.35	10.635	9.986	9.394	8.853	8.358	7.904	7.487	7.103	6.750	6.424	6.122	5.842	5.583	5.342	4.910	4.533	3.78
14	12.11	11.296	10.563	9.899	9.295	8.745	8.244	7.786	7.367	6.982	6.628	6.302	6.002	5.724	5.468	5.008	4.611	3.82
15	12.85	11.938	11.118	10.380	9.712	9.108	8.559	8.061	7.606	7.191	6.811	6.462	6.142	5.847	5.575	5.092	4.675	3.86
20	16.35	14.877	13.590	12.462	11.470	10.594	9.818	9.129	8.514	7.963	7.469	7.025	6.623	6.259	5.929	5.353	4.870	3.95
25	19.52	17.413	15.662	14.094	12.783	11.654	10.675	9.823	9.077	8.422	7.843	7.330	6.873	6.464	6.097	5.467	4.948	3.99
30	22.40	19.600	17.292	15.372	13.765	12.409	11.258	10.274	9.427	8.694	8.055	7.496	7.003	6.566	6.177	5.517	4.979	4.00

Example: The Present Value of £500 a year for the next 10 years, at 12 per cent discount rate of interest = 500 x 5.650 = £2,825. This is the same answer that would be obtained by multiplying 500 by each discount factor (at 12 per cent) in Table A for each year from 1 to 10, and adding together the ten resulting figures.

To obtain the Discounted Yield of a constant annual net cash flow, divide this into the original investment and look up the resulting figure in the table above, against the number of years. Example: an investment of £1,000 is estimated to produce £80 a year additional profit over 10 years (before charging interest). Add £100 depreciation a year = £180 annual net cash flow. 1000 /180 = 5.56. This equals just over 12 per cent (the 10 years /12 per cent figure being 5.650).

COMPOUNDING TABLE

The Future Money Value of £1 after n Years with no additional payments made

Rate of Interest

Year	2%	3%	4%	5%	6%	7%	8%	9%	10%	11%	12%	13%	14%	15%	16%	18%	20%	25%
1	1.02	1.03	1.04	1.05	1.06	1.07	1.08	1.09	1.10	1.11	1.12	1.13	1.14	1.15	1.16	1.18	1.20	1.25
2	1.04	1.06	1.08	1.10	1.12	1.14	1.17	1.19	1.21	1.23	1.25	1.28	1.30	1.32	1.35	1.39	1.44	1.56
3	1.06	1.09	1.12	1.16	1.19	1.23	1.26	1.30	1.33	1.37	1.40	1.44	1.48	1.52	1.56	1.64	1.73	1.95
4	1.08	1.13	1.17	1.22	1.26	1.31	1.36	1.41	1.46	1.52	1.57	1.63	1.69	1.75	1.81	1.94	2.07	2.44
5	1.10	1.16	1.22	1.28	1.34	1.40	1.47	1.54	1.61	1.69	1.76	1.84	1.93	2.01	2.10	2.29	2.49	3.05
6	1.13	1.19	1.27	1.34	1.42	1.50	1.59	1.68	1.77	1.87	1.97	2.08	2.19	2.31	2.44	2.70	2.99	3.81
7	1.15	1.23	1.32	1.41	1.50	1.61	1.71	1.83	1.95	2.08	2.21	2.35	2.50	2.66	2.83	3.19	3.58	4.77
8	1.17	1.27	1.37	1.48	1.59	1.72	1.85	1.99	2.14	2.30	2.48	2.66	2.85	3.06	3.28	3.76	4.30	5.96
9	1.20	1.30	1.42	1.55	1.69	1.84	2.00	2.17	2.36	2.56	2.77	3.00	3.25	3.52	3.80	4.44	5.16	7.45
10	1.22	1.34	1.48	1.63	1.79	1.97	2.16	2.37	2.59	2.84	3.11	3.39	3.71	4.05	4.41	5.23	6.19	9.31
11	1.24	1.38	1.54	1.71	1.90	2.10	2.33	2.58	2.85	3.15	3.48	3.84	4.23	4.65	5.12	6.18	7.43	11.64
12	1.27	1.43	1.60	1.80	2.01	2.25	2.52	2.81	3.14	3.50	3.90	4.33	4.82	5.35	5.94	7.29	8.92	14.55
13	1.29	1.47	1.67	1.89	2.13	2.41	2.72	3.07	3.45	3.88	4.36	4.90	5.49	6.15	6.89	8.60	10.70	18.19
14	1.32	1.51	1.73	1.98	2.26	2.58	2.94	3.34	3.80	4.31	4.89	5.53	6.26	7.08	7.99	10.15	12.84	22.74
15	1.35	1.56	1.80	2.08	2.40	2.76	3.17	3.64	4.18	4.78	5.47	6.25	7.14	8.14	9.27	11.97	15.41	28.42
20	1.49	1.81	2.19	2.65	3.21	3.87	4.66	5.60	6.73	8.06	9.65	11.52	13.74	16.37	19.46	27.39	38.34	86.74
25	1.64	2.09	2.67	3.39	4.29	5.43	6.85	8.62	10.83	13.59	17.00	21.23	26.46	32.92	40.87	62.67	95.40	264.7
30	1.81	2.43	3.24	4.32	5.74	7.61	10.06	13.27	17.45	22.89	29.96	39.12	50.95	66.21	85.85	143.4	237.4	807.8

COMPOUNDING TABLE B

The Future Money Value of £1 after n Years*

									Rate of Interest									
Year	2%	3%	4%	5%	6%	7%	8%	9%	10%	11%	12%	13%	14%	15%	16%	18%	20%	25%
1	1.02	1.03	1.04	1.05	1.06	1.07	1.08	1.09	1.10	1.11	1.12	1.13	1.14	1.15	1.16	1.18	1.20	1.25
2	2.06	2.09	2.12	2.15	2.18	2.21	2.25	2.28	2.31	2.34	2.37	2.41	2.44	2.47	2.51	2.57	2.64	2.81
3	3.12	3.18	3.25	3.31	3.37	3.44	3.51	3.57	3.64	3.71	3.78	3.85	3.92	3.99	4.07	4.22	4.37	4.77
4	4.20	4.31	4.42	4.53	4.64	4.75	4.87	4.98	5.11	5.23	5.35	5.48	5.61	5.74	5.88	6.15	6.44	7.21
5	5.31	5.47	5.63	5.80	5.98	6.15	6.34	6.52	6.72	6.91	7.12	7.32	7.54	7.75	7.98	8.44	8.93	10.3
6	6.43	6.66	6.90	7.14	7.39	7.65	7.92	8.20	8.49	8.78	9.09	9.40	9.73	10.07	10.41	11.1	11.92	14.1
7	7.58	7.89	8.21	8.55	8.90	9.26	9.64	10.03	10.44	10.86	11.30	11.76	12.23	12.73	13.24	14.3	15.50	18.8
8	8.75	9.16	9.58	10.03	10.49	10.98	11.49	12.02	12.58	13.16	13.78	14.42	15.09	15.79	16.52	18.1	19.80	24.8
9	9.95	10.46	11.01	11.58	12.18	12.82	13.49	14.19	14.94	15.72	16.55	17.42	18.34	19.30	20.32	22.5	24.96	32.3
10	11.17	11.81	12.49	13.21	13.97	14.78	15.65	16.56	17.53	18.56	19.65	20.81	22.04	23.35	24.73	27.8	31.15	41.6
11	12.41	13.19	14.03	14.92	15.87	16.89	17.98	19.14	20.38	21.71	23.13	24.65	26.27	28.00	29.85	33.9	38.58	53.2
12	13.68	14.62	15.63	16.71	17.88	19.14	20.50	21.95	23.52	25.21	27.03	28.98	31.09	33.35	35.79	41.2	47.50	67.8
13	14.97	16.09	17.29	18.60	20.02	21.55	23.21	25.02	26.97	29.09	31.39	33.88	36.58	39.50	42.67	49.9	58.20	86.0
14	16.29	17.60	19.02	20.58	22.28	24.13	26.15	28.36	30.77	33.41	36.28	39.42	42.84	46.58	50.66	60.0	71.04	109
15	17.64	19.16	20.82	22.66	24.67	26.89	29.32	32.00	34.95	38.19	41.75	45.67	49.98	54.72	59.93	71.9	86.44	137
20	24.78	27.68	30.97	34.72	38.99	43.87	49.42	55.76	63.00	71.27	80.70	91.47	103.8	117.8	133.8	173	224.0	429
25	32.67	37.55	43.31	50.11	58.16	67.68	78.95	92.32	108.2	127.0	149.3	175.8	207.3	244.7	289.1	404	566.4	1318
30	41.38	49.00	58.33	69.76	83.80	101.1	122.3	148.6	180.9	220.9	270.3	331.3	406.7	500.0	615.2	933	1418	4034

* Equal payments made at the beginning of each year.

AMORTISATION TABLE

Annual Charge to write off £1,000

Write-off Period	2	3	4	5	6	7	8	9	10	11	12	13	14	15	16	18	20
5 years	212	218	225	231	237	244	250	257	264	271	277	284	291	298	305	320	334
6	179	185	191	197	203	210	216	223	230	236	243	250	257	264	271	286	301
7	155	161	167	173	179	186	192	199	205	212	219	226	233	240	248	262	277
8	137	142	149	155	161	167	174	181	187	194	201	208	216	223	230	245	261
9	123	128	134	141	147	153	160	167	174	181	188	195	202	210	217	232	248
10	111	117	123	130	136	142	149	156	163	170	177	184	192	199	207	223	239
11	102	108	114	120	127	133	140	147	154	161	168	176	183	191	199	215	231
12	95	100	107	113	119	125	133	140	147	154	161	169	177	184	192	209	225
13	88	94	100	106	113	120	127	134	141	148	156	163	171	179	187	204	221
14	83	89	95	101	108	114	121	128	136	143	151	159	167	175	183	200	217
15	78	84	90	96	103	110	117	124	131	139	147	155	163	171	179	196	214
16	74	80	86	92	99	106	113	120	128	136	143	151	160	168	176	194	211
17	70	76	82	89	95	102	110	117	125	132	140	149	157	165	174	191	209
18	67	73	79	86	92	99	107	114	122	130	138	146	155	163	172	190	208
20	61	67	74	80	87	94	102	110	117	126	134	142	151	160	169	187	205
25	51	57	64	71	78	86	94	102	110	119	127	136	145	155	164	183	202
30	45	51	58	65	73	81	89	97	106	115	124	133	143	152	162	181	201
40	37	43	51	58	66	75	84	93	102	112	122	131	141	151	160	180	200

**Rate of Interest**.

Example: £30,000 is borrowed to erect a building. The annual charge to service interest and capital repayment on the £30,000, repayable over 10 years at 12%, is 30 x £177 = £5,310. Where the write-off period of the building (10 years) is equal to the repayment period of the loan, then the average annual depreciation plus interest will equal £5,310.

The proportion of the total annual charge representing the average amount of capital repaid per annum can be readily determined by dividing the sum borrowed by the number of years of the loan: (in the above example this is £30,000 ÷ 10 = £3,000/year). The remainder is clearly the average amount of interest paid per annum: (in the above example, £5,310 — £3,000 = £2,310/year). The year to year variations between the two items (i.e. capital repaid and interest) are shown in the Mortgage Repayment Data tables (2 pages further on), which demonstrate the way the capital repayment part increases and the interest part decreases over time.

SINKING FUND TABLE

The sum required to be set aside at the end of each year to make £1,000

Rate of Interest

No. of Years	2	3	4	5	6	7	8	9	10	11	12	13	14	15	16	18	20
5	192	188	185	181	177	174	170	167	164	161	157	154	151	148	145	140	134
6	159	155	151	147	143	140	136	133	130	126	123	120	117	114	111	106	101
7	135	131	127	123	119	116	112	109	105	102	99	96	93	90	88	82	77
8	117	112	109	105	101	97	94	91	87	84	81	78	76	73	70	65	61
9	103	98	94	91	87	83	80	77	74	71	68	65	62	60	57	52	48
10	91	87	83	80	76	72	69	66	63	60	57	54	52	49	47	43	39
11	82	78	74	70	67	63	60	57	54	51	48	46	43	41	39	35	31
12	75	70	67	63	59	56	53	50	47	44	41	39	37	34	32	29	25
13	68	64	60	56	53	50	47	44	41	38	36	33	31	29	27	24	21
14	63	59	55	51	48	44	41	38	36	33	31	29	27	25	23	20	17
15	58	54	50	46	43	40	37	34	31	29	27	25	23	21	19	16	14
16	54	50	46	42	39	36	33	30	28	26	23	21	20	18	16	14	11
17	50	46	42	39	35	32	30	27	25	22	20	19	17	15	14	11	9
18	47	43	39	36	32	29	27	24	22	20	18	16	15	13	12	10	8
19	44	40	36	33	30	27	24	22	20	18	16	14	13	11	10	8	6
20	41	37	34	30	27	24	22	20	17	16	14	12	11	10	9	7	5
25	31	27	24	21	18	16	14	12	10	9	7	6	5	5	4	3	2
30	25	21	18	15	13	11	9	7	6	5	4	3	3	2	2	1	1
40	17	13	11	8	6	5	4	3	2	2	1	1	1	1	—	—	—

MORTGAGE REPAYMENT DATA

Items per £1000 invested; where I = Interest, P = Principal repaid, L = Loan outstanding

Loan of 5 years	3%			4%			5%			6%			8%			10%		
	I	P	L	I	P	L	I	P	L	I	P	L	I	P	L	I	P	L
1	30	188	812	40	185	815	50	181	819	60	177	823	80	170	830	100	164	836
2	24	194	618	33	192	623	41	190	629	49	188	635	66	184	645	84	180	656
3	19	200	418	25	200	424	31	200	424	38	199	435	52	199	447	66	198	458
4	13	206	212	17	208	216	21	210	220	26	211	224	36	215	232	46	218	240
5	6	212	0	9	216	0	11	220	0	13	224	0	19	232	0	24	240	0
10 years																		
1	30	87	913	40	83	917	50	80	920	60	76	924	80	69	931	100	63	939
2	27	90	823	37	87	830	46	83	837	55	80	844	75	75	856	94	69	868
3	25	93	730	33	90	740	42	88	749	51	85	758	69	81	776	87	76	792
4	22	95	635	30	94	646	37	92	657	46	90	668	62	87	689	79	84	709
5	19	98	537	26	97	549	33	97	561	40	96	572	55	94	595	71	92	617
6	16	101	436	22	101	448	28	101	459	34	102	471	48	101	494	62	101	516
7	13	104	332	18	105	342	23	107	353	28	108	363	39	110	384	52	111	405
8	10	107	224	14	110	233	18	112	241	22	114	249	31	118	266	40	122	282
9	7	111	114	9	114	119	12	117	123	15	121	128	21	128	138	28	134	148
10	3	114	0	5	119	0	6	123	0	8	128	0	11	138	0	15	148	0

MORTGAGE REPAYMENT DATA (CONTINUED)

Loan of	3%			4%			5%			6%			8%			10%		
20 years	I	P	L	I	P	L	I	P	L	I	P	L	I	P	L	I	P	L
1	30	37	963	40	34	966	50	30	970	60	27	973	80	22	978	100	17	983
5	25	42	802	34	39	818	43	37	833	53	34	847	72	30	872	92	26	893
10	19	49	573	26	48	597	33	47	620	41	46	642	58	44	683	76	41	722
15	11	56	308	15	58	328	20	60	347	26	61	367	38	64	407	51	66	445
20	2	65	0	3	71	0	4	76	0	5	82	0	8	94	0	11	107	0
25 years																		
1	30	27	973	40	24	976	50	21	979	60	18	982	80	14	986	100	10	990
5	27	31	854	36	28	870	45	25	884	55	23	897	75	19	920	95	15	938
10	22	36	686	30	34	712	38	33	736	47	31	760	66	27	802	86	24	838
15	16	41	490	22	42	519	29	41	548	37	41	576	54	40	629	72	39	677
20	9	48	263	13	51	285	18	53	307	23	55	330	35	59	374	48	62	418
25	2	56	0	2	62	0	3	68	0	4	74	0	7	87	0	10	100	0

MORTGAGE REPAYMENT DATA (CONTINUED)

Loan through	4%			5%			6%			8%			10%			12%		
	I	P	L	I	P	L	I	P	L	I	P	L	I	P	L	I	P	L
30 years																		
1	40	18	982	50	15	985	60	13	987	80	9	991	100	6	994	120	4	996
5	37	21	903	47	18	917	57	16	929	77	12	948	97	9	963	118	7	974
10	32	25	786	42	23	811	51	21	833	71	18	872	92	14	903	113	11	927
15	27	31	643	35	30	675	44	29	706	63	26	760	83	23	807	104	20	846
20	20	38	469	27	38	502	34	38	535	51	38	596	69	37	652	88	36	701
25	12	46	257	17	49	282	21	51	306	33	56	355	46	60	402	61	63	448
30	2	56	0	3	62	0	4	69	0	7	82	0	10	96	0	13	111	0
40 years																		
1	40	11	989	50	8	992	60	6	994	80	4	996	100	2	998	120	1	999
5	38	12	943	48	10	954	58	8	964	79	5	977	99	3	986	119	2	992
10	36	15	874	45	13	896	56	11	915	76	8	944	97	5	964	118	4	977
15	32	18	789	42	16	821	52	15	850	73	11	895	94	9	928	115	6	951
20	28	22	687	37	21	726	47	20	762	67	17	823	88	14	871	110	11	906
25	24	27	562	32	27	605	40	26	645	59	24	718	80	22	778	102	20	826
30	18	33	410	24	34	450	31	35	489	48	36	563	66	36	628	86	35	685
35	11	40	225	15	43	252	20	47	280	31	53	335	45	58	388	60	61	437
40	2	49	0	3	56	0	4	63	0	6	78	0	9	93	0	13	108	0

Note—All figures rounded to nearest £.

6.   FARM RECORDS

The following records should be kept for management purposes:

BASIC WHOLE FARM FINANCIAL POSITION

1.   Cash Analysis Book, fully detailed.

2.   Petty Cash Book.

3.   Annual Valuation, including physical quantities of

    i.   Harvested crops in store

    ii.   Livestock (breeding and fattening) at (near) market value, less any variable costs yet to be borne.

    iii.   Fertilisers, seeds, sprays, casual labour or contract work applied to growing crops should be recorded, but "cultivations" and manure residues can be ignored for management purposes.

    iv.   Fertiliser, seed, sprays and other sundry direct items in store,

4.   Debtors and creditors at the end of the financial year.

OTHER FINANCIAL AND PHYSICAL RECORDS

5.   Output (quantities and value) of each crop and livestock enterprise for the "harvest year" (or production cycle). It may be possible to get information of sales from a fully detailed cash analysis book (although, for crops, the financial year figures will then have to be allocated between crops from the current harvest and those from the harvest in the previous financial year, in order to check on the accuracy of the opening valuation of crops in store; this is particularly a problem with Michaelmas ending accounts). The following records of internal transfers and consumption will also be required:

    (a)   Numbers and market value of livestock transferred from one livestock category to another, e.g. dairy calves to dairy followers or beef enterprise, or dairy heifers to dairy enterprise.

    (b)   Quantity and market value of cereals fed on farm and used for seed.

    (c)   Quantity and market value of milk and other produce consumed by the farmer or his employees, used on the farm (e.g. milk fed to calves), or sold direct.

6.   A monthly record of livestock numbers; preferably reconciled with the previous month according to births, purchases, deaths, sales and transfers.

7.   Costs and quantities of concentrate feed to each category of livestock, including home-grown cereals fed on the farm.

8.   Allocation of costs of seed, fertiliser, sprays, casual labour and contract work specific to an enterprise. This is in order to calculate gross margins, where required.

9.   Breeding record for cows, including bulling dates, date(s) served, type of bull used, pregnancy testing, estimated calving date, actual calving date, and date when dried off.

10. For each crop, total output and yield per hectare, in both quantity and value. Include each field where the crop has been grown and its approximate yield, where this can be satisfactorily obtained.

11. For each field, keep one page to cover a period of say, ten years. Record on this, each year, crop grown, variety sown, fertiliser used, sprays used, date sown, date(s) harvested, approximate yield (if obtainable), and any other special notes that you feel may have significance for the future.

12. A rotation record. On a single page, if possible, list each field down the side and say, ten years along the top. Colour each field-year space according to the crop grown, e.g. barley yellow, potatoes red, etc.

13. It is important to note that other farm records are required for legislative and cross compliance purposes including:

     i.   Livestock movements, identification, flock and herd records etc.

     ii. Nitrate Vulnerable Zone (NVZ) records and calculations including livestock loadings, manure storage, fertiliser plans and usage etc.

     iii. Pesticide application and storage records, risk assessments

     iv. Farm waste storage and disposal records and necessary exemptions / permits / transfer certificates

     v.   Integrated Pollution and Prevention Controls (IPPC) records (for pig and poultry units)

     vi. Soil Protection reviews and risk assessments

     vii. Financial (HMRC) records including VAT, PAYE, NI etc.

IX. MISCELLANEOUS DATA

1. CONSERVATION COSTS

Note: Costs vary widely, depending on geographical location and the type and size of the job. Markets for such services can be highly localised, sparse in some areas, competitive in others.

Hedges

Hedge Cutting. Flailing £32/hour to £325 per day at an average of 3 miles per day (refer also to contracting charges on page 195).

Hedge Laying (Making hedges stock proof and rejuvenated by selective cutting and positioning). Depends on hedge thickness (single or double), amount of timber to clear, access to hedge, style of hedge and varieties in hedge. Manual hedge laying approximately 20m/day at £13.00 to £15.70/metre (contract).

Hedge Planting. Single row = 3-4 plants per metre, double row 6 plants per metre

- Plants average £50p - £1.25 each (mixed species); spiral guards 36p; canes 13p.

- Fencing (labour and materials): stock proof £4.70/metre, rabbit proof (dug in) up to £6.90/metre (per side).

- Labour: Planting up to £2.70-£3.20/metre, professional contractor up to 100-150 metres/day. Preferably October/March.

- Overall from £3.20/metre; unfenced, single width, self-planted;
   to £23.50/metre; double width & double rabbit fenced, contract planted.

Hedge Coppicing. By hand: 2 men and a chain saw, £5.80-6.85 per metre plus burning debris. Contractor: tractor mounted saw, driver and 2 men, 12.5 metres per hour, £42.00/hour.

Devon Hedges. Maintenance, flailing annually and occasional mechanical recasting banks when eroded. Flailing costs as above and recasting with Backhoe excavator £25.50/hr.

Fencing

Fencing (labour and materials): stock proof £4.70/metre, rabbit proof (dug in) up to £6.80/metre (per side)

Dry Stone Walls

Dry Stone Walling. This is one of the most variable costs depending on stone type, stone grading availability, structure, vehicular access to site and local competition (people pay more for private walls in gardens than fields). As a guide, the following figures apply: Cost of graded stone approximately £143/tonne, varying regionally and depending on local stone, type and availability. Cost of wall building is (normally quoted per square meter but grants awarded per linear meter) from as low as £37 (highlands) to £195 (Cotswolds) per square metre. Most are around £85-95/m^2. Partial grants are available in ELS, UELS, HLS and some local grants e.g. within National Parks.

Trees

Amenity tree planting; (half acre block or less)

- Transplants average £1.07; shelter plus stake and tie £1.30; stake 56p; whip 82p. rabbit spiral guard 36p; netlon guard 54p; cane 15p.
- Trees per man day: farmer 200, contractor 400; (large-scale, 33 man days/ha). Optimal time November to April.

Shelter Belts; Per 100 metre length

- 100 large species (oak, lime, etc.) £55; 66 medium species (cherry, birch, etc.) £47; 100 shrubs, £38;
- 166 tree stakes, shelters and ties, £290;

  (site preparation, weed control, labour and fencing extra)

Woodland Establishment.

- Conifers £225/1,000 (2m spacing), broadleaves £440/1000 (3m spacing).
- To supply and plant transplants; conifer £3.20/tree, oak or beech £3.80-£4.40 each, (2-3ft tall) in tubes dependent on shelter size and species.
- Rabbit fencing £6.80/metre (dug in), deer fencing £8.50/metre, deer and rabbit fencing £10.50/metre
- Contract planting labour: Conifers at 2m £1,600/ha; broadleaves at 3m £1,100/ha; forest transplants £310/1,050.

Forestry, General.

- 2-man tree surgery team £550/day
- Contract labour: chain sawing £25/hr,
- brush cutting £15.00/hr,
- extracting timber/pulp £5.30-£12.00/tonne,
- chemical spot weeding 11p-15p/tree, or £320/hectare
- Rhododendron control range from £690-£2,585/hectare dependant on stem diameter (largest over 7cm) and accessibility.

Pollarding and Tree Surgery.

- Pollard: £97/mature tree; Pollarding: 2 or 3 trees/day. Pollard every 20-40 years.
- Tree surgery from £180/tree. Dependant on size and number. Best in winter.

Ponds and Ditches

Pond Construction. Butyl lining (0.75mm) £6.00/m²; other linings up to £4.20/m². Contract labour: 150 Komatsu £31/hr.; bulldozer D6 LGP £50/hr, 13t 360° excavator £43/hr (excluding haulage), Flail-mowers from £19.00/hr (machine only). Autumn (dry ground conditions).

Pond Maintenance. Hymac £44/hr.; Backhoe £24.00/hr. 100 m²/day (contractor). Timing: probably winter; time depends on ground condition and species whose life cycles may be disturbed. Every 15 to 50 years.

Ditch Maintenance. Backhoe excavator £24.00/hr; 13t 360° excavator £43/hr (excluding haulage), labour £12.70/hr. preferably in winter. Every 3 to 7 years on rotation.

Grassland

Permanent Grass Margins at Field Edges. To provide wildlife benefits and help control pernicious weeds, reducing herbicides at the field edge. (A sterile strip provides virtually no wildlife benefit and the initial establishment costs may be offset by savings in maintenance costs in future years.)

Costs per 100 metres of seeds as follows.

- Establishment: 2m grass margins, £1.80-£2.50;
- 6m grass margins, £5.30-£7.20;
- beetle banks, £5.85 (6m wide) (£4.00/kg, 25kg/ha).
- Maintenance: 2m margins, 75p to £1.00p;

6m margins, £1.60-£2.70.

Establishment of Wildlife Grassland Meadow. £180-275/ha for ground preparation, depending on weed burden and total area, more for heavy land or exceptional weed burden. Seed costs very variable, but as a guide:

- Native Perennial wild flowers and grasses, £15.25/kg, 25kg/ha = £370/ha
- Nectar mix for bumble bees and butterflies £15.00/kg, 25kg/ha = £350/ha
- Bird Seed sward £6.00/kg, 12kg/ha = £72/ha for single year crop, £4.20/kg, 50kg/ha = £210 for longer sward.
- Single species native grass seeds vary from £3.30/kg (e.g. Creeping Red Fescue) to £60/kg (Sweet Vernal).
- Single species native perennial wild flower seeds vary from £50/kg (Lady's Bedstraw) to £450/kg (Cowslip)
- Buffer strip grass margin mix for cross compliance, ELS and HLS compliance, £4.00/kg drilled at 25kg/ha = £100/ha. Costs of ground preparation and drilling are usually higher than the seed.

Acknowledgement: Thanks to Cotswold Seeds, 0800 252 211 and the Forestry Commission http://www.forestry.gov.uk/forestresearch

2.   FERTILISER PRICES

Compounds		Analysis		Price Per Tonne
	N	P_2O_5	K_2O	£
	0	26	26	285
	0	24	24	263
	0	18	36	283
	0	20	30	267
	0	30	15	258
	0	30	20	281
	5	24	24	302
	8	24	24	325
	10	26	26	361
	11	15	20	276
	13	13	20	279
	15	15	20	307
	16	16	16	302
	22	4	14	267
	20	10	10	269
	25	5	5	255
	26	0	15	278

Straights	Price per tonne £
Ammonium Nitrate: UK (34.5% N)	265
Ammonium Nitrate: Imported (34.5% N)	254
NS grade: UK (27% N, 30% SO_3)	259
Sulphate of Ammonia (21% N, 60% SO_3)	265
Urea (46% N.): granular/ prills	353
Liquid Nitrogen (26% N, 5% SO_3)	208
Triple Superphosphate (TSP) (46% P_2O_5)	275
DAP (18/46/0)	413
Muriate of Potash (MOP) (60% K_2O)	275

Average price (p) per kg:			
	N :	76.8	(UK AN)
	P_2O_5 :	59.8	(TSP)
	K_2O :	45.8	(MOP)

The prices above are for fertiliser delivered in 600kg bags; delivery in bulk averages £7.00/tonne less; collection of bags by farmers £8/tonne less. They are based on forward prices in October 2014 and spring 2015; they vary according to area and bargaining power. They assume delivery in 25-27 tonne loads; add approximately £3.50/tonne for 10 tonne loads, £8.50 for 6-9 tonne loads, £20 for 4-5 tonne loads.

3.   MANURE VALUE OF SLURRY

Nutrient Values of Common Farm Yard Manure Types

	Dry Matter %	(kg N/t) Total N	(kg N/t) *Available N*	(kg P₂O₅/t) Total P	(kg P₂O₅/t) *Available P*	(kg K₂O/t) Total K	(kg K₂O/t) *Available K*
Cattle FYM *	25	6.0	*0.6*	3.2	*1.9*	8.0	*7.2*
Pig FYM	25	7.0	*1.0*	6.0	*3.6*	8.0	*7.2*
Sheep FYM	25	7.0	*0.7*	3.2	*1.9*	8.0	*7.2*
Duck FYM	25	6.5	*1.0*	5.5	*3.3*	7.5	*6.8*
Horse FYM	30	7.0	*N/a*	5.0	*3.0*	6.0	*5.4*

*For manure stored for 3 months or more.   FYM = Farmyard Manure

Note: these nutrient contents are for guidance only and will vary between different livestock systems and storage methods. Analysis should be performed to understand the specific values of manure.

Manure Output per Head during the Housing Period

	Undiluted Excreta t or m³	Total Kg N	Total Kg P₂O₅	Total Kg K₂O
1 dairy cow ~ *6,000 to 9,000 litres milk yield*	11.6	60	26	46
1 beef cow ~ *>500 kg*	8.2	41	15.5	33
1 finishing pig ~ *per place ~ 86% occupancy*	1.6	10.6	5.6	5.6
1,000 broiler hens ~ *per hen place ~ 85% occupancy*	19	330	220	340

Note: These figures should not be used for calculating NVZ compliance as they only allow for the time spent in the buildings and therefore exclude manure deposited in fields during grazing. Refer to the DEFRA NVZ guidance booklets for NVZ calculation methodology and annual manure output tables.

Lime

Prices average around £22 delivered and spread per tonne with an application rate of 6 tonnes per hectare per application, typically every 4 years, or 1.25 tonnes per hectare of arable land per year.

Lime price varies according to type of dressing, grade of mineral (such as particle size and consistency), location and ease of spreading. And could be as low as £2 per tonne ex quarry to £20 ex quarry. A short haul would cost about £5.50 and spreading approximately £4.50 per tonne, adding £10 to the ex-quarry cost.

Biosolids (Sewage Sludge)

Biosolids act as good soil conditioner and fertiliser to farmers, whilst providing the most environmentally favourable method for water companies to dispose of the sludge. Biosolids vary in nutritional composition depending on processing and location, but RB209 describes its content as follows:

Biosolid Key Composition

	Digested Cake	Thermally Dried Pellets	Lime Stabilised
Dry Matter	25%	95%	40%
Total Nitrogen *kg/t*	11	40	8.5
Total Phosphate (P2O5)	18	75	26
Total Potash	0.6	2	0.8
Available N *kg/t*	1.6	2	0.9
Available P_2O_5 *kg/t*	9	35	13
Available K_2O *kg/t*	0.5	1.8	0.7
Available SO_3 *kg/t*	6	23	8.5
Guideline Price £/t applied	£4.00	£35	£3.75

Nutrient data taken from Fertiliser Manual RB209 (2010)

Application rates vary according to terrain, soil analysis and plant need, but an application of 25 tonnes dry solids per hectare is the typical maximum rate.

4.   AGROCHEMICAL COSTS

Only the names of the active ingredients are given below, with their principal use. These materials should only be applied in accordance with the manufacturers' recommendations.

Application rates vary and there are differences between the prices of various proprietary brands. The list is not intended to be exhaustive and there is no implied criticism of materials omitted.

The variation in costs per hectare is because of varying application rates rather than price variation between suppliers. It is priced on the purchase of chemical alone, i.e., not the agronomy service.

Crop	Function		Material	Cost £/ha per application
Cereals	Herbicides	General	Mecoprop-P	5.90-13.50
			Ioxynil+Bromoxynil	5.50-15.00
			Metsulfuron-methyl	17.60
			Mesosulfuron + Iodosulfuron	35.00
			Diflufenican	4.20 - 7.00
		Cleavers	Fluroxypyr	5.90 - 7.80
			Amidosulfuron	9.20 – 13.80
			Florasulam (Placeholder1)m + Fluroxypyr	12.40-18.60
		Wild Oats	Pinoxaden	20.00-52.00
		Wild Oats & Blackgrass	Clodinafop-propargyl	31.25
			Fenoxaprop-P-ethyl	20.00-30.00
			Flurasulam + Pyroxsulam	27.50
	Growth Regulator		Chlormequat	3.40
			2-chloroethylphosphonic acid	6.70-13.30
			2-chloroethylphosphonic acid + Mepiquat Chloride	11.00-22.00
			Trinexapac-ethyl	6.60-13.20
	Fungicides		Azoxystrobin	30.00
			Fenpropimorph	19.00-25.50
			Epoxiconazole	20.00
			Tebuconazole	10.00
			Prothioconazole	18.50-37.00
			Chlorothalonil	5.50
			Epoxiconazole & Boscalid	27.50
			Pyraclostrobin	33.50
			Prothioconazole & bixafen	33.00 - 41.00
			Epoxiconazole & Fluxapyroxad	30.00 – 37.50
			Epoxiconazole & isopyrazam	30.00 – 40.00
			Chlorothalonil & propiconazole	11.00 – 22.00

Crop	Function		Material	Cost £/ha per application
		Seed Dressing	Fuberidazole + Triadimenol	6.50-10.00
			Fuberidazole + Triadimenol + Imidacloprid	11.50-18.00
			Prothioconazole + Clothianidin	11.80-19.00
			Silthiofam	24.00-38.00
			Imidacloprid + Tebuconazole + Triazoxide	13.00-21.00
			Fluquinconazole	13.00 – 21.00
			Fludioxonil + Tefluthrin	13.00 - 22.00
			Triticonazole + Prochloraz	6.50 – 10.50
			Manganese	6.50 – 10.70
	Aphicide		Pirimicarb	9.25
			Chlorpyrifos	7.00-14.00
			Lambda-Cyhalothrin	3.60
	Slug Killer		Metaldehyde	8.40
			Ferric-Phosphate	19.25
Oilseed Rape	Herbicides		Propyzamide	27.30
			Metazachlor	22.50-37.50
			Clomazone	20.00
	Insecticide		Deltamethrin	4.75
			Pirimicarb	9.25-13.90
			Lambda-Cyhalothrin	5.40
	Fungicide		Iprodione + Thiophanate-methyl	26.00-39.00
			Tebuconazole	5.00-10.00
			Metconazole	20.80
			Boscalid	17.00 – 34.00
	Dessicant		Glyphosate	8.25
Potatoes	Herbicides:		Metribuzin	18.80-37.50
			Linuron	19.00-35.70
			Diquat	8.50-17.00
			Clomazone	23.00
	Blight Control		Cymoxanil + Mancozeb	10.40
			Cymoxanil + Famoxadone	13.00-18.20
			Fluazinam	9.00
			Mancozeb + Metalaxyl	28.50
	Insectaicides		Oxamyl	44.40-66.60
	Haulm Dessicant		Diquat	34.00
Sugar Beet				
	Herbicides:	Pre-emergence	Chloridazon:	11.60-27.2
		Post-emergence	Phenmedipham:	3.60-6.00

Crop	Function	Material	Cost £/ha per application
		Triflusulfuron-methyl	23.00
	Insecticide	Oxamyl	44.40-66.60
		Pirimicarb	9.30
Beans	Herbicide	Bentazone	70.40
		Pendimethalin	16.80-20.10
		Clomazone	20.00
	Fungicide	Chlorothalonil	16.50
		Tebuconazole	10.00
		Azoxystrobin	30.00
Peas and Beans			
	Herbicide	Pendimethalin + Imazamox	42.00
	Insecticide	Pirimicarb	9.25
		Lambda-Cyhalothrin	5.50
Maize	Herbicide	Nicosulfuron	21.00 - 32.00
		Bromoxynil	23.00
		Mesotrione	34.00
Brassicas	Herbicides	Metazachlor	36.00
		Pyridate	78.00
Broadleaved Grass weeds and volunteer Crops			
	Cereals	Fluazifop-P-butyl	25.00 - 37.50
		Propaquizafop	12.60 – 27.00
		Cycloxydim	25.50 - 42.50
Grassland	Herbicides	MCPA	9.60 - 16.00
		Dicamba +Mecoprop-P + MCPA	21.00-26.00
General	Weed and Grass Killer		
	Couch Grass Control	Glyphosate	8.00 - 11.00
		Clopyralid + Fluroxypyr + MCPA	30.00 - 60.00

The above prices are based on retail prices paid by farmers (August 2014) and reflect the discounts available where there are competing products from several manufacturers. The range in prices per hectare reflects the varying application rates. This is the price for the product, not including the agronomic advice that often comes with it.

Average rates for agronomy only are £12.75/ha for cereals or maize only and rising to £21-£32/ha for potatoes and other vegetable and perishable crops.

Acknowledgement: Thanks to Frontier 01767 680 351

5. AGROCHEMICAL RATES

This table summarises the agrochemical spend for the main crops in Chapter 1, with a breakdown of what each figure is comprised from. Clearly the variation can be considerable between soil-types, regions, farms and even fields, but this offers a starting point from which individual costings can be derived.

Agrochemical Breakdown (excluding seed treatments) £/ha

	Herb-icides	Fung-icides	Insect-icides	PGR	Other	Total Ag-chemical
Feed Wheat	95	110	7	16	5	233
Milling Wheat	95	115	7	16	8	241
Second Wheat	105	115	7	16	5	248
Spring Wheat	60	50	7	16	5	138
Red Wheat	66	90	7	16	27	206
Feed Barley	75	75	7	16	5	178
Malting Barley	75	75	7	16	5	178
S. Malting Barley	60	50	7	16	5	138
Winter Oats	55	42	7	16	5	125
Spring Oats	35	32	7	8	5	87
Winter Rape	90	70	7	16	13	196
Spring Rape	70	50	7	16	13	156
Winter Beans	50	45	7	0	9	111
Spring Beans	50	40	10	0	9	109
Blue Peas	55	50	10	0	9	124
Marrowfats	65	88	10	0	15	178
Maincrop Potatoes	30	180	45	0	448	703
Sugar Beet	160	45	10	0	15	230

6. SEED ROYALTY RATES

Farm-saved seed payment rates for autumn 2014 and spring 2015

	£/ha	£/tonne
Wheat	7.57	42.99
Winter Barley	6.96	42.19
Spring Barley	8.62	47.35
Oats	5.69	36.02
Peas	9.06	38.73
Beans	12.23	53.63
Oilseed Rape	10.07	2,143
Linseed	7.16	135.09
Triticale	7.38	45.56

Seed purchased from a merchant includes a component of royalty for the seed breeder. Those farmers who save seed from the previous season (farm saved seed) are legally obliged to pay the royalty. If the seed is cleaned and dressed, the royalty payment is taken at this point (per tonne), if not, the farmer is responsible for paying (per hectare). Many older varieties no longer have royalty payments payable. It is illegal to sell or buy seed unless under license. View eligible varieties at www.bspb.co.uk .

7. HOME SAVED SEED COSTS

	Value of Old Crop £/t	Cleaning & Dressing £/t	Testing £/t	Royalty £/t	Total Cost £/t
Feed Wheat	135	73	1.10	43	**252**
Milling Wheat	158	73	1.10	43	**275**
Spring Wheat	158	78	0.90	43	**279**
Winter Feed Barley	125	78	2.20	42	**247**
Winter Malting Barley	142	78	2.20	42	**264**
Spring Malting Barley	152	78	2.20	47	**280**
Winter Oats	125	81	4.30	36	**246**
Spring Oats	125	81	4.10	36	**246**
Winter Rape	265	4,450	68.6	2143	**6,927**
Spring Rape	265	4,450	126	2143	**6,984**
Winter Beans	229	54	2.80	54	**339**
Spring Beans	245	54	2.80	54	**355**
Blue Peas	275	49	2.80	39	**366**
Marrowfats	345	60	3.80	83	**491**

The old crop seed is the value of sales not made from 2014 harvest. Cleaning and dressing figures are based on costs for a mobile cleaner on a 350 hectare farm, and likely amounts of seeds required for each crop (the lower the tonnage, the higher the cost). Single purpose or basic seed treatments included. Testing costs assume a single test (one variety) per species (Germination only; £32/test). Royalty rates as above.

8. SEED DRILLING RATES

		Thousand Grain Weight (g/1000 grains)											
		35	38	41	44	47	50	53	56	59	62	65	68	71
	150	53	57	62	66	71	75	80	84	89	93	98	102	107
	175	61	67	72	77	82	88	93	98	103	109	114	119	124
	200	70	76	82	88	94	100	106	112	118	124	130	136	142
	225	79	86	92	99	106	113	119	126	133	140	146	153	160
Seeds Planted per m^2	**250**	88	95	103	110	118	125	133	140	148	155	163	170	178
	275	96	105	113	121	129	138	146	154	162	171	179	187	195
	300	105	114	123	132	141	150	159	168	177	186	195	204	213
	325	114	124	133	143	153	163	172	182	192	202	211	221	231
	350	123	133	144	154	165	175	186	196	207	217	228	238	249
	375	131	143	154	165	176	188	199	210	221	233	244	255	266
	400	140	152	164	176	188	200	212	224	236	248	260	272	284
	425	149	162	174	187	200	213	225	238	251	264	276	289	302
	450	158	171	185	198	212	225	239	252	266	279	293	306	320

Measured in Kg/Ha

9.   FEED PRICES

£ per tonne

Cattle	Dairy:	High Energy Parlour	260
		Dairy Concentrate	230
		Medium Energy Blend	255
	Beef	Pellets (16% CP)	235
		Concentrate	250
	Calf	Milk Substitute (bags)	1,700
		High Fat replacer (bags)	1,200
		Calf Weaner Pellets	275
		Calf Rearer Nuts	270
Sheep		High Energy Lamb Pellets.	260
		Medium energy sheep	245
		Sheep/lamb cake	250
		Ewe cake	255
Horses		Horse and Pony Pencils/Cubes (bags)	375
Goats		Goat Nuts	275
Pigs		Piglet Weaner	315
		Sow Nuts	265
		Early Grower Pellets (20-24% protein)	325
		Grower/Finisher Pellets (17-21% protein)	280
		Sow Concentrate	375
		Grower Concentrate	380
Poultry		Chick and Rearer Feeds	260
		Layers Feeds	270
		Broiler Feeds	325
		Turkey Feeds	280
Straight Feeds		Fishmeal (66/70% CP)	1,130
		Soya Bean Meal (Hipro; 50% CP)	400
		Rapeseed Meal (34-36% CP)	245
		Palm Kernel Meal/Cake (17% CP)	150
		Sunflower Seed (30/33% CP)	205
		Citrus Pulp Nuts/Pellets	195
		Wheatfeed Meal (14-18% CP)	130
		Wheatfeed Pellets (14-18% CP)	140
		Maize Gluten (19-20% CP)	190
		Molasses (Cane) (5% CP)	180
		Sugar Beet Pulp (Molassed Nuts/Pellets)	225
		Brewers' Grains	50
		Distillers wheat grain	225
		Distillers Barley Grain	210
		Distillers Maize Grains	220

Compound feed prices are from July 2014; there will be a range incorporating differences in the ingredients and delivery destinations on any one occasion. The market prices are also likely to move (possibly considerably) throughout the year. They are delivered prices for hauls more than 10 miles in 25 tonne loads. The additional farm delivered cost for bags ranges from £20.00 to £28.00 a tonne.

10.   FEEDSTUFF NUTRITIVE VALUES

Typical Energy and Protein Contents of Some Common Feeds and cost per unit

Type of Feeds	£/T	Dry Matter g/kg	ME MJ/kg DM	CP g/kg DM	p/kg DM	p/MJ ME	p/g CP
Forages:							
Barley Straw	65	860	7	10	7.56	1.08	0.76
Grass Silage (typical clamp)	24	250	10.8	150	9.73	0.90	0.06
Hay (typical meadow)	61	850	8.8	100	7.15	0.81	0.07
Maize Silage	19	300	11	90	6.31	0.57	0.07
Pasture (rotational grazed)	6	180	11.5	160	3.22	0.28	0.02
Whole-crop Wheat (fermented)	43	350	10.5	95	12.21	1.16	0.13
Cereals:							
Barley (home grown *)	125	860	13.2	120	14.53	1.10	0.12
Oats (home grown *)	125	860	12.5	120	14.53	1.16	0.12
Wheat (home grown *)	135	860	13.6	130	15.70	1.15	0.12
Maize	155	880	13.8	90	17.61	1.28	0.20
Roots:							
Fodder Beet	7	180	12	60	3.84	0.32	0.06
Potatoes	30	200	13.3	100	15.00	1.13	0.15
Wet By-Products:							
Brewers Grains	50	260	11.5	250	19.23	1.67	0.08
Pressed Sugar Beet Pulp	225	880	11.5	100	25.57	2.22	0.26
Straights:							
Cane Molasses	180	750	12.7	40	24.00	1.89	0.60
Distillers Barley Grains	210	900	12.2	260	23.33	1.91	0.09
Distillers Maize Grains	220	900	14	310	23.33	1.75	0.08
Distillers Wheat Grains	225	900	13.5	340	25.00	1.85	0.07
Dried Citrus Pulp	195	900	12.6	70	21.67	1.72	0.31
Dried Molassed Sugar Beet Pulp	225	900	12.5	100	25.00	2.00	0.25
Field Beans	205	880	13.3	290	23.30	1.75	0.08
Maize Gluten Feed	190	880	12.8	210	21.59	1.69	0.10
Palm Kernel Meal	150	900	11.4	200	16.67	1.46	0.08
Wheat-feed	130	880	11.3	190	14.77	1.31	0.08

* Home grown feed should be costed to the livestock enterprise at the value the grain
   could otherwise be sold at, i.e. the opportunity cost of the crop.

11.   AGRISTATS

These basic agricultural statistics relate to the UK farming and food sectors. The main source of data is the Defra Publication 'Agriculture in the UK 2013'. This can be found online at - www.defra.gov.uk/statistics/foodfarm/cross-cutting/auk/. All figures are for the UK and relate to the 2013 year unless otherwise stated.

INDUSTRY STRUCTURE

Agriculture's Economic Contribution	UK	England	Wales	Scotland	N.I.
Gross Output (£m)............................	25,715	19,126	1,529	3,138	1,921
Total Income from Farming* (£m) ...	5,464	4,120	218	829	298
Agriculture's Share of the Economy**	0.62%	0.60%	0.51%	0.93%	1.32%
Agriculture's Share of Employment .	1.44%	1.08%	3.94%	2.59%	5.84%

*   *Total Income from Farming (TIFF) is essentially the profit of the farming sector. These are provisional figures (and considered high by the Editor, thought likely to fall in next update).*

** *Based on agriculture's share of gross value-added – 2012 data.*

The wider agri-food sector (including farming, food manufacturing, wholesaling, retailing and catering) contributed £97.1bn or 7.2% to national gross value-added in 2012, and employed 13% of the total UK workforce (14% in 2011).

Agricultural Workforce (2013)	2011	2012	2013
Regular Full-time....................................	*64,000*	*65,000*	63,000
Regular Part-time*.................................	*39,000*	*41,000*	39,000
Seasonal, Casual and Gang....................	62,000	67,000	61,000
Salaried Managers	11,000	11,000	11,000
Total Employees.....................................	176,000	184,000	173,000
Farmers, Partners Directors and Spouses			
Full-time...	140,000	141,000	138,000
Part-time*...	159,000	158,000	152,000
Farmers, Partners Directors & Spouses .	299,000	298,000	290,000
Total Labour Force	476,000	481,000	464,000

*   *Part-time is less than 39 hours in England and Wales, less than 38 hours in Scotland and less than 30 hours in Northern Ireland.*

UK Farmed Areas '000 Hectares

	2006	2010	2012	2013	2014 est.
Wheat	1,833	1,939	1,992	1,615	1,985
Barley	882	922	1,003	1,213	1,015
Oats	122	124	122	177	110
Mixed Corn, Triticale, Rye	24	29	26	24	26
Total Cereals (excl. maize)	**2,861**	**3,014**	**3,143**	**3,029**	**3,136**
Oilseed Rape	500	642	756	716	722
Linseed	40	45	29	37	30
Peas (harvested dry)	46	42	24	29	28
Field Beans	185	166	96	118	125
Potatoes	140	138	149	139	145
Sugar Beet	130	118	120	117	118
Veges & Salad grown in open	117	119	124	116	122
Top & Soft Fruit	33	34	33	33	34
Other Horticulture	14	14	15	15	14
Maize	137	164	158	194	165
Other Arable Crops	140	102	102	123	105
Set-aside (inc. non-food crops)	422	-			
Bare Fallow	233	174	153	255	155
Total Tillage	**4,998**	**4,772**	**4,902**	**4,921**	**4,899**
Temporary Grass (<5 years)	1,137	1,232	1,357	1,390	1,350
Total Arable	**6,135**	**6,004**	**6,259**	**6,311**	**6,249**
Permanent Grass (>5 years)	5967	5925	5799	5802	5864
Total Grass*	7,104	7,157	7,156	7,192	7,214
*Total Tillage & Grass**	**12,102**	**11,929**	**12,058**	**12,113**	**12,113**
Sole Right Rough Grazing	4,354	4,055	3,926	3,940	3,940
Common Rough Grazing	1,236	1,228	1,200	1,197	1,200
Total Rough Grazing	**5,590**	**5,283**	**5,126**	**5,137**	**5,140**
Land for Outdoor Pigs		10	7	9	10
Utilisable Agric.l Area (UAA)	**17,692**	**17,222**	**17,191**	**17,259**	**17,263**
Woodland	583	774	827	865	875
Other Land on agric.l holdings	289	274	332	324	325
Total Agricultural Area	**18,564**	**18,270**	**18,350**	**18,448**	**18,463**

* *Excluding Rough Grazing*

** *2014 Estimate provided by The Andersons Centre*

The Utilisable Agricultural Area (UAA) comprises around 71% of the total UK land area. Of the remaining 29%, 4% is woodland and other land on agricultural holdings. The 25% of 'non-agricultural' land broadly splits equally between forest land, urban areas and 'other' land uses. The latter category includes villages, small towns, transport infrastructure, non-urban wasteland, and inland water. The total UK land area is approximately 24.3 million hectares.

Livestock Numbers (June)

'000 Head	2005	2010	2012	2013	2014*
Total Cattle and Calves...............	10,770	10,112	9,900	*9,844*	*9,875*
of which: Dairy Cows	1,998	1,847	1,812	*1,782*	*1,800*
Beef Cows.............	1,751	1,657	1,657	*1,611*	*1,575*
Total Sheep and Lambs	35,416	31,084	32,215	*32,856*	*33,000*
of which .... Female Breeding	16,935	14,740	15,229	*15,561*	*15,500*
Total Pigs	4,862	4,460	4,481	*4,885*	*4,950*
of which Female Breeding ...	470	427	425	*350*	*375*
Poultry Broilers..................	111,475	105,309	102,558	*104,576*	*105,000*
Laying Flock	29,544	47,107	46,633	*47,024*	*47,000*
Other Poultry.........	10,928	11,451	10,870	*11,008*	*11,000*
Farmed Deer...............................	33	31	31	*32*	*32*
Goats	96	93	98	*99*	*99*

* 2014 Estimate provided by The Andersons Centre

Size Distribution of Holdings - 2013

By Area on Holding	Holdings - '000	Area - '000 Ha	% of Holdings	% of Area
Under 20 hectares............................	106	701	47.5	4.1
20 to 50 hectares..............................	42	1,380	18.8	8.0
50 to 100 hectares............................	33	2,349	14.8	13.6
100 hectares and over	42	12,820	18.8	74.3
Total	223	17,250	100	100

Average Size of Enterprises

Hectares	2005	2011	Number	2005	2011
Cereals (excl. maize)	49.4	59.0	Dairy Cows	68	80
Oilseed Rape..............	34.4	46.6	Beef Cows.......... ...	27	28
Potatoes	11.6	15.2	Breeding Sheep	217	218
Sugar Beet	20.3	23.6	Breeding Pigs.........	80	72
			Broilers	37,953	42,692

Data not updated since 2011.

Age of Farm Holders

	2000	2003	2005	2007	2010
Under 35 years	5	3	3	3	3
35-44 years	18	15	14	12	11
45-54 years	26	24	23	23	25
55-64 years	26	29	29	29	29
65 years and over	25	29	31	33	32
Median age	56	58	58	59	59

DEFRA data. Does not measure amount of farming controlled by each age group, or who the active decision maker is. Neither has it been updated since 2010.

FINANCE

Total Income From Farming (TIFF)

	Real Terms 2013		Current Values	
	TIFF (£ million)	TIFF per AWU (£)	Gross Output	Total Income from Farming (£ million)
1985	3,081	11,253	12,964	1,363
1986	3,525	12,928	13,256	1,609
1987	3,995	14,830	13,445	1,914
1988	3,672	13,852	13,768	1,864
1989	3,823	14,661	14,895	2,078
1990	3,150	12,273	15,248	1,828
1991	3,214	12,628	15,638	1,989
1992	4,260	16,818	16,202	2,718
1993	5,900	23,472	17,555	3,831
1994	6,439	25,939	18,173	4,229
1995	7,429	30,434	19,786	5,000
1996	6,662	27,614	20,053	4,609
1997	3,939	16,468	17,911	2,774
1998	2,726	11,593	16,471	1,956
1999	2,792	12,236	15,960	2,048
2000	2,100	9,547	14,984	1,552
2001	2,195	10,227	15,281	1,659
2002	2,802	13,322	15,510	2,169
2003	3,452	16,774	16,137	2,731
2004	3,197	15,800	16,797	2,589
2005	2,984	14,900	14,777	2,465
2006	2,890	14,542	14,663	2,456
2007	3,076	15,602	15,897	2,672
2008	4,521	23,164	19,919	4,055
2009	4,589	23,849	19,583	4,207
2010	4,414	22,992	20,659	4,172
2011	5,501	28,247	23,633	5,319
2012	4,834	24,791	24,218	4,756
2013	5,464	28,426	25,715	5,464

* *TIFF per full-time entrepreneur equivalent*

** *average 1976 = 100*

TIFF is the business profits plus remuneration to farmers, partners and directors and others with an entrepreneurial interest in the business. It is calculated on a calendar year basis and is the main aggregate measure of UK farming's income (profitability). There are no imputed charges (such as a rental value for owned land or value of the farmer's own labour).

TIFF Accounts - Inputs and Outputs (2013 Provisional)

Inputs	£m	Outputs	£m	%
Animal Feed	5,608	Wheat	2,085	8.1
Seeds	814	Barley	1,125	4.4
Fertilisers	1,488	Oats and other cereals	164	0.6
Pesticides	856	Oilseed rape	741	2.9
Hired Labour	2,379	Potatoes	940	3.7
Depreciation: equipment	1,680	Sugar beet	266	1.0
Depreciation: buildings	886	Fresh vegetables	1,314	5.1
Depreciation: livestock	1,347	Fruit	596	2.3
Maintenance: materials	919	Plants and flowers	1,097	4.3
Maintenance: buildings	572	Other crops	960	3.7
Fuels	1,069	Cattle	3,767	14.7
Electricity	414	Sheep	1,373	5.3
Agricultural services	1,055	Pigs	1,287	5.0
Veterinary expenses	441	Poultry	2,521	9.8
Net rent	451	Milk	4,271	16.6
Interest and Finance Fees	396	Eggs	718	2.8
Other goods and services	3,081	Other livestock	304	1.2
		Other agricultural	1,055	4.1
		Non-ag income	1,110	4.3
Total Inputs	**22,456**	**Total Gross Output**	**25,694**	100.0
Total Income From Farming	5,464	Single Payment & subsidies	3,226	
	28,920	**Total Output**	**28,920**	
		Total crops	6,281	24.4
		Total horticulture	3,007	11.7
		Total livestock	9,252	36.0
		Total livestock products	4,989	19.4
		Other	2,165	8.4

Average English Farm Business Income (FBI) (Real Terms 2013/14 Prices)

Farm Type	2010/11	2011/12	2012/13	2013/14 (prov.)
Dairy	73,500	92,000	52,500	101,000
Grazing Livestock (LFA)	24,000	31,000	20,000	26,000
Grazing L'stock (Lowland)	24,000	34,000	17,000	19,000
Cereals	94,500	99,500	69,500	49,000
General Cropping	124,000	106,500	93,500	84,000
Specialist Pigs	49,500	40,500	42,000	78,000
Specialist Poultry	76,000	49,500	96,500	103,000
Mixed	57,000	78,500	39,000	35,000

FBI is the main farm-level measure of farming income (profitability). It is similar to TIFF but is based on a March to February year. *There has been a change in methodology of the series which means data prior to 2011/12 is not strictly comparable to more recent years. UK data is not currently available.*

Balance Sheet of UK Agriculture (2012 – latest data)			£m	£m
Assets:	Fixed:	Land	193,705	
		Buildings, plant and machinery ...	24,485	
		Breeding livestock	7,587	
		Total Fixed Assets:		*225,776*
	Current	Trading livestock	4,005	
		Crops and stores	4,003	
		Debtors and cash deposits	8,432	
		Total Current Assets:		*16,440*
	Total Assets:			***242,217***
Liabilities:	Long &	Bank and Building Society loans.	9,820	
	Med-term:	AMC and SASC	1,760	
		Other (inc. family loans)	729	
		Total Long and Medium Term Liabilities		*12,307*
	Short-term	Bank overdrafts	3,519	
		Trade credit	3,431	
		Hire purchase and leasing	1,893	
		Other	86	
		Total Short-term Liabilities:		*8,930*
	Total Liabilities:			***21,238***
Net Worth:				**220,979**

% Equity (Net worth as a % of Total Assets): ... 91.2%

Total Income from Farming (TIFF) 2012 as % of   a) Net Worth: 2.2%
b) Total Assets: 2.0%
c) Tenants Cap' 9.8%

Note: no charge has been made for farmers' own labour or management

PRODUCTIVITY

UK Crop Yields (tonnes per hectare)	2008	2009	2010	2011	2012	2013	Average 08-13
Wheat	8.3	7.9	7.7	7.7	6.7	7.4	7.6
Barley (all)	6.0	5.8	5.7	5.7	5.5	5.9	5.8
Winter Barley	6.7	6.4	6.4	6.1	6.4	6.4	6.4
Spring Barley	5.4	5.5	5.2	5.4	5.0	5.7	5.4
Oats	5.8	5.8	5.5	5.6	5.1	5.5	5.6
Oilseed Rape	3.3	3.4	3.5	3.9	3.4	3.0	3.4
Linseed	1.8	2.0	1.6	2.0	1.5	1.8	1.8
Field Beans	4.5	3.7	3.0	3.4	3.3	3.2	3.6
Dried Peas	4.0	3.6	3.5	4.1	2.4	3.7	3.5
Potatoes (all)	42.8	44.3	43.8	42.3	31.3	40.8	41.0
Early Potatoes	13.3	15.4	23.2	23.3	15.4	15.5	17.7
Maincrop Potatoes	46.7	47.7	45.5	45.1	32.8	43.3	43.5
Sugar Beet*	63.8	74.0	55.1	75.4	60.7	72.1	66.9

* *Adjusted to 16% sugar*

UK Livestock Output		average (harvest year)					Average
(kg unless stated)	2008	2009	2010	2011	2012	2013	08-13
Milk Yield (litres/cow)*	6,943	7,031	7,273	7,528	7,442	7,535	7,292
Beef Carcase Wgt**	349	342	347	345	347	342	345
Lamb Carcase Wgt ∆....	18.7	18.8	18.9	19.0	19.1	19.0	18.9
Pig Carcase Wgt ♦	76.4	77.8	78.1	78.0	78.0	79.0	77.9

* litres per annum   ** steers, heifers & young bulls
∆ clean sheep and lambs   ♦ clean pigs

FOOD

Self Sufficiency* (%)	2003	2013		2003	2013
All Food........................	64	60	Indigenous-type Food	77	73
Crops:...........................			Livestock:		
Wheat	124	83	Beef and Veal.........	70	83
Barley	120	110	Mutton and Lamb...	86	100
Oats	124	95	Pig-meat.................	49	61
Total Cereals..................	113	85	Poultry-meat...........	91	90
Oilseed Rape	108	114	Milk	102	103
Potatoes	82	75	Hen Eggs................	87	87
Sugar	76	60			
Fresh Vegetables	63	55			
Fresh Fruit	8	10			

* ratio of UK production to UK human consumption

Food Spending*	2007	2008	2009	2010	2011	2012
Household Expenditure	22.14	23.00	23.86	24.50	24.92	25.98
Eating-Out Expenditure	7.96	8.16	8.26	8.54	8.79	8.95
All Expenditure	30.10	31.17	32.12	33.04	33.71	34.93

* expenditure on Food and Non-alcoholic Drinks (£ per person per week) DEFRA

Producers Share*	1990	1995	2000	2005	2010	2011	2012
Basket of Goods	43	48	35	35	36	39	39
Wheat (bread)........	16	16	10	7	8	11	11
Potatoes	31	62	27	22	20	22	22
Carrots....................	31	44	38	43	41	46	47
Apples	51	48	40	43	42	40	44
Milk.......................	35	39	28	30	32	34	35
Beef.......................	57	57	44	44	48	53	54
Lamb	57	58	43	45	56	57	53
Pork.......................	55	57	47	37	39	39	40
Chicken..................	44	46	37	42	38	39	39
Eggs.......................	36	31	29	32	27	26	31

* farmer's share of retail price (per cent) DEFRA. 2012 = latest figures

12.   RATE OF INFLATION; PRICE AND COST INDICES

INFLATION DATA

Calendar Year	RPI*: % yearly change	RPI: Index 1987=100	CPI** % yearly change	CPI Index 2005=100	*Agricultural Prices Index, 2010 = 100*	
					Outputs	*Inputs*
1987..............	4.2	100	-	-	-	-
1988..............	4.9	107	-	-	*69.4*	*53.0*
1989..............	7.8	115	5.2	67	*74.0*	*55.8*
1990..............	9.5	126	7.0	72	*75.3*	*58.4*
1991..............	5.9	134	7.5	77	*74.1*	*60.5*
1992..............	3.7	139	4.3	80	*74.1*	*62.1*
1993..............	1.6	141	2.5	82	*78.2*	*64.7*
1994..............	2.4	144	2.0	84	*78.8*	*64.8*
1995..............	3.5	149	2.6	86	*85.9*	*66.3*
1996..............	2.4	153	2.5	88	*83.7*	*69.9*
1997..............	3.1	158	1.8	90	*73.1*	*68.1*
1998..............	3.4	163	1.6	91	*68.4*	*65.3*
1999..............	1.5	165	1.3	92	*65.6*	*65.1*
2000..............	3.0	170	0.8	93	*63.6*	*66.3*
2001..............	1.8	173	1.2	94	*68.8*	*68.2*
2002..............	1.7	176	1.3	95	*65.7*	*67.8*
2003..............	2.9	181	1.4	97	*70.1*	*69.0*
2004..............	3.0	187	1.3	98	*71.6*	*72.9*
2005..............	2.8	192	2.1	100	*69.6*	*75.3*
2006..............	3.2	198	2.3	102	*72.3*	*78.1*
2007..............	4.3	207	2.3	105	*82.2*	*84.8*
2008..............	4.0	215	3.6	109	*98.9*	*103.2*
2009..............	-0.5	214	2.2	111	*95.0*	*95.9*
2010..............	4.6	224	3.3	115	*100.0*	*100.0*
2011..............	5.2	235	4.5	120	*113.1*	*112.2*
2012..............	3.2	243	2.8	123	*118.7*	*113.8*
2013..............	3.0	250	2.0	126	125.5	117.0
2014 (so far)..		*256 (Jun)*		*128 (Jun)*	*122.8*	*114.2*

* *Retail Price Index*

** *Consumer Price Index*

Inflation of food-based Component of CPI

Per Cent	1998	2000	2005	2010	2011	2012	2013	2014 to June
CPI (Overall Index)	1.6	0.8	2.1	3.3	4.5	2.8	2.0	1.9
All goods	0.3	0.8	0.3	3.1	4.6	2.3	1.7	1.4
All Services	3.8	3.3	4.1	3.6	4.3	3.5	2.4	2.5
Food & non-alcoholic drinks	1	0.5	15	3.4	5.5	3.2	1.9	-0.6*
Food	0.6	0.4	1.7	3	5	3.1	2.1	-0.6*
Bread & Cereals	-0.1	-0.2	1.3	2.1	6.4	2.2	3.3	0.4
Meat	-3.4	0.4	0.7	0.9	5.4	3.7	2.5	0.6
Fish	8.3	2.2	1.6	6.6	9.2	3.6	5.2	2
Milk, Cheese & Eggs	-1.4	-0.6	2.7	0.2	2.6	0.9	1.8	0.8
Oils & Fats	0.8	-1.2	-2.2	6.7	11.8	2.4	0.9	1.2
Fruit	1.3	0.4	1.2	7.9	3.7	1.7	-0.1	-0.3
Vegetables Inc. potatoes	7	-3.5	3	2.9	3.4	3.3	2.3	-4.8
Sugar, Jam & Sweets	1.2	0.7	2.8	5.6	7.5	5.0	0.1	2.9
Food Products	2.3	-0.3	-0.5	0.7	3.2	5.0	2.9	-4.6

* = May 2013 figures

Weighting of food-based Component of CPI

parts per 1000	1998	2000	2005	2010	2011	2012	2013	2014
CPI (Overall Index)	1000	1000	1000	1000	1000	1000	1000	1000
All goods	462	591	536	549	561	555	534	540
All Services	358	409	464	451	439	445	466	460
Food & non-alcoholic drinks	144	121	106	108	118	112	106	112
Food	129	109	93	96	103	98	93	99
Bread & Cereals	23	19	15	16	17	17	16	17
Meat	30	27	23	22	22	22	21	22
Fish	6	5	4	4	4	4	4	4
Milk, Cheese & Eggs	19	14	13	14	15	14	13	14
Oils & Fats	3	2	2	2	2	2	2	2
Fruit	9	9	8	9	12	9	9	10
Vegetables Inc. potatoes	18	18	14	15	16	15	14	15
Sugar, Jam & Sweets	14	12	12	11	12	12	11	12
Food Products	7	3	2	3	3	3	3	3

DETAILED AGRICULTURAL PRICE AND COST INDICES

Producer Prices	2008	2009	2010	2011	2012	2013
Feed Wheat	120.0	89.5	100.0	141.0	143.7	152.8
Feed Barley	126.0	86.3	100.0	155.5	159.9	158.6
All Cereals	124.0	89.6	100.0	144.8	149.7	153.1
Oilseed Rape	118.7	91.5	100.0	143.3	139.1	127.0
Potatoes (all)	108.7	86.6	100.0	107.1	121.9	155.7
Sugar Beet	93.6	99.0	100.0	96.5	101.7	108.0
Desert Apples	92.1	96.6	100.0	107.0	118.0	117.1
All Fresh Vegetables	91.9	87.8	100.0	92.7	108.6	110.5
All Fresh Fruit	96.6	95.6	100.0	98.7	103.7	104.8
All Crop Products	*103.6*	*89.1*	*100.0*	*118.1*	*124.2*	*128.5*
Milk	105.2	96.1	100.0	111.0	113.8	128.2
Cattle	198.4	104.9	100.0	116.4	129.3	137.7
Sheep	72.1	91.1	100.0	112.3	105.1	102.0
Wool	32.4	47.1	100.0	121.6	75.5	145.1
Pigs	89.5	103.1	100.0	102.1	106.3	116.7
Poultry	89.5	99.5	100.0	102.9	105.0	109.3
Eggs	103.2	105.7	100.0	99.9	124.0	130.8
All Animal Products	*95.6*	*99.3*	*100.0*	*109.5*	*114.7*	*123.3*
All Products	*98.9*	*95.0*	*100.0*	*113.1*	*118.7*	*125.5*
Input Prices						
Seeds	111.2	105.0	100.0	105.8	98.5	110.2
Fertilisers	148.5	102.3	100.0	130.4	125.2	113.1
Agro-chemicals	100.9	102.8	100.0	99.8	97.0	98.8
Energy and Lubricants	107.0	88.3	100.0	118.2	122.4	123.4
Animal Feeding Stuffs	103.7	95.4	100.0	120.7	128.5	139.4
Plant Maint' & Repair	91.6	95.8	100.0	104.9	106.5	108.3
Machinery & Equip'	97.4	99.7	100.0	103.8	94.3	96.8
Building Maintenance	94.0	93.8	100.0	107.4	109.8	110.1
General Expenses	93.0	93.3	100.0	106.0	107.2	109.6
All Inputs	*103.2*	*95.9*	*100.0*	*112.2*	*113.8*	*117.0*

(2010 = 100)

13.   METRIC CONVERSION FACTORS

Metric to Imperial   *Imperial to Metric*

Area

1 hectare (10,000m^2).... 2.471 acres	1 acre .... 0.405 ha
	1 square mile .... 259 ha
1 square km ....0.386 sq. mile	1 square mile .... 2.590 sq. km
1 square m ....1.196 sq. yard	1 square yard .... 0.836 sq. m
1 square m .... 10.764 sq. feet	1 square foot .... 0.093 sq. m

(m = metre, km = kilometre)

Length

1 mm..............................0.039 inch	1 inch. ....25.4 mm
1 cm...............................0.394 inch	1 inch ....2.54 cm
1 m................................. 3.281 feet	1 foot.......................................0.305 m
1 m................................ 1.094 yard	1 yard ....0.914 m
1 km........................... 0.6214 mile	1 mile ....1.609 km

(mm = millimetre, cm = centimetre)

Volume

1 millilitre.............. 0.0352 fluid oz	1 fluid oz...............................28.413 ml
1 litre .... 35.2 fluid oz	1 fluid oz............................ 0.028 litre
1 litre ....1.76 pints	1 pint................................... 0.568 litre
1 litre .... 0.22 gallon	1 gallon ....4.546 litres
1 cubic m...................35.31 cu feet	1 cubic foot .... 0.028 cu m
1 cubic m ....1.307 cu yard	1 cubic yard........................0.765 cu m
1 cubic m ....220 gallons	1 gallon ....0.005 cu m
1 ha of 10mm water . 22,000gallons	1 acre-inch .... 102.75m^3

Weight

1 gram.............................0.0353 oz	1 oz ....28.35 gm
1 kg..................................35.274oz	
1 kg................................. 2.205 lb	1 lb.......................................0.454 kg
50 kg...............................0.984 cwt	
1 tonne (1,000 kg)...........19.68 cwt	1 cwt. ....50.80 kg
1 tonne........................... 0.984 ton	1 ton .... 1.016 tonne

Milk

1 litre 1.03kg	
1kg..................................0.971 litre	
1 litre ....1.709 pints	1 pint.......................................0.585kg
I tonne..................... 213.63 gallon	1 gallon 4.681kg

Yields and Rates of Use

1 tonne/ha. ....0.398 ton/acre	1 ton/acre ....2.511 tonnes/ha
1 tonne/ha. ....7.95 cwt/acre	1 cwt/acre.................... 0.125 tonne/ha
1 gram/ha..................0.014 oz/acre	1 oz/acre............................70.053 g/ha
1 kg/ha......................0.892 lb/acre	1 lb/acre .... 1.121 g/ha
1 kg/ha....................0.008 cwt/acre	1 cwt/acre............................125.5 g/ha
1 kg/ha (fert.)..........0.797 unit/acre	1 unit/acre ....1.255 kg/ha
1 litre/ha.................0.712 pint/acre	1 pint/acre ....1.404 litre/ha
1 litre/ha..................0.089 gal/acre	1 gal/acre........................ 11.24 litres/ha

Power, Pressure, Temperature

1 kW................................ 1.341 hp	1 hp ....0.746 kW
1MW 1,000kW	
1 kilojoule......................0.948 Btu	1 Btu ....1.055 kilojoule
1 therm ....10,000 Btu	1 Btu ....0.0001 therm
1 lb f ft........................... 1.356 Nm	1 Nm ....0.738 lb f ft
1 bar......................14.705 lb/sq.in.	1 lb/sq.in ....0.068 bar
°C to °F.........................x1.8, + 32	°F to °C .... -32, ÷ 1.8

INDEX

00781559

296